P9-ARI-750

WITHDRAWN
No longer the property of the
Boston Public Library.
Sale of this material benefits the Library.

OMNIVM LVX CIVIVM

BOSTON
PUBLIC
LIBRARY

Explorations
in the History of Psychology
in the United States

Explorations
in the History of
Psychology
in the United States

Edited by Josef Brožek

Lewisburg
Bucknell University Press
London and Toronto: Associated University Presses

© 1984 by Associated University Presses, Inc.

Associated University Presses, Inc.
440 Forsgate Drive
Cranbury, NJ 08512

Associated University Presses Ltd
25 Sicilian Avenue
London WC1A 2QH, England

Associated University Presses
2133 Royal Windsor Drive
Unit 1
Mississauga, Ontario,
Canada L5J 1K5

Library of Congress Cataloging in Publication Data
Main entry under title:

Explorations in the history of psychology in the
United States.

  Includes bibliographical references.
  1. Psychology—United States—History—Collected
works.   I. Brožek, Josef M.
BF108.U5E96   1983   150′.973   81-72024
ISBN 0-8387-5039-7

Printed in the United States of America

Dedicated to the Memory of
DAVID JAYNE HILL
President of the University at Lewisburg
(later Bucknell University)
1879–1888
Professor of Psychology and Ethics,
1881–1888
and author of
Elements of Psychology (1888)

Contents

FOREWORD   11
Dennis O'Brien and Douglas K. Candland
PREFACE   13
Josef Brožek
THE ORIGINS OF AMERICAN ACADEMIC PSYCHOLOGY   17
Rand B. Evans
  Introduction   17
  Psychology in the Scholastic Curriculum   19
  The New Learning   22
  The Rise of Scottish Thought in America   29
  Scottish Philosophy and Academic Orthodoxy   34
  Consolidation and Development of Academic Psychology   42
  Academic Reform and the Coming of the "New Psychology"   48
JONATHAN EDWARDS'S THEORY OF THE MIND: ITS APPLICATIONS
  AND IMPLICATIONS   61
James G. Blight
  Introduction   61
  The Theory of the Mind   62
    "First Awakenings": Creating a Need for Conversion   63
    "Legal Strivings": The Fruitless Search for God and Salvation   67
    "A Sense of the Heart": A Preface to the Operation of the Spirit in
      Conversion   69
    The "Principles" of Psychology: The Discovery of Divine Love   73
  The Dilemma: The Psychological Basis of Spiritual Uncertainty   78
    "False Affections and True": The Need for Criteria   79
    "Marks" and "Signs" as Evidence   81
    Denouement: "Solemn Inward Pain of Truth"   85
  Epilogue: Edwards's Achievement   87
  Supplement: The Psychological Thought of Jonathan Edwards
    (1703–1758)—A Historiographical Review   97
DAVID JAYNE HILL: BETWEEN THE OLD AND THE NEW PSYCHOLOGY   121
Josef Brožek
  Introduction   121
  General Chronological Framework   123
  The University at Lewisburg (Bucknell)   123
    Learning at Lewisburg   125
    Teaching at Lewisburg   125
    Presidency at Lewisburg   126

The University of Rochester   127
Thinking and Writing   128
  Hill's Publications   128
  The Elements of Psychology   129
  Genetic Philosophy   136
  From Dualism toward Monism   139
Applying Psychology   142
Synopsis   143
WILLIAM JAMES'S PSYCHOLOGY OF WILL: ITS REVOLUTIONARY IMPACT
  ON AMERICAN PSYCHOLOGY   148
  William R. Woodward
William James's Psychology of Will   149
  Habit and Ideo-Motor Action   149
  Fiat as Inhibition and Consent   151
  Subjective Interest and Attention   151
  Feelings of Innervation Refuted on Empirical Grounds   153
  The Meynert Scheme Revised: A "Functionalist" Critique of the
    Association of Ideas   155
The Impact on American Psychology   158
  Physiological Psychology: G. T. Ladd   158
  Cognitive Development: J. M. Baldwin   160
  Attention and Volition: John Dewey and J. F. Angell   165
  Learning: E. L. Thorndike   167
  Motivation: R. S. Woodworth   171
  Emotions: W. B. Cannon   172
  Personality: Mary W. Calkins and Gordon Allport   175
  Social Psychology: G. H. Mead   177
  Abnormal Psychology: Morton Prince, Boris Sidis, and J. J. Putnam 181
Overview   184
Conclusion   186
PIONEER PSYCHOLOGY LABORATORIES IN CLINICAL SETTINGS   196
  John A. Popplestone and Marion White McPherson
University Laboratories: A Preamble   196
Psychological Research in Psychiatric Settings   207
  Institutional Personnel: Boris Sidis, W. O. Krohn, S. I. Franz, F. L.
    Wells   209
  Academic Personnel: J. W. Baird, F. B. Barnes   226
  An Overview   227
Psychological Research in the Context of Mental Deficiency   228
  The Laboratory Era: G. E. Johnson, A. R. T. Wylie   230
  Between the Experimental Laboratory and the Testing Room: Lightner
    Witmer, H. H. Goddard, E. B. Huey, J. E. W. Wallin, Fred
    Kuhlmann   235
  The Mental Testers: Naomi Norsworthy, Isabel Lawrence, L. P.
    Ayres, C. H. Town, L. M. Terman   253
JAMES MCKEEN CATTELL AND AMERICAN PSYCHOLOGY IN THE 1920S   273
  Michael M. Sokal
Introduction   273
Mental Testing   276
Industrial Psychology   283

Certification of Consulting Psychologists   290
Financial Support of Child Psychology   292
The Psychological Community and E. B. Titchener   294
The Ninth International Congress of Psychology   295
Gestalt Psychology in America   297
Closing Comments   307
NOTES ON CONTRIBUTORS   324
INDEX   327

Foreword

The late 1970s and the early 1980s have been recognized by the psychological community as rounding out a century of scientific psychology, the most evident birth date being the foundation of the first psychological research laboratory by Wilhelm Wundt at the University of Leipzig in 1879.

Bucknell University recalled a contemporaneous local event. David Jayne Hill, a capable young man of twenty-nine, was elected on March 11, 1879, to the presidency of the University at Lewisburg. The election signified a major step in the life of the Lewisburg professor, who had graduated from the university only five years earlier. It proved to be a significant event in the history of his alma mater as well, since Hill contributed much to the University at Lewisburg (soon renamed Bucknell) before he was called to the presidency of the University of Rochester in 1888.

In 1974 the question of how best to commemorate the approaching anniversary of Hill's election engaged the attention of Charles H. Watts, then president of Bucknell. The conviction prevailed that the cause would best be served by the publication of a scholarly work dealing with a field in which Hill pioneered as both teacher and writer.

Dr. Josef Brožek, a friend of Bucknell University, strongly supported the idea and developed a proposal to initiate and, eventually, to publish a collection of small monographs devoted to various facets of the history of psychology in the United States. The present volume is the fruit of the joint efforts of Dr. Brožek, the authors of the individual essays, the Office of the President of Bucknell University, and the Bucknell University Press.

Dennis O'Brien
President
Bucknell University

Douglas K. Candland
Professor of Psychology
Bucknell University

Preface

The foundation, in 1965, of the *Journal of the History of the Behavioral Sciences* provided a welcome and urgently needed medium for the publication of journal articles on the history of psychology. Unresolved remained the problem of finding a proper mechanism for the publication of monographic studies, too long to qualify as journal articles and not long enough and, by design, too narrow in scope to be published as books.

While it does not provide a long-term solution of the problem, the editor of the present volume has welcomed the opportunity to bring out a collection of research monographs on various facets of the history of psychology in the United States.

The initial monograph, entitled "The Origins of American Academic Psychology," provides a general framework for much of what follows. It covers the period of some 250 years, from the 1630s (marked by the establishment of Harvard College in 1636) to the 1880s. The establishment of a three-year course in experimentally-oriented psychology at The Johns Hopkins University, described in 1886 by G. Stanley Hall, and the foundation of the *American Journal of Psychology* by Hall in 1887 mark the beginnings of a self-consciously "New Psychology."

The monograph "Jonathan Edwards's Theory of the Mind: Its Applications and Implications" explores, in depth, the psychological thought of a major figure of the eighteenth century. Crucial for Edwards is his deep concern about the validity of conversion. It is in this context that his inquiry into the nature of man's mind was carried out. A critical review of the literature on the psychological thought of Jonathan Edwards is presented in the form of an appendix.

Two of the contributions deal with individuals belonging to the transitional period of American psychology: David Jayne Hill, a minor figure as far as the history of psychology is concerned, a teacher and a textbook writer, and William James, an intellectual giant.

The explorations pursued in "David Jayne Hill: Between the Old and the New Psychology" focus on two of Hill's books, *The Elements of Psychology* (1888) and *The Genetic Philosophy* (1893). In terms of the history of the institutionalization of psychology, it is noteworthy that in 1881 Hill's academic title was changed from "Professor of Metaphysics and Mental Philosophy" to "Professor of Psychology and Ethics." It appears that this was the first professorship of psychology in the United States (and perhaps in the world), be it a professorship of psychology and ethics. In his teaching at the University of Rochester (1889–96) Hill introduced his students to the best of contemporary thought in psychology—American, French, and German.

William James, author of the brilliant *Principles of Psychology* (1890), is one of the most important bridges between the philosophical and empirical, and the experimental, American psychology, together with John Dewey (*Psychology,* 1886), G. T. Ladd (*Elements of Physiological Psychology,* 1887), and J. M. Baldwin (*Handbook of Psychology,* vol. 1, 1889; vol. 2, 1891). Selected aspects of James's thought are examined in "William James's Psychology of Will: Its Revolutionary Impact on American Psychology."

Nothing symbolized the "new" psychology more distinctly than the provision of facilities for experimental, quantitative studies. This topic is explored in "Pioneer Psychology Laboratories in Clinical Settings." Following a brief account of the university laboratories, the authors examine in detail the psychological laboratories operating in the psychiatric setting and in the context of mental deficiency.

The closing monograph," James McKeen Cattell and American Psychology in the 1920s," brings us to the twentieth century. In his approach to historiography, the author stresses the *social* history of psychology, contrasted with the *immanent,* content-oriented history of ideas.

The present series of monographs, followed by monographic explorations of other aspects of American psychology and supplemented by journal articles, will facilitate the writing of a systematic scholarly history of the development of psychology in the United States. At the same time, the individual presentations are of interest and value as portraits of selected facets of that fascinating, complex process through which American psychology, under the stimulus of ideas brought over to these shores from Europe, developed from meager beginnings into the position of world leadership in this field.

Josef Brožek

Explorations
in the History of Psychology
in the United States

The Origins of American Academic Psychology

RAND B. EVANS

Texas A & M University

Introduction

In 1929 the Ninth International Congress of Psychology was held at Yale University with J. McKeen Cattell as president. Since this was the first such congress to meet in America, Cattell took as the theme of his presidential address the development of American psychology. Cattell's view was that a history of psychology in America prior to the 1880s

> would be as short as a book on snakes in Ireland since the time of St. Patrick. In so far as psychologists are concerned, America was then like Heaven, for there was not a damned soul there.[1]

To Cattell psychology was synonymous with scientific, experimental psychology, the psychology of Wundt's laboratory and, to some degree, of Williams James's *Principles of Psychology*. The earlier work in this country was discounted as mere mental and moral philosophy, not *real* psychology. The entire address, entitled "Psychology in America," was to be devoted to developments after 1880.

It is understandable that a psychologist trained in the "new psychology" of experimentation would regard the earlier work as not worthy of mention under the name of psychology. Many of these first- and second-generation "new" psychologists found themselves doing constant battle in their classrooms against the "faculty" psychologies and the theologically tinged views that permeated the thinking of their students. The "man-on-the-street" psychologies that youngsters brought with them to college in the early 1900s was nothing more than the mental and moral philosophies of the preexperimental period. E. B. Titchener, one of the chief warriors on the side of experimental psychology, saw the separation of experimental psychology from its earlier philosophical apron strings as an absolute necessity. To Titchener, the American psychologies prior to the 1880s—and much since then—were little more than watered-down Cartesianisms, codified phrenologies, or worst of all, thinly disguised theology.[2]

Cattell's confusion was in not separating a particular form of institutionalized psychology, in his case experimental psychology, from the matrix of psychological thought in general. To deny that there was psychological thought before the 1880s in America is to deny that it existed in Europe before Wilhelm Wundt opened the Leipzig laboratory or in England before Francis Galton opened his laboratory in London. There were in all these places long histories of psychological thought that acted as the substrata for the establishment of the various experimental psychologies of the twentieth century. What happened in the 1880s was not the creation of psychology itself but the institutionalization of psychology as an independent, experimental discipline, an institutionalization that was not completed until well into the second decade of the twentieth century—if, indeed, it has ever been completed.

Nothing emerges from nothing. Before there emerged courses, professorships, and departments in American colleges labeled "psychological," there were people with other titles talking about much the same things, although often under different rubrics and with different intents than those of the twentieth-century psychologist. Anyone who doubts this needs only to compare the topics in Thomas Upham's *Mental Philosophy,* published in 1831, with any of the texts current in 1929 when Cattell made his statement or for that matter, with present-day texts used for the introductory course in psychology.

The emergence of psychology as an independent discipline is closely linked to the development of the American academic scene. We tend today to use the term *psychologist* to refer to someone who has a degree in psychology, a person who has gone through a particular course of study. Psychology-as-curriculum, then, is the central concern of this paper and, particularly, the dynamics that led psychology from scattered and vague classifications within the physics and theology of the seventeenth-century scholastic curriculum of the American college to the emergence of modern departments of psychology in the late 1880s.

The concepts that make up modern academic psychology, reflecting different emphases and methods than those of a century or two ago, still have a great deal in common with the earlier forms. Psychological thought, whether of today or of the distant past, can be represented in terms of three basic questions: (1) How do I come to know the things I know? This includes the topics of sensation, perception, learning, memory, cognition and similar topics. (2) How do I come to feel the things I feel? This category includes the spectrum of internal emotive states as well as motivation, beliefs, and attitudes. (3) How do I come to do the things I do? This "doing" includes the behavioral side of life, from simple reflexes to coordinated activities and social interactions. For the sake of this paper, at least, academic subjects that relate to these three questions, whether they are enmeshed in topics called physics, metaphysics, intellectual philosophy, moral philosophy, pneumatology, or whatever will be considered "psychological" so long as there is evidence of some linkage with the eventual emergence of twentieth-century thought.

Psychology in the Scholastic Curriculum

Since it is usually best to begin with the beginning or near to it, let us go back to the 1630s, when a major influx of colonists from England to America occurred. This immigration centered around Boston under the charter of the Massachusetts Bay Colony. The new colony was populated by a militant breed of religious dissenters from the Anglican confession, the Puritans. For all their stern reputation, the Puritans, with respect to their education as in other respects, were fairly representative of the population of England they came from. Graduates of both Oxford and Cambridge were represented in the colony, but there was a particularly strong representation of graduates of Emmanuel College, Cambridge, the Puritan college from which most of the colony's ministers came.[3] This group recognized the importance of education—at least of an educated clergy. In the *New Englands First Fruits* we find the following:

> After God had carried us safe to New England, and wee had builded our houses, provided necessaries for our livli-hood, rear'd convenient places for Gods worship, and setled the Civill Government; One of the next things we longed for, and looked after was to advance *Learning* and perpetuate it to Posterity; dreading to leave an illiterate Ministery to the Churches, when our present Ministers shall lie in the Dust.[4]

The result of this longing was the establishment of Harvard College in 1636.

For all the expressed purpose of ministerial preparation, at least half of the graduates of seventeenth-century Harvard were not headed for the ministry but took on other roles of the educated class in the colony. This probably represented a larger proportion of secular graduates than would have been found at Oxford or Cambridge at the same time.[5] These secular graduates became an important factor in New England life, particularly when the flow of educated English immigrants to the colony virtually stopped after the 1640s.

The curriculum of the new college was taken over bodily from its English counterparts. As such, the Harvard curriculum was bound by the scholastic tradition then still current in England. William Dunster (1609–59), first president of Harvard, put forth the curriculum of the college in 1642, much in line with the education he had encountered at Cambridge. It was, in short, the medieval arts and sciences curriculum which William Costello describes as follows:

> The undergraduate arts at Cambridge were three: logic, which taught the student correct patterns of thinking; rhetoric, which taught him to express himself according to the very-long-established principles of eloquentia; and ethics, which taught him the principles of moral behavior, as these principles are discoverable by reason and natural law. . . .
>
> University rhetoric included . . . wide reading in, and memorizing of, Greek and Latin orators, historians and poets; and, above all, required written exercises in imitation of whatever author the tutor should assign.
>
> Ethics, the third undergraduate art, considered virtue . . . the proficiency in willing what is conformed to right reason. The Aristotelian virtues were first considered singly in themselves (morals); then . . . as they affect social relationships (family economy) . . . or finally, between group-units themselves (politics).[6]

The sciences were divided by the seventeenth-century scholastic systematists into four provinces: physics, metaphysics, mathematics, and cosmography. Matters that we are defining as psychological were considered largely under the context of physics. Costello describes the *physica* as

> concerned with extended being, so far as it was qualified or modified according to the Categories of Aristotle. . . . In the first part of physics (physica generalia . . .) the student considered such concepts as change itself, time, place, quantity. . . , and the specific aspects of matter and form. This is physica as Aristotle limited it.
> The second part of physica, as presented by the late scholastic manualists, lumped the other Aristotelian tractates on extended being . . . which the Philosopher himself had kept distinct from his *Physica* into a hodgepodge of astronomy, chemistry, biology, psychology, physics, anatomy, meteorology, and geology.[7]

Hornberger has analyzed the course of study at Harvard as described by Dunster as though a modern "hour credit" system were used, giving one hour credit for attending one class once a week for one term. The Harvard students' program between 1640 and 1652 looked something like the following:[8]

Logic and Disputations (in Latin)	30 hours
Greek	24
Hebrew, Aramaic, and Syriac	24
Rhetoric and Declamations	24
Divinity and Commonplaces	16
Arithmetic and Geometry	6
Physics (including psychological topics)	2
The Nature of Plants	2
Astronomy	2
History	2

This was for Dunster's three-year bachelor's curriculum. For the masters' degree, the author of *New Englands First Fruits* says:

> Every Scholar that giveth up in writing a Synopsis or summa of Logicke, Naturall and morall Philosophy, Arithmeticke, Geometry, and Astronomy, and is ready to defend his thesis or positions, withall Skilled in the originals as aforesaid . . . shall bee capable of the second degree of Master of Arts.[9]

The synopsis usually consisted of the student's abstract of the classical works, usually those of Aristotle or of a scholastic commentator. Clearly, the master's student got a bit more psychological subject-matter under the heading of "morall Philosophy" than the bachelor's student, but the content of the early curriculum at Harvard had little to offer in terms of psychological fare.

In a manuscript dated 1690, we find a bit more detail of the Harvard scheme after the bachelor's curriculum was expanded to four years. A few changes had already begun at Harvard. In the first year the freshman class would study the Latin and Greek classics: Tully, Vergil, Homer, and the like, along with the New

Testament in Greek. One of the scholastic rhetoric books, usually that of Dugard or Farnham, was used as a guide. The nearest thing the freshman encountered to something psychological was the study of logic, quite likely using the text of Peter Ramus, the Puritans' favorite logician, or perhaps that of Burgerdius.[10] In the sophomore year, Burgerdius's logic would be studied for sure, along with the logic of LeGrand. Theology would be broached with Wollebius's *Abridgement of Christian Divinity,* Herebard's *Meletemata* and other such works.[11]

In the third year Wollebius would still be much in evidence, but the student of 1690 would also encounter Charles Morton's physics text, the *Compendium Physicae,* one of the earliest departures from the scholastic monolith.[12] Morton's physics was a transitional work between Aristotle's thought and that of Newton. It replaced Johannes Magirus's *Physiologiae Peripatetica,* published in 1597, a scholastic work so hopelessly out of date that the junior sophisters of the class of 1671 finally revolted and refused to read it.[13] Ethics was studied in the third year as well, making use of More's *Ethicks.* In the late 1690s William Brattle introduced, in manuscript form, his *Compendium Logicae . . . ,* also a transitional work, showing some familiarity with Cartesian logic.[14]

In the fourth year, the senior sophisters would recite works of geometry, astronomy, grammar, logic, and natural philosophy, debating once a week on philosophical and astronomical questions. Copernicus had replaced Ptolemy by the end of the century in matters of astronomy.[15] Theology was stressed to the utmost over all four years of instruction, the seniors receiving a double dose in the form of William Ames's *Medulla Theologicia* (the *Marrow of Sacred Divinity*) and his *Cases of Conscience.* In general, then, even though Descartes, Newton, and Copernicus were piercing the armour of the medieval curriculum, the corpus of scholastic education was very much alive in seventeenth-century New England.[16] What little that can be called of psychological concern was introduced in strongly theological contexts or jumbled up in a wide variety of other topics under the headings of physics, metaphysics, and logic. J. W. Fay sums up the level of psychological information that was transmitted to the student at seventeenth-century Harvard when he calls it:

> . . . the science of a Platonic soul, endowed with Aristotelian faculties, Christianized by St. Paul and St. Augustine, systematized by Thomas Aquinas, divorced from the Catholic Church by Luther and Calvin, and transmitted, enmeshed in various philosophic disciplines . . . through the Protestant Colleges of Oxford and Cambridge.[17]

There was no such thing as specialization in the colonial college. It made no difference if a student were planning to be a minister or to sell goods in a shop, the topics of instruction were the same for all. There were no separate classes with different professors teaching specialty topics. The scholastic regenting system was employed, in which the instruction of the entire freshman class (which might not be more than a dozen students) was undertaken by one tutor, who would stay with that class through its entire four years of college.

The isolation that enveloped the American colonies of New England after the 1640s greatly limited the influence of the new developments in Britain and Europe.

While not all the developments were unknown, the writings of Bacon, Descartes's *Traité des passions de l'âme,* Hobbes's *Human Nature* and *Leviathan,* Locke's *Essay concerning Human Understanding,* even Newton's *Principia Mathematica* and *Optics* made no significant impact on the colleges until a full generation after they were written. In general, if the masters and tutors in the New England colleges knew anything of the revolutionary changes going on across the Atlantic, the students were hearing little of it.

I have dwelt on the Harvard program in such detail because it was, by and large, the model for the other colonial colleges. The College of William and Mary, founded by the Anglicans in 1693, the only other college founded in America in the seventeenth century, followed the same basic plan, as did Yale with its founding in 1701. The products of these colleges in turn made up the bulk of tutors and professors for the other colleges that were founded in the eighteenth century.[18]

Yale opened with a Harvard-trained rector and Harvard-trained tutors. For more than a decade after its founding as a Congregational college, Yale was even further behind than was Harvard. Samuel Johnson (1692–1772), later president of King's College (Columbia) and one of the first American students whose thinking was altered by the "New Learning" of Newton and Locke, recalled of his training at Yale:

> There was nothing but the scholastic cobwebs of few little English and Dutch systems . . . Indeed there was no such thing as any books of learning to be had in those times under a 100 or 150 years old, such as the first settlers of the country brought with them 70 or 80 years before . . .[19]

The New Learning

The year 1714 represents a benchmark in the history of American education and in the beginnings of modern psychological considerations in the American college. It was that year that the seeds of the American Enlightenment arrived on these shores, neatly packed in nine crates. Jeremiah Dummer, the colonial agent for Connecticut, had spent a good bit of his time in England collecting books to be sent to the new College of Connecticut, not yet called Yale and not yet moved to New Haven. These nine hundred volumes represented the whole spectrum of science and philosophy. Newton personally contributed his *Principia* and his *Optics.* Francis Bacon's *Advancement of Learning* was included and, most significant of all for the history of psychology, there was a copy of John Locke's *Essay Concerning Human Understanding.*[20]

The books arrived in Boston in September of 1714, and shortly after they reached their final destination at Saybrook, Connecticut, the location then of the soon-to-be-called Yale College, a senior sophister called Samuel Johnson was allowed to peruse the contents of many.[21] Johnson later recalled that students were cautioned against many of the books for fear that "the new philosophy would soon bring in a new divinity and corrupt the pure religion of the country."[22] How right the tutors were! In Samuel Johnson's notebook for the entry dated November 11, 1714, "Finitum Opus, Thanksgiving Day's Night," is found in parenthesis an addendum in Johnson's hand, stating "And by next Thanksgiving, November

16, 1715, I was wholly changed to the New Learning."[23] The Enlightenment had been loosed in America.

The "wholly changed" Samuel Johnson became a tutor at Yale in 1717 when it was moved to New Haven. The influence of what Johnson called the "New Learning" was clearly discernible in Johnson's treatment of the scholastic curriculum for the class under his charge. As L. L. Tucker relates it:

> Upon becoming a tutor, he swept out much of the accumulated scholastic rubbish and began to introduce into the curriculum the empiricism of Locke, the inductive method of Bacon, and the cosmology of Kepler, Copernicus, and Newton. He also introduced the vitally necessary adjunctive mathematical studies. He himself was obliged to acquire a teachable knowledge of "Euclid, Algebra and Conic Sections"; such instruction had not been provided during his own undergraduate career.[24]

Johnson left Yale in 1719, but the beginnings were made. The thought of Newton and Locke, along with the personal contacts later with the Irish philosopher George Berkeley, led Johnson to produce the first philosophy text in America, his *Elementa Philosophica,* published in 1752.[25] Newton and Locke would also continue to influence Yale students. A youthful Jonathan Edwards (1703–58) would encounter Locke's *Essay* in the Yale library, quite likely the same volume that so changed Johnson's outlook. The implications of Locke's thought on Edwards would bear fruit in the form of his own philosophy, as well as his classic book on the will, which would later be used in the course of study at Yale and at other American colleges. Edwards continued to carry on the precepts of much of the New Learning while himself a tutor at Yale (1724–26). Thomas Clap took over as rector at Yale in 1739 and established the scientific aspects of the Enlightenment on firm ground in the Yale curriculum. Clap, although a religious conservative, had been exposed to Newton while a student at Harvard (1718–22), under the tutorship of Thomas Robie (1689–1729).[26] The emphasis on mathematics and modern "experimental philosophy" begun by Samuel Johnson would be further supported by Clap during his years at Yale. Clap's rectorship saw the addition to the Yale library of the extensive collection of George Berkeley, an addition that made Yale's library the best in New England, particularly in psychological topics. Even with the presence of the works of Berkeley, Hume, and other "forward looking" philosophers, however, Locke's works remained the staple of psychological information at Yale and in all New England colleges until the takeover of American philosophical thought by Scottish realism in the nineteenth century.

Locke's *Essay* was also a starting point for general changes in the way the academic disciplines were arranged. In the last chapter of Locke's *Essay* he lists his "Division of the Sciences." While Locke's arrangement was still based on the Aristotelian and scholastic arrangements of the seventeenth-century Cambridge curriculum, there were some differences to set minds like that of Samuel Johnson awhirl. Locke called for a division of the "body of knowledge"—Locke's definition of the term "philosophy"—into three branches: *physica, practica,* and *logica.*[27] *Physica,* to Locke, was natural philosophy, which dealt with the knowledge of Things, as they are in their own proper Beings, their Constitutions, Properties, and Operations, whereby I mean not only Matter and Body, but Spirits also. . . .[28]

Practica was something like moral philosophy,

the Skill of Right applying our own powers and Action, for the Attainment of Things good and useful. The most considerable under this Head, is *Ethicks,* which is the seeking out those Rules, and Measure of humane Actions, which lead to Happiness, and the Means to practise them.[29]

Logica was the term by which Locke meant the "Doctrine of Signs" or logic,

the business whereof, is to consider the Nature of Signs, the Mind makes use of for the understanding of Things, or conveying its Knowledge to others.[30]

In Locke's arrangement, aspects of psychological thought are present in all three divisions, but primarily in *physica*. The immediate influence of this arrangement can be seen in Samuel Johnson's early manuscript of his *Cyclopedia,* probably dating from 1715.[31] Following Locke, Johnson divides philosophy into three parts, rational, natural, and moral. Johnson defines rational philosophy as that branch which

1st Teaches us to cultivate our Rational powers of thinking & Speaking, that in the right use of them we may know the Truth & (being Sociable Creatures) may communicate our knowledge one to another. . . .[32]

Natural philosophy in Johnson's scheme is that part of philosophy which

instructs us in the knowledge of things, i.e. all the Truths that concern us, as being the objects in the Knowledge of which a great part of our happiness consists. . . .[33]

Moral philosophy, according to Johnson,

teaches us from the Knowledge of things the rules of behaving ourselves, i.e. chusing & acting in such a manner as will make us completely happy. . . .[34]

Rational and natural philosophy "beatifies" the understanding, and moral philosophy, the will and affections. In this early scheme, still somewhat scholastic in flavor, natural philosophy, *Physica,* contains pneumatology, which "Treats of the Nature and powers of our own Souls.& . . . Inquires concerning other Tribes of Intelligence."[35]

Samuel Johnson thought over the arrangement of education during most of the remainder of his life. By the 1752 printing of his *Elementa Philosophica,* Johnson appended his final form of the enlightened education, reproduced here.[36]

A more accurate TABLE, for the Partition of the Sciences, than that, Page xix.

CYCLOPÆDIA, is the whole Circle of Learning, or the Knowledge of every Thing that may contribute to our Happiness, both in Theory and Practice, and consists of two Parts.

I. Philology, or the Study of Language or Signs, called also *Humanity*, and the *Belles Lettres*, and is,

- 1. *General*, or common to all Kinds of Speaking, in
  - 1. *Grammar*, of pure Language.
  - 2. *Rhetorick*, of figurative Speech.
- 2. *Special*, of particular Kinds of Speaking or Writing, as
  - 1. *Oratory*, which treats of Eloquence.
  - 2. *History*, which relates real Facts.
  - 3. *Poetry*, which describes Things in an elevated Manner, whether real or imaginary; and to all these belongs the Art of *Criticism*.

II. Philosophy, or the Study of Wisdom, being the Knowledge of *Things*, together with Practice correspondent thereto, in both which consists our Happiness. All Things or Beings are,

- 1. *Bodies*, or sensible Things, which constitute the natural World, the Knowledge of which is, in a large Sense, called *Physicks*, or *Natural Philosophy*, and is,
  - 1. *General*, of the common Affections of Bodies, Number and Magnitude, in *Mathematicks*, including *Arithmetick* and *Geometry*.
  - 2. *Special*, of all particular Things in the natural World: Particularly,
    - 1. *Natural History*, which gives an Account of Facts in all Nature.
    - 2. *Mechanicks*, of the Laws of Motion.
    - 3. *Geology*, of this terraqueous Globe, and all Things in it, inanimate and animate. And,
    - 4. *Astronomy*, of the Heavens and Stars, and the whole Mundane System.
  - Under each of which Heads there are many practical Matters.

Or,

- 2. *Spirits*, or intelligent moral Beings, which constitute the intelligent or moral World, the Knowledge of which, in a large Sense of the Words, may be called *Metaphysics*, and *Moral Philosophy*, and is,
  - First, *Speculative*, or what relates to the Knowledge of intellectual Things.
    - 1. In *General*, the *Noetics* or *Logic*, including both *Ontology* and *Dialectic* of the Conduct of the Mind in Thinking or Reasoning.
    - 2. In *Special*, *Pneumatology*, of the several Kinds of created Intelligences.
    - 3. *Theology*, of the DEITY, the Father and Lord of them all.
  - Second, *Practical*, or what relates to Life and Conduct, in our several Capacities, personal and social.
    - 1. *Ethics*, of the Conduct of our Temper and Behaviour in general, in order to Happiness.
    - 2. *OEconomics*, of the Conduct of Families. And,
    - 3. *Politics*, of the Government of States, *Civil* and *Ecclesiastical*; to which relate *Biography*, and Civil and Ecclesiastical *History*.

While the influence of Locke's division is still in evidence in the general classes, Johnson's arrangement shows a definite break with the past in the details. The components that made up rational philosophy in Johnson's 1715 division, grammar, rhetoric, oratory, history, and poetry, are now removed from philosophy altogether and reclassified as "Philology," "Humanity," or "Belles lettres," the study of language and signs.

Philosophy, on the other hand, is defined as "the study of Wisdom . . . the Knowledge of Things." Philosophy is now divided into two major components, natural and moral. Natural Philosophy deals with "bodies," the things of the material world; moral philosophy deals with "spirits," the things of the mental and theological world. The "special" topics that make up natural philosophy are those familiar to us as the natural sciences: physics, biology, geology, and astronomy. Mathematics is the "general" study, a tool through which the sciences may be understood. Moral philosophy is divided into two parts: speculative, "what relates to the Knowledge of Intellectual Things," and practical, "what relates to Life and Conduct, in our several Capacities, personal and social."

Speculative moral philosophy deals with "Knowledge of intellectual Things" and includes the special cases of pneumatology, knowledge "of the several Kinds of created Intelligences," and theology, "of the DEITY. . . ." The general study that allows us to understand speculative moral philosophy is logic, called by Johnson "Noetics." It is parallel to the use of mathematics in natural philosophy. *Noetics* is used more broadly than our modern use of logic. In Johnson's definition *Noetics* includes "both Ontology and Dialectic of the Conduct of the Mind in Thinking or Reasoning." Between noetics and pneumatology we have the equivalent of what would become intellectual philosophy in the nineteenth century. The fact that theology is listed along with pneumatology shows how close was the linkage in Johnson's thought between religious and intellectual matters.

Practical moral philosophy covers three special cases: *ethics,* "of the Conduct of our Temper and Behavior in general"; *oeconomics,* "of the Conduct of Families," and *politics,* "of the Government of States, Civil and Ecclesiastical." It contains the behavioral side of future psychological concern in "Ethics," dealing not only with how man should behave, but how, in fact, he does behave. The remaining topics make up the subject matter that would evolve into the various social sciences during the nineteenth century.

Samuel Johnson's own text, *Elementa Philosophica,* was divided into the two sections he recommended in his division of the sciences, speculative and practical, although he used the names *"Noetica"* and *"Ethica."*[37] The content of the book itself is not remarkable, being primarily his own formulation of the ideas of John Locke and George Berkeley. The book had disappointing sales at first and its publisher, Benjamin Franklin of Philadelphia, quite likely lost money on it. It is Johnson's organizational scheme that has had such great importance to the history of American academics and American psychology. Franklin was impressed with Johnson's educational ideas and attempted to entice him to accept the presidency of the College of Philadelphia, later to become the University of Pennsylvania, but Johnson refused.[38]

Johnson did have another chance to apply his philosophical and educational ideas, however, when he accepted the presidency of the newly established College of New York, later to be King's College and finally Columbia. In most respects, Johnson attempted to live up to the concepts he had laid out in his "More accurate Table for the Partition of the Sciences," published with the *Elementa*.

In broad outline, the scholar at King's College was exposed in his first year to philology, particularly Latin grammar, since the King's College freshman was considered "very raw" in such matters. It was, as Johnson put it, "a Course of Rhetoric & Oratory & making Theories."[39] A solid dose of the new logic was presented as well, with William Duncan's *Elements of Logic* (1748) as the text. This was quite likely the most up-to-date book in logic available in the colonies at the time.

In the second year the student was exposed to the general "tools" topics of natural and moral philosophy, including more of Duncan's *Logic*, along with John Locke's *Essay* and also the *Noetica* of Johnson's *Elementa*, "things relating to the Mind or Understanding." Mathematics, including geometry, was included also in the second year course of study.

The third year was devoted primarily to natural science, using the Newtonian *Compendious System of Natural Philosophy* by John Rowning.

In the senior year, Johnson took the students through moral philosophy using his own *Elementa Philosophica*, or at least the *Ethica* of it, "things relating to the Moral Behavior." The division of the psychological material into two courses, *Noetica* and *Ethica*, clearly presaged the nineteenth-century courses of Intellectual Philosophy and Moral Philosophy as separate entities.

Johnson was never fully able to realize his hopes for the college curriculum at King's College, largely because of the limitations of the students, difficulties with the ruling body of the college, and also, to some degree, because of a loss of intellectual nerve on his own part. All his life, Johnson had tried to balance religious conscience—whether Puritan or Anglican—against the influences of the New Learning that led so many educated Americans to deism and atheism. In the end the strain was too much, and Johnson withdrew into the safety of the Old Testament in Hebrew, looking for Moses' "Principia."[40] Although he turned his back on the consequences of the ideas of Newton and Locke, Johnson's students still were exposed to the gems of the New Learning.

A major innovation that Johnson introduced at King's College was to reject the regenting system that had been such a part of the scholastic education. No longer would a tutor carry his class through all the departments of knowledge. Whether the impetus for this change came from a similar system adopted at the College of William and Mary a few years earlier or from the reforms of the Scottish universities is of less importance than its impact on the college system.[41] The regenting system had forced the tutors to be complete generalists, covering all facets of the curriculum. Most tutors kept the position only for a few years until they could take over a congregation somewhere as ministers. The rare tutor who looked on the position as a career soon became a pedantic drudge who went through the motions of the academic exercises with little more variety than a recorded textbook. With a few exceptions, college education was perfunctory and shallow. With the removal of regenting, instructors were able to specialize in various fields—even if the "specialization" was as broad as natural philosophy or moral philosophy. This encouraged study in depth. While it did not do away with the boring or mechanical pedant, it improved the quality of teaching and the transmission of more current information.

When the instructors were allowed to specialize, college teaching as a career became more desirable. Many of the major developments in late eighteenth- and early nineteenth-century science may be directly attributed to this sort of long term professional commitment on the part of college instructors. The next thing to follow was the special title. Rather than being listed as the "tutor," the man who taught moral philosophical topics became the "Professor of Moral Philosophy." Endowed professorships also came into being, as gifts of wealthy ex-students. Within the "chairs" in natural philosophy or moral philosophy or political economics were the germs of modern departments. As the student body increased markedly, as it did in the mid-1800s, and more than one person was required to teach an individual subject, the professor holding the chair would become the head of a department. By 1800, King's College, renamed Columbia, had twenty-six different "departments of knowledge," although several departments were sometimes represented by one man.[42]

In Johnson's curriculum, the ancient works of William Ames and similar religious tracts were removed from the course of study. What replaced them was an approach to moral behavior through the broader context of ethics and moral philosophy.[43] While Johnson's King's College could hardly be called secular in atmosphere, it marked the beginning of some degree of separation between the strictly theological and the philosophical principles of morality. The dropping of religious tests for faculty and students was carried out under Johnson and was soon typical in private American colleges, no matter what their religious affiliation.

Much of what has been said about Samuel Johnson's King's College can also be said of William Smith's College of Philadelphia—later to become the University of Pennsylvania. William Smith accepted the presidency in 1754 after Samuel Johnson had refused it. Smith was a Scot, a graduate of the University of Aberdeen, and was something of an educational reformer. Just as Benjamin Franklin had been attracted by Samuel Johnson's *Elementa Philosophica,* he was also attracted by William Smith's *A General Idea of the College of Mirania* (1753).[44] This utopian work depicts Smith's view of the perfect college, containing many of the same innovations Johnson would introduce at King's College and which were being instituted at Aberdeen.

Smith was installed not only as president of the College but also as professor of natural history. His vice-provost, Francis Alison, also a Scot, was listed as professor of moral philosophy. Professors were listed in oratory, languages, and mathematics as well. William Smith is best known for his emphasis on applications of learning, urging the introduction of useful studies into the curriculum. In topics we would call psychological, however, Smith did not go so far as did Johnson, although Philadelphia did make use of Johnson's *Elementa Philosophica* as a text, along with Locke's *Essay* as a suggested reading.[45] Johnson's shift of psychological concerns from the category of physics to moral philosophy seems to have been followed at Philadelphia. Smith appears to have shared Samuel Johnson's view of placing the study of man's knowing faculties in logic, and that of his willing and doing faculties in moral philosophy. Smith's division of the departments of knowledge is clearly seen in the following:

> Now the genuine branches of this Philosophy . . . may be included under the following general heads, it appearing to me that the nature of things admits of no more. (1) Languages & c, . . . rather as an Instrument or Means of Science than a Branch thereof. (2) Logic and Metaphysics, or the Science of the Human mind; unfolding its powers and directing its operations and reasonings. (3) Natural Philosophy, Mathematics and the rest of her beautiful train of subservient arts; investigating the Physical properties of Body, explaining the various phenomena of Nature; and teaching us to render her subservient to the ease and ornament of Life. (4) Moral Philosophy, applying all the above to the business and bosoms of men, deducing the laws of our conduct from our situation in life and connextions with the Beings around us, settling the whole Economy of the Will and Affections establishing the predominancy of Reason and Conscience, and guiding us to Happiness, through the practice of Virtue.[46]

By the close of the eighteenth century, then, psychological thought had progressed considerably beyond the vagueness of the scholastic curriculum, finally having one foot in logic and one in ethics. This general arrangement, found both at Columbia and Pennsylvania, would be repeated in innumerable colleges, particularly in the years after the American Revolution. The consolidation of psychological topics into a single course would largely have to wait until the consolidation of the Scottish philosophy in the nineteenth century.

The Rise of Scottish Thought in America

If the first century or so of the American college and its psychological subject-matter was characteristically English in origin and influence, the second century or more was just as characteristically Scottish. The Scots had begun coming to America in the early eighteenth century—particularly the Scotch-Irish, those Scots once transplanted on Ulster Plantation in Ireland. The Scotch-Irish came to America in a number of waves between 1717 and 1775.[47] There was an unusually high concentration of educated people in these groups, largely Scotch Presbyterian ministers, but also medical men and teachers. These Scotch-Irish and mainland Scots brought with them attitudes and ideas that deeply affected the American educational scheme and with it the way psychology would be treated in the college classroom.

The Scotch Presbyterians had a deep concern for education, not only for their prospective ministers but also for their congregations. The result of this concern was the establishment of large numbers of Presbyterian academies and colleges. With the reformation of the educational system in most of the Scottish Universities, the immigrants after the 1750s brought with them an education far superior to that of Oxford or Cambridge graduates of the same years. The result was a flood of modern learning, both theoretical and applied, into the middle colonies and western frontier, checked against the excesses of Berkeley and Hume by the firm limits of Calvinist orthodoxy.

The beginnings of Scottish influence have already been demonstrated in the reforms at Columbia and Philadelphia by Samuel Johnson and William Smith. Johnson and Smith were both influenced by the article on moral philosophy by David Fordyce and that on logic by William Duncan in Robert Dodsley's *Preceptor*.[48] Both Fordyce and Duncan were at the very heart of the Scottish reforms at Aberdeen. Duncan's text in logic was used both at Columbia and Philadelphia. William Smith was himself a Scot, although an Anglican, and was a product of the prereform University of Aberdeen. Francis Alison, Smith's vice-provost was a Presbyterian Scot and was in charge of the courses in moral philosophy at Philadelphia. The educational reforms by Smith and Johnson laid the basis for the expansion of the college curriculum in the nineteenth century. The differentiation of psychology from the other social disciplines was dependent on that expansion.

The first educational fruits of the Presbyterian Scots' influx was the College of New Jersey, founded in 1746 and later called Princeton. The college was a product of the repercussions of the surge of "fire and brimstone" revivalism that took place in the 1740s, called the "Great Awakening." All of the Calvinistic churches were involved in one way or the other, but the Presbyterians were particularly split between the "Old Lights," the more traditional Calvinists, and the "New Lights," or the more evangelical branch. The Great Awakening had been prompted by a number of concerns, but one that was of major significance was the rise of "natural religion" and other rationalistic and even irreligious lines of thought. The drift away from fundamentalist Calvinism was the realization of the predicted "new divinity" that would "corrupt the pure religion of the country," about which the tutors of Samuel Johnson had been so concerned in 1714.[49] Newton's and Locke's view of the lawful universe, originally viewed with favor by Calvinist leaders as evidence of the existence and work of God, led ultimately to the view that God does not intervene in the everyday affairs of men. If the universe is so lawful, minute intervention is unnecessary. God, then, becomes a lawgiver, a being who set up the laws of the universe and, like a clockmaker who has completed his creation and set it in motion, goes on to other things. The colonial college students began to lean toward such views, even at staid Yale, overwhelming the best efforts of President Clap to prevent that. The leaders of the Great Awakening hoped that the revival would prove to be a great antidote to the poison of irreligion. In some cases, however, the wild emotionality of the revivalists often encouraged just the opposite reaction, particularly when, after the fervor died down, people were the same as before, if not worse.[50]

After the initial spread of the Great Awakening, the "New Light" Presbyterians felt more and more isolated from the teachings of the supposedly Calvinistic colleges at New Haven and Cambridge. Although Thomas Clap at Yale did not approve of blatant deism, he also did not approve of the excesses of the New Light revivalists. Clap ordered the New Light literature removed from the Yale library, so great was his hostility. When Clap expelled a student of the New Light persuasion for saying, after hearing one of a Yale tutor's sermons, that the tutor had "no more grace that the chair I am leaning upon,"[51] it became clear that the New Light Presbyterians needed a college of their own, free from the limitations of the "Old Lights" and Congregationalists. Aaron Burr, one of the founders of

Princeton, who defended the student in his hearing before the Yale trustees, is supposed to have said later that "if it had not been for the treatment received by Mr. Brainerd at Yale College, New Jersey College would never have been erected."[52] Quite likely, however, Princeton would have come about with or without the rejected Mr. Brainerd. The New Lights had already begun to set up their log colleges on the frontier, as well as in New Jersey, in order to supply a sufficient number of ministers for the growing Presbyterian congregations flooding into the west.

The first twenty years of Princeton's history is not of major concern to the topic at hand. In 1768, however, John Witherspoon (1723–94), a widely respected minister of the Church of Scotland with evangelical leanings, arrived in America to take up the somewhat jinxed presidency of Princeton.[53] Witherspoon was well chosen to do battle against the rationalistic, deistic, and idealistic trends so much afoot in the Colonies at the time. Witherspoon's distaste for the Anglican rationalists and the deists may be seen in his satirical representation of a deist's beliefs, which he called the "Athenian Creed":

I believe in the beauty and comely proportions of Dame Nature and in almighty Fate, her only parent and Guardian. . . . I believe that the universe is a huge machine, wound up from everlasting necessity, and consisting of an infinite number of links and chains, each in a progressive motion towards the zenith of perfection and meridian of glory; that I myself am a little glorious piece of clockwork, a wheel within a wheel, or rather a pendulum in this grand machine, swinging hither and thither by the different impulses of fate and destiny; that my soul (if I have any) is an imperceptible bundle of exceedingly minute corpuscles, much smaller than the smallest Holland sand. . . . I believe that there is no ill in the universe, not any such thing as virtue, absolutely considered; that those things, vulgarly called sins, are only errors in judgment, and foils to set off the beauty of nature, or patches to adorn her face.[54]

Such a satirist could hold his own in any verbal exchange, and he did.

Witherspoon had been a student at Edinburgh (1730–36) and had kept in close touch with the flowering of the Scottish Enlightenment. He was clearly influenced by the writings of the new realist philosophy and held strongly to the view that empirical knowledge, the knowledge by way of the senses, is of a more accurate nature than deduction from reason. He was clearly in the camp of Thomas Reid and is said to have brought a copy of Reid's *Inquiry Into the Human Mind* over with him to his new home. Witherspoon believed that he was the first to introduce the Scottish philosophy of common sense to America. He was certainly espousing ideas similar to those of Reid at a very early date.[55]

On his arrival at the College of New Jersey, Witherspoon found that Berkeley's philosophy and that of Jonathan Edwards was very much alive at Princeton. Edwards had been president of Princeton for a few weeks before dying of smallpox inoculation, and his son was a tutor there. The tutors, particularly one Joseph Periam, espoused a form of Berkeleyan idealism. Samuel Stanhope Smith (1750–1819), later to become Witherspoon's son-in-law and successor as president of Princeton, was then a student at Princeton and a fervent believer in the Berkeleyan view. According to an observer of the time:

The Berkeleyan system of metaphysics was in repute in the college when he [Witherspoon] entered. The tutors were zealous believers in it, and waited on the president with some expectation of either confounding him, or making him a proselyte. They had mistaken their man. He first reasoned against the system, and then ridiculed it till he drove it out of the college.[56]

Witherspoon had just the antidote for Berkeley. Frederick Beasley (1777–1845), later provost and professor of moral philosophy at the University of Pennsylvania, recalled of Witherspoon's Princeton that:

after the fanciful theory of Bishop Berkeley, as a kind of philosophical day-dream, had maintained its prevalence for a season; the principles of Reid and the Scottish metaphysicians superseded it, and during the period of our residence in the seminary, acquired and maintained undisputed sway. At that time, I, together with all those graduates who took any interest in the subject, embraced without doubt or hesitation the doctrines of the Scottish school.[57]

Needless to say, Periam and the other offending tutors left Princeton not long after Witherspoon's coming, leaving positions open for tutors of a theoretical position more compatible with that of the president.[58]

For all his orthodox views of Calvinism, Witherspoon was an enthusiastic supporter of learning and was responsible for the expansion of the Princeton curriculum to include practical and scientific topics, even at the expense of some of the classical topics. This was much in line with the Scottish university reforms. The percentage of Presbyterian ministers produced at Princeton actually dropped during the Witherspoon years to approximately 28 percent of the graduates, this largely due to a stiff dose of science and literature and the heightened standards of instruction under Witherspoon and his successor, Samuel Stanhope Smith.[59] Witherspoon did not alter the structure of the philosophical instruction as concerns psychology so much as alter its contents; anything psychological at Princeton was bound to be Scottish realism. Witherspoon viewed the psychological subject matter in the following way:

The faculties of the mind are commonly divided into these three kinds, the understanding, the will and the affections; though perhaps it is proper to observe, that these are not three qualities wholly distinct, but different ways of exerting the same principle. It is the soul or mind that understands, wills, or is affected with pleasure and pain.[60]

This was very much the Scottish "party line," and Witherspoon made few alterations. The study of the faculties was still divided between courses in logic and moral philosophy. Witherspoon still defined the subject of moral philosophy as "that branch of Science which treats of the principles and laws of Duty and Morals."[61]

It was Samuel Stanhope Smith, Witherspoon's successor at Princeton, who would begin to cast the Americanized Scottish psychology into the form that would be so common in the nineteenth-century college. Smith shifted the psychology of knowing out of the course in logic and into the course in moral philosophy.

In this way the three basic aspects of human psychology, knowing, feeling, and doing, were finally put under the single rubric of moral philosophy. Samuel Stanhope Smith defined moral philosophy as:

> . . . an investigation of the constitution and laws of mind, especially as it is endowed with the power of voluntary action, and is susceptible of the sentiments of duty and obligation . . . . The science of moral philosophy begins with the study of the human mind—its sensations, perceptions, and generally, its means of acquiring knowledge—its sentiments, dispositions and affections, and generally, its principles of action or enjoyment—its present state, and reactions to other beings—its future hopes and fears.[62]

Smith's method was inductive, based on the direct knowledge of the real world. Smith and the other Scottish writers had no argument with the empirical side of Locke, just with his view that we are aware of things only through the senses, and not of the objects themselves. The reliance on senses and induction over reason and deduction is at the heart of the "Baconian" method that underlined so much of Scottish influence in American science.

> No law should be admitted on hypothesis but should rest solely on an induction of facts . . . . Laws collected from an ample and accurate induction of facts should be deemed universal, till other facts occur to invalidate, or limit the conclusions which have been drawn from them.[63]

The influence of Witherspoon and Samuel Stanhope Smith was great. During their terms at Princeton, a large number of students were imprinted with the logic and moral philosophy of the Scottish realists. Many of these students would also become tutors or professors of moral philosophy themselves or otherwise be of influence in the founding and expansion of American colleges. These students, and the professors directly imported from the fountainhead of realism in Scotland, quickly filled the newly created professorships in moral philosophy in the expanding college curriculum after the Revolution.[64]

And how the American colleges expanded! Between the founding of Harvard in 1636 and the Revolution only nine colleges were founded, of which six were under the control of the Presbyterians.[65] By 1851, two-thirds of the colleges in the United States were directly or indirectly under the control of the Presbyterian Church.[66] By the start of the Civil War, a total of 49 permanent colleges had been founded by the Presbyterians or were under their control. The growth of other denominational colleges in the half-century after the Revolution, while not so spectacular as that of the Presbyterians, was still very great. All in all, 182 colleges were in operation by the start of the Civil War. With the founding of those new colleges on the frontier went the ideas of the Scottish philosophy, which, after Witherspoon and Samuel Stanhope Smith, had been accepted virtually as the official philosophy of the Presbyterians in much the same way as Aquinas's writings served the Catholics. The Scottish philosophy spread quickly beyond Presbyterian strongholds to other Protestant colleges.

The Scottish philosophy was pervasive. Even Frederick Beasley, provost of the University of Pennsylvania, himself a product of Witherspoon and Smith, who defended the writings of Locke against the attacks of Reid, produced a book that was much nearer to the Scottish philosophy than to the views of Locke.[67]

By the 1820s Scottish philosophy was the norm in the American college. Even at Yale, John Locke's *Essay* was supplanted in 1825 by Dugald Stewart's *Essays*.[68] By 1829, James Marsh, the president of the University of Vermont could write:

> The works of Locke were formerly much read and used as text books, in our colleges; but of late have very generally given place to the Scotch writers; and Stewart, Campbell and Brown are now almost universally read as the standard authors on the subjects of which they treat.[69]

Scottish Philosophy and Academic Orthodoxy

The reasons underlying this phenomenally widespread acceptance of the Scottish philosophers in American colleges are complex and go beyond the mere expansion of Presbyterianism and the Protestant college. The Enlightenment and the American Revolution had brought about dizzying changes in the culture of the old colonies and the values underlying it. Intellectual movements seem destined to lead to extremism. One line of thought seems to run its full course until it reaches such an extreme point that it loses popular support and is checked by an opposing line which, in turn, runs to its extreme. The New Learning that so excited Samuel Johnson and other college-trained men of the late eighteenth century followed such a course. Rationalism and deism, along with various forms of unconventional religious thought, had not been stamped out by the Great Awakening. In fact, they were more prevalent after the Revolution than ever. The view that God did not intervene in everyday affairs of men again became popular, leading many to believe that the lawful universe of Newton did not require the presence of God at all.

Locke's attempt to put knowledge on an empirical basis contained within it the seeds of skepticism. George Berkeley, in an attempt to protect man from the skeptical consequences of Locke, created his idealism, with its dependence on the act of God in the perception of reality and in the creation of what would later be called associative bonds. Rather than succeeding in his task, Berkeley's view led to David Hume's work, which reduced everything to ideas and habit. By disposing of the nexus of cause and effect, Hume also succeeded in weakening the Aristotelian concept of first cause—at least in the minds of many—with the result that the basic refuge for the proof of the existence of God disappeared. To those who followed this line of thought skepticism was inevitable. Along with this intellectual turmoil the disruption of life during the Revolution led to a loosening of absolutist views of all kinds, including those on morals and religion.

The students who came back to the colleges after the Revolution were a different lot from those before. The unyielding edifice that was New England Puritanism was crumbling. New ideas were sweeping in from the European continent, particularly France. If not presented to the students in the college classroom, such writings as those of Rousseau and Voltaire were available in the literary society libraries. Only the most isolated or orthodox of students would have missed the new ideas. The deistic writings of Thomas Paine were widely read. At Yale and elsewhere, students adopted the affectation of calling each other by the names of the leaders of the French revolution.[70] Civil unrest came to the colleges around the turn of the century, with riots and vandalism becoming commonplace on previously placid campuses. Religious affiliation was at the lowest ebb in the history of the nation. Irreligion became common on the postwar campus.

> In the 1790's the typical Harvard student was an atheist. A few years later students at Williams College were conducting mock celebrations of the Lord's supper. At Princeton the infidel leader of the undergraduate deists led his followers in burning the Bible of the local Presbyterian church.[71]

Lyman Beecher recalled from the experiences of his youth, perhaps with some exaggeration, that

> Yale College was in a most ungodly state. The College church was almost extinct. Most of the students were skeptical, and rowdies were plenty. Wine and liquors were kept in many rooms, intemperance, profanity, gambling and licentiousness were common. . . . Most of the class before me were infidel.[72]

After the French Revolution, French Jacobinism, deism, and even atheism became the rage on the campus, as attested by Bishop William Meade:

> . . . the College of William and Mary was regarded as the hot bed of French politics and religion. I can truly say that then and for some years after in every educated young man in Virginia whom I met I expected to find a sceptic, if not an avowed unbeliever.[73]

In 1802, Samuel Stanhope Smith watched Nassau Hall burn to the ground at Princeton, the work, so he and his trustees believed, of "Jacobin infidels" stimulated by "those irreligious and demoralizing principles which are tearing the banks of society asunder."[74] The conservative reaction to all this was inevitable. Even leaders like John Adams who had flirted with deism and revolution in their younger days denounced the influences of French deism and atheism, materialism and revolutionary attitudes. Adams said in 1798:

> We have had too many French philosophers already, and I really begin to think, or rather to suspect, that learned academies, not under the immediate inspection and control of government, have disorganized the world, and are incompatible with social order.[75]

Americans were, at root, conservative. The American Revolution had not been universally supported in the colonies. A fear of anarchy after the defeat of the British was in the minds of many of the landed gentry who had a vested interest in a rejection of democracy and egalitarianism. Had a vote been taken among the population of the colonies who had the right to vote in the 1770s, a motion to revolt would quite likely have lost. In the French Revolution, with the horrors of the guillotine and confiscation of property, the worst fears of this powerful conservative class were realized. The frightening influx of ideas from France and the unruly events on the once calm campuses seemed to confirm the coming of a cultural Armageddon in America.

The antidote that failed in the 1740s to dispel the spectre of deism and irreligion was again given a try. The second Great Awakening started on the frontier, with its camp meeting format, and began to sweep the nation during the first decade of the nineteenth century. Once unleashed, the religious fervor continued in wave after wave until the time of the Civil War.

This new emphasis on fundamentalist religion and the rejection of the rationalist positions of the deists, coupled with the fast creation of new colleges, particularly along the frontier, left most classrooms by the 1820s under the control of college presidents and trustees firmly resolved that the seeds of infidelity would never again get a chance to take root.

At Yale, Timothy Dwight instituted the religious revival as a means of draining off his students' emotions, but in most institutions the emphasis was on discipline, "keeping the lid on."[76] At Princeton after the riots of 1807, 125 of the student body were expelled by order of the trustees. "We will probably have fewer students," said a Princeton trustee, "but a few under discipline is better than a mob without any."[77] President Timothy Dwight of Yale lauded the Princeton decision, believing that such action would "ultimately serve to strengthen the bonds of discipline and to put down that impatience of control which we also lament as a strong characteristic of the rising generation."[78] At about the same time as the Princeton riots, the Harvard trustees expelled 29 students for disorderly conduct.[79] When the violence continued at Princeton, the trustees finally forced Samuel Stanhope Smith to resign.[80] Clearly, discipline was the order of the day.

Discipline extended beyond student activities. It reached into the intellectual sphere as well. The professor, particularly the professor who taught moral philosophy, had to be "safe," holding to the orthodox tenets of the trustees, one who could present the facts of moral philosophy without the danger of leading students to irreligion or skepticism. The Scottish philosophy, with its appeal to common sense, was quite amenable to this new orthodox fervor, since its concepts avoided the skeptical pitfalls of an unrestrained Locke, Berkeley, or Hume.

The chill was on. I. Woodbridge Riley has referred to the rise of Scottish philosophy in the 1820s as the "glacial age," "an overwhelming mass of cold orthodoxy" grinding out all opposition.[81]

The orthodox attitude can be seen clearly by comparing the way instruction was handled before and after the orthodox "chill." When Samuel Stanhope Smith lectured to his students in the 1790s, he defined philosophy as

an investigation of the constitution and laws of nature both in the physical and moral world, so far as the powers of the human mind, unaided by the light of revelation, are competent to discover them.[82]

Even this statement is more conservative than most at the time. The rationalist view held that man can know all things through reason, if he seeks hard enough. This is not to say that there was freewheeling speculation in the classroom of the moral philosophy course in the eighteenth century—although such speculation certainly existed in student discussion groups, literary societies and debating clubs, particularly in the immediate post-Revolutionary period. The student of the middle to late eighteenth century did, however, receive the bulk of his psychological information from original sources. Students would read Locke or Berkeley or even Hume unexpurgated, very often with line-by-line recitation in the classroom. Even if such works were not available in the classroom, the local literary society library, often larger than the college library itself, would fill the void.

The orthodox view of the early nineteenth-century college was more paternalistic. Confidence in the ability of youth to distinguish truth from error had been tarnished by the apparent irrationality of the post-Revolutionary student. Now the view seems to have become that the student should be protected from new ideas that might confuse him or lead him astray. Thomas Cogswell Upham (1799–1872), professor of mental and moral philosophy at Bowdoin College on the frontier of Maine, expressed a common view in the 1820s.

> Place before the student a mass of crude and conflicting statements, his mind becomes perplexed. To be able to resolve such a mass into its elements, and to separate truth from error, implies an acquaintance with the laws of the intellect, and a degree of mental discipline, which he is not yet supposed to have acquired; and hence, instead of obtaining much important knowledge, he becomes distrustful of everything.
> . . . It belongs rather to professional men and to public instructors, to engage in this minute and laborious examination, and to present those, whom they instruct, with the results of their inquiries. It may indeed be desirable to give them some knowledge of the history of a science, and to point out such authors as are particularly worthy of being consulted by those, whose inclinations and opportunities justify more particular investigations. But this is all that is either demanded, or can be profitable in the ordinary course of education.[83]

There were some "safe" books. Thomas Reid's two volumes of *Essays,* which became available in America in the early nineteenth century, were soon followed by editions of Dugald Stewart. American editions of all the major Scottish realist philosophers were available by the 1820s. In 1825, the Harvard senior received his psychological dosage straight from the texts of Dugald Stewart and Thomas Brown. In his junior year he would have been prepared with Levi Hedge's *Elements of Logick: A Summary of the General Principles and Different Modes of Reasoning,* a mildly Scottish guide to the intellect. His course in moral philosophy used William Paley's *Principles of Moral and Political Philosophy.* Paley's books in natural theology and moral philosophy were popular in the 1820s until replaced by even safer texts.[84]

It is perhaps significant that in the annual reports from many colleges in the 1820s more emphasis seems to be put on the list of texts used than on the title of the courses. The text, in fact, appears to have begun to define the course of study. The study of philosophy was no longer presented as an investigation of natural or moral laws to the limits available to the human mind, but became instead the contents of a given book. What better way to limit the possibilities of skepticism than by presenting the course as the contents of the text? That text would either be by one of the "safe" Scots or the lecture notes of a professor of moral philosophy, made up of carefully gleaned explication of the safe aspects of philosophical thought. In many respects, this is the way we still run courses. "The whole scheme" as Louis Snow points out, "is governed by text books."[85]

Most of the major colleges were firmly in the hands of the Scots, whose influence was felt not only through their own books but also through the packaged textbooks prepared by American professors.

In the 1820s there was further reason for the academic college to gird its loins. New idealisms were coming across the Atlantic by way of Americans studying in Europe and bringing back with them the writings of Kant, Fichte, Schelling, and Lotze. By 1829, James Marsh of the University of Vermont introduced Americans to Samuel Taylor Coleridge's interpretation of the German idealism in the American edition of *Aids to Reflection*. In these new ideas, many conservatives thought, were contained the seeds of skepticism and irreligion. Clearly, the orthodox colleges saw a duty no less important than that of a parent to protect their charges from intellectual danger. The packaged textbook in psychological subjects was clearly the way to handle the problem.

The form the early texts took, and through them the way the courses were taught, was influenced mightily by the appearance in America of Thomas Reid's *Essays on the Intellectual Powers of Man* and his *Essays on the Active Powers of the Human Mind*. As the titles suggest, Reid divided moral philosophy into intellectual powers and active powers. The organization of the subject matter may be seen more clearly in the partial reproduction of the tables of contents of the two works:

I. Intellectual Powers
  1. Of the Powers we have by means of our external senses
  2. Concerning Memory
  3. Of Conception (simple apprehensions)
  4. Of Abstraction
  5. Of Judgment
  6. Of Reasoning
  7. Of Taste (Esthetics)
II. Active Powers
  1. Of the Will
  2. Of the Principles of Action
    a. Mechanical—Instinct and Habit
    b. Animal Principles—appetites, desires, affections, passions, disposition, opinion
    c. Rational Principles of Action—duty, moral obligation, sense of duty, conscience
  3. Of morals

What is immediately evident in this organization is that the subject matter is almost entirely psychological—intellectual powers, dealing with understanding, active powers dealing with feeling and doing. The traditional handling of moral philosophy included a much larger group of topics that today could be referred to as political science, sociology, anthropology and the like. These nonpsychological topics had already begun to differentiate in some institutions into separate courses. Political economy was an area that separated off quite early, with its own professorship in some institutions.[86] The modelling of the moral philosophy course after the arrangement of Reid's topics led to an even faster differentiation of social sciences.

The general outline of Reid's intellectual and active powers would strongly influence the arrangement of college texts in psychological topics for the greater part of a century. Thomas Cogswell Upham of Bowdoin College is usually regarded as the author of the first American textbook in psychology. Samuel Johnson might be given the same credit, although his *Elementa Philosophica* went beyond the topics that would become identified as purely psychological. Johnson usually gets credit for writing the first American text in philosophy. There are other authors who could vie with Upham for the credit of producing the first American psychology text. Ezra Stiles Ely's *Conversations on the Science of the Human Mind* (1819), Frederick Beasley's *A Search of Truth in the Science of the Human Mind* (1822), and even Asa Burton's *Essay on Some of the First Principles of Metaphysicks, Ethicks, and Theology* (1824) have arguments in their favor. What sets Upham's series of books apart from these is the degree to which its content defines the course of psychology as it finally evolved, the degree of systemization exhibited, and the genuine spirit of eclecticism that permeates the entire work.

Upham was one of those "safe" professors. His primary recommendation for the position of professor of moral philosophy and metaphysics at Bowdoin College was that he could probably draw students to Maine from his native New Hampshire and that he could be trusted to stand by orthodox principles.[87] Upham issued his Bowdoin lecture notes for the period 1824–27 under the title *Elements of Intellectual Philosophy* (1827). The title clearly derives from Reid's *Essays*. To say that Upham's book was merely a discourse on Reid, however, is to make the oversimplification that has misrepresented the whole line of American textbook writers in the nineteenth century. As a matter of fact, Upham's 1827 volume is based more on Locke than on the Scots, although the influence of Reid and Stewart is clearly present. Fay, in analyzing the 1827 volume, noted sixty-six basic sources. These sources ranged from Locke to the Scots to more diverse authors such as Montaigne, Descartes, Malebranche, Condillac, Helvetius, Cabanis, Pinel, Esquirol, and de Gerando, to name only a few.[88] Upham was blessed with a talent for languages and an interest in learning modern tongues which, in many ways, gave him access to wider sources of information than were available to any other of the early American writers on psychological matters.

Upham was careful to avoid falling into the easy, uncritical approach of merely summarizing the teachings of a single school. He makes his intent quite clear when he tells the reader that he seeks to

avoid becoming pledged and holden in support of any writer or system. The great object we have before us is to ascertain the facts in regard to the mind; the arrangement of those facts, and any speculations which are not directly founded upon them, are subordinate points of consideration. And there is the greater reason for pursuing this course, when it is remembered that men have ever discovered a strong tendency to make premature generalizations. It flatters their pride; and in thus doing they are urged forward by the influence of a puerile vanity more than by the love of truth.[89]

This was written during the high-water mark of American Baconianism, with its supreme reliance on observation, description, and induction, and its abhorrence of hypotheses and a prioiri statements. That Upham did not always live up to his high standards is excusable because of the monumental efforts he took to be inductive.

In 1832, Upham changed the title of his book, by now expanded to two volumes, to *Elements of Mental Philosophy,* judging that the term *intellectual philosophy* was too narrow to encompass the intellect and the sensibilities. Upham's use of *mental philosophy* would prove quite useful, since moral philosophy was thought of in a number of different ways, from being largely psychological, as with Samuel Stanhope Smith, to a general coverage of what today would be called social science and law. In 1834, Upham added a third volume, the *Philosophical and Practical Treatise on the Will,* completing his three-part system. The later editions of the *Mental Philosophy* became more strongly influenced by the Scots. Fay finds in the 1840 edition heaviest citations of Reid (375 lines), Stewart (175), Brown (84), Locke (165), Cudworth (98), and Buffon (one citation of 145 lines).[90] In many respects, Upham shows in epitome the shifts in American academic psychology from Locke to the Scots. Still, Upham attempted to be objective. In the 1840 edition of the *Mental Philosophy,* Upham tells the reader that the book

is essentially Eclectic in its character; and, as such, can neither incur the discredit, nor claim the honour, of belonging exclusively to any of the great Philosophical Schools, although it does not hesitate to acknowledge its indebtedness to all.[91]

Upham also includes in his *Mental Philosophy* material on abnormal psychology, under the heading of "Imperfect and Disordered Intellectual Action." At the request of Harper Brothers, Upham wrote in 1840 a separate book on abnormal psychology under the title *Outlines of Disordered Mental Action.* This is certainly the first abnormal psychology text to appear in America.[92] By 1861, Upham had come to a final arrangement of his text in the form of an abridgment of his three-volume *Mental Philosophy,* intended as a textbook for academies and high schools. A listing of the topics will give a "feel" for perhaps the clearest arrangement of psychological topics in early nineteenth-century mental philosophy.[93]

Division I: The Intellect or Understanding
Part I: Intellectual States of External Origin
1. Origin of Knowledge in General
2. Sensation and Perception
3. Sense of Hearing
4. Senses of Smell and Taste
5. Sense of Touch

      6. Sense of Sight
      7. Habits of Sensation and Perception
      8. Conceptions
      9. Simplicity and Complexness of Mental States
    10. Abstraction
    11. Of Attention
    12. Dreaming

Part II. Intellectual States of Internal Origin
      1. Internal Origin of Knowledge
      2. Suggestion
      3. Consciousness
      4. Relative Suggestion or Judgment
      5. Association: Primary Laws
      6. Association: Secondary Laws
      7. Memory
      8. Duration of Memory
      9. Reasoning
    10. Demonstrative Reasoning
    11. Moral Reasoning
    12. Practical Directions in Reasoning
    13. Imagination
    14. Disordered Intellectual Action: Excited Conceptions or Apparitions
    15. Disordered Intellectual Action: Insanity

Division II. The Sensibilities
  Part I: Natural or Pathematic Sensibilities
    Class I: Emotions or Emotive States of the Mind
      1. Nature of the Emotions
      2. Emotions of Beauty
      3. Associated Beauty
      4. Emotions of Sublimity
      5. Emotions of the Ludicrous
      6. Instances of Other Simple Emotions
    Class II: The Desires
      1. Nature of the Desires
      2. Instincts
      3. Appetites
      4. Propensities
      5. The Malevolent Affections (Anger, Peevishness, Envy, Jealousy, Revenge, etc.)
      6. The Benevolent Affections (Love, Patriotism, Friendship, Pity, Gratitude, etc.)
      7. The Benevolent Affections: Love to the Supreme Being
      8. Habits of the Sensibilities

    Part II. The Moral Sensibilities or Conscience
           1. Emotions of Moral Approval and Disapproval
           2. Relations of Reasoning to the Moral Nature
           3. Feelings of Moral Obligation
           4. Uniformity of Action in the Moral Sensibilities
           5. Moral Education
    Part III. Imperfect or Disordered Sensitive Action
           1. Disordered and Alienated Action of the Appetites and Propensities
           2. Sympathetic Imitation
           3. Disordered Action of the Affections
           4. Disordered Action of the Moral Sensibilities
Division III. The Will
           1. General Nature of the Will
           2. On the Laws of the Will
           3. Laws of the Will Implied in the Prescience of Foresight of the Deity
           4. Laws of the Will Implied in the Prescience of Men
           5. On the Freedom of the Will
           6. Freedom of the Will Implied in Man's Moral Nature
           7. On the Power of the Will

Upham's outline, the main divisions of which are given here, consists of a total of 495 separate topics.

Upham's textbooks were widely used throughout the country well into the 1870s and did much to standardize the form of the mental philosophy course. The numerous references to the Deity point up the essentially religious side of Upham, a trait common to just about all the writers on mental philosophy before William James. Virtually all the textbook writers were trained as ministers, Upham included. The appeal to the study of the relationship of man to God was an almost obligatory exercise in the mental philosophies of the nineteenth century, particularly before the Civil War. This concern for religious matters was one of the reasons, of course, why orthodox religion was so congenial to textbook writers like Upham. Education in America was still the handmaiden of the Protestant establishment.

Consolidation and Development of Academic Psychology

In the 1820s and 1830s, the tendency for a differentiation of the curriculum continued. The old natural philosophy course was subdivided into specific sciences. The philosophy of the human mind was being more clearly separated in most colleges from logic on one side and social science aspects of the old moral philosophy course on the other. During the winter semester in the 1820s, for instance, the Princeton senior would take

Belles Lettres, Composition, Mechanics, Chemistry, Exper. Philosophy, Gr. & Lat. Class., Logic, Phil. of Human Mind, Political Economy.[94]

The curriculum began to show the faint outlines of the form that was to come. Textbooks began to reflect this differentiation. Francis Wayland (1799–1865), professor of moral philosophy and president of Brown, wrote both an intellectual philosophy and a moral philosophy. Wayland's *Elements of Intellectual Philosophy* covered psychology in its narrow sense of "knowing, feeling, and doing," in terms of mental states. His *Elements of Moral Science* also touched on psychological matters, but was more concerned with ethics and general concepts of morality—how man should behave rather than how he does behave. Wayland also wrote *Elements of Political Economy,* dealing with a variety of social science topics from the old form of the moral philosophy course. Similarly, Joseph Haven (1816–74) wrote immensely popular texts covering mental philosophy and moral philosophy as separate topics with the psychological material primarily in the mental philosophy. Such attempts by one person to cover both the psychological and ethical aspects of the field lasted well into the proliferation of courses after the introduction of the elective system in the 1870s. Noah Porter (1811–92), professor of moral philosophy and metaphysics and president of Yale, brought this model to its apex with *The Human Intellect* (1868) and *The Elements of Moral Science: Theoretical and Practical* (1885). What is important is that psychological topics were becoming clearly distinguished from the other social sciences. Mark Hopkins made this distinction clear in his own lectures:

> What man ought to do will depend on what he is, and the circumstances in which he is placed. Mental science, or psychology, will therefore, be conditional for moral science, which will make use of the first, and is the higher of the two. The province of psychology will then be to show what the faculties are; that of moral philosophy to show how they are to be used for the attainment of their end. Both have to do with the faculties of the mind, but in different aspects; as both the botanist and the agriculturist have to do with wheat, and the astronomer and navigator with the heavenly bodies. The botanist classifies wheat; the agriculturist raises it, and cares for a knowledge of its class only as it will enable him to do that.[95]

Between 1827 and 1860 the number of textbooks on mental philosophy proliferated as quickly as did the colleges. There are a number of reasons for this, but one major influence was certainly the change from the recitation system to a lecture system. Instead of merely drilling students on the assigned readings for the day, the professor often talked about the material itself or, more typically, read to the class his lecture notes on the subject. Lectures had been used in America since the time of John Witherspoon and William Smith, but the technique did not gain widespread use until the 1820s. It may well have been the push for orthodoxy that encouraged the use of the method. When even the safest books contained material to which the professor objected, there was a need for correction. The lecture provided for that. Certainly a common justification found in the preface of the American textbooks in mental philosophy for the author's adding yet another book to the market was some disagreement with the available texts, often Scottish, or with commentators such as William Paley or Lord Kames. Whatever the justification of using the lecture system, the result was that professors found themselves with extensive lecture notes that could easily be converted into textbooks and a source of income to boot.

It is easy to oversimplify and regard the products of the textbook writers for the nineteenth-century college as rigid Scottish faculty psychologies. Scottish thought did predominate through much of the century, but such a broad generalization gives an incorrect picture of psychological thought both in America and Scotland during that period. It is a mistake to think that the professors of mental, intellectual, or moral philosophy (whatever they were called at a given location) were content merely to paraphrase the orthodox Scots. Upham, for instance, while following the basic outlines of Reid and Stewart, did not agree with them in every detail, even in the most "Scottish" versions of his texts. Virtually all the writers of texts of the "Scottish type," after Upham, selected from ideas beyond England and Scotland. The use of exotic sources was not highly publicized in most cases. There were still more rewards for appearing orthodox and "safe" than being labeled as controversial. The "Baconian" vogue of being descriptive and inductive rather than explanatory allowed some degree of safety, as did the rather sparse referencing of sources that was common in most textbooks of all kinds in the early nineteenth century.

The phrase "orthodox Scottish philosophy" should be restricted to the ideas of Reid and Stewart. Thomas Brown, whose books were exceptionally popular in America after their appearance in the 1820s, was attempting to go beyond Reid and Stewart and make union with the concepts of the psychology of association. Sir William Hamilton, whose books appeared somewhat later, attempted to find rapport between Scottish and Kantian thought. Reid, Stewart, Brown, and Hamilton were all Scots and their thought often has been lumped together under the general term "Scottish philosophy," but the latter two are markedly different from the former. In short, by the 1830s not even the Scottish School was orthodox. As Stewart replaced Locke, so Brown replaced Stewart and finally, just before the Civil War, Hamilton began to replace Brown in the American college as the standard source for Scottish philosophy.

By the 1840s, the homogeneity of British thought, whether that of Locke or Stewart, had largely disappeared in many of the American colleges. An English observer of the American philosophical scene in the 1840s described the influences on American textbooks as being Anglo-Scottish and Franco-German.[96] By Anglo-Scottish he meant the Locke-Reid-Stewart-Brown influence and by Franco-German, the influence of Kant and the post-Kantians, such as Schelling, Fichte, and Hegel, through the interpretations of the French eclectics, such as Victor Cousin, and the English poet and philosopher Samuel Taylor Coleridge.

The Kantian and post-Kantian philosophers, about whom Thomas Upham's trustees at Bowdoin had been so concerned, slipped into the country before the door of orthodoxy could be slammed shut. As a matter of fact, it was James Marsh (1794–1842), a classmate of Upham at Andover Theological Seminary, who was largely responsible for leaving the door ajar. Marsh was professor of moral philosophy and president of the University of Vermont. In the late 1820s Marsh came across a copy of Samuel Taylor Coleridge's *Aids to Reflection,* an explication of Coleridge's idealism with sources in Berkeley but primarily in Kant and the post-Kantians. Being surprised to find his ideas so similar to those of Coleridge, Marsh wrote requesting permission to put out an American edition of the work, which appeared in 1829.[97] Marsh's intent was to introduce the Kantian views to an American public, largely ignorant of their existence. Marsh wrote to Coleridge that

> the German philosophers, Kant and his followers, are very little known in this country; and our young men who have visited Germany, have paid little attention to that department of study while there. I cannot boast of being wiser than others in this respect; for though I have read a part of the works of Kant, it was under many disadvantages, so that I am indebted to your own writings for the ability to understand what I have read. . . . To me, it seems a point of great importance to awaken among our scholars a taste for more manly and efficient mental discipline. . . .[98]

As Marsh pointed out, the German writings came into America only gradually. Many colleges like Bowdoin had trustees violently opposed to anything that smacked of idealism, for fear that it would foster a new wave of skepticism and irreligion. Marsh also attributed the lack of American familiarity with Kant and his followers to the rather negative treatment Dugald Stewart gave the Germans in his *History of Philosophy*.[99] Stewart has since been criticized for his treatment of Kant, in his history and in his article in the *Encyclopaedia Britannica,* as due to misinformation on Kant's views, "whose works he knew only from translations and imperfect compends."[100] The major problem, however, then as now, was the tendency of Americans to be monolingual, at least in modern languages. What little Americans knew of the German philosophy was, for a number of years, through Coleridge's writings. Even the English translations of Kant, when they appeared, proved difficult for Americans to understand. Mark Hopkins of Williams College admitted that the only exposure he had to Kant was through Bohn's translation, and even then he was "never able to get beyond the first paragraph of the *Critique of Pure Reason,* which he could not understand."[101] Since Hopkins related that he used ideas of "Kant and Coleridge" in the formulation of part of his lectures, we must surmise that his knowledge of Kant was solely through Coleridge.[102] It was only as contacts between Americans and Europeans increased in the 1830s and 1840s that the flow of French and German ideas increased as well.

Marsh's course at Vermont appears to be the first point of direct contact between German philosophy and the American classroom. Marsh used the term *psychology* in his classes, although its coverage represented only a section of the course of philosophy.[103] The term *psychology* was in common use in Germany in the 1820s, of course, and had been for decades. Marsh's lectures on psychology have the flavor of Sir William Hamilton's thought in many respects, which should not be surprising, since they were both attempting a similar synthesis. Unfortunately, Marsh died before publishing his lectures and therefore much of the potential of his own thought was never realized in the wider American intellectual sphere.[104]

Friederich Augustus Rauch (1806–41) was another source of German philosophical ideas in America. Rauch was educated in Giessen and Heidelberg. He is said to have been a favorite pupil of the Hegelian philosopher Daub at Heidelberg. Rauch earned his Ph.D. in 1827 and reached the rank of *Professor Extraordinarius* before political problems caused him to come to America in 1831. Rauch was ordained as a minister in the German Reformed Church and in 1836 became the first president of Marshall College (later combined with Franklin College to form Franklin and Marshall College).[105] Rauch's textbook, *Psychology; or, A View of the Human Soul, Including Anthropology,* was published in 1840. The book appears to be the first American text to make use of the term *psychology* in its title. Herbart had used the word in the title of his *Psychologie als Wissenchaft,* but other American and British writers still preferred *mental philosophy* or *pneumatology.* The word would become common only after the appearance of Herbert Spencer's *Principles of Psychology* in 1855.

Rauch's use of the term *anthropology* had to do with a consideration of mind-body relationships and was very much in the German academic tradition. Anthropology included considerations of environmental effects, such as climate, on mental actions. Individual differences were also considered in this section, such as sex and race. Aging was also studied in this context, as well as the mind-body relations, including phrenological considerations.

"Psychology" in Rauch's usage dealt with the internal mental functions, Reason and Will. "Reason" embraced (1) Sensation, (2) Conception, Fancy, and Imagination, and (3) Pure Thinking, while "Will" was treated also in three sections, (1) Desires, (2) Inclinations and Passions, and (3) Emotions. Rauch's psychology emphasized mind as a process rather than in terms of independent faculties. Reason and will were considered to be inseparable functions of a unitary mind.[106]

> . . . They are both two sides of the same coin. Reason is nothing else than will with prevailing consciousness, and will is reason with a prevailing practical tendency.[107]

Rauch emphasized the growth of the mind as a continuing process. It was his objective to merge German with American philosophy. All this was done with a careful consideration of the religious predilection of his American audience. A review at the time described Rauch as "embracing fully the transcendental speculations of Schelling and Hegel," but having labored to reconcile them with the religion of the Bible."[108] The book was quite popular. Fay tells us that the first edition was sold out in a matter of a few weeks.[109] Rauch died the year following the publication of his *Psychology,* which may partly explain his lack of lasting influence.

Typical of the texts of the time, Rauch's *Psychology* was based on his lectures at Marshall College in the late 1830s. Between 1836 and 1839 Rauch's junior course was titled "Intellectual Philosophy," but in 1840 with the appearance of Rauch's book, the course title was changed to "Psychology."[110] This course given in 1840 at Marshall was quite likely the first course to bear the name "Psychology" in an American college.

Another source of German idealistic concepts was Victor Cousin (1792–1867). Cousin's eclectic psychology was a composite of post-Kantian German romantic philosophy and British views. Although some French editions of Cousin's writings were in the United States by the 1830s, it was Caleb Sprague Henry, professor of philosophy at New York University, who translated and edited Cousin's writings and issued in 1834 *Victor Cousin's Elements of Psychology: Included in a Critical Examination of Locke's Essay*. Cousin's impact was greater on the nonacademic transcendentalists than on the academicians at first, but in years to come Cousin would be found commonly in the college library and classroom.

Perhaps the most widely read early American textbook writer of the German idealist tradition was Laurens Perseus Hickok (1798–1888). Herbert Schneider calls Hickok "the first American theologian and professor to become a systematic expositor of German idealism."[111] While Rauch might well deserve this credit, Hickok was certainly widely read and was influential in the shift of American academic thought toward German idealism as the century progressed. Hickok's best known psychological works are his *Rational Psychology* (1848) and his *Empirical Psychology* (1854). Hickok defined psychology as the "Science of Mind."

> Empirical Psychology attains the facts of mind and arranges them in a system. The elements are solely the facts given in experience, and the criterion of their reality is the clear testimony of consciousness . . . .
> Rational Psychology is a very different process for attaining a science of Mind . . . . It is truly a transcendental philosophy inasmuch as it transcends experience and goes up to those necessary sources from which all possible experience must originate . . . . It enters into the very essence of Rational Psychology to make this *a priori* investigation of the human intellect; to attain the idea of intelligence, from the *a priori* conditions which make an intellectual agency possible, and thereby determine how, if there be intelligence, it must be both in function and operation; and then find the facts which shall evince that such intellectual agency is not only possible in void thought, but is also actual being in reality.[112]

Hickok, while clearly and strongly influenced by Kantian thought, was still eclectic. Hickok perhaps did more than any American textbook writer to open the door left ajar by James Marsh and let in the Kantian and post-Kantian idealisms. While the early editions of Hickok's books, particularly the *Rational Psychology,* were criticized by some conservative elements for their emphasis on German idealism, Hickok was careful to demonstrate that there was no conflict between Kantian thought and religion. He seems to have satisfied enough academicians, since his texts, particularly the *Empirical Psychology,* were widely used both in their original editions and in the revisions by Seelye as late as the 1880s.[113]

By the 1850s American philosophers were beginning to make the trek to Europe to visit the authors whose books they were reading. In 1852 for instance Henry Philip Tappan toured England, Scotland, and France, making contacts with William Hamilton and Victor Cousin.[114] In 1853, Noah Porter spent half a year in Europe, taking particular care to attend the fall lectures of Adolf Trendelenburg, the Aristotelian scholar and teacher of Franz Brentano.[115] Porter also came to know Schelling and Alexander von Humboldt.

Even though the taking of doctoral degrees in Germany by Americans would become popular only after the Civil War, such contacts did much to widen the perspective of American philosophical psychologists on Continental thought and, through them, of their students.

In general, however, the German influence of Kant and the post-Kantians slipped into the American classroom—at least in the first half of the century— quite indirectly, through the texts of the general, eclectic American textbook writers. As Cousin's and Hamilton's eclectic psychologies came to be commonly used in the antebellum classroom, the fear of the German idealisms began to wane in all except the most conservative institutions. After the Civil War, the neo-Humean idealisms of John Stuart Mill and the evolutionary psychology of Herbert Spencer made Kant appear almost "safe" by contrast.

There were major influences outside of academia on the side of Hegelian idealism in the form of the St. Louis movement. The *Journal of Speculative Philosophy,* the organ of the school, containing as it did translations of both "classic" and new German philosophy as well as commentaries by American authors, was another major introduction of the American student to German thought.

By the time of the Civil War, the freeze of orthodoxy had largely thawed. All manner of new ideas were coming into the college classroom. The number of courses had expanded to the degree that President Quincy of Harvard admitted as early as 1841 that the topics in the arts and sciences had so multiplied as to make it impossible for a student to study everything.[116] Some sort of elective system was necessary. The concept of electives had been broached on many occasions over the previous eighty years or so. William Smith's University of Pennsylvania had tried it; Thomas Jefferson's William and Mary had done likewise, as had Eliphalet Nott's Union College, Wayland's Brown, and a number of other institutions. Often these electives took the form of parallel courses leading not to a diploma but to a certificate of attendance. In general, however, up until the massive reforms at Harvard in the 1870s, only a limited number of options were possible in the American colleges. In 1839, for instance, the Harvard faculty had agreed to allow the substitution of science, modern languages, and history for the required Latin and Greek, at least after the first year. Theological seminaries represented something of an alternative subject matter, as did the scientific schools like the Sheffield Scientific School at Yale and the Lawrence Scientific School at Harvard.

Academic Reform and the Coming of the "New Psychology"

The more frequent contact with European universities led to calls for academic reform in the American college. Henry Philip Tappan, president of the University of Michigan, called for a university system with specialties and electives.

> With the vast extension of science, it came to pass that the course of study was vastly enlarged. Instead of erecting Universities, we have only pressed into our four years' course a greater number of studies. The effect has been disastrous. We have destroyed the charm of study by hurry and unnatural pressure, and we have rendered our scholarship vague and superficial . . . . We have not disciplined the mind by guiding it to a calm and profound activity, but we have stimulated acquisition to preternatural exercitations, and have learned as it were from an encyclopedia the mere names of sciences without gaining the sciences themselves.[117]

A thorough reform would have to wait for Eliot's changes at Harvard. The rise of

natural science after the Civil War and the tendency to separate theological matters from general academic programs doubtlessly aided in the transition. Eliot, for
instance, who took the presidency in 1869, was a chemist rather than a theologian
or philosopher. The creation of the Land Grant Colleges in the 1860s also set the
stage for a secularization of education in America.

The thaw of orthodoxy was evident in the increased breadth of education and in
the heterogeneity of psychological thought in the classroom. G. Stanley Hall, a
student at Mark Hopkins's Williams College in the 1860s, recalled that during the
time that Hopkins was using Sir William Hamilton's *Lectures on Metaphysics* in
his classes, John Bascom, one of the lecturers and later president of the University of Wisconsin,

> encouraged me to break away from Sir William Hamilton, whose system was
> taught by the president and to become interested in Mill, Mansel, Jouffroi and
> the Associationists. The divergences of his standpoint from that of the president
> were marked and a source of great interest to us students in the later college
> years, as most of us took sides with one or the other.[118]

Such diversity of thought in a college a few decades earlier would have been
unheard of. Hopkins's rather open attitude was certainly part of the phenomenon
at Williams. Hopkins encouraged questions in class and even challenges to the
line of thought he was promoting. Hall recalled the kindly way in which Hopkins
dealt with his enthusiastic attempt to level John Stuart Mill's criticisms at the
Hamiltonian view as expounded in Hopkins's lectures.[119]

The new liberality was not confined to a few idyllic colleges like Hopkins's
Williams College. The Harvard trustees' boast of 1854 that the Harvard student
was aquainted with "a variety of intricate systems and theories, which from age to
age have tasked the most acute intellects" appears to have become the goal of
most of the major colleges and many of the lesser ones.[120]

Charles W. Eliot's implementation of an elective system in 1874 further encouraged a liberality and diversity of thought. The system initially required
courses only during the freshman year, except for rhetoric, philosophy, history,
and political science. Other than that, the Harvard student could select courses as
they appealed to him. Except for the fact that advanced courses had prerequisites
in basic courses which had to be taken first, the Harvard curriculum was completely open. The effect was to allow the Harvard student to go beyond the
general course in a given topic and begin explorations of the subject matter in
depth. By the late 1870s the philosophy curriculum at Harvard was the largest in
the country. The general philosophy course in 1877 included required readings in
Jevons's *Logic* and Locke's *Essay*. In addition, however, elective courses were
available beyond the general course. First was a course on Cartesianism, Descartes, Malebranche, Berkeley, and Hume. The first elective was on Spinoza's
History of Modern Philosophy and *Lectures on French and German Philosophy*.
The second elective was a course on German Philosophy of the present day,
which used Schopenhauer's *Die Welt als Wille und Vorstellung* and Hartmann's
Philosophie des Unbewussten as texts. The third elective was a course titled
"Psychology" using Taine's *On Intelligence*. The fourth elective was Ethics, mak-

ing use of Grote's *Treatise on the Moral Ideals* and Cicero's *De officiis*. Each of these courses was given for three hours per week throughout the entire school year.[121] This sort of selection can hardly be called typical in the American college of the 1870s, but it is certainly the direction in which the philosophical curriculum was moving.

Francis Bowen (1811–90), Alford Professor of Philosophy at Harvard, was head of the Department of Philosophy in the 1870s and was one of the three great conservatives in the Harvard, Yale, Princeton triad who saw psychology come into its own. The other two members were Noah Porter of Yale and James McCosh of Princeton. Porter and McCosh were philosophers and were both presidents of their respective institutions. All three of these men opposed to some degree the extent of Eliot's wide-open elective system, yet their departments of philosophy developed largely due to the creation of the system. In a way, these three conservatives point up just how far the new attitudes toward a liberal education had gone in the American college of the 1870s and 1880s.

Bowen was a theist and a strong supporter of the views of Sir William Hamilton. Yet, when John Stuart Mill published his *Examination of the Philosophy of Sir William Hamilton,* a scathing analysis and attack on Hamilton, Bowen offered an elective course using Mill's book as a text.[122] While one can be sure that Bowen made use of Mill's book as a foil for his lectures, the important point is that students had a chance to read the potentially "dangerous" work in the original rather than being fed an eviscerated synopsis of it in a partisan Hamiltonian-oriented textbook. The material was presented and, along with Bowen's critique, was allowed to compete openly for the students' allegiance. When Bowen proposed a similar elective on Kant, some New England newspapers expressed a fear that the result would be agnosticism at Harvard.[123] The course was offered nevertheless. Even though Bowen's stance was basically one of philosophical conservatism, it did not include the ironbound paternalism of the 1820s. There was a greater appreciation of the ability of the undergraduate to judge views for himself. The atmosphere of the 1870s was much more like that of the 1770s than the 1820s.

Bowen's Philosophy 1 course was almost entirely psychological. In 1872 it went under the title "Psychology," requiring readings in Locke's *Essay,* Cousin's *Philosophie sensualiste* and *Philosophie de Locke* as well as Mill's *Examination of the Philosophy of Sir William Hamilton.*[124] In 1878, however, Bowen opposed the introduction of William James's elective titled "Psychology." The reason might be that James had previously used Spencer's *Principles of Psychology* in his Natural History 2 course, "Physiological Psychology," and was viewed as a supporter of evolution. More than likely, the crucial fact was that James had no formal training in philosophy, but had done his undergraduate work at the Lawrence School of Science and had an M.D. degree. Whatever the basis of Bowen's objections, they were overruled by President Eliot and the course was instituted in the Department of Philosophy.[125] G. Stanley Hall, who reported these developments a couple of years later, noted that the course

was admitted not without some opposition into the department of philosophy, and is up to the present time the only course in the country where students can be made familiar with the methods and results of recent German researchers in physiological psychology: the philosophical standpoint of Dr. James is essentially that of the modified new-Kantianism of Renouvier.[126]

James had first offered his course on physiological psychology in the graduate curriculum in 1875 titled "The Relations between Physiology and Psychology" and including a demonstrational laboratory. In 1876 the course was offered for undergraduates.[127] All this was in the Department of Natural History, however. The "Psychology" of 1877 was the first of James's offerings in the philosophy curriculum.[128]

At Yale the elective system was late in coming. Noah Porter opposed the concept and as president was in a position to resist its coming. Even with Porter's opposition, however, electives began to creep into the Yale curriculum during the mid-1870s under the guise of "optionals." These "optionals" could be taken beyond the required courses but could not be substituted for them.[129] Later on, even Porter would admit that optional courses provided

> the opportunity for courses of study for those who have in view special occupations in life and also for those who desire to perfect themselves by continuous application in one or more favorite or specially desirable departments of knowledge.[130]

The elective system allowed for specialization and professionalization of the various fields of study and of the subfields, such as psychology.

The increase in available courses at Yale due to "optionals" and later electives was important in the further development of psychological courses. Another important factor at Yale was the creation of the professorship of political and social sciences in 1872. William Graham Sumner occupied the chair. This removed the last vestige of the "social science" aspects of the old moral philosophy course offered in the Department of Philosophy. Porter's course had been titled "Psychology" for some years but now took the subject matter over exclusively. In time the course would be transferred to George Trumbull Ladd, who joined the department in 1881.[131]

Porter has often been represented as a hard-line conservative, and in matters of educational curriculum and religious standards he was. In many ways, Noah Porter was Yale's Thomas Clap of the nineteenth century. In religious matters and in his defense of the orderly required curriculum, Porter was as hard and fast as Thomas Clap ever was. Like Clap's however, Porter's mind was not closed to advancements in thought. Porter was one of the early generation of philosophers to go to Europe to discover the new philosophies at first hand, and dedicated his *Human Intellect* to Adolf Trendelenburg. Even the layout of *The Human Intellect* demonstrates Porter's wish to give the student more than one side of the question.

Porter's book was laid out in different typefaces. The basic definitions and propositions were printed in the largest type. Explanatory material and illustrations of the major lines of thought were in a smaller type, and Porter's own criticisms and other "controversial material" were printed in the smallest type. Porter's *Human Intellect* was called "a thesaurus of its subject, containing in outline the results of the best thinking which had been done in all ages on the human mind."[132] True to the American tradition, Porter's book is genuinely eclectic, drawing on different lines of thought as they served the topic at hand. Although the most conservative of our three conservatives, Porter sought to present all sides of the question and let the student decide the truth of the matter.

George Trumbull Ladd (1842–1921) was appointed instructor in philosophy at Yale in 1881. Ladd, a Congregationalist minister, was conservative in much the same way as was Porter, which may explain his selection to the post. Ladd was not close-minded, however, and as the new German psychology of Wundt became known, he steeped himself in the new experimentalism. In 1887 Ladd published his *Elements of Physiological Psychology,* based heavily on the 1880 edition of Wundt's *Grundzüge der physiologischen Psychologie.*[133] For a number of years, until the translations of Wundt appeared, Ladd's book would be the initial introduction of most American students to Wundt and experimental psychology. The book was not all Wundtian. Ladd's religious predilection led him to represent the mind as a real unit-being, a substantive entity. Ladd eventually took over the Department of Philosophy in the late 1880s and continued to forward the new experimental psychology. In 1892 Ladd hired Edward Scripture (1864–1943), fresh from Wundt's laboratory. In the same year Scripture founded Yale's experimental psychology laboratory and the *Studies from the Yale Psychological Laboratory,* a house organ for the results of Yale researches. For more than a decade to follow, Yale would be a leader in the new experimental psychology.[134]

The third conservative force in the last quarter of the nineteenth-century American college was James McCosh. If Noah Porter was the Thomas Clap of nineteenth-century Yale, then McCosh was certainly the John Witherspoon of nineteenth-century Princeton. Like Witherspoon, McCosh was a native Scot, deeply committed to the Scottish School. McCosh was a student of Sir William Hamilton. A conservative in things religious, McCosh, like Witherspoon, had an open mind to matters of science and learning. McCosh was elected president of Princeton in 1868, just a century after Witherspoon. In his inaugural address, McCosh called for an expansion of the curriculum and a beginning of an elective system.

> I say, if you are to admit . . . the new branches without excluding the old, then you must allow a choice. If our years were as many as those of the antediluvians, one might require all of every student, but to do so in a four year course, would give but a smattering of all without a real knowledge of any.[135]

While McCosh strongly disagreed with the wide-open system of electives available at Harvard, his program was far more liberal that that at Yale and close in some respects to the "concentration and distribution" system so widely practiced today. McCosh provided a place for curricular expansion by beginning one of the greatest building sprees in the history of the American college up to that time. With sufficient buildings, McCosh then proceeded to build up the Princeton faculty. Like the term of Witherspoon, McCosh's tenure was filled with a flood of new ideas into America, many of which were likely to tempt students to infidelity. Darwin's evolutionary theory was much in evidence, as was the thought of John

Stuart Mill and Herbert Spencer. McCosh's response to the new ideas was surprising for a "conservative":

> Ours is an age in which there is a fierce attack on Christianity and not a little infidelity in many of the colleges of Europe and America. I am happy to report that there is little disposition in this college towards scepticism or scoffing. I do my best to guard against these. But I do this not by keeping the young men ignorant of prevailing errors, or by an empty denunciation of them—from a large observation I am able to say that this is the most effective of all means to produce infidelity. I encourage freedom of thought and expression among the students and seek to guide it aright. I state the errors of the day and then show the students how to meet them.[136]

McCosh saw no conflict between religion and Darwin's concepts of evolution. McCosh's view of Darwin as showing a picture of God's handiwork is an interesting parallel to that of Cotton Mather on Newton's picture of the lawful universe.[137]

In his own teaching on philosophical and psychological topics, McCosh held fast to the Scottish view, calling for a return to the pristine view of Reid. McCosh in his *Psychology,* published in two volumes in 1886, two years before he stepped down as president of Princeton, gives the last gasp of psychology as the study of soul. McCosh's attempt to revive Scottish realism simply came too late.

Of the three conservatives, McCosh appears to have been most open to new ideas, although he seems to have found it necessary to justify each new idea as really being an extension of the Scottish philosophy. McCosh was particularly interested in the new experimental psychology. In 1882 McCosh wrote that

> last winter in Princeton College half a dozen of the younger officers formed a club to study Wundt's work on physiological psychology, and his anatomical experiments were repeated by skillful anatomists with a well-prepared apparatus. I have sought in correspondence with one of our young professors, Dr. Osborn, to make all my students take an interest in the curious investigations which have been made by Dr. Galton of London, as to the Visualizing Faculty, as he calls it . . . and we have sent the answers to queries on to Dr. Galton
> The tendency of the day is certainly towards physiology. This should not be discouraged, but rather furthered. Physiology has already made many interesting discoveries bearing on mental action.[138]

James Mark Baldwin recalled his student days at Princeton concerning McCosh and this course on Wundt:

> President McCosh taught his Natural Realism vigorously, and the nucleus of all his instruction was empirical psychology. . . . McCosh . . . had insight which was for that time prophetic . . .: he had seized upon the project of scientific psychology as announced in Wundt's *Physiologische Psychologie,* then just out, and had also pronounced in favor of the theory of biological evolution, holding it to be consistent with the "divine government of the world." . . . Furthermore, I was brought into the circle of interest through the tradition of a course of readings in Wundt, arranged by McCosh, with the demonstrations given by W. B. Scott and H. F. Osborn, young members of the Princeton faculty.[139]

Laboratory psychology was on its way at Princeton. Baldwin would later found research laboratories in psychology at Toronto and at Johns Hopkins.

During the tenure of each of these philosophical conservatives, Harvard, Yale and Princeton became universities and issued degrees at the doctoral level. In 1878, G. Stanley Hall (1842–1924) was the first Harvard student to receive a Ph.D. degree from the Department of Philosophy. Hall's major advisor was William James.[140] In March of 1882, after a series of lectures begun in the fall of 1881, Hall was offered the position of lecturer of psychology and pedagogy at the earliest American University, Johns Hopkins. Hall appears to have been in competition with William James, George Sylvester Morris, and Charles S. Peirce for the full-time professorship. Morris and Peirce were part-time lecturers, and James had given a series of lectures at Hopkins. In April 1884, Hall was officially appointed to the full professorship.[141] Hall had spent the time since receiving his Harvard degree studying in Europe with Wundt, Ludwig, and Helmholtz. At Hopkins, Hall reports being given a budget of $1,000 a year for laboratory equipment.[142] There were students at Hopkins like J. McKeen Cattell, John Dewey, H. H. Donaldson, Joseph Jastrow and E. C. Sanford.[143] Between 1882 and 1888, the spirit of the new experimental psychology was very much alive at Hopkins. In 1887 Hall began publication of the *American Journal of Psychology,* the first journal in English to be devoted entirely to research in psychology.

The psychology course Hall taught at Hopkins "was almost entirely experimental and covered for the most part the material that Wundt had set forth in the later and larger edition of his *Physiological Psychology*".[144] Hall's psychology course was described in the *Eleventh Annual Report of Johns Hopkins (1886)* as follows:

A three years' course in Psychology, consisting of two lectures with reading club and seminary weekly and daily laboratory work. The first year is devoted to the senses considered experimentally and anatomically, but from the standpoint of Psychology, with reference to aesthetical and educational applications and to morbid phenomena, and concluding with an extended treatment of the field of binocular vision, with parallel reading of Helmholtz and Hering. The second year takes up first the four topics of space, the time-sense, physiological time, and the psychophysic law, on each of which the vast body of recent experimental literature is epitomized as far as possible. The last half of the second year is devoted to association, memory, habit, attention, the will, and feelings successively, and treated experimentally. The third year is occupied with the topics of instinct in animals, psychogenesis in children, the psychological parts of anthropology (including animism, the chief mythic cycles, traditions, rites, and ceremonies), and morbid psychology (especially aphasia, hypnotic and allied states, paranoia, epilepsy, hysteria, paralysis, etc.) with constant reference to their anatomical correlations where such are made out, and to their educational, hygienic, and prophylactic applications.[145]

Not all of this was Wundtian, of course. Hall, like the preexperimental psychologists before him was eclectic, selecting the aspects of the new experimental psychology of Wundt that appealed to him and selecting, from whatever sources were at hand, other topics—such as "morbid psychology"—that were of interest to him. In many respects, Hall's course at Johns Hopkins in 1886 was the experimental realization of Thomas Upham's program of 1831.

During the 1870s and 1880s the course in psychology, now most commonly offered under the name "Psychology," became standard in the curriculum of even the smallest college. In the larger colleges, entire departments were being created for philosophy, and in the 1890s the curriculum would expand sufficiently for the creation of departments of psychology. The trek to Germany for advanced training in psychology had become almost obligatory for those who could afford it. Hall could write in 1878 that

> scores of American students may be found in nearly all the larger German universities. Most of even the smaller (American) colleges have one or two professors who have spent from one to three or four years in study in that country.[146]

A new day was dawning for American psychology. Those who studied in Germany in the 1880s and 1890s, particularly those with Wundt, would bring back with them the new psychology of experimentation. The market for these new experimental psychologists increased in America. A peculiar thing happened to those experimentalists from Wundt's laboratory, however. When they left Wundt they were fired up with the promise of mind-as-contents, but after coming back to America they soon found themselves talking in the Scottish terms of mind-in-use. The veneer of Wundt's content psychology was not thick enough to survive through immersion in the intellectual atmosphere of America. It is reasonably safe to say that hardly a single American student remained faithful to the precepts of Wundtian content psychology for more than a few years. Their courses, in their new American positions, sounded remarkably like the subject matter of Upham's *Mental Philosophy* or Porter's *Intellectual Philosophy*. What did survive the trip was the basic experimental method. The applications of that method were to problems beyond the realm of contents of experience and more in the context of mental functions.

The new experimental psychology was responsible for a major shift in the academic philosophy and psychology curriculum, but it must be emphasized that it was *just* a shift and not a new creation. The arrival of laboratory psychology brought about as great a change as had the arrival of Lockean philosophy in the eighteenth century and Kantian philosophy in the nineteenth century, but the problems of psychological investigation continued to be the same with only another switch of terms and method. The laboratory approach was not universally accepted, however, and departments of philosophy were often split on the funding of laboratories. The philosophical psychologist often considered that the laboratory offered no insights that the traditional "armchair" approach did not. The result was often great friction, which may well have accelerated the separation of departments of psychology. That final separation of psychology departments from the matrix of mother philosophy and the battle of the laboratory over the armchair, however, is in the domain of J. McKeen Cattell's fifty years of "real" American psychology.

In 1882, James McCosh had also called for an American psychology:

> It is time that America had a philosophy of its own. . . . It should not seek to be

independent of European thought. . . . It may be Scoto-German-American school. It might take the method of the Scotch, the high truths of the German, and combine them by the practical invention of the Americans. But no: let it in fact, in name and profession, be an independent school. As becometh the country it may take, not a monarchical form under one leader, like the European systems, let it rather be a republican institution, with separate states and a central unity.[147]

What McCosh was calling for, of course, was just the sort of thought that had existed in America throughout the nineteenth century. What better name for the movements of the nineteenth century than a "Scoto-German-American school" with "separate states and a central unity"? By the time McCosh wrote his appeal, however, this electic American psychology was already blending into the new experimental psychology being imported from Germany. The new American psychology would bring together the methods of experimental research from Wundt's laboratory and the underlying concepts of mind-in-use from the Scottish philosophical traditions. What developed during much of that fifty years between McCosh's appeal and J. McKeen Cattell's presidential address before the Ninth International Congress of Psychology was the development of a new amalgam of experimental, functional psychology. This amalgam has continued to work its way in American psychology to the present time, adapting each new movement as it comes along, but continuing to emphasize mind-in-use (under whatever guise or rubric is acceptable at a given time) as central to psychological consideration.

NOTES

I wish to thank Dr. John J. McDermott for his suggestions on the clarification of a number of issues addressed in this work.

1. J. McKeen Cattell, "Psychology in America," in *Proceedings and Papers: Ninth International Congress of Psychology* (Princeton, N.J.: Psychological Review Company, 1929), p. 12. Cattell espoused this view as early as 1898, except that he substituted Iceland for Ireland. "The Advance of Psychology," *Proceedings of the American Association for the Advancement of Science* 47 (1898): 3. Both articles are reprinted in *James McKeen Cattell: Man of Science* (Lancaster, Pa.: Science Press, 1947), vol. 2, p. 110.

2. It is ironic that Titchener has so often been represented as a philosophical rather than a scientific psychologist. One of Titchener's major tasks during his time in America was to separate psychology from its philosophical underpinnings.

3. George P. Schmidt, *The Liberal Arts College* (New Brunswick, N.J.: Rutgers University Press, 1957), p. 4.

4. *New Englands First Fruits* (London: Henry Overton, 1643), reprinted in Samuel Eliot Morison, *The Founding of Harvard College* (Cambridge, Mass.: Harvard University Press, 1935), p. 432.

5. Schmidt, *Liberal Arts College*, p. 24.

6. William T. Costello, *The Scholastic Curriculum at Early Seventeenth-Century Cambridge* (Cambridge, Mass.: Harvard University Press, 1958), pp. 147–48.

7. Ibid., pp. 148–49.

8. Theodore Hornberger, *Scientific Thought in the American Colleges: 1636–1800* (Austin, Tex.: University of Texas Press, 1946), p. 23.

9. Morison, *Founding of Harvard College*, p. 337.

10. Harvard College Papers, vol. 1 (1650–1736), no. 31, cited in Louis Franklin Snow, *The College Curriculum in the United States* (New York: Teachers College, Columbia University, 1907), pp. 32–34.

11. Petrus Ramus, *Dialecticae* (1560). Ramus is also sometimes found under Pierre de la Ramée. Franco Burgersdicius, *Logicae* (Leyden, 1626). Herebard was an alternative spelling of Adrianus

Heereboord, *Meletemata Philosophica* (Amsterdam, 1680). One could also get Burgersdicius at second hand from Heereboord in his *Synopsis Logicae Burgersdicianae* (Cambridge, 1680). Johann Wollebius, *The Abridgment of Christian Divinity* (London, 1660).

12. Charles Morton, *Compendium Physicae*. Harvard adopted Morton's physics as a manuscript textbook in 1687.

13. Johannes Magirus, *Physiologiae Peripatetica* (1597). Magirus's book was a century old when it was used at Harvard and even then was a paraphrase of Aristotle's *De Anima*. One of Heereboord's books was used between the time Magirus's book was rejected and Morton's book was adopted. See Joseph J. Ellis, *The New England Mind in Transition: Samuel Johnson of Connecticut, 1696–1772* (New Haven, Conn.: Yale University Press, 1973), pp. 15–33; Hornberger, *Scientific Thought*, p. 40.

14. William Brattle, *Compendium Logicae secundum Principia D. Renati Cartesii* (Boston, 1758).

15. Hornberger, *Scientific Thought*, pp. 38–39.

16. William Ames, *Medulla Theologica (Marrow of Sacred Divinity)* (1643); *De Conscientia et ejus Iure, ve Casibus (The Cases of Conscience)* (1631).

17. Jay Wharton Fay, *American Psychology before William James* (New Brunswick, N.J.: Rutgers University Press, 1939), p. 10.

18. Snow, *College Curriculum*, pp. 32, 37–38.

19. Samuel Johnson, quoted in Fay, *American Psychology*, p. 13.

20. Edwin Oviatt, *The Beginnings of Yale, 1701–1726* (New Haven, Conn.: Yale University Press, 1916), pp. 298–300.

21. Ellis, *New England Mind*, pp. 34–36.

22. I. Woodbridge Riley, *American Philosophy: The Early Schools* (New York: Dodd, Mead and Co., 1907), p. 210.

23. Fay, *American Psychology*, p. 13.

24. Louis L. Tucker, *Puritan Protagonist: President Clap of Yale College* (University of North Carolina Press, 1962), p. 24.

25. Samuel Johnson, *Elementa Philosophica: Containing Chiefly, Noetica, or Things Relating to the Mind or Understanding, and Ethica, or Things Relating to the Moral Behavior* (Philadelphia: B. Franklin and D. Hall, 1752).

26. Tucker, *Puritan Protagonist*, p. 24.

27. Richard I. Aaron, *John Locke*, 3d ed. (Oxford: Clarendon Press, 1971), p. 74.

28. John Locke, *An Essay concerning Human Understanding* (1690; reprint ed., Oxford: Clarendon Press, 1971), book 4, chap. 21, lines 9–11.

29. Ibid., lines 18–22.

30. Ibid., lines 27–29.

31. Johnson, *Cyclopaedia of Learning*, quoted in Riley, *American Philosophy*, pp. 64–67.

32. Ibid., p. 65.

33. Ibid.

34. Ibid.

35. Ibid., p. 66.

36. Johnson, *Elementa Philosophica*, reverse of p. 103.

37. The division of the sciences into speculative and practical is clearly derived from Aristotle, differentiating the theoretical from the applied. See, William Hamilton, *Lectures on Metaphysics and Logic*, 4 vols. (London: William Blackwood and Sons, 1859), vol. 1, Lecture 7.

38. Ellis, *New England Mind*, pp. 171–72.

39. David C. Humphrey, *From King's College to Columbia 1746–1800* (New York: Columbia University Press, 1976), pp. 163–64.

40. Johnson had come to believe in John Hutcheson's contention, as published in his *Moses' Principia* (1724), that all scientific truths are present in linguistic cues in the original Hebrew form of the Old Testament. See Ellis, *New England Mind*, pp. 228–33.

41. Douglas Sloan, *The Scottish Enlightenment and the American College Ideal* (New York: Teachers College, Columbia University, 1971), pp. 23–24.

42. Hornberger, *Scientific Thought*, p. 31.

43. Ellis, *New England Mind*, p. 240.

44. William Smith, *A General Idea of The College of Mirania* (1753; reprint ed., New York: Johnson Reprint Corp., 1969), 86 pp.; Horace Wemyss Smith, *Life and Correspondence of the Rev. William Smith, D.D.* (Philadelphia: S. A. George & Co., 1879), vol. 1, pp. 23–26.

45. Horace Wemyss Smith, *Life and Correspondence*, p. 59.

46. William Smith, quoted in Riley, *American Philosophy*, p. 233.

47. James G. Leyburn, *The Scotch-Irish* (Chapel Hill, N.C.: University of North Carolina Press, 1962), p. 169.

48. Sloan, *Scottish Enlightenment, p. 85n.*

49. *Thomas Jefferson Wertenbaker, Princeton 1746–1896* (Princeton, N.J.: Princeton University Press, 1946), pp. 3–24.

50. Douglas Sloan, ed., *The Great Awakening and American Education* (New York: Teachers College Press, 1973), pp. 1–53.

51. Wertenbaker, *Princeton*, pp. 17–18. For the student side of the story, see Sloan, *Great Awakening*, pp. 129–33.

52. J. F. Stearns, quoted in Wertenbaker, *Princeton*, p. 18.

53. Jonathan Dickinson, the first president of Princeton, survived only four and a half months in office, and Jonathan Edwards only a few weeks.

54. John Witherspoon, quoted in Riley, *American Philosophy*, p. 485.

55. Sloan, *Scottish Enlightenment*, pp. 129–31. By "Scottish philosophy" I mean the philosophical thought of Thomas Reid and those identified with his thought.

56. Ashbel Green, quoted in James McCosh, *The Scottish Philosophy* (London, 1875; reprint ed., Hildesheim: George Olms Verlag, 1966), p. 188.

57. Frederick Beasley, quoted in Fay, *American Psychology*, p. 191.

58. Sloan, *Scottish Enlightenment*, p. 115.

59. Sloan, *Scottish Enlightenment*, pp. 111–14.

60. John Witherspoon, quoted in Fay, p. 60.

61. Ibid., p. 59.

62. Samuel Stanhope Smith, *The Lectures, Corrected and Improved, Which Have Been Delivered for a Series of Years, in the College of New Jersey; on the Subjects of Moral and Political Philosophy* (Trenton, N.J.: Daniel Fenton, 1812), p. 13., quoted in Fay *American Psychology*, p. 62.

63. Ibid., p. 62.

64. Sloan, *Scottish Enlightenment*, pp. 182–83.

65. Donald G. Tewksbury, *The Founding of American Colleges and Universities before the Civil War* (New York: Teachers College Press, 1932), p. 58.

66. Tewksbury, *Founding of American Colleges*, pp. 60, 92.

67. Frederick Beasley, quoted in George P. Schmidt, *The Old Time College President* (New York: Columbia University Press, 1930), p. 123.

68. Noah Porter, "Mental and Moral Science in Yale College," in William L. Kingsley, ed., *Yale College: A Sketch of Its History* (New York: Henry Holt & Co., 1879), vol. 1, p. 389.

69. James Marsh, Letter to Samuel Taylor Coleridge, March 23, 1829, quoted in Joseph Torrey, ed., *The Remains of the Rev. James Marsh D.D.* (1843; reprint ed. Port Washington, N.Y.: Kennikat Press, 1971), p. 136.

70. Tewksbury, *Founding of American Colleges*, p. 60.

71. Frederick Rudolph, *The American College and University* (New York: Alfred A. Knopf, 1962), p. 38.

72. Lyman Beecher, quoted in Tewksbury, *Founding of American Colleges*, p. 60. Such problems seem to run in cycles. For similar problems in the 1690s, see Perry Miller, *Errand into the Wilderness* (New York: Harper & Row, 1956), pp. 7–8.

73. Bishop William Meade, *Old Churches, Ministers and Families of Virginia*, Vol. 1, p. 29 (1857). Quoted in Tewksbury, *Founding of American Colleges*, p. 60.

74. Samuel Stanhope Smith, quoted in Sloan, *Scottish Enlightenment*, p. 180.

75. John Adams, quoted in Merle Curti, *The Growth of American Thought*, 2d ed. (New York: Harper and Brothers, 1951), p. 185.

76. Sloan, *Scottish Enlightenment*, p. 180.

77. Wertenbaker, *Princeton*, p. 144.

78. Timothy Dwight, quoted ibid., pp. 142–43.

79. Ibid., p. 142.

80. Ibid., pp. 151–52.

81. I. Woodbridge Riley, *American Thought* (New York: Henry Holt & Co., 1915), p. 121.

82. Samuel Stanhope Smith, quoted in Schmidt, *Old Time College President*, p. 117.

83. Thomas Cogswell Upham, *Elements of Mental Philosophy*, 3d ed. (Portland, Me.: William Hyde, 1839), pp. 3–4.

84. Snow, *College Curriculum*, p. 129.

85. Ibid., p. 124.

86. Gladys Bryson, "The Comparable Interests of the Old Moral Philosophy and the Modern Social Sciences," *Social Forces* 10 (1932): 20–21. See also Bryson, "The Emergence of the Social Sciences from Moral Philosophy," *International Journal of Ethics* 42 (1932): 304–23.

87. Alpheus S. Packard, *Address on the Life and Character of Thomas C. Upham, D.D.* (Bruns-

wick, Me.: Joseph Griffin, 1873), pp. 7–8. Upham's title was later changed to Professor of Mental and Moral Philosophy.

88. Fay, *American Psychology*, p. 196.
89. Upham, quoted in ibid., p. 92.
90. Ibid., p. 196.
91. Thomas C. Upham, *Mental Philosophy* (New York: Harper & Bros., 1856) p. iii.
92. Jacques Quen gives this "first" to Isaac Ray, whose *A Treatise on the Medical Jurisprudence of Insanity* appeared in 1838. See Quen, "Isaac Ray and His 'Remarks on Pathological Anatomy,'" *Bulletin of the History of Medicine* 38 (1964): 113.
93. Upham, *Abridgment of Mental Philosophy* (New York: Harper & Bros., 1861), pp. v–xviii. (Reprint ed, Scholars Facsimile Press, 1979.)
94. Snow, *College Curriculum*, p. 120.
95. Mark Hopkins, *Lectures on Moral Science* (Boston: Gould & Lincoln, 1870), pp. 79–80.
96. Robert Vaughn, "American Philosophy," *British Quarterly Review* 5 (1847): 98–99.
97. Joseph Torrey, *The Remains of the Rev. James Marsh, D.D. (1843)*. Reprint (Port Washington, N.Y.: Kennikat Press, 1971), pp. 91–92, 103.
98. Marsh to Coleridge, in Ibid., p. 137.
99. Ibid.
100. James McCosh, *The Scottish Philosophy* (1874). Reprint (Hildesheim: Georg Olms Verlagsbuchhandlung, 1966), pp. 287, 304–5.
101. G. Stanley Hall, *Life and Confessions of a Psychologist* (New York: D. Appleton & Co., 1923), p. 169.
102. Mark Hopkins, *Lectures on Moral Science* (Boston: Gould and Lincoln, 1870), p. viii.
103. Marsh's lectures on psychology are published in Torrey, *Remains*, pp. 239–367.
104. John Dewey, "James Marsh and American Philosophy," *Journal of the History of Ideas* 2 (1941): 131–50.
105. H. J. B. Ziegler, *Friedrich Augustus Rauch: American Hegelian* (Lancaster, Pa.: Franklin and Marshall College, 1953). The author thanks Mr. David Lewis, reference librarian at Franklin and Marshall College, for materials on Rauch.
106. R. C. Davis, "American Psychology,, 1800–1885," *Psychological Review* 43 (1936): 479–80; Gabriel Darrow Ofiesh, "The History, Development, Present Status, and Purpose of the First (Introductory) Course in Psychology in American Undergraduate Education" (Ed.D. dissertation, University of Denver, 1959), pp. 124–25.
107. Friedrich Augustus Rauch, *Psychology; or, A View of the Human Soul; Including Anthropology* (New York: M. W. Dodd, 1840).
108. James Murdock, *Sketches of Modern Philosophy* (1842), quoted in Davis, "American Psychology" p. 480.
109. Fay, *American Psychology*, p. 114.
110. *Catalogue of the Officers and Students in Marshall College*, 1839–40, p. 13; 1840–41, p. 19.
111. Herbert W. Schneider, *A History of American Philosophy*, 2d ed., (New York: Columbia University Press, 1969), p. 379.
112. Laurens P. Hickok, quoted in Fay, *American Psychology*, p. 121.
113. Schneider, *History of American Philosophy*, p. 384.
114. Charles M. Perry, *Henry Philip Tappan: Philosopher and University President* (Ann Arbor, Mich.: University of Michigan Press, 1933), pp. 147–48, 158–64.
115. W. W. Andrews, "Study at Berlin," in George S. Merriam, *Noah Porter: A Memorial by Friends* (New York: Charles Scribner's Sons, 1893), pp. 94–98.
116. John S. Brubacher and Willis Rudy, *Higher Education in Transition*, 3d ed. (New York: Harper & Row, 1976), p. 106.
117. Henry Philip Tappan, quoted in Brubacher and Rudy, p. 108.
118. Hall, *Life and Confessions*, p. 157.
119. Ibid., p. 170.
120. Overseers Report on Francis Bowen, Jan. 1854, quoted in Bruce Kuklick, *The Rise of American Philosophy: Cambridge, Massachusetts 1860–1930* (New Haven, Conn.: Yale University Press, 1977), p. 120.
121. Hall, "Philosophy in the United States," *Mind* 6 (1879): 97.
122. Kuklick, *Rise of American Philosophy* pp. 31–32.
123. Ibid., p. 32.
124. Robert S. Harper, "The Laboratory of William James," *Harvard Alumni Bulletin* 52 (1949): 169.
125. Kuklick, *Rise of American Philosophy* p. 135. Kuklick incorrectly states that James used

Spencer's *Principles of Psychology* as the text in his Philosophy 4 course, "Psychology." He used Taine's *On Intelligence*. This is a commonly stated error, most likely derived from a misreading of Ralph Barton Perry, *The Thought and Character of William James* (Boston: Little, Brown and Co., 1935), vol. 1, pp. 475–76.

126. Hall, "Philosophy in the United States," p. 97.

127. The title was changed to "Physiological Psychology." There is some controversy about the "first" psychological laboratory in the United States. Whether James, Peirce, or Hall was first depends largely on one's criterion of laboratory. What is important is that by the late 1870s the laboratory was becoming part of American academic psychology.

128. James appears not to have used Spencer in a philosophy course until 1879, when he offered "The Philosophy of Evolution," using Spencer's *First Principles*.

129. Brooks Mather Kelley, *Yale: A History* (New Haven, Conn.: Yale University Press, 1974), pp. 240–41; George Wilson Pierson, *Yale College: An Educational History 1871–1921* (New Haven, Conn.: Yale University Press, 1952)

130. Porter, "Additional Notices respecting Instruction and Discipline," in Kingsley, *Yale College*, vol. 2, pp. 507–8. A coverage of the topic for other colleges may be found in Brubaker and Rudy, pp. 100–119.

131. Kelley, *Yale*, pp. 182–83.

132. George M. Duncan, "Dr. Porter as a Philosopher," in Merriam, pp. 199–200.

133. George Trumbull Ladd, *Elements of Physiological Psychology: A Treatise on the Activities and Nature of the Mind* (New York: Charles Scribner's Sons, 1889), p. 1v.

134. Pierson, *Yale College*, pp. 147–49.

135. McCosh, quoted in Wertenbaker, *Princeton*, p. 293.

136. Ibid., p. 311.

137. Ellis, *New England Mind*, pp. 53–54.

138. McCosh, "The Scottish Philosophy as Contrasted with the German," *Princeton Review* 10 (1882): 334.

139. J. Mark Baldwin, "Autobiography," in Carl Murchison, ed., *History of Psychology in Autobiography* (Worcester, Mass.: Clark University Press, 1930), vol. 1, pp. 1–2.

140. Dorothy Ross, *G. Stanley Hall: The Psychologist as Prophet* (Chicago: University of Chicago Press, 1972), p. 79.

141. Ibid., 136.

142. Hall, *Life and Confessions*, p. 227.

143. Ibid., p. 232.

144. Ibid., p. 234.

145. Ibid., p. 255.

146. Hall, "Philosophy in the United States," p. 104.

147. McCosh, "The Scottish Philosophy as Contrasted with the German," pp. 343–44.

Jonathan Edwards's Theory of the Mind: Its Applications and Implications

JAMES G. BLIGHT

Harvard University

Introduction

"Jonathan Edwards," it has been remarked, "was a Christian and a genius. But many of his contemporaries were so blinded by his Christian orthodoxy that they failed to recognize his genius."[1] This is no longer true; today, Edwards's genius is fully recognized, though his contribution to the history of psychology has yet to be investigated thoroughly.[2] In this essay I have tried to interpret for historians of psychology both sides of this Edwardsean paradox: the soaring intellect used, in "the Age of Reason," to justify a medieval conception of Christianity. It was his fervent, evangelical Calvinism, and the accompanying urgent necessity of knowing the state of his soul that created in Edwards the impetus to theorize about psychology. The son of a typical Calvinist parson on the New England frontier, Edwards (1703–58) was from his earliest youth concerned that he experience a valid conversion, a visitation from the Holy Spirit of God. In addition, Edwards was a typical Calvinist of his time and place in his earnest pursuit of assurance that whatever spiritual experiences he had were valid works of God rather than self-delusions or works of the devil. After his graduation from Yale in 1722 and his ascendance to the pulpit in Northampton, Massachusetts, in 1729, Edwards began to transform his personal search for salvation into a much more intellectualized inquiry into the nature of the mind and its transformation during conversion.

In the practice of speculating about psychological matters Edwards was hardly exceptional; Protestant theologians had for centuries sought to explicate the nature of the mind in order that they might comment intelligibly about the nature of what it is that is transformed in conversion. Edwards's speculations had an important practical application—to guide clergymen as they assisted their parishioners in the determination of the validity of their spiritual experiences. In his relentless search for assurance of personal salvation, in his speculations about the nature of mental functioning in conversion, and in his determined attempt to apply his theory of the mind to the spiritual experiences of his parishioners, Edwards was the very prototype of an educated parson serving his people on the frontier of colonial Massachusetts. He never met a great scientist or philosopher; he never visited Europe. He preached in Northampton to a largely uneducated congregation and his last years were spent, for the most part, tending to the needs of an Indian tribe at a mission in Stockbridge, Massachusetts. Yet, while his need to theorize about psychological issues was perfectly unexceptional, the nature of his theorizing reflects quite clearly the work of genius. From his own era down to the present day Edwards's commentators have marveled that a mind of such precision, scope and power should have arisen in the backwoods of colonial New England.

A central assumption of this essay is that Edwards, whose psychological theory is virtually unknown to historians of psychology, is worth reading. I shall not be concerned with the question of Edwards's influence on others, though in fact it seems certain that, however one defines "influence," Edwards was the most influential psychologist in America prior to James. Rather, I hope to show that, as Robert MacLeod once said of James, "The proper question is: can we still read . . . [him] and get good ideas from him? The answer . . . is that we can."[3] For we may witness in Edwards an unusually powerful enactment of the age-old, fundamental drama of psychology. It is described variously as "mind-body problem," "relationship between reason and emotion," "freedom in a determined universe," "the place of value in a world of facts." It is the attempt to formulate a conception of mind, and its relation to brains, bodies, and other aspects of the physical world in a way such that the puzzling dichotomies of existence are resolved in an intelligible synthesis. Each great psychologist has attempted solutions to these intractable problems, and Edwards, like the others, did so in accordance with the contingencies of his time and place. For Edwards, the central burning question, the anvil on which solutions to all the fundamental dichotomies were forged was this: *Can one know with certainty when a mind (one's own or that of another) has been altered by the Spirit of God?* His answer was "No!"; his explanation and its implications occupy the remainder of this essay.

The Theory of the Mind

> . . . . he went his way
> down among the lost people like Dante, down. . . .
>
> and showed us what evil is, not, as we thought,
> deeds that must be punished, but our lack of faith,
>   our dishonest mood of denial . . .
>
> but he would have us remember most of all
> to be enthusiastic over the night
>   . . . for the sense of wonder
> it alone has to offer. . . .
>
>   W. H. Auden,
>   "In Memory of Sigmund Freud"

Much of the literature which emerged from the Great Awakening in the American colonies (ca. 1736–46), that remarkable explosion of religious enthusiasm and controversy, is notable for its bombast, accusations and extravagant self-righteousness. The evangelical preachers George Whitefield and James Davenport were laying siege to the spiritual life of the American colonies; in the churches and in open fields people in unprecedented numbers were seen to shout, sweat, scream, and faint in the name of God. Many ministers, encouraged and excited by the dramatic increase in converts, actively supported and even fomented the Awakening. Others, however, recoiled in horror at what they regarded as lunacy, as evidence that vast numbers of people had taken leave of their reason and acquiesced in devilish enthusiasm. It is commonly believed that the supporters of the Awakening ("New Lights") and the opponents of the Awakening ("Old Lights") engaged in a kind of political combat with each side keenly aware of its friends, enemies, slogans, and leaders, and each side serenely impervious to the arguments of the other. In this view, the "Old Lights" were as irrational in their defense of reason as the "New Lights" were in their pursuit and defense of emotion, or "raised affections."

In this religious and political ferment, Jonathan Edwards occupied an anomalous position. He was an active, though relatively restrained, participant in the Awakening. In his *Faithful Narrative* he astonished many readers with accounts of the "surprizing conversions" of a young child and a dying woman, he welcomed Whitefield to his pulpit in Northampton, and, of course, his sermon, "Sinners in the Hands of an Angry God," filled with terrifying imagery, became the most famous evangelical sermon ever preached in America. Yet Edwards was also, in common with some opponents of the Awakening, a precocious child of the Enlightenment, conversant with Newtonian mechanics and thoroughly immersed in the philosophy of Locke. He was a logician and a philosopher of power and originality. Most importantly, Edwards was a psychological theorist. After reading Locke, and perhaps Berkeley, as a young boy, Edwards became, and was to remain, preoccupied with the nature of the mind and its operation in conversion.

Conversion, the event to be explained by Edwards's psychological theory, is usually said to be both a human activity and more than a human activity. It involves the interaction of a human mind with a supernatural spirit. According to Edwards, it is God Himself who transforms the core of the human mind in a true conversion. Edwards once acknowledged that "there is a vast variety, perhaps as manifold as the subjects of the operation [of conversion]." He quickly added, however, that "in many things there is a great analogy in all."[1] We shall now examine the details of Edwards's "great analogy"—the theory of the mind which he formulated to account for the phenomenon of religious conversion.

"First Awakenings": Creating a Need for Conversion

The "great analogy" or morphology of conversion was presented most clearly and positively in Edwards's *Faithful Narrative*. This remarkable work, an elaboration of a letter to his fellow minister Benjamin Colman of Boston, reveals a side of Edwards that is seldom obvious in his adult writings.[2] It contains an array of firsthand and secondhand accounts, along with Edwards's commentary, of conversions which occurred during the early days of the Great Awakening in the Connecticut Valley. Edwards organizes his evidence, bit by bit, and emerges with a composite formula for conversion which is not so much a "how to do it" manual as a simple generalization. The colorful anecdotes and enthusiastic lack of defensiveness in the *Faithful Narrative* easily differentiates it from his later, relatively abstract, argumentative tracts like *Original Sin* and *Freedom of the Will*.[3]

In those early days of the Awakening, in 1735 and 1736, Edwards was utterly convinced that the Holy Spirit had taken up temporary residence in the Connecticut Valley. Many "surprizing conversions" had been accomplished and he was eager to tell the world exactly how the wonderful work had occurred. In the *Faithful Narrative* he had only to describe what he had seen and organize that data as coherently as possible. He thus discussed with feeling and in great detail the series of events which usually led up to a true conversion.

According to Edwards, God first makes His presence felt by creating a need for conversion. People who are satisfied with, or uninterested in the state of their soul, will not be motivated to seek God, and hence they will never find Him. Edwards believed that most of the inhabitants of his own town of Northampton, in the period immediately preceding the Awakening, were typical of the complacent, corrupt, degenerate types who have no room in their life for God.

> Licentiousness for some years greatly prevailed among the youth of the town; there were many of them very much addicted to night-walking, and frequenting the tavern, and lewd practices, wherein some, by their example exceedingly corrupted others. It was their manner very frequently to get together in conventions of both sexes, for mirth and jollity, which they called frolics. . . .[4]

The validity of Edwards's rather stern yet quaint judgment of the worth of "frolicking" is of course not at issue here. The point is that Edwards believed such complacent individuals could never be receptive to the Holy Spirit because they perceived no incongruity between their actual state and some ideal or desired condition. Until they felt a sense of spiritual inadequacy, the "licentious" citizens of Northampton would continue to frolic rather than organize a plan to seek their salvation. Seen through Edwards's Calvinist eyes, his parishioners were spiritually asleep, and sleeping men and women are frightfully unaware of imminent dangers which surround them. Clearly, the spiritually slumbering townspeople would have to be awakened, be made aware of their own inadequacy, before they would begin to plan for salvation rather than frolics.

During the period of what Edwards calls "first awakenings," smug self-assurance is transformed into nervous insecurity.[5]

> Persons are first awakened with a sense of their miserable condition by nature, the danger they are in of perishing eternally, and that it is of great importance to them that they speedily escape, and get into a better state. Those that before were secure and senseless, are made sensible how much they were in the way to ruin in their former courses.[6]

Persons suddenly find themselves, or actually perceive themselves, out of favor with God and in imminent danger of burning forever in the devil's fiery pit. A wide gulf separates an "awakened" individual's sorry spiritual status and the goal of saving grace. Clearly, there is serious business to attend to.

By what means does God create the sense or need to seek conversion? What, for example, eventually moved the degenerate Northampton youths to religion? Chiefly, according to Edwards, *fear*. In the Connecticut Valley, for instance, the violent death of a youth in Pascommuck in the spring of 1734 "much affected many young people."[7] This was followed by the death of a young woman who, on her deathbed, counseled others on the means to grace. "This," claims Edwards, "seemed much to contribute to the solemnizing of the spirits of many young persons."[8] There was also fear of a more abstract sort in the form of Arminianism, the traditional New England "Bogy-Man."[9] Edwards, and many of his ministerial colleagues predicted that the New England Congregational way would decline into chaotic heterodoxy if Arminian principles were not unilaterally renounced. If Congregationalism declined, it was claimed, the awful fate of all New Englanders would be sealed. The point was that all concerned had better act quickly if the devil and his Arminian army were to be defeated.

Although fear was an especially effective method of motivating complacent frolickers to act in behalf of their souls, Edwards also believed that God created spiritual incongruity in another manner. God sometimes saw fit to convert a few renowned sinners, thereby focusing attention on the practical benefits of coming to grace. If one person's life could be miraculously transformed from a miserable existence into a vital, useful, secure one, then many other people might be moved to duplicate that transformation. They would be motivated by attraction to the godly life in addition to being repelled by the prospect of eternal damnation. In the *Faithful Narrative,* Edwards describes just such a "surprizing work of God" which, he claims, had a profound, positive impact on the progress of the Great Awakening in the entire Connecticut Valley. It involved the apparent conversion of

> a young woman, who had been one of the greatest company keepers in the whole town. When she came to me, I had never heard that she had become in any wise serious, but by the conversation I then had with her, it appeared to me that what she gave an account of was a glorious work of God's infinite power and sovereign grace; and that God had given her a new heart, truly broken and sanctified. I could not then doubt of it, and have seen much in my acquaintance with her since to confirm it.[10]

According to Edwards, this remarkable event helped open the spiritual floodgates in Northampton and surrounding communities. It was "the greatest occasion of awakening to others, of anything that ever came to pass in the town."[11] She was convincing; her behavior had changed remarkably. Observing this astonishing transformation in the "company keeper," many others became convinced that God was among them. They quickly made plans to seek grace, to reduce the incongruity between their own sinful ways and the saintly life as exhibited by the reformed "company keeper."

Edwards supports these generalizations concerning God's *modus operandi* with

two case studies drawn from his Northampton parish. One of these, Phebe Bartlet, is held by Edwards to illustrate God's use of fear to create the need for
conversion. Phebe, a child of four, seemed to be growing up in quite an ordinary
fashion until her "hopefully converted" eleven year old brother "seriously talked
to her about the great things of religion."[12] After these discussions with her
brother she became withdrawn and began spending much time alone in her room
praying. Then one day,

> when the child had done prayer, she came out of the closet, and came and sat
> down by her mother, and cried out loud. Her mother very earnestly asked her
> several times what the matter was, before she would make any answer; but she
> continued exceedingly crying, and wreathing her body to and fro, like one in
> anguish of spirit. Her mother then asked her whether she was afraid that God
> would not give her salvation. She answered, "Yes, I am afraid I shall go to hell!"
> Her mother then endeavored to quiet her, and told her she would not have her
> cry; she must be a good girl, and pray every day, and she hoped God would give
> her salvation. But this did not quiet her at all . . . .[13]

In Edwards's view, God, working perhaps through Phebe's brother, had fright-
ened the youngster into an awareness of her need for salvation.

In the case of Abigail Hutchinson, God created the same need in quite a different manner; He made her envious of the "company keeper." Abigail was a frail
young woman who was dying from some sort of blockage of the throat. "But her
infirmity," Edwards quickly adds, "had never been observed at all to incline her to
be notional or fanciful, or to occasion anything of religious melancholy."[14] It was
probably God, therefore, not "melancholy" which caused her reaction to "the
news of the conversion of the young woman before mentioned [the "company
keeper"] . . . ."[15]

> This news wrought much upon her, and stirred up a spirit of envy in her towards
> this young woman, whom she thought very unworthy of being distinguished
> from others by such a mercy; but withal it engaged her in a firm resolution to do
> her utmost to obtain the blessing."[16]

Abigail's first step would be to plan a strategy for reaching her goal; that is, she
would determine more precisely the nature of "her utmost."

This, then, according to Edwards, is how God begins His dispensation of grace:
by motivating those who were created in His image but have gone astray, so that
they eventually escape the eternal fires of the Evil One. People begin to plan and
act, according to Edwards, only when they perceive an incongruity between their
depraved condition and their goal of saving grace. God simply "awakens" individuals by providing them with clearer, more accurate pictures of their condition
and their goal. Persons become fearfully aware that they are in dire spiritual straits
and if they don't *do* something about it they will burn forever in hell. That is their
unfortunate status. Preconverts also become increasingly aware of the nature of
their goal through their observation of inspired demonstrations, such as that of the
"company keeper." The more that awakening persons discover about their actual
and ideal selves, the more the gulf between the two seems to widen. When the

discrepancy becomes unbearable, their equilibrium is destroyed, and they initiate a plan, or a group of plans, which are designed to eliminate the perceived incongruity in their spiritual system. Thus the search for God and His grace begins.

"Legal Strivings": The Fruitless Search for God and Salvation

After being awakened to their precarious spiritual state, people begin casting about trying, so it appears, to make up for lost time. They become pious, read scripture voraciously, go to church often, and do good. During this frenzied period of what he called "legal strivings," Edwards observed that awakened persons expend nearly all their physical and psychological energy in pursuit of their salvation. This sudden shift from careless complacence to earnest performance of good works had certain practical advantages, as Edwards, the minister of an often raucous frontier settlement, was eager to point out:

> These awakenings when they have first seized on persons have had two effects: one was that they have brought them immediately to quit their sinful practices, and the looser sort have been brought to forsake and dread their former vices and extravagancies. When once the Spirit of God began to be so wonderfully poured out in a general way through the town, people had soon done with their old quarrels, backbitings, and intermeddling with other men's matters; the tavern was soon left empty, and persons kept very much at home; none went abroad unless on necessary business, or on some religious account, and every day seemed in many respects like a Sabbath day. And the other effect was, that it put them on earnest application to the means of salvation—reading, prayer, meditation, the ordinances of God's House, and private conference; their cry was "What shall I do to be saved?" The place of resort was now altered; it was no longer the tavern, but the minister's house, that was thronged far more than ever the tavern had wont to be.[17]

Awakened persons try to proceed toward their goal as quickly as possible. There is, in their view, no time to lose. Phebe Bartlet, for instance, prayed alone "five or six times in a day" at the height of her "legal strivings."[18] Abigail Hutchinson, on the other hand, undertook to educate herself:

> . . . she thought she had not a sufficient knowledge of the principles of religion to render her capable of conversion; whereupon she resolved thoroughly to search the scriptures; and accordingly immediately began at the beginning of the Bible, intending to read it through.[19]

Abigail's decision clearly illustrates the philosophy of the newly awakened: it is better to do something rather than do nothing. Many activities are carried on simultaneously, in the hope that one or more will work.

Unfortunately, according to Edwards, none of the elaborate plans and activities ever work. The newly awakened are destined for failure after failure until they become wrung out, exhausted, disillusioned, and more convinced than ever of their own worthlessness. Why does God lead them through such a frustrating, hopeless ordeal? Because, in Edwards's view, God is not just there for the taking. Arrogant people, with their confident schemes and plans, must learn through hard experience the humility that is appropriate to those who are utterly dependent on Him:

> The drift of the Spirit of God in his legal strivings with persons, has seemed most evidently to be, to make way for, and to bring to, a conviction of their absolute dependence on his sovereign power and grace, and universal necessity of a Mediator, by leading them more and more to a sense of their exceeding wickedness and guiltiness in his sight; the pollution and insufficiency of their own righteousness, that they can in no wise help themselves, and that God would be wholly just and righteous in rejecting them, and all that they do, and in casting them off forever . . . .[20]

The purpose of the frustrating period of "legal strivings" is therefore to make people really feel an urgent need for spiritual awakening. The whole process of planning and searching for God is initiated by some perceived incongruity between one's present state and a state of saving grace. Yet this need is what Edwards often called "notional"; it involves only an intellectual, detached assent to a proposition. The need felt by persons who have striven and struggled and failed utterly is far more urgent and direct than this. It is a need that is felt in the viscera and documented with the data of their own wretched experience. Like Abigail Hutchinson, all awakened seekers after grace must acknowledge that the absolute corruption of their hearts is such "that the sin which she brought into the world with her was alone sufficient to condemn her."[21] The need to *obtain* grace is thus transformed into a need to *receive* it; all human plans must be relinquished in favor of God's Plan. The discovery of God always comes on God's terms.

After awakened persons conclude that they cannot save themselves, they lay their fate at God's doorstep. The frantic phase of seeking gives way to patient waiting:

> . . . a general hope arises that some time or other God will be gracious, even before any distinct and particular discoveries of mercy; and often they then come to a conclusion within themselves, that they will be at God's feet and wait his time, and they rest in that, not being sensible that the Spirit of God has now brought them to a frame whereby they are prepared for mercy.[22]

This is the "frame" of mind in which, as Edwards put it, "gracious discoveries . . . are given."[23]

What is the result of relinquishing a plan or plans? If the relinquishment is preceded by vigorous planning, as it clearly must be for Edwards's converts, the result is often a creative insight, a new way of looking at things.[24] It is now common, following Freud, to attribute creative insights to a fusion of emotional, unconscious needs with logical, conscious considerations. It is here, but perhaps only here, that Edwards and contemporary analysts of the creative act part company altogether. For Edwards, the intrusions come not from an unconscious mind or from peripheral aspects of the environment but from his Calvinist God. Poets, scientists, musicians, and artists *make* discoveries. To the converts of Edwards, however, "gracious discoveries . . . are *given*."[25]

When Jesus invited men to "seek and ye shall find," he had in mind, according to Edwards, a search that is arduous and complex. After God establishes some initial incongruity, after persons become awakened and concerned about their spiritual state, they are confronted with a problem which they alone cannot possibly solve. Gradually, they become aware of their incompetence. Their elaborate planning and activity brings only frustration and anxiety. Finally, these frustrated, humiliated people give up as they are "brought to the borders of despair, and it looks as black as midnight to them a little before the day dawns in their soul."[26] They wait, quiet, desperate, and hopeless. When the Spirit comes, unexpectedly and swiftly, their minds will be fundamentally altered by "gracious discoveries." This profound psychological alteration brought by the spirit is the core of Edwards's psychological system, and it is his remarkable explanation of this phenomenon that we shall now examine.

"A Sense of the Heart": A Preface to the Operation of the Spirit in Conversion

In Edwards's view, conversion represents a remarkably simple, though fundamental, alteration of the mind. In order to appreciate the importance of the psychological change wrought by conversion, however, it is necessary to understand the essential attribute of the Edwardsean mind: *unity*. In this section, therefore, we shall make a brief, but vitally necessary, digression into Edwardsean mental mechanics. We shall examine, in detail, his concept of mind.

Thinking, feeling, and willing are not, in Edwards's view, isolated human activities each of which originates in a separate source in the mind. Augustine had been right. The mind is more like a New World melting pot than an Old World ghetto. The constituents have lost their identity through intermarriage and the sharing of responsibilities. To Edwards, the most significant mental miscegenation is between reason and emotion. Human beings are rational-emotive unities, and it is this union which makes them appear disarmingly simple in theory, and hopelessly complex in practice.

Perhaps the most characteristically "rational" activity is the act of consciously weighing two or more alternative actions and eventually choosing one over the others. From Edwards's day down to the present, those who have claimed that people have "free will" have emphasized the importance of the capacity for rational judgment and choice. Of course, if there is such a thing as an absolutely rational choice, or act, then Edwards's position is false. He had to prove, therefore, that

> The will, and the affections of the soul, are not two faculties; the affections are not essentially distinct from the will, nor do they differ from the mere actings of the will and inclination of the soul, but only in the livliness and sensibleness of exercise.[27]

If he could demonstrate conclusively that every act of will, every rational choice, has an emotional component, he would effectively refute any effort to treat them as independent "faculties." If willing and the affections *always* appear together, that is, it would then be quite obvious that the two "faculties" are completely integrated and unified.

Edwards undertook to defend two extremely unpopular notions: the determination of "the will," and the fundamental importance of human irrational capacities.[28] Of course, he agreed, people weigh alternatives and decide, without coercion, the course of action they will take. If for example, I decide to take a walk, then, in one sense, my decision is both free and rational.[29] My motive, according to this position, is the physical object in view: my awareness of the need to walk or, perhaps, the attraction to walking. Thus far in his argument Edwards had offered nothing threatening or objectionable to the Arminian "free willists"; he had simply summarized their position.

In fact, Edwards never actually disagreed with the Arminian analysis of will. Instead, he discarded it as superficial and irrelevant. The rational or "free will" position failed, according to Edwards, to notice a pervasive commonality among the infinite number of "motives" that impel people to action.[30] It failed to recognize that

> . . . the will is as the greatest apparent good is, . . . that volition has always for its object the thing which appears most agreeable; it must be carefully observed, to avoid confusion and needless objection, that I speak of the direct and immediate object of the act of volition; and not some object that the act of will has not an immediate, but only an indirect and remote respect to.[31]

In Edwards's view, the particular choice—to walk, talk, etc.—is of secondary importance. Whatever the conscious goal, there exists an incontrovertible law of human nature which necessitates that a person always choose the alternative which seems to provide the greatest good or pleasure, and least pain. There are no exceptions. Thus,

> . . . the will is *determined* by the greatest apparent good, or by what seems most agreeable; because an appearing most agreeable or pleasing to the mind, and the mind's preferring and choosing, seem hardly to be properly and perfectly distinct.[32]

Paradoxically, people choose between alternatives, but they have no alternative to choosing that which they like. Thus, by Edwards's definition of "motive," the freedom of conscious "choices" is a mere illusion.

Unlike the conscious, considered choice of an "indirect" object, the selection of likes and dislikes is always made unconsciously. Edwards acknowledged that "reason," or conscious choice, sometimes contributes to the determination of whether an object appears agreeable or disagreeable. Often, however, it does not, as Edwards notes in a ponderous but significant restatement of the dilemma articulated by St. Paul in Romans 7:15–21.

> When it [reason] concurs with other things, then its weight is added to them, as put into the same scale; but when it is against them, it is as a weight in the opposite scale, where it resists the influence of other things: yet its resistance is often overcome by their greater weight, and so the act of the will is determined in opposition to it.[33]

"Other things" often determine a course of action. When choices are made, an object is sought for its beauty or ugliness, symmetry or asymmetry, harmony or discord, for its sweet smell or pungent stench.[34] Each of these, and an infinity of "other things," aesthetic considerations, usually register, if at all, as vague but vitally important *feelings*.[35]

Edwards redefined the common-sense conception of motivation. A motive is not that which is consciously desired or "in the view of the mind," as Edwards often put it. Rather, a motive is a group of emotional considerations which either attract us toward or repel us from a "rational" alternative:[36]

> We see the world of mankind to be exceedingly busy and active; and the affections of men are the springs of the motion: take away all love and hatred, all hope and fear, all anger, zeal, and affectionate desire, and the world would be, in a great measure, motionless and dead; there would be no such thing as activity amongst mankind, or any earnest pursuit whatsoever.[37]

Every human action is a complex mixture of reason and emotion. This simple fact represents to Edwards a kind of behavioral expression of the underlying, psychological reality:

> I humbly conceive that the affections of the soul are not properly distinguished from the will, as though they were two faculties in the soul. All acts of the affections of the soul are in some sense acts of the will, and all acts of the will are acts of the affections. All exercises of the will are in some degree or other, exercises of the soul's appetition or aversion; or which is the same thing, of its love or hatred. The soul wills one thing rather than another, or chooses one thing rather than another, no otherwise than as it loves one thing more than another; but love and hatred are affections of the soul: and therefore all acts of the will are truly acts of the affections.[38]

Edwards thus made his point forcefully and unambiguously. All our plans and acts are in some measure a function of our likes and dislikes, love and hatred, of our own peculiar sense of what is beautiful and what is ugly.

The Puritan and Neoplatonic churchmen from whom Edwards inherited the terminology of faculty psychology drew a portrait of human psychology that was theoretically complex but practically quite simple. A stimulus was said to be passively received and its resulting "phantasm" thereafter leapfrogged through a host of independent faculties until it reached a kind of executive faculty: "Reason." The rational faculty could make its decisions independently of the affections. People were thus seen as complicated pieces of psychological machinery whose conduct, conversely, was a rather simple function of the choices made by the rational faculty. In spite of an ornate, Byzantine concept of mind, human thinking and behavior was rendered quite explicable and even predictable.[39] Edwards, however, inverted this arrangement. His conception of the mind was starkly simple; he acknowledged only two faculties: "understanding" and "will-affections," and then only as convenient fictions rather that as quasi-autonomous entities. Furthermore, by uniting the will and affections, the structurally simple Edwardsean person emerges as one whose thinking and behavior is caused mostly by complex, uncontrollable, even unknowable unconscious "other things," i.e., by emotional forces.

Thus far we have considered only what might be called experiential indices of Edwards's unified conception of the human mind. Since rational acts of will like planning, choosing, and acting are motivated by emotional needs, then it may be inferred that human mental structure is a rational-emotive unity. For Edwards's rigorous, relentless mind, however, mere inference was fallible and insufficient. He therefore undertook to analyze the precise nature of the relationship between the two mental functions (not structures) which he acknowledged, understanding and will-affections.

At first glance, Edwards analysis of mind is decidedly unexceptional except for the poverty of "faculties" and the integrated conception of "will-affections":

> God has indued the soul with two faculties: one is that by which it is capable of perception and speculation, or by which it discerns and judges of things; which is called the understanding. The other faculty is that by which the soul does not merely perceive and view things, but is in some way inclined with respect to the things it views or considers . . . either as liking or disliking, pleased or displeased, approving or rejecting. This faculty is called by various names: it is sometimes called the *inclination:* and, as it has respect to the actions that are determined and governed by it, is called the *will:* and the *mind,* with regard to the exercises of this faculty, is often called the *heart.*[40]

Some commentators have jumped to the false conclusion that this statement proves that Edwards was a mere modified "faculty psychologist" who had honed Occam's razor to an uncommonly sharp cutting edge.[41] These misinterpreters have simply failed to grasp Edwards's essential message concerning the relationship between these "faculties."

Edwards distinguished between two kinds of understanding. A person can possess a "mere notional understanding, wherein the mind only beholds things in the exercise of a speculative faculty."[42] This level of understanding, which implies a minimum of personal participation and involvement, is held by Edwards to be inadequate at best, and at worst representative of serious pathology. A person who does not get involved with the object of attention, who does not take a position with regard to it, to experience it, has, according to Edwards, somewhat artificial, rarefied knowledge. Such knowledge seldom leads to constructive action because emotional involvement, absent in a "notional understanding," motivates the will. So-called rationalists, therefore, those who seek to keep their emotions in check, are guilty of denying a basic human function.

This highly intellectual "notional understanding" must be contrasted with the understanding which Edwards called "a sense of the heart":

> I say a sense of heart; for it is not speculation merely that is concerned in this kind of understanding: nor can there be a clear distinction made between the two faculties of understanding and will, as acting distinctly and separately, in this matter. When the mind is sensible of the sweet beauty and amiableness of a thing, that implies a sensibleness of sweetness and delight in the presence of the idea of it: and this sensibleness of the amiableness or delightfulness of beauty, carries in the very nature of it, the sense of the heart; or an effect and impression the soul is the subject of as a substance possessed of taste, inclination and will.[43]

Scholastic distinctions between "faculties" of reason and emotion must, in Edwards's view, be discarded. It cannot be denied, asserted Edwards, that "he that has perceived the sweet taste of honey, knows much more about it, than he who has only looked upon and felt of it."[44] "A sense of the heart" implies a simultaneous dispensation of heat and light: the receiving of information that is deeply cared about and experienced directly.[45] In the sort of understanding he tried to express with "a sense of the heart" Edwards found conclusive evidence that the human mind functions as a fully integrated rational-emotive unity that transcends the artificial boundaries erected by common sense and assumed by "faculty" psychology.

Edwards held that human beings are creatures whose every act and every perception is emotionally motivated, and that true understanding, therefore, consists in a sense of the heart—a total grasp involving not only speculative judgment but loving and/or hating. Persons constructed in such a manner can come to know God, then, in only one way: with a total commitment of all their intellectual and emotional resources. Spiritual understanding is but a very special case of a sense of the heart.

> Spiritual understanding primarily consists in this sense, or taste of the moral beauty of divine things; so that no knowledge can be called spiritual, any further than it arises from this, and has this in it. But secondarily, it includes all that discerning and knowledge of things of religion, which depends upon, and flows from such a sense.[46]

Both before and after conversion people are attracted to that which they like and repelled by that which they dislike. They are "free" to consciously choose among alternatives but, at a deeper level, they must choose that which appears more attractive or lovely to them. Before conversion, due to their originally sinful nature, persons can have only a "notional understanding" of "divine things," at best. They do not love or relish God and the beauty of divine works in such a way that they cannot do otherwise. They need, according to Edwards, to have their affections made more congruent with those of God Himself so that their thinking, perceiving, and acting more closely approximate the manner in which God might accomplish these tasks. This psychological transformation occurs during the "gracious discoveries" of conversion.

The "Principles"
of Psychology: The Discovery of Divine Love

It is commonly supposed that the conversion experience has no proper analogue. It is said neatly to divide a person's life into two discrete units: sinner and saint, dead and reborn, lost and saved; spiritual weakness is miraculously transformed into spiritual strength. Many individuals believe they are so fundamentally different after conversion that, like St. Paul, they may change their residences, their occupations, and even their names. These uniquely decisive *effects* of conversion, combined with its hypothesized supernatural origins, have generally discouraged investigation into the precise nature or *essence* of the event. William

James for example, called off his investigation of conversion far short of trying to isolate its essence:

> If the grace of God miraculously operates, it probably operates through the subliminal door, then. But just *how* anything operates in this region is still unexplained, and we shall do well now to say good-by to the *process* of transformation altogether—leaving it, if you like, a good deal of a psychological or theological mystery—and to turn our attention to the fruits of the religious condition, no matter in what way they may have been produced.[47]

How, one might sensibly inquire, can the mental operations of conversion be explained when the mind, the conversional arena, can never be observed directly, and the supernatural stimulus cannot be observed at all? Edwards rushed in where James and many other psychologists of religion have feared to tread.[48] In his attempt to describe and explain as precisely as he could the psychological change incurred at conversion, Edwards culminated his courageous yet ultimately frustrating entry into cognitive psychology.

To Edwards, as well as most other orthodox Christians, it was baldly obvious that sinners and saints behave differently. Edwards was merely restating what seemed to be an ancient truism when he drew the obvious conclusion from this:

> Hence it will follow, that the sense of things of religion that a natural man has, is not only not to the same degree, but nothing of the same nature with that which a true saint has.

> The reason why natural men have no knowledge of spiritual things is because they have nothing of the Spirit of God dwelling in them.[49]

Converted persons, they who have the Holy Spirit dwelling within them, differ in some absolutely fundamental way from persons who lack the Spirit.

But wherein, exactly, lay the saintly psychological monopoly? How does the Spirit interact with the mind of the converted person? Edwards usually refers to the presence of the Spirit in conversion as a "principle," "principles," or sometimes an "indwelling vital principle."[50] "There is some one holy principle in the heart," he said in a typical passage, "that is the essence and sum of all grace, the root and source of all holy acts of every kind."[51] The establishment of the new principle is an affair of the heart, which is Edwards's way of saying that it has something to do with the affections. Moreover, the emotional reorientation produced by the spiritual principle is no simple usurpation by God of human functions. Nothing in the mind is replaced, yet the entire mind is reorganized and given a new direction.[52] Although he admitted the vagary and inadequacy of his notion of "principle," there is little doubt that it is what is now commonly called a cognitive-attitudinal structure:

> I use the word "principles," for want of a more determinate signification. By a principle of nature in this place, I mean that foundation which is laid in nature, either old or new, for any particular manner or kind of exercise of the faculties of the soul: or a natural habit or foundation for action, giving a person ability and disposition to exert the faculties in exercises of such a certain kind; so that

to exert the faculties in that kind of exercises, may be said to be his nature. So this new spiritual sense is not a new faculty of understanding, but it is a new foundation laid in the nature of the soul.[53]

The "natural habits or foundations" in the soul, or cognitive structures, represent mental categories or rubrics which permit us to interpret and organize our experience.[54] It seems clear that the Edwardsean "principle" accomplishes a fundamental alteration and reorganization of the manner in which converts structure and interpret their experience.

For converts, behavioral changes are a function of their new psychological "principles"; their conceptions of themselves and their place in the universe has changed. The "gracious discoveries" of God's beauty and the love of Him are accompanied, quite literally, by the discovery of a world which seems startlingly new. The world is now structured and interpreted in part, that is, through the eyes of God. In the following very significant psychological statement, we see Edwards struggling to describe the psychological significance of the newness, the sense of creative discovery, inherent in conversion. The vital indwelling principle emerges quite clearly as a principle of cognitive reorganization:

> If grace be . . . an entirely new kind of principle; then the exercises of it are also entirely a new kind of exercises. And if there be in the soul a new sort of exercises which it is conscious of, which the soul knew nothing of before, and which no improvement, composition or management of what it was before conscious or sensible of, could produce, or anything like it; then it follows that the mind has an entirely new kind of perception or sensation; and here is, as it were, a new spiritual sense that the mind has, or a principle of a new kind of perception or spiritual sensation, which is in its whole nature different from any former kinds of sensation of the mind.[55]

The "new kind of exercises" imparted by the "principle" are thus interpretive and organizational exercises of the mind. The discoveries of conversion, according to Edwards, like other creative discoveries, consist, not primarily in the novel manipulation of the physical environment, but first and significantly in a new vision of the commonplace.

Like cognitive psychologists of all eras, Edwards was frustrated by the invisibility of the mind. Neither he nor his readers had the means with which to evaluate his theory of mental functioning. No one had ever seen, nor would they ever see, a "mind" in operation, and certainly none had observed directly and objectively, the Edwardsean "principle." When he attempted to describe the actual activity of the "principle," therefore, Edwards resorted to the use of analogy; he tried to explain, that is, not what the mind *is,* but rather what it *is like.* In all the analogies which Edwards draws between the mysterious conversion "principle" and familiar, observable phenomena, he stresses the fundamental nature of the change. Something in the essence, or the core, of converts is altered. They not only act and think differently than before; they literally possess different minds.

"The word of God," Edwards remarked, "abides in the heart of a regenerate person as a holy seed, a Divine principle there, though it may be but as a seed, a small thing." But, he reminds us, "the seed is a very small part of the plant, and is its first principle."[56] Edwards, of course, knew nothing of modern genetics but, if he had, he might have carried the analogy even further. The infusion of the divine "principle," he might have said, is like giving a person a new set of genes. The "principle" represents no mere face lift which gives the appearance of youth; converts literally are transformed into spiritual babes: vigorous, clean, and new. They are, as evangelists have long been fond of saying, born again. In another place, Edwards referred to the principle as a "divine, supernatural spring of action" in which converts ". . . don't only drink living water, but this living water becomes a well or fountain of water, in the soul, springing up into spiritual and everlasting life."[57] In still another analogy, Edwards remarked: "The light of the Sun of Righteousness don't only shine upon them, but is so communicated to them that they shine also, and become little images of that Sun which shines upon them."[58] Converted persons, that is, are not like the planets which derive their energy from elsewhere, but rather they resemble something like comets, each containing the vital glow of the energy source which spawned it.

The conversion "principle" represents an utterly fundamental aspect of mind. It therefore must involve or influence the most basic aspects of human nature. Recall that Edwards held that all human thinking and action begin with the affections, with loving and hating. We see and do that which we like and avoid that which does not please us. The "principle" of grace, therefore, must accomplish a revolution in the affectional system; it must redistribute a person's deepest loves and hates. Furthermore, since it is the Holy Spirit of God which is "united to the faculties of the soul," the basic, motivating love of the convert must, in Edwards's view, be redirected toward God and all his works:[59]

> That principle in the soul of the saints, which is the grand Christian virtue, and which is the soul and essence and summary comprehension of all grace, *is a principle of Divine love.*[60]

> Divine love, as it has God for its object, may thus be described. 'Tis the soul's relish of the supreme excellency of the Divine nature inclining the heart to God as the chief good.[61]

Whereas before the infusion of the divine light individuals might be inclined toward card playing, drinking, "frolicking," and other "debaucheries," the reason and emotion of reborn converts is inclined toward God and godliness. That is, it is *necessarily* inclined. After conversion persons have a deeply felt "sense" of God's beauty; they must yearn for, relish, and love God simply because their minds are now constructed so that they must.

Although the divine "principle" is passively received from God, human mental activity, according to Edwards, is normally active and strenuous. The laborious "exercises" which he describes are now generally referred to as information processing—the sorting, selecting, and depositing of information into cognitive categories. Each new experience is interpretable only within the context provided by the altered cognitive-attitudinal structures which give meaning to experience. Potential experience can never become actual until an appropriate cognitive structure has been created. As an example of the sort of mental realignment Edwards had in mind, consider the following trivial example of the importance of cognitive structures. You are asked to connect the following set of dots with four straight lines without lifting your pencil from the paper (Figure 1).

Fig. 1. The dot problem.

Let us suppose that you try to solve the problem, fail repeatedly, and conclude that it is insoluble. You inform your neighbor of your difficulty and seek her sympathy. Instead of offering consolation, however, she takes your pencil and solves the problem with four deft strokes (Figure 2).
You are amazed at your neighbor's brilliance until she tells you that she learned the solution in a psychology class she took years ago.[62] Even after your amazement dissipates, however, you will still possess a fundamentally different view of the problem than you did before. You will have discovered the areas outside the "dot box" which escaped your notice initially, and in any future encounters with the problem the solution will seem as obvious to you as it does to your neighbor. The acquisition of a new cognitive structure has permitted the discovery of an entirely new, if trivial, realm of experience.[63]

Edwards claimed that the infusion of the "principle" of divine love led the mind to a "new sort of exercises" which permits persons to perceive things they have never seen before. Yet the world itself changes little; conversion is intrapsychic. The "gracious discoveries" cause us to refocus our attention and reorganize familiar information. For Edwardsean converts, godly beauty and truth are eagerly received into their appropriate, valid, and newly acquired categories:

> Persons after their conversion often speak of things of religion as seeming new to them; that preaching is a new thing; that it seems to them they never heard preaching before; that the Bible is a new book: they find there new chapters, new psalms, new histories, because they see them in a new light.[64]

We see, think, and act, according to Edwards, so as to maximize our pleasure and minimize our pain. Although much human activity appears rational and goal directed, we are always attracted to that which we love and repelled by that which

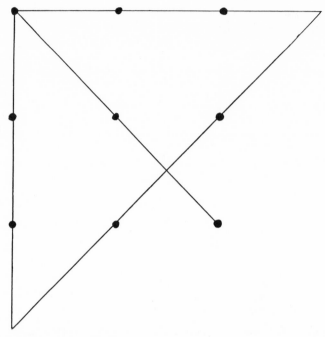

Fig. 2. Solution to the dot problem.

we hate. We are rational-emotive unities. The "vital, indwelling principle," a new cognitive structure or principle of mental reorganization, is rooted ultimately, therefore, in a reorientation of the emotions. Converts think, act, and view the world differently because they feel differently; they are drawn by their love of God inexorably toward godliness. When this occurs, Edward says that God is apprehended with a "sense of the heart," with the total commitment of our combined rational and emotional resources. We take a close look at aspects of the world and ourselves to which we were formerly blind and we are amazed at what we find. This is perhaps the essence of all cognition which results in what we call "discovery."

The Dilemma: The Psychological Basis of Spiritual Uncertainty

> And I will build a citadel
> Too beautiful to tell
> O too austere to tell
> And far too beautiful to see. . . .
> Making the spirit leap and burn
>
> For the hard intellectual light
> Kills all delight
> And brings the solemn, inward pain
> Of truth into the heart again.

Richard Eberhart,
"In a Hard Intellectual Light"

In his model of the mind, Edwards argued for the singular importance of the emotions or affections. In all our plans and acts, in our basic understanding and perception of the world, emotional considerations play a vital role. In Edwards's view, human rationality is only an illusion; a substratum of emotional needs determines every act we commit, every direction we look, and every inference we make.

Why did Edwards seek to demonstrate the superordinate significance of the emotions? What reason was there to construct an elaborate psychological theory that was nearly incomprehensible but apparently in opposition to nearly every "enlightened" view of the day? It was simply this: Edwards believed the affectionate outbursts of the Great Awakening represented, for the most part, a valid work of God and not a dance of lunatics, as some would have it. It was true that there had been many emotional excesses which could hardly be interpreted as works of the Holy Spirit. Yet he resolutely refused to believe that the emotional outbursts were unnecessary, even harmful, artifacts. Emotion must be an integral component of coming to grace. Somewhere, far beneath the raving and ranting, the shouting, sweating, and speaking in tongues, Edwards thought he discerned a profound truth: "true religion, in great part, consists in holy affections."[1] The entire psychological system of Edwards is meant to justify the equating of true religion with emotional involvement.

"False Affections and True": The Need for Criteria

But what, one may ask, are the signs of a valid conversion? How deep must one look to discern the validity of a conversion experience? Since Edwards viewed the cognitive-attitudinal alteration in conversion as fundamentally a revolution in the affections, an individual's emotional responses probably yield the most important insights into the validity of the experience. In particular, Edwards believed that the "sense of the heart" was most reliably exhibited in what he called "religious affections" or "holy affection." ". . . There is no true religion," he claimed, "where there is no religious affection."[2] The surest sign that a conversion is valid, then, is an emotional outpouring of love for God and godliness.

The equation between valid conversion and the affections did not, however, provide a very useful criterion against which conversions might be evaluated. It merely focused attention on the affections by contending that in the absence of "raised affections," or emotional intensity, a conversion cannot occur. Yet it seemed obvious to Edwards that the presence of emotional disturbances hardly guaranteed the presence of the Holy Spirit. People become emotionally aroused for many reasons, most of which are unrelated to conversion or even to religion; all are capable of raising the affections to an extraordinary degree. Chief among these artificial stimulants to the affections were the tricks of fanatical ministers, as the infamous James Davenport vividly demonstrated one evening in July 1741:

Divers women were terrified and cried out exceedingly. When Mr. Davenport had dismissed the congregation some went out and others stayed; he then went into the broad alley [aisle], which was much crowded, and there he screamed out, "Come to Christ! Come to Christ! Come away!" Then he went into the third

pew on the women's side, and kept there, sometimes singing, sometimes praying; he and his companions all taking their turns, and the women fainting and in
hysterics. This confusion continued until ten o'clock at night. And then he went
off singing through the streets.[3]

That God should operate in such a fashion was, to Edwards, unproven, even
improbable. Raving and ranting are no sure signs of grace. Bizarre episodes like
those involving Davenport, in fact, merely discredited all raised affections.
". . . False religion," said Edwards, "consisting in the counterfeits of the operations of the Spirit of God . . . tends greatly to wound and weaken the cause of vital
religion. . . ."[4] There was a desperate need, in other words, to distinguish between
the affections:

> There are false affections and there are true. A man's having much affection,
> don't prove that he has any true religion: but if he has no affection it proves that
> he has no true religion. The right way, is not to reject all affections, nor to
> approve all; but to distinguish between affections, approving some and rejecting
> others; separating between the wheat and the chaff, the gold and the dross, the
> precious and the vile.[5]

A theory was needed which could establish a causative link between the essence
of conversion—the restructuring of the mind—and its behavioral and experiential
indices—certain aspects of emotional arousal.

Often, Edwards believed, a minister must provide the final assurances through
favorable interpretations of his parishioners' experiences.

> Many continue a long time in a course of gracious exercises and experiences,
> and don't think themselves to be otherwise; and none knows how long they
> would continue so were they not helped by particular instruction.[6]

It was impossible to instruct people concerning the state of their immortal souls,
however, until a checklist of observable holy affections had been constructed.
Until the affections were distinguished, the minister could offer only moral support to tormented but hopeful parishioners. "Particular instruction" to an aspiring
convert without particular instructions for the minister would, to a person of
Edwards's relentlessly logical mind, constitute an irresponsible and dangerous
game.

Although certainly less important than the removal of the tormenting anxiety
associated with individual conversions, a set of signs, or rules, would also help
make life more fulfilling for the ministers. Edwards and his "New Light" colleagues were in the business of bringing souls to Christ; that was their primary
function.[7] While all individuals in the congregation agonized over the state of their
souls, the minister was often right beside them, lamenting his own inability to tell
his parishioners the joyous words they desperately wanted to hear. Even Jonathan
Edwards, the epitome of ruthless Puritanism, yearned to relax and celebrate the
accomplishment of his goal—salvation for members of his congregation:

> Yet I should account it a great calamity to be deprived of the comfort of

rejoicing with those of my flock when there seems to be good evidence that those that were dead are alive.[8]

Edwards, like his "flock," was often in an uncomfortable situation. It would be devastating to labor so long and hard and have no true converts. He needed "the comfort of rejoicing" over the fruits of his labor and God's mercy, and for this he needed "good evidence," which might be obtained only after the affections had been distinguished.

In the period of the Great Awakening (ca. 1736–46), therefore, a set of criteria for evaluating the validity of conversion experiences was needed for a variety of reasons. Many people thought they had been converted, but they needed to know for sure. Conscientious evangelical ministers, like Edwards, also needed to be sure, lest they mislead an unwitting soul into hell. Edwards, in addition, had a unique interest in distinguishing between holy and spurious affections. He was the acknowledged leader and spokesman of a group of minister-theologians who sought to defend a middle position against rationalists led by Charles Chauncy of Boston, on the one hand, and fanatical enthusiasts like Davenport on the other.[9] Both sides needed to be shown that "raised affections" are the core of religious experience and that false affections can be distinguished from true.

"Marks" and "Signs" as Evidence

Edwards's initial task was to demonstrate that valid, reliable, and *observable* signs of conversion are theoretically possible. For this assignment, he was well armed with his theory of a unified mind: ". . . All acts of the will," he said, "are truly acts of the affections."[10] Human functioning consists in a unified rational-emotive process which begins with conscious and unconscious feeling and culminates in goal-directed, volitional activity. Conversion is essentially the fundamental reorientation of the affections; God and godliness is loved and relished above all else. A direct, immutable, and instantaneous causative sequence begins, therefore, with the infusion of the Divine Light in conversion. Converts love Divine things, conceptualize the world differently, and finally they think and behave in a saintly fashion. Most assuredly, for Edwards, there must be visible evidence of conversion which can be traced directly to the invisible essence of the process: the reorientation of the affections; the apprehension of God with a "sense of the heart."

What is the nature of this evidence, then, which allows one to label certain affections as holy and others as spurious? Edwards elaborated the distinctions between the affections twice, once during the heat of the Awakening, in the *Distinguishing Marks* (1741), and again shortly after the spiritual furor had subsided, in the *Religious Affections* (1746).[11] A summary of the reliable evidence of conversion is presented in Table 1, while the potentially spurious evidence is found in Table 2.[12]

Most of these "signs" and "marks" are derived from scripture and from orthodox Puritan commentary. Theologically, Edwards's position on conversion evidence is quite unexceptional. Psychologically, however, his discussion of the indices of a valid conversion is most peculiar. As tools for evaluating the truth or falsity of conversion, the lists are decidedly inadequate. In the first place, the distinguishing marks and positive signs are innocuously vague and subjective. How high, for instance, does esteem of Jesus Christ (first distinguishing mark) have to be raised? How tender is a Christian tenderness of spirit (ninth positive sign)? Even if it is granted that all the marks and signs are true, that is, that they occur if and only if they are accompanied by a valid conversion, their importance is still restricted to theological disputation and biblical interpretation. There is virtually no way for aspiring converts to evaluate whether their experiences are valid conversions. Edwards, in other words, provided what today might be called an untestable theory. There is no common ground where theoretical criteria and data can meet. In science, untestable theories are inadmissible, but then Edwards was no scientist. An eighteenth-century Calvinist had neither the means nor the propensity to test the edicts which were attributed to his God. The ultimate result of arid theorizing was much the same for Edwards, however, as it is for the modern scientist. Scientists tend to ignore theories which have no behavioral referents. Likewise, thoughtful, aspiring converts would be forced to turn elsewhere for a more useful, if less eloquent and well-reasoned, method of evaluating their experiences. In the absence of testable criteria they would probably ask their ministers or perhaps even their friends for a simple yes or no.[13]

A second difficulty with Edwards's marks and signs lay in the confounding of reliable and unreliable evidence. It might well be the case that the negative instances and signs could act as imperfect vehicles for the expression of the positive marks and signs. If, for example, a person experiences an increased regard for Holy Scripture (third distinguishing mark), he or she is likely to make a great deal of noise about religion (third negative instance). And certainly the exercise and fruit of Christian practice (twelfth positive sign) includes godly, charitable behavior (twelfth negative sign). Edwards had demonstrated that, in theory, "there are undoubtedly sufficient marks given to guide the church of God in this great affair of judging of spirits."[14] For the worried constituents of that church, however, Edwards's categories did little to assist them in the evaluation of the validity of their conversions. He had demonstrated that holy affections can, in theory, be distinguished from polluting artifact. Unfortunately, Edwards did not provide instructions for accomplishing this delicate distillation in practice.

His hands were tied, as he would have it, by the devil. The Evil One played a critical role in Edwardsean psychology, for it was he who effectively frustrated any attempt to successfully evaluate the validity of a conversion.[15] That "he can't *exactly* imitate divine operations in their nature" was small consolation.[16] All other aspects of conversion, those which are available to introspective analysis and observation, can be flawlessly reproduced by the Evil One. "First," Edwards pointed out, ". . . the devil can counterfeit all the saving operations and graces of the Spirit of God . . . those effects of God's Spirit which are special, divine and sanctifying."[17] Like God himself, the devil can infiltrate people, "possess" them, and produce any or all of the conversion effects that also follow the infusion of the Divine light. "Secondly," admitted Edwards, ". . . if Satan can imitate the things themselves, he may easily put them one after another, in such a certain order."[18] Progression through the conversion sequence, then, from need to seeking to despair to apparent discovery, is no guarantee of a valid conversion. The devil can imitate the exact order as well as all the effects of a valid conversion. "Thirdly," Edwards concludes, "we have no certain rule to determine how far God's own spirit may go in those operations and convictions which in themselves are not spiritual and saving."[19] The wheat and the chaff, alas, are inextricably mixed; the usefulness of the distinguishing marks and positive signs must be negated in order that the devil be paid his due.

Not all of Edwards's ministerial and theological colleagues were so pessimistic. For radical enthusiasts like Davenport, the overflow of emotion was evidence enough that the Lord was at work. To rationalists like Charles Chauncy of Boston, conversion was a much more reasonable enterprise, something like passing a university examination.[20] Edwards's peculiarly generous respect for the ability of the devil to camouflage successfully the nature of religious experience is rooted in his psychology. In a true conversion, he maintained, God's divine light illuminates every corner of the soul; the convert cannot doubt its divine origin:

When there is an actual and lively discovery of this beauty and excellency, it will not allow of any such thought as that it is the fruit of man's invention. This is a kind of intuitive and immediate evidence. They believe the doctrine of God's word to be divine, because they see a divine, and transcendent, and most evidently distinguishing glory in them; such a glory as, if clearly seen, does not leave room to doubt of their being of God, and not of men.[21]

Edwards is saying here that the truth of the light must be inferred immediately and be intuitively obvious—that is a test of its validity. An implication of this remarkable contention is that if the inference is immediate, and the convert concludes that the divine light principle which is fused with the mind is true, then no further examination is necessary.[22] The decision rules contained in the *Distinguishing Marks* and the *Religious Affections* are therefore superfluous.

Recall that, according to Edwards, one can never be an objective, "rational" observer of personal experience or the behavior of another. That which appears beautiful or delightful must also, and immediately, be perceived as true. A "sense of the heart" implies that reason and the emotions are acting in unison. Thus, if the divine light is beheld in the way Edwards suggests, with a "sense of the heart," then no amount of disconfirming evidence afterward is likely to convince hopeful converts that their experiences were invalid. They *know* they are saved. Furthermore, since we have also seen that the devil can imitate every aspect of the conversion sequence except the divine principle itself, any rules for evaluating information about a conversion are problematic for three reasons: (1) the data to which they apply may be unaccountably spurious; (2) the event to which they apply is strictly cognitive and thus too private to be evaluated by an outsider; and, (3) the event to which they apply is apprehended in such a way as to make it impervious to objective evaluation even by the person who has experienced it. If persons are not convinced totally and immediately that their experiences were valid conversions, then, logically, they have not been converted. But even extreme confidence is insufficient. Edwards's eleventh negative sign is unmistakably clear on this:

> This is no sign that affections are right, or that they are wrong, that they make persons that have them, exceedingly confident that what they experience is divine, and that they are in a good estate.[23]

The devil is quite capable of inducing supreme confidence even in those whose affections have been raised spuriously.

Edwards faced a difficult problem. He had conceived of people as complex, dynamic beings who are *always* motivated by an array of mostly unconscious emotions. In order to transform the whole person, then, a true conversion must consist in an absolutely inward, cognitive-attitudinal, reorientation that is not subject to objective evaluation. The existence of the new, divinely oriented mind must always be inferred from signs which, unfortunately, the devil can also produce. "The devil has special advantage," Edwards admitted, " . . . with respect to the inward experiences of Christians themselves; and . . . with respect to the external effects of experiences."[24] In his reflective moments he must have thought it a grossly unfair advantage, unfair to hopeful converts and unfair to well-meaning ministers.

As people initiate evaluation of their conversion experiences, they are confronted with an impossible task. This or that sign which they have observed in their own experiences may be a reliable index of a valid conversion, and then again, it may not. "It is like giving a man rules," said Edwards, "how to distinguish visible objects in the dark."[25] It is impossible to reach a conclusion concerning any apparent conversion, based strictly on the external "evidence."

Edwards faced squarely the principal problem of all cognitive psychologists: the mind, the great organizer of experience and action, is inscrutable. Like Edwards, contemporary cognitive theorists are necessarily interested in behavior, and with Edwards they believe that behavior is only a very rough and unreliable indicator of human functioning.[26] If Jonathan Edwards had been a contemporary cognitive psychologist, he would probably have attached statistical probabilities to his distinguishing marks and positive signs. "If all behavioral and experiential indices are considered together," he might have jargonized, "then the probability of an individual exhibiting all these traits without the presence of the divine light is less than one in a hundred." The devil would become the capricious chance factor, the intervening, uncontrolled, but sometimes effective causative agent. In fact, Edwards's reasoning followed a similar line. He sought to discover a way of discriminating true religion from false which has some specifiable reliability. His own set of presumably valid criteria could not accomplish this because his ultimate dependent variable (entrance into heaven) was as inaccessible as his independent variable (presence or absence of the divine light). Edwards had access to neither cause nor effect.

Denouement: "Solemn Inward Pain of Truth"

Edwards needed to know the unknowable. The manner in which he faced this predicament, over a frenzied period where the need became increasingly urgent, is the result of the interaction between a psychological theory and spiritual upheaval. In 1734, before the Great Awakening got into full swing, Edwards delivered and published his brilliant sermon on "The Divine and Supernatural Light." In it he announced that he would "show what this divine light is."[27] This is clearly a misstatement of purpose; Edwards, in fact, attempted to examine the *effects* of the divine light. These effects, he noted in 1734, are purely cognitive and attitudinal:

> . . . he, [the Holy Spirit] unites himself with the mind of a saint, takes him for his temple, actuates and influences him as a new supernatural principle of life and action. . . . The Holy Spirit operates in the minds of the godly, by uniting himself to them, and living in them, and exerting his own nature in the exercise of the faculties.[28]

It was enough, at this point, to elaborate the principal cognitive effects of conversion: the acquisition of "a *sense* of the loveliness and beauty of that holiness and grace."[29] Although this "sense" would undoubtedly be reflected in "action," as Edwards called it, all that need be said about it is that it is "godly."

Edwards, and before him his grandfather Solomon Stoddard, had long urged that emotionalism was not a desirable artifact in conversion. The sudden and complete reorientation of a person's emotional system toward love of an awesome God is a shattering experience which might easily be accompanied by fainting, shrieking, and sweating. By 1741, however, what had long been the rule in Northampton had spread and was engulfing all the American Colonies in turmoil. Davenport had laid siege to New England, and Whitefield was preaching to enthusiastic thousands from Maine to Georgia.[30] Some envisioned the entire British Empire in America disintegrating in the spiritual smoke of burning religionists. It was in part to allay these fears that Edwards, the acknowledged leader of the New-Light supporters of the Awakening, produced the *Distinguishing Marks*. It is a curious document, exceedingly confident in the beginning, but ending in apparent contradiction and confusion. On the second page he stated his goal:

> My design therefore at this time is to show what are the true, certain, and distinguishing evidences of a work of the Spirit of God, by which we may proceed safely judging of any operation we find in ourselves or see in others.[31]

Yet in his conclusion to this treatise, after carefully presenting the distinguishing marks and negative instances, Edwards implicitly acknowledged his insoluble dilemma. In order to achieve his stated goal, he would have either to embrace an alternative system of psychology and conception of conversion or, alternatively, give false assurances to hopeful converts. He admitted, finally, that "we must allow the scriptures to stand good, that speak of everything in the saint, that belongs to the spiritual and divine life, as hidden."[32] Though he adroitly chose not to emphasize the point, he saw clearly that there are no marks of God's grace which ordinary mortals can distinguish.

As leader of the supporters of the Awakening, Edwards was in a difficult situation. He would do nothing directly to dampen the fires of the Awakening. His intuition told him that the "uncommon concern and engagedness of mind about the things of religion is, undoubtedly, in the general, from the Spirit of God."[33] To the enemies of the Awakening, Edwards, never diplomatic, was disarmingly blunt. He remarked matter-of-factly, as though it could be proven, that "Christ is come down from heaven into this land," and he reminded them of the Bible's clear warning that they who do not aid in the work of the Spirit "should take heed that they ben't guilty of the unpardonable sin against the Holy Ghost."[34] In other words, opponents of the Awakening should count themselves among the unfortunate majority of humanity who are destined for the eternal torments of hell. On the other hand, he admonished preachers who were supporters of the Awakening to practice "humility and self-diffidence, and an entire dependence on our Lord Jesus Christ."[35] This is the most important message in the *Distinguishing Marks,* though it appears as but a whisper next to the marks themselves. "Trust my psychological analysis of the operation of the divine light," he might have said; "do not believe in the usefulness of the distinguishing marks." Yet he did not actually say anything of the kind. The Lord should be given benefit of the doubt. He provided a number of distinguishing marks; all should pray earnestly that He grant His earthly disciples His power of discernment.

One of the basic postulates of Edwardsean psychology is that people selectively attend to that which pleases them and avoid that which appears painful. Edwards undoubtedly believed that hopeful converts and New Light ministers would focus their attention on the marks, at the expense of his muted pleas for humility and moderation. In 1741, it seemed as if a new order might be at hand. Edwards himself had seen members of the Enfield, Connecticut, congregation shriek and faint upon hearing one of his sermons, delivered in his usual calm, deliberate manner.[36] And after Whitefield addressed Edwards's Northampton congregation, he recorded in his journal that even Edwards wept uncontrollably from the beginning to the end of the sermon.[37] The devil seemed to be in retreat. In his more sober moments, however, Edwards quietly offered the devil his profound respect. The preservation of Edwards's psychological system in the *Distinguishing Marks,* the maintenance of conversion as an absolutely cognitive-attitudinal event, represents a courageous and grudging tribute to the power of the Evil One.

By 1746, the Great Awakening was over. The energy was spent and bitter controversy prevailed. God seemed to have forsaken his flock when they needed Him most. From all the disappointment and charges and countercharges of enthusiasm, chicanery, and hard-heartedness, Edwards extracted one implication of overriding significance: people are incapable of distinguishing between charlatans and saints. He presented the positive signs in the *Religious Affections* not so much for their practical value, but rather to demonstrate that his psychological views are rooted in Holy Scripture:

... I am far from undertaking to give such signs of gracious affections, as shall be sufficient to enable any certainly to distinguish true affection from false in others; or to determine positively which of their neighbors are true professors, and which are hypocrites.[38]

Furthermore,

No such signs are to be expected, that shall be sufficient to enable those saints certainly to discern their own good estate.[39]

Those in search of a manual which would help them evaluate the validity of their conversion experiences need not have read on. Those who read on to the end of the *Affections* would find a boldly stated conclusion which had been only an implicit assumption prior to the Awakening and a surreptitious afterthought in heat of that remarkable event: sainthood is a purely cognitive phenomenon.

Christian or holy practice is spiritual practice; and this is not the motion of a body, that knows not how, nor when, nor wherefore it moves. . . . To speak of Christian experience and practice, as if they were two things, properly and entirely distinct, is to make a distinction without consideration or reason. Indeed all Christian experience is not properly called practice; but all Christian practice is properly called experience.[40]

All that is essentially Christian is the reorientation of the mind toward love of the divine.

If the *Distinguishing Marks* is Edwards's tribute to the power of the devil in a time when God seemed to be roaming the New England countryside, the *Religious Affections* is his acknowledgment of God's awesomeness in a period of apparent godlessness. "God," Edwards declared in the title of his first published sermon, is "Glorified . . . by . . . Man's Dependence upon Him."[41] In the *Affections* Edwards attempted to demonstrate the absolute nature and psychological basis of that dependence. The inscrutable, emotional human mind is where the battle between the forces of light and darkness takes place. Calvinist theology thus became rooted in cognitive psychology. We must depend on God's benevolence not only for grace, but also for the assurance of grace. In Edwards's view, ultimate causes of human behavior can never be known because the structure of the mind will not permit it. God and the devil perform their transformations in the unconscious.

Epilogue: Edwards's Achievement

But as for certain truth, no man has known it,
Nor shall he know it, neither of the gods
Nor yet of all the things of which I speak.
For even if by chance he were to utter
The final truth, he would himself not know it:
For all is but a woven web of guesses.

Xenophanes
(translation by Karl R. Popper)

What was Edwards's achievement? In attempting to answer this question scholars have searched for analogous contributions in the mainstream of Western philosophy. The idealistic metaphysics of Edwards's *Notes on the Mind* has reminded many commentators of Berkeley, while the current fashion, following up a number of suggestions made by Perry Miller, is to find in Edwards a kind of Calvinistic, evangelical, applied Lockean sensationalism.[1] The latter view holds that Edwards found in Locke's doctrine—that the mind is structured and derives its contents solely through the senses—a justification for evangelical preaching and for the sensuous emotionalism of the Great Awakening. Edwards, it will be recalled, used the Lockean phrase "new simple idea" to describe the operation of the Holy Spirit on the human mind.

Without denying Edwards's profound debt to Locke or his early affinity to Berkeleian idealism, I suggest that for the historian of psychology the proper analogue to Edwards is Hume, the third great figure of classical empiricism and, in the indelicate phrase of Bertrand Russell, empiricism's "dead end."[2] Hume demonstrated logically, and perhaps permanently, that the central postulate of empiricism—that all human knowledge originates with sensory input and is therefore traceable, in principle, to the observable, empirical world—is absolutely incompatible with the attainment of certain, rationally demonstrable knowledge. This conclusion, with which neither he nor subsequent generations of empiricists are by any means comfortable, forced him into philosophical skepticism, the paradoxical view that the only conceivable rational judgment is to withhold all judgment. Hume's argument for philosophical skepticism may be viewed as having three related components: (1) human reason is fallible; (2) the mind is a unified mixture of (what are called, for convenience) reason and emotion; (3) judgments, which must inevitably be made, cannot be fully rational. I will illustrate Hume's reasoning with three characteristic passages from his *Treatise*, begun in 1734.[3]

1. *Human reason is fallible.*

    In all demonstrative sciences the rules are certain and infallible; but when we apply them, our fallible and uncertain faculties are very apt to depart from them, and fall into error. . . . By this means all knowledge degenerates into probability; and this probability is greater or less, according to our experience of the veracity or deceitfulness of our understanding and according to the simplicity or intricacy of the question.

2. *The mind is a rational-emotive unity.*

    When any affecting object is presented, it gives the alarm, and excites immediately a degree of its proper passion. . . . This emotion passes by an easy transition to the imagination; and diffusing itself over our idea of the affecting object, makes us form that idea with greater force and vivacity, and consequently assent to it. . . . The first astonishment . . . spreads itself over the whole soul, and so vivifies and enlivens the idea, that it resembles the inferences we draw from experience. This is a mystery. . . .[4]

3. *Human judgments cannot be rationally justified.*
   But as experience will sufficiently convince anyone, who thinks it worthwhile to try, that tho' he can find no error in the foregoing arguments, yet he still continues to believe, and think, and reason as usual. . . .

Hume, in firm possession of one of the most rational of minds and the most empirical of theories, reached the disastrous (for him) but inescapable conclusion that a rational response to the empirical world is just not possible. His conclusion was forced upon him by a logic so impeccable that, to this day, he remains the embarrassing vexation of his fellow empiricists.

Edwards's problem situation was of course, in many respects, much different from that of Hume. Philosophical skepticism was utterly foreign to Edwards, as it had been to Locke and Berkeley. Locke had failed to take sufficient note of the rather glaring inconsistency between his empiricist principles and his belief in primary qualities existing in the empirical world which can be known with certainty, unclouded by the vicissitudes of human sensory and nervous systems. Berkeley extended the domain of empiricism to what Locke had called primary qualities, but he was subsequently saved from skeptical doubt by virtue of his faith in God. For although, according to Berkeley, all our knowledge of the world is "secondary" (i.e., knowledge of our *ideas* of the world) and we should therefore doubt all that is not momentarily perceived, we are, in Berkeley's view, saved from skeptical doubt because God, the "Great Perceiver," is always directly aware of everything. Thus everything is perceived at all times and may therefore be said to exist, with allowance for human imperfection, pretty much as it appears. Hume, more logical than Locke but less faithful than Berkeley, became a skeptical philosopher.[5]

Edwards, guided by his relentless logic and driven by his Calvinist faith, rejoiced where Hume fretted. As a boy at Yale, Edwards, after reading Locke and those aspects of Newton accessible to one devoid of higher mathematics, concluded:

God . . . causes all changes to arise, as if these things had actually existed in such a series, in some created mind, and as if created minds had comprehended all things perfectly . . . although created minds do not. . . .[6]

We cannot, according to Edwards, know with anything like certainty that things are as they appear and that the causes and effects which we observe actually exist. Only God, the determinant of all events (including mental events) past, present, and future has such knowledge, and only God, in His austere perfection, should have such knowledge. "And we need not," reasoned young Edwards, "perplex our minds with a thousand questions and doubts that will seem to arise. . . . For the corporeal world is to no advantage but to the spiritual."[7] It is the place of human beings to trust in God; it is God's place to have certain knowledge. In this respect, Edwards's initial encounter with Locke was very similar to that of Berkeley.

That Edwards went beyond Berkeley's idealism to an achievement comparable
to that of Hume is attributable to a number of circumstances, including his settlement in a frontier pulpit, the events of the Great Awakening, and the maturation of
his ruthlessly logical mind. Baldly stated, Edwards's journey from his ivory tower
in New Haven to the wooden church in Northampton forced him to address three
urgent practical questions: (1) Was he (Edwards) truly converted; had God caused
his own "awakenings?" (2) Which of his parishioners were truly converted; which
of their "awakenings" had God caused to happen? (3) To what extent was the
entire Great Awakening caused by God? At no time, it must be emphasized, did
Edwards become a *philosophical* skeptic. Rather, his complete inability to answer
with certainty any of these questions which absorbed his attention forced upon
him what I would call a profound *practical* skepticism and a devastating critique
of rationality.

He presented his position concisely and in almost its final form in his justly
famous sermon "A Divine and Supernatural Light," preached (and later published) at Northampton in 1734, the year in which Hume began his *Treatise*.
Edwards's argument for practical skepticism, like Hume's for a more pervasive
sort of doubt, has three parts: (1) human reason is fallible; (2) the mind is a unified
mixture of (what are called for convenience) reason and emotion; (3) judgments
can never be fully rational. The following illustrative passages are taken from
Edwards's sermon on the "Divine Light."

1. *Human reason is fallible.*
   There is . . . understanding . . . which is merely speculative and notional; as
   when a person only speculatively judges that anything is, which, by the agreement of mankind, called good or excellent, VIZ., that which is most to general
   advantage, and between which and a reward there is a suitableness, and the
   like. . . . [This is but] having an opinion . . . [which] rests only in the head . . .
   [and] may be obtained by hearsay.[8]

2. *The mind is a rational-emotive unity.*
   He that is truly enlightened truly apprehends it [the divine light] and sees it, or
   has a sense of it. He does not merely rationally believe that God is glorious, but
   he has a sense of the gloriousness of God in his heart. . . . [The divine light] not
   only removes the hindrances of reason, but positively helps reason. . . . It
   engages the attention of the mind, with more fixedness and intenseness to that
   kind of objects; which causes it to have a clearer view of them, and enables it
   more clearly to see their mutual relations, and occasions it to take more notice
   of them.[9]

3. *Human judgments cannot be rationally justified.*
   There arises from this sense of divine excellency of things contained in the
   word of God, a conviction of the truth and reality of them.[10]
       . . . this light is immediately given by God, and not obtained by natural
   means . . . though the faculties are made use of, it is as the subject and not as
   the cause.[11]

Unlike Hume, Edwards was not driven, by the force of his own logic, to a position of despairing skepticism concerning human knowledge. Indeed Edwards saw in perpetual human ignorance God's greatest glorification.

Yet for historians of psychology the interest in Edwards must reside in his refutation of the concept of certain, empirically verifiable knowledge, just as it must with Hume. For each of them, human reason *is* fallible *because* the mind is a rational-emotive unity (rather than, as common sense suggests, a collection of "faculties" or "powers"), and *therefore* judgments cannot be rationally justified. This is the essence of their logic and at its core lay a conception of mind which is at once compelling and obviously anathema for seekers after certain, verifiable knowledge. Knowing is, in this view, accomplished not by "the reason" or "a mind" but by whole persons who are inextricably part of the process they seek to analyze. Certainty, in this view, is entirely personal, an affair, as Edwards said, "of the heart," or in Hume's phrase, "the sensitive part of our nature." "Impersonal truth" thus becomes a contradictory phrase.

"Hume's philosophy," Russell has contended, "whether true or false, represents the bankruptcy of eighteenth-century reasonableness. . . . It was inevitable that such a self-refutation of rationality should be followed by a great outburst of irrational faith . . . [which] thought the heart superior to reason."[12] In Russell's view, the transition from Hume, the rational inquirer after empirical truth, to Rousseau, the champion of the wisdom of the "noble" savage, marks the "dead end" of empiricism in its pure form and the birth of the Romantic Movement, with its passion, its visions, and its poetry. I suggest that the philosophical distance between Hume and Rousseau is roughly that which also separates Edwards from Emerson; the implications inherent in the psychological theory of Edwards, that is, became the psychological postulates of Emerson.[13] Indeed, the distance between the ambivalent anti-intellectualism of transcendentalism and a similar feature in the pragmatism of James is small.[14] Thus I further suggest, in conclusion, a half-informed but wholly serious proposition. If one were to begin with Edwards's psychological theory, subtract from it his Calvinism, add a dash of Darwin and (perhaps) Hodgson's phenomenology, the yield is William James.[15] The psychological core remains, as does the skepticism, though James, like Edwards, is usually (and, I think, mistakenly) held to be anything but skeptical. With James, of course, we enter the modern period of American psychology and, thus, so does Edwards.

ACKNOWLEDGMENT

This essay has benefited immensely from the intense interest and line-by-line scrutiny of my wife, Janet Marie Lang. The essay, and our mutual life, owe whatever quality they have to her courageous devotion to openness and truth. My profound gratitude is also extended to the editor of this volume, Josef Brožek, for exhibiting courage in conceiving the project and selecting the "Explorers," and for patient but firm guidance in seeing the manuscript through to its appearance in print.

NOTES

Introduction

1. Paul K. Conkin, *Puritans and Pragmatists: Eight Eminent American Thinkers* (New York: Dodd, Mead, 1968), p. 39.

2. The supplement to this essay, "The Psychological Thought of Jonathan Edwards (1703–1758): A Historiographical Review," is my attempt to introduce historians of psychology to the vast, diffuse literature which is concerned with Edwards's psychology. In writing the appendix I have had three goals: (1) to introduce historians of psychology to the most influential of Edwards's modern commentators; (2) to extract and organize the bits and pieces of scholarship concerned with Edwards's psychology; (3) to provide a *critical* analysis—that is, to evaluate the quality and pertinence of each contribution with which I have dealt. The reader who is interested, therefore, only in my own opinions of Edwards's psychological theory, can safely ignore the supplement. The person who would attempt to evaluate what I have written, however, and, perhaps, use it as a spur to further research on Edwards's psychology, must, I think, become familiar with the secondary literature.

3. Robert B. MacLeod, ed., *William James: Unfinished Business* (Washington, D.C.: American Psychological Association, 1969), p. vii.

The Theory of the Mind

1. *A Faithful Narrative of the Surprising Work of God,* in C. C. Goen, ed., *The Great Awakening* (New Haven, Conn.: Yale University Press, 1972), p. 160.

2. See Goen, "Editor's Introduction," pp. 32–46, for a textual history of the *Faithful Narrative.*

3. Goen points out that Isaac Watts and John Guyse, who collaborated on a preface to the first edition of the *Faithful Narrative,* found it to be too colorful. They carefully omitted some passages and apologized for others which in their judgment, might offend readers ("Editor's Introduction," p. 39).

4. *Faithful Narrative,* p. 146.

5. Ibid., p. 164.

6. Ibid., p. 160.

7. Ibid., p. 147.

8. Ibid., p. 148.

9. "Arminianism," according to Clyde Holbrook, " . . . is a complex of notions involving an elevated confidence in freedom of choice, a sharply upward revised estimate of human nature, and a form of common sense moralism. . . ." ("Editor's Introduction" to Jonathan Edwards, *Original Sin,* New Haven, Conn.: Yale University Press, 1970, p. 4). There is a good deal of controversy concerning whether or not "Arminianism" was a real and powerful enemy of the Congregational way or merely an illusion. Goen ("Editor's Introduction," pp. 4–18) makes a strong case for the reality of the Arminian threat, while the illusion hypothesis is advanced by Edmund S. Morgan in his *The Gentle Puritan: A Life of Ezra Stiles, 1727–1795* (New Haven, Conn.: Yale University Press., 1961), pp. 15–19, and Gerald J. Goodwin, "The Myth of 'Arminian-Calvinism' in Eighteenth Century New England," *New England Quarterly* 41 (1968): 213–37.

10. *Faithful Narrative,* p. 149.

11. Ibid., p. 149.

12. Ibid., p. 199.

13. Ibid., p. 200.

14. Ibid., p. 191.

15. Ibid., p. 192. On Edwards and the notion of melancholy see Gail Thain Parker, "Jonathan Edwards and Melancholy," *New England Quarterly* 41 (1968): 192–212.

16. *Faithful Narrative,* p. 192.

17. Ibid., pp. 160–61.

18. Ibid., p. 199.

19. Ibid., p. 192.

20. Ibid., pp. 163–64. Edwards made this point most starkly in an early, important sermon, "God Glorified in the Work of Redemption, by the Greatness of Man's Dependence upon Him, in the Whole of It." In Sereno E. Dwight, ed., *The Works of President Edwards,* 10 vols. (New York: Carvill, 1830), 6: 149–62.

21. *Faithful Narrative,* p. 193.

22. Ibid., pp. 169–70.

23. Ibid., p. 171. At various times Edwards referred to the essence of conversion as "mercy," "the divine and supernatural light," "divine love," "grace," "a vital, indwelling principle," and, after Locke, "a new simple idea."

24. A very influential theory of the creative process is that of Graham Wallas. In his view, the process traverses four stages: preparation, incubation, illumination, and revision. This theory is similar, in its basic aspects, to Edwards's description of conversion. See *The Art of Thought* (London: Jonathan Cape, 1926).

25. *Faithful Narrative*, p. 171, my italics.

26. Ibid., p. 162.

27. Jonathan Edwards, *A Treatise Concerning the Religious Affections,* ed. John E. Smith (New Haven, Conn.: Yale University Press, 1959), p. 97. (1746)

28. When he was faced with a similar dilemma 150 years later, Freud's strategy was first to ingratiate himself with his incredulous, even hostile audience, and then to slowly and subtly destroy their basic assumptions. Edwards followed the same strategy.

29. Jonathan Edwards, *Freedom of the Will,* ed. Paul Ramsey (New Haven, Conn.: Yale University Press, 1957), p. 147. (1754)

30. On Edwards's definition of motive, see Joseph Haroutunian, *Piety versus Moralism* (New York: Harper & Row, 1962), pp. 220–29. On the same topic, but emphasizing the influence of Locke on Edwards's concept of motive, see Paul Ramsey, "Editor's Introduction" to Edwards's *Freedom of the Will,* pp. 47–64.

31. Will, p. 143.

32. Ibid., p. 144; Edwards's italics.

33. Ibid., p. 148.

34. See *Will,* pp. 145–46, for Edwards's list of reasons why objects appear agreeable or disagreeable.

35. Much later, of course, Freud would deal much more specifically with these emotionally laden "other things."

36. *Will,* p. 141.

37. *Affections,* p. 101.

38. *Some Thoughts Concerning the Present Revival of Religion in New England,* in Goen, *Great Awakening,* pp. 291–530, p. 297.

39. See Perry Miller, *The New England Mind: Seventeenth Century* (Boston: Beacon, 1961), chap. 9, "The Nature of Man."

40. *Affections,* p. 96 (Edwards's italics).

41. Cf. J.W. Fay, *American Psychology Before Williams James* (New Brunswick, N.J.: Rutgers University Press, 1939) and A. A. Roback, *A History of American Psychology* (New York: Collier, 1964).

42. *Affections,* p. 272.

43. Ibid., p. 272.

44. Ibid., p. 272.

45. Edwards's notion of "a sense of the heart" has much in common with what William James later called "Knowledge of Acquaintance"; cf. *Principles of Psychology,* 2 vols. (New York: Holt, 1890). 1: 220–21.

46. *Affections,* p. 273.

47. William James, *The Varieties of Religious Experience* (New York: Collier, 1962), p. 219. (1902)

48. Of course, many "faculty" psychologists offered opinions on conversion. These were hardly explanations, however. They usually stated merely that certain mythical entities ("faculties") had somehow been miraculously transformed. The question, of course, is how does this occur; and how is it reflected in perception and behavior? Edwards addressed himself to these more difficult questions.

49. *Treatise on Grace,* ed. Paul Helm (London: Clarke, 1971), p. 29.

50. Cf. *Affections,* pp. 200–207 for many examples of Edwards's use of the term *principles.*

51. *Grace,* p. 40.

52. Cf. *Affections,* p. 206.

53. *Affections,* p. 206.

54. For a good general introduction to the concept of cognitive structures, see Ezra Stodtland and Lance Canon, *Social Psychology: A Cognitive Approach* (Philadelphia: Saunders, 1972), chap. 1. A more technical introduction to the topic may be found in Ulric Neisser, *Cognitive Psychology,* (New York: Appleton-Century-Crofts, 1967), pp. 286–92. In addition, one may consult the introduction to Howard Gruber and J. Jacques Voneche, eds., *The Essential Piaget* (New York: Basic Books, 1977) for a sophisticated discussion of Piaget's use of the term "cognitive structure."

55. *Affections,* pp. 205–6.

56. *Grace,* p. 32.
57. *Affections,* p. 200.
58. Ibid., pp. 200–201.
59. Ibid., p. 200.
60. *Grace,* p. 40; Edwards's italics.
61. Ibid., pp. 48–49.
62. This is a simple example of the Gestalt principle of "functional fixedness." Solving difficult problems often involves reorganizing the entire field, or gestalt; i.e., looking at the problem in a way which is fundamentally different from the original approach. To the extent that persons are incapable of such cognitive flexibility, they are said to be functionally fixated.
63. Perhaps Edwards was approaching a psychological premise similar to that established in the twentieth century by Jean Piaget. In each case, persons with inscrutable but apparently malleable minds are said to develop through stages which are defined by cognitive principles or structures appropriate to each. The alteration of these structures, moreover, is said to signify an invisible yet profound personal revolution. See Jean Piaget, *The Construction of Reality in the Child* (New York: Basic Books, 1954).
64. *Faithful Narrative,* p. 181.

The Dilemma: The Psychological Basis of Spiritual Uncertainty

1. *Affections,* p. 95.
2. Ibid., p. 120.
3. *The Diary of Joshua Hempstead of New London, Connecticut* (New London, Conn., 1902), p. 379; quoted in Goen, "Editor's Introduction," p. 52.
4. "True Grace Distinguished from the Experience of Devils," in Dwight, ed., *Works,* 6: 232–61, p. 259. (1752)
5. *Affections,* p. 121.
6. *Faithful Narrative,* p. 175.
7. This was especially true in Northampton, where Edwards's grandfather and predecessor in the pulpit, Solomon Stoddard, had been conducting revivals, or "harvests," for fifty years. Stoddard's relationship to Edwards's psychological views is dealt with indirectly by Smith, "Editor's Introduction," pp. 57–60, and more specifically in my "Solomon Stoddard's *Safety of Appearing,* and the Dissolution of the Puritan Faculty Psychology," *Journal of the History of the Behavioral Sciences* 10 (1974): 238–50.
8. *Faithful Narrative,* p. 176.
9. Other important "New Lights" were Gilbert Tennent and Jonathan Dickinson, both of New Jersey. An analysis of their views may be found in William Warren Sweet, *Revivalism in America* (New York: Scribner, 1944); excerpts from their writings are in Alan Heimert and Perry Miller, *The Great Awakening* (New York: Bobbs-Merrill, 1967).
10. Edwards, *Some Thoughts,* p. 297; see also *Affections,* p. 96, and *Will,* pp. 141–48.
11. *The Distinguishing Marks of a Work of the Spirit of God.* In Goen, *Great Awakening,* pp. 226–88 (1741). Many of Edwards's other treatises and sermons are also concerned with this problem; cf. "True Grace Distinguished" and *A Treatise on Grace.* The *Distinguishing Marks* and *Religious Affections,* however, are devoted almost entirely to the systematic distinction between the affections.
12. The "distinguishing marks" and "negative instances" in Tables 1 and 2 are adapted from Goen, "Editor's Introduction," p. 54. The "positive signs" and "negative signs" in these tables are taken directly from the *Affections.* Edwards seems to have derived these lists, in part, from Thomas Shepard's *The Parable of the Ten Virgins* (London, 1660) and from 1 John 4:1. For an analysis of the "marks," see Goen, "Editor's Introduction," pp. 24–43, and pp. 53–57 for a discussion of Shepard's influence on Edwards.
13. This is precisely the approach taken by many of Thomas Shepard's parishioners; see George Selement, ed., *The Confessions of Thomas Shepard* (Worcester, Mass: Massachusetts Historical Society, 1975).
14. *Marks,* p. 228.
15. After his fall from heaven, the devil was alleged to have retained most of his former powers because, as Edwards put it, "sin destroys spiritual principles but not the natural faculties" ("True Grace Distinguished," p. 237).
16. *Affections,* p. 159.
17. Ibid., p. 158.

18. Ibid., p. 159; see also Edwards's most extensive exposition of the devil's powers in "True Grace Distinguished."

19. *Affections*, pp. 159–60; see also *Some Thoughts*, pp. 458–59.

20. The emotional aberrations of the Awakening were catalogued by Chauncy in his *Seasonable Thoughts on the State of Religion in New England, a Treatise in Five Parts* (Boston, 1743). Two-thirds of this large book (424 pages) is devoted to the documentation of seizures, faintings, and other examples of raised affections associated with New Light preaching. In an often-quoted passage Chauncy remarked, "an enlightened mind and not raised affections ought always to be the guide of those who call themselves men; and this in the affairs of religion as well as other things" (p. 327). It was Perry Miller, I believe, who first clearly demonstrated that Chauncy's psychological position, as shown in the previous passage, cannot refute that of Edwards. Chauncy was an orthodox "faculty" psychologist; the "mind" addressed by his view is composed of discrete, partially autonomous entities. To Chauncy, acts which are entirely rational are possible and desirable. Edwards, on the other hand, believed the "will" and "affections" to be unified; thus an "enlightened mind" need not be, as Chauncy assumed, an alternative to "raised affections." The so-called debate between these spokesmen, far from being a dialogue, was in fact a collection of parallel monologues. To Edwards, a pure "enlightened mind" was an ethereal abstraction, while Chauncy equated "raised affections" with lunacy.

21. "A Divine and Supernatural Light, immediately imparted to the Soul by the Spirit of God, shown to be both a Scriptural and Rational Doctrine." In Dwight, ed., *Works,* 6: 171–88, p. 178. (1734)

22. Theologically, this position is unexceptional; it corresponds to one of the five tenets of Calvinism contained in the *Westminster Confession*—irresistible grace. It was characteristic of Edwards, however, to find a root or referent in his theory of the mind for even the most commonplace dogma.

23. *Affections*, p. 167; see also "True Grace Distinguished," p. 245.

24. *Some Thoughts*, p. 458.

25. *Affections*, p. 195.

26. Psycholinguists, for instance, distinguish between *competence* and *performance*. People are said to be far more competent in a language than their performance can ever indicate. We can, in theory, construct an infinite number of grammatical sentences, the vast majority of which we have neither heard nor spoken before. This remarkable and uniquely human ability is attributed in part to transformational rules which are embedded in "deep structures" of the mind. See Noam Chomsky, *Aspects of the Theory of Syntax* (Cambridge, Mass: MIT Press, 1965) and his much more readable *Language and Mind*, rev. ed. (New York: Harcourt Brace Jovanovich, 1972). The postulation of rarefied constructs like "deep structures" irks the arch-behaviorist, B. F. Skinner. His behavioristic account of language may be found in *Verbal Behavior* (New York: Appleton-Century-Crofts, 1958). See also Chomsky's classic, vituperative rebuttal to Skinner in *Language* 35 (1959): 26–58. Their "debate" has much in common with that of Edwards and Chauncy; in their most parochial moments, Skinner's position seems to be—"Mind? No matter!", while Chomsky's "refutation" is "Matter? Never mind!"

27. "Divine Light," p. 273.

28. Ibid., p. 174.

29. Ibid., p. 177.

30. The American career of Whitefield is traced by Joseph Tracy in his classic, *The Great Awakening: A History of the Revival of Religion in the Time of Edwards and Whitefield* (Boston: Tappan, 1842) and by Whitefield in his *Journals*, ed. by L. Murray (London: Banner of Truth, 1960).

31. *Marks*, p. 227.

32. Ibid., p. 285.

33. Ibid., p. 260.

34. Ibid., p. 270 and p. 275.

35. Ibid., p. 277.

36. Rev. Eleazar Wheelock reported that "there was such a breathing of distress, and weeping, that the preacher was obliged to speak to the people and desire silence, that he might be heard." In Benjamin Trumbull, *A Complete History of Connecticutt, Civil and Ecclesiastical, 1630–1764*, 2 vols. (New Haven, Conn., 1818), 2: 145.

37. *Journals*, p. 477.

38. *Affections*, p. 193.

39. Ibid., p. 193.

40. Ibid., pp. 450–51.

41. "God Glorified in the Work of Redemption, by the Greatness of Man's Dependence upon Him, in the Whole of It." In Dwight, ed., *Works,* (1731) 6: 149–62.

Epilogue: Edwards's Achievement

1. Cf. *Jonathan Edwards* (New York: Sloane, 1949), especially the chapter entitled "Naturalism," and "Jonathan Edwards on 'a Sense of the Heart,'" *Harvard Theological Review* 41 (1948): 123–45.

2. *A History of Western Philosophy* (New York: Simon and Schuster, 1945), p. 659. Edward H. Davidson, in his provocative, yet highly readable, *Jonathan Edwards: The Narrative of a Puritan Mind* (Cambridge, Mass: Harvard University Press, 1966), is the only writer of whom I am aware who has noticed similarities between Hume and Edwards. "Into this gap between the objectivity of things and the tantalizingly questionable ideas in the mind," writes Davidson, "both Hume and Edwards moved with devastating logic" (p. 48). See also chapters 3 and 7 for stimulating discussions of aspects of Edwards's psychology.

3. *A Treatise of Human Nature*, ed. by L. A. Selby-Bigge (London: Oxford University Press, 1888), I, iv, 1; I, iii, 10; I, iv, 1.

4. See also *Treatise*, II, iii, 3: "Reason is . . . the slave of the passions."

5. Still the best summary for psychologists of the progression of empiricism from Locke through Berkeley to Hume is to be found in Edna Heidbreder, *Seven Psychologies* (New York: Appleton-Century-Crofts, 1933).

6. "Notes on the Mind," in Clarence H. Faust and Thomas H. Johnson, eds., *Jonathan Edwards: Representative Selections* (New York: Hill and Wang, 1962), p. 30.

7. Ibid., p. 30.

8. "Divine Light," pp. 176–77.

9. Ibid., pp. 176–78.

10. Ibid., p. 177.

11. Ibid., pp. 178–79.

12. *History*, pp. 672–73.

13. Edwards's relationship to American transcentalism has been described by Perry Miller, "From Edwards to Emerson," in *Errand into the Wilderness* (New York: Harper & Row, 1964), and by Conkin, *Puritans and Pragmatists*, chapter 5, "Ralph Waldo Emerson: Poet-Priest."

14. Valuable analyses concerning this important thread of rigorous irrationalism in American intellectual history may be found throughout the work of Morton White. Cf. his *Pragmatism and the American Mind* (New York: Oxford University Press, 1973) and *Science and Sentiment in America: Philosophical Thought from Jonathan Edwards to John Dewey* (New York: Oxford University Press, 1972).

15. I have recently become convinced of the importance of Shadworth Hodgson's influence on James through the work of Richard P. High. His unpublished doctoral dissertation, done at the University of New Hampshire, explores the relationship between Hodgson's phenomenology and certain aspects of James's *Principles*.

Table 1
Reliable Marks and Signs of a Valid Conversion

"Distinguishing Marks"

1. Raised esteem of Jesus Christ as Son of God and Saviour of the world.
2. Turning away from corruptions and lusts to the righteousness of God.
3. Increased regard for Holy Scripture.
4. Minds are established in the objective truths of revealed religion.
5. Genuine love for God and man.

"Positive Signs"

1. Influences and operations on the heart are *spiritual, supernatural,* and *divine.*
2. The Divine is loved for itself.
3. An appreciation of the moral excellency of divine things.
4. The mind is enlightened, rightly and spiritually to understand divine things.
5. A certainty of divine things.
6. A sense of evangelical humiliation.
7. A change of nature.
8. Meekness and mercy.
9. A Christian tenderness of spirit.

10. Beautiful symmetry and proportion.
12. The exercise and fruit of Christian practice.
11. The higher the affections are raised, the greater the longing that they be increased.
12. The exercise and fruit of Christian practice.

Table 2
Unreliable Marks and Signs of a Valid Conversion

"Negative Instances"

1. The work is carried on in an unusual or extraordinary way.
2. Strong effects are produced in the body.
3. A great of noise about religion is occasioned.
4. Lively impressions are induced on people's imaginations.
5. The work is promoted too much by the influence of example.
6. Imprudent and irregular conduct.
7. Errors in judgment and delusions of Satan.
8. Professed converts falling into scandal.
9. Preachers insist too much on God's wrath.

"Negative Signs"

1. High affections.
2. Bodily effects.
3. Talking of the things of Religion.
4. Persons did not contrive affections.
5. Texts of scripture are remarkably brought to mind.
6. An appearance of love in the affections.
7. Many kinds of affections.
8. The affectionate joy seems to follow a certain order.
9. Persons are much engaged in worship and church duties.
10. Much praising and glorifying God.
11. Confidence in the validity of the conversion experience.
12. Godly, charitable behavior.

Supplement
The Psychological Thought of Jonathan Edwards (1703–1758):
A Historiographical Review

> What are the roots that clutch, what branches grow
> Out of this stony rubbish? . . .
> I will show you something different . . .
>
> T. S. Eliot, *The Waste Land*

The dominant view of the history of European psychology may be characterized for the most part as progressionist. This view holds, following E. G. Boring, that all psychologists whose thought did not lead *directly* to Gustav Fechner's application of psychophysical methods to the mind-body problem and Wilhelm Wundt's first experimental psychology laboratory shall be conceived of as preparing the way for the advent of scientific psychology.[1] Philosophical thought beginning with Locke, or perhaps Hobbes, and early physiological investigations, especially those of Johannes Müller, are seen in this perspective as two tributaries that led inevitably into a common stream of thought which culminated in *the* event—the founding by Fechner and Wundt of psychology as a science.[2] The history of American psychology is usually viewed in a slightly different way. It is commonly thought to have been spontaneously generated with the publication of William James's *Principles of Psychology* in 1890.[3] It is hardly progressionist, however. James, though an American, is usually characterized as European in spirit and as the American popularizer, critic, and integrator of the European (chiefly German) experimental work prior to 1890.[4] It is quite safe to assume, in fact, that many, perhaps most, contemporary American psychologists would be incapable of identifying a single person or publication of psychological importance in America in the two hundred sixty years of American thought before James. Pre-Jamesian, or pre-"scientific" psychology in America is thought of, if at all, as a myth.[5]

The dominant assumptions of this review essay are that psychology in America before James (long before James, in fact) is no myth, and that the most profound and influential expositor of this "indigenous American psychology" was Jonathan Edwards.[6] My goal is to organize and introduce the large but diffuse and widely dispersed literature concerned with the psychology of Edwards. Some of it is "stony rubbish" written by historians of psychology whose only discernible motive has been to mock Edwards's religiosity. Other commentaries on Edwards's psychology are confusing blends of sensitive research and wild-eyed speculation—a function, in most cases, of having profound acquaintance with Edwards and equally profound ignorance of psychology. Although most of the research reviewed here is in many respects inadequate, it must nevertheless be read and digested by anyone interested in the history of American psychology before William James. For although Edwards's psychology may, as some have claimed, lie at the foundation of his system, that foundation cannot be encountered until one has worked through a complex, unfamiliar web of Calvinist theology, mystical aesthetics, revivalist practices, and an extravagantly legalistic style of discourse. This review is intended to serve as an introductory aid to an arduous but rewarding scholarly journey into the psychology of Edwards, and the entire shadowy American epoch which precedes James.

The Centrality of Jonathan Edwards

There are a number of fascinating parallels between the lives and professional careers of Wilhelm Wundt and Jonathan Edwards. Both were sons of Protestant ministers and each matured into an austere, industrious, combative thinker. Wundt chose to alienate a brilliant student, Oswald Külpe, rather than bend his own system to accommodate the "imageless thoughts" discovered at Külpe' laboratory.[8] Edwards chose virtual banishment to a frontier outpost in Stockbridge, Massachusetts, rather than "cheapen" the requirements for membership in his Northampton congregation.[9] Though neither ever set foot in England, the philosophy of British empiricism, chiefly that of Locke, played a decisive role in the formulation of their mature theories. Wundt saw his task as the integration of empiricist philosophy with the experimental methods of German physiology while Edwards tried to unite Lockean empiricism with the Christian theology of Augustine and Calvin. More important than these coincidental similarities is the manner in which certain historians have evaluated their importance. The hour glass is the appropriate metaphor for historians' judgment of both Wundt and Edwards.

To Boring, all psychological roads lead to, through, and away from Wundt.

Wundt is the senior psychologist in the history of psychology. He is the first man who without reservation is properly called a psychologist.[10]

"Descartes, Leibniz, and Locke on the philosophical side" are included in Boring's narrative only because "the genetic account requires the explanation of the new movement in terms of its ancestry."[11] Likewise, "almost all the new schools of psychology have been founded as a protest against some one or another characteristic of Wundt's psychology."[12] Wundt is thus seen as a kind of narrow neck of a historical hourglass, integrating material from diverse strains of thought into an intellectual system which became the standard of agreement and disagreement for generations.

To most historians of American theology Edwards, like Wundt in experimental psychology, represents a synthetic culmination of the past that became a beacon light of the future. Most would still agree with George Bancroft's famous remark that "he that would know the workings of the New England Mind in the middle of the last century and the throbbings of its heart, must give his days and nights to the study of Jonathan Edwards."[13] It has been contended, for instance, that Edwards's synthesis of Lockean empiricism and Calvinist theology contributed to the development of a tradition of American fundamentalism, transcendentalism, and even the American Revolution.[14] In addition, the rise of the "New England Theology," an apologia for Edwards written by his descendants (chiefly), served much the same function as Wundt's psychology. Its doctrines were so complex and its conclusions so objectionable to some that it gave intellectuals something to argue over for generations.[15]

Like Wundt, Edwards understood his mission; he knew what he was up to. His self-imposed task was to restore New England Puritanism to its former purity.[16] This would require strenuous disputations against deistic and Arminian types who were clamoring that man had a "free will." It would necessitate cleansing the churches of those who could not demonstrate publicly that they had been visited by the Holy Spirit. And most importantly, it would demand a skillful, delicate weaving together, in theory and in practice, of the traditional Puritan emphases upon heartfelt piety and the rational intellect. As the storm of the Great Awakening was raging in and around Edwards, he recognized that the warring fundamentalists and rationalists represented traditional polarities within Puritanism that needed to be united if the faith was to survive intact. In order to show that the act of faith, and in fact all human perception, is both rational and emotional, he needed to go beyond the traditional disjunctive faculty psychology he inherited and the Lockean psychology he adopted.

Psychology on the Periphery of the New England Mind: Perry Miller

For the intellectual historian of psychology, one who views psychology as a series of questions about human nature, it is extremely difficult to be both historically accurate *and* comprehensible to historically minded behavioral scientists. Ideally, the historian should have exhaustive knowledge of an era of special interest and good facility with the contemporary usage of psychological terms. Unless some agreed-upon conceptual scheme exists which can accommodate the historical theory and the modern viewpoint, the conceptual historian should be capable of providing the framework. Since at present no widely accepted conceptual scheme exists for the historian of psychology, the burden of striking a balance between antiquarian irrelevance and presentist distortion rests on the shoulders of the individual historian. Unfortunately, but perhaps not surprisingly, interpreters of the psychological views of American Puritanism, the tradition from which Edwards emerged, do not satisfy these rigorous and diverse requirements. Some, like Perry Miller, were intimately familiar with the Puritans and Puritanism but blissfully ignorant of modern psychology and terribly sloppy in their usage of psychological terms.[17] Others, such as A. A. Roback, have been competent professional psychologists who apparently never read carefully anything written by colonial Puritans.[18] Still another, J. W. Fay, seems to have understood a little about the Puritans and a little about contemporary psychology.[19] This unfortunate situation must be reviewed briefly, not out of malice toward those brave scholars who have ventured wholeheartedly but half-informed into American Puritan psychology, but because most of the deficiencies of Puritan psychological scholarship are also present in the more extensive work on Edwards. This review represents the beginning of a demonstration that a new approach to pre-Jamesian psychology in America is needed, especially with regard to Edwards, its most important and provocative theorist.

It has been remarked that the historian cannot hope to get inside the "mind" of the Puritans.[20] We believe events are caused by atoms, molecules, cells, gravity, ids, egos, and other unseen agents. The New England Puritan, on the other hand, attributed events to God, devils, angels, archangels, animal spirits, saintly intervention, and a host of other causal constructs.[21] Probably no one ever succeeded in entering the forbidden ground inside the Puritan mind to the extent that Perry Miller did. He claimed often, and arrogantly, to have read, digested, and integrated everything of importance ever written by Puritans on both sides of the Atlantic. His books and articles are the starting point for every aspiring Puritan scholar; they are monuments of erudition, complexity, insight, creativity, and frustration. The density of his convoluted style has much in common with the expository form of *Finnegans Wake*. Thoreau inadvertently spoke to the reader of Miller when he issued his dictum that a reader should take as long to read a book as it took the author to write it. In reading Miller's *New England Mind*, one simply must either go slowly or drown in a sea of words.

Miller's formal analysis of Puritan psychology is confined principally to a lengthy chapter on "the Nature of Man" in *The New England Mind: The Seventeenth Century*.[22] Psychology, generally speaking, is for Miller "a certain method of the soul," used to elucidate "the method of grace" (i.e., conversion).[23] There were no psychologists in Puritan New England. There were, however, inventive scholars who were willing to employ a scholastic faculty psychology to explain the dualistic dilemma inherent in the conversion experience.[24] Miller summarized the

Puritan notion of the mechanics of conversion in a manner that is more fanciful, yet also more concise than typical Puritan expressions of the topic:

> If original sin is a dislocation of the faculties, then regeneration must set them right again. If in nature the original sequence of sensation, common sense, fancy, reason, memory, will, and affection is now broken, it follows that in a converted nature the reflex must be reconstructed. When conversion was described in the vocabulary of psychology it became in effect a realignment of twisted pulleys and tangled ropes, permitting the blocks once more to turn freely and the tackle to run smoothly, in accordance with the first plan of the rigging.[25]

God was said to work through "means," i.e., through the mechanical organization of the faculties; and most importantly the work of regeneration consisted in a regeneration of the rational faculty. A regenerated reason would be capable of rationally comprehending the will of God, although God, of course, remained sovereign and need not reveal His intentions even to a converted person. Reason was vitally important because the will, the passions, and all the other numerous faculties attributed to the mind were said to follow, for the most part, the dictates of the rational faculty. Thus Miller would hold that the "vocabulary of psychology," as he called the various hypothethical faculties, and views concerning human nature, were inextricably intertwined. A theorist who emphasized the importance of the faculty of reason in the conversion experience would necessarily hold that human nature is primarily rational. One who claimed that the reorientation of the will and affections (or emotions) was central to conversion might be said to view human nature as primarily emotional or irrational.

In holding that psychology is concerned with questions of human nature, Miller followed Brett.[26] It is unfortunate that Miller did not go beyond Brett to provide an explicit conceptual scheme with which to define and interpret psychological views of human nature. With rare exceptions, Miller was content to quote and catalogue each theorist's arrangement of, or comments upon, the faculties. The mind is portrayed somewhat like a jigsaw puzzle with hundreds of sets of directions. The "New England Mind," like any conglomerate construct, is complex, and Miller described that complexity in remarkable detail. Yet we normally do not need a guide to inform us that there are many trees in the forest, all slightly different from each other. We would rather be shown a path that leads through it. What, one must ask after reading Miller's long chapter on "The Nature of Man," *is* the Puritan conception of human nature?

Instead of providing a synthesis of Puritan psychology, Miler preferred to offer speculations concerning why the Puritan treatises were not very psychological in nature. This may appear odd, since Miller also claimed that ". . . in Puritan writing there are almost enough passing allusions to each part of the psychological reflex to furnish the material for extended chapters."[27] Yet speculation was Miller's forte, and his treatment of Puritan psychology is riddled with the implication that certain "unconscious" motives dictated the alleged scanty volume of Puritan psychological inquiry. He indicates that the Puritans had a "vague sense" of the incongruities in their system, especially regarding the manner in which the conversion experience could be both "an irresistible seizure and a rationl transaction."[28] Miller asked,

> . . . was it possibly because they sensed, however obscurely, that there were
> further difficulties within it [their psychology] which, if exposed too openly,
> would raise uncomfortable queries in more important regions?[29]

Was it, in other words, some vague sense of insecurity which held the Puritans at arm's length from the systematic and careful investigation which characterized most of their intellectual endeavors?

Miller's flights of fancy into the unconscious motivations of the Puritans are both suggestive and frustrating. His detours far beyond the available evidence often are stimulating and productive of further investigation.[30] The frustration occurs, however, when one attempts to evaluate the validity of some of his claims. There are two sources of frustration. First, in the case of Puritan psychology, the object of inquiry lacks even a simple definition. How can psychology, which by Miller's own admission is concerned with "The Nature of Man," be defined as a "certain method of the soul"? Neither the dimensions of human nature, nor the explicit relationship between human nature and the "method" is revealed. The flights of fancy have no firm base from which to embark. When we are told that the Puritans unconsciously refrained from indulging in detailed psychological analyses, we do not know what it was that they weren't doing. The second source of frustration is Miller's fertile imagination. He was attempting a sort of psychohistory devoid of the theoretical framework of psychoanalysis (or any other structure). Miller knew the New England mind better perhaps than anyone will ever know it again. Yet Puritan psychology remains mostly shrouded in mystery because he lacked a conceptual scheme which could define psychology in a way that bridges the gap of centuries. He talked around the issues rather than to them. Some structure certainly would have helped prevent excursions into a Puritan-in-Wonderland where nobody says what apparently is said and no one's conscious motives are the functional ones.[31]

Psychology on the Periphery of The New England Mind: Roback and Fay

Prior to the revival of interest in Puritanism early in this century, the very word "Puritan" had an unsavory connotation, even among scholars.[32] Puritans were those nasty, narrow-minded forebears of ours who attached scarlet letters to the chests of passionate young women, executed so-called witches, dressed in black and worried a lot about whether or not they were going to heaven. Their intellectual pinnacle was reached, it was often thought, with Michael Wigglesworth's abominable poem, "Day of Doom," which described the road to hell as paved with the skulls of young children.

Perry Miller and his colleagues rejected this simple-minded, vindictive approach to the Puritans and attempted to meet them on their own terms and treat them as complex individuals who grappled with some of the most important intellectual issues of their day. If Miller's analysis of the psychological system of the Puritans is of limited usefulness to a historian of psychology, it is because his approach lacks a psychological perspective, not because Puritanism is perceived as a psychological wasteland, devoid of raw material.

No such claim can be made for the two remaining analysts of New England Puritan psychology whose work will be reviewed in this section: A. A. Roback and J. W. Fay. To these writers, the Puritan revival never happened; the colonial New England intellectuals are objects of subtle scorn and curious amazement rather than serious scholarship. This is unfortunate because, unlike Miller, Roback was very knowledgeable about modern psychology and, had he therefore taken the Puritans seriously, he might have helped tell us just what those odd philosopher-pastors share with us in the twentieth century and which of their psychological ideas are peculiarly their own.

Roback's attitude toward Puritan psychology is best described as shallow, condescending amusement. There is no indication that Roback ever read carefully anything written by a colonial Puritan.[33] He mentions a few theses done at Harvard in the seventeenth century which, along with William Brattle's logic digest, are said to contain "a sprinkling of psychological facts, as they were then known."[34] Just what these "facts" are, however, and what makes them "psychological" remains unknown to the reader. His chief argument against the Puritans seems to be that they were religious, and that they therefore *must* have possessed an inferior system of psychology.[35] Speaking of the colonial Puritans, he wrote:

> If psychology is handed down to us on a golden catechistic platter, then what need is there for seeking more information? The definitions, vague and hazy, as they were, made sense to the students of the time, and saved them the bother of thinking . . .
> It is clear that no empirical science could advance on the basis of postulates and definitions alone. So long as psychology remained the succubus of theology, as was the case throughout the seventeenth century and during the early decades of the eighteenth century, it could only rest on the accepted authority of the past.[36]

Roback was willing, like Brett, to consider the thought of many individuals outside the mainstream which led through Fechner and Wundt to twentieth-century experimental psychology. Yet instead of defining the history of psychology as past inquiries into human nature, Roback tends to evaluate colonial thinkers in a Boring-like fashion: in terms of the extent to which their views approximate some trend or other in experimental psychology. Thus, after haranguing "pastoral psychologist" Cotton Mather for "taking stock in the absurdities of witchcraft," Roback offers the backhanded compliment that he "managed to introduce some observations which could be considered psychological and which must have particularly impressed the listeners."[37] The nature of the psychological views of Mather remains a mystery, for by definition almost, in Roback's confused scheme, neither Mather nor any of his contemporaries are permitted to have significant psychological views. Roback wished to elucidate the neglected psychological thought of the "nebulous colonial days," as he calls the era, yet the thinkers of the period were religious men concerned with, among other things, human nature. Roback, on the other hand, viewed religion, or Christianity at any rate, as a plague on psychology, which he implicitly defined in terms of twentieth-century conceptions which prevented him from obtaining even a glimmering of Puritan psychology.

Somewhere between Miller and Roback, but certainly closer to Roback, stands J. W. Fay. His monograph demonstrates a much more careful reading of the sources than is shown by Roback, although it is admittedly sketchy when compared to Miller's glossy erudition.[38] Yet if Miller looked forward from his seventeenth-century vantage point in search of modern "Puritans," Fay, like Roback though to a lesser extent, looked back in American history in search of colonial "psychologists." Fay states:

> . . . the science had not yet taken shape, and ideas which belong properly to that field [psychology] are disguised and hidden beneath a theological terminology that is most misleading. Interminable discussions of "predestination," will be found to involve conceptions of the will, and the momentous question of "original sin" is weighted with consideration of heredity and the transmission of original and acquired characteristics.[39]

There is a problem with this statement. Theological concerns are misleading only to the historian who ignores the theological context out of which the psychological ideas arose. Fay sought to prove, in effect, that the theological psychology of America's first two and a half centuries made important contributions to American psychology after William James. His failure to articulate the dimensions of "psychology," however, prevented Fay from demonstrating any relationship between James's antecedents and descendants. Yet if Fay's analysis is inconclusive, he is no more than benignly neglectful. The early thinkers, Fay holds, were "strong in philosophical insight into some of the most real and important problems of an empirical science, both introspective and behavioristic. . . ."[40] Roback, it will be recalled, came not to praise the religious psychologists, but to bury them.

Fay's book is far more valuable than Roback's. Unlike Roback, Fay was not a psychologist, but a philosopher. Like many philosophical students of psychology, he viewed modern psychology as in many respects coterminous with its philosophical roots. In this view modern psychology is just a new method for studying old problems like "will" or "the mind-body problem," and it is not the new method but the old problems that should occupy the focus of attention. Thus, when Fay looked backward into colonial Puritanism, he saw old friends where Roback saw only new enemies.

The Debate over Edwards's Psychological Theory

Most of the confusion surrounding Edwards's psychology concerns two broad dimensions of human nature: (1) Are human beings functional, fully integrated unities, or well-oiled collections of complementary but disjunctive parts? (2) Are human beings primarily active or reactive as they perceive and conceive aspects of the universe? It must be pointed out that commentators upon Edwards's psychology have not dichotomized their dispute in this way; indeed there is no evidence that differences of opinion have even been clearly perceived. This is to be expected since one must have some clear notion of "psychology" in mind, and a particular view toward the psychology of Edwards, before it can be determined that a definitional criterion has been violated or a personal position attacked. Those who thus far have presumed to describe and judge the psychology of Edwards have lacked both.

Human Nature: An Integrated Unity or Collection of Parts?

It is curious that those historians who are least acquainted with Edwards have no trouble whatever in describing his psychology in a couple of brief remarks, categorizing him, and dispensing with him. According to Roback, "Edwards takes it for granted that there are only two departments of the mind: (1) understanding, or as we call it, cognition, (2) volition and affection."[41] Fay agrees with Roback: "Edwards follows the scholastic division of mental operations into cognitive and appetent."[42] In classifying Edwards's psychology as "scholastic," Roback and Fay deny, in effect, that Edwards upheld the unity or integrity of the self. The Puritan version of Thomistic psychology had the human mind (or soul) divided into separate, interacting, but functionally autonomous entities. This was especially true of the intellect and the will.[43] Roback and Fay place Edwards squarely in the Aristotelian-Thomistic tradition.

A number of historians, however, including the majority of recent Edwards scholars, believe that Edwards was one of those brave thinkers who chose to remain uncomfortably ambiguous rather than apply scholasticlike distinctions to the human mind.[44] In his attempt to preserve the unity of the mind Edwards faced an almost insurmountable difficulty. The very language he used to express himself was the disjunctive terminology of faculty psychology. Puritan psychological theology had always emphasized either the reason or the volition in conversion, in spite of the conviction that the whole person must obviously be involved. Conrad Cherry mentions, for instance, Thomas Shepard as a proponent of reason and William Ames as an advocate of will.[45] Cherry describes Edwards's dilemma this way:

> Edwards was thus handed by his theological forbears a clear *effort* to account for personal unity in the act of faith, but he was also handed a *way* of accounting for that unity which continually frustrated the effort. With man so divided into distinct faculties, the temptation was to describe the nature of the faith-act in terms of their distinct operations rather than in terms of the unity of the human subject.[46]

The "way" referred to by Cherry is, of course, the doctrine of the separate faculties. It is clear that few Puritan theologians could resist the temptation to break down the human mind into distinct parts and to emphasize the importance of one or another of these quasi-mythological entities in conversion. Whether or not their readership agreed with their conclusions was, in a sense, unimportant. By appealing to a common-sense doctrine of faculties, an author could be reasonably certain that writer and reader understood each other.

There have been some thinkers, however, who have resisted the temptation of a rigid partitioning of human nature and psychological activity, and hence have never been clearly understood. Augustine and Locke were two of these brave but ambiguous thinkers who were important influences upon Edwards.[47] The doctrines of Augustine had always been an important part of Puritan piety and they came to Edwards's special attention through the writings of a Dutch theologian, Peter van Mastricht.[48] Augustine held that the rational and emotive capacities operate in a unified, inseparable fashion.

> For there are some things which we do not believe unless we understand them, and there are other things which we do not understand unless we believe them. . . . Our understanding therefore contributes to the comprehension of that which it believes, and faith contributes to the belief of that which it comprehends.[49]

Locke, whose terminology is to be found throughout Edwards's works also registered his objection to an artificially dichotomized human mind. In a famous passage he sarcastically remarked:

> For, if it be reasonable to suppose and talk of faculties as distinct beings that can act, (as we do, when we say the will orders, and the will is free,) it is fit that we should make a speaking faculty, and a walking faculty, and a dancing faculty. . . . And we may as properly say that it is the singing faculty sings, and the dancing faculty dances, and that the will chooses or that the understanding conceives.[50]

Locke, and later Edwards, reduced the ponderous list of faculties to two, understanding and will, which Locke viewed as interacting processes rather than as structural entities.[51]

The group of scholars who believe that, to Edwards, the mind is an integrated rational-emotive unity generally portray Edwards's attempt to express this unity as a little more comprehensible than Augustine's and a little less comprehensible than Locke's. One theologian has stated that

> he [Edwards] agreed with Locke that we should not attempt to divide the mind into separate compartments, but simply recognize the several interacting mental processes. But Edwards perceived more than this. He saw an aesthetic element in every act of understanding as well as a cognitive element in every act of will.[52]

That is, Edwards went beyond Locke to Augustine in asserting that mental processes not only interact but are rational and emotional components of a superordinate, unified mental process.

While Augustine's vision is incisive and vast, his explanations are intuitive rather than explicit. Most scholars give Edwards credit for at least trying to explain what he meant. Edwards called the end product of this unified process "a sense of the heart."

> I say, a sense of heart; for it is not speculation merely that is concerned in this kind of understanding: nor can there be a clear distinction made between the two faculties of understanding and will, as acting distinctly and separately, i

this matter. When the mind is sensible of the sweet beauty and amiableness of a thing, that implies a sensibleness of sweetness and delight in the presence of the idea of it.

And yet there is the nature of instruction in it; as he that has perceived the sweet taste of honey, knows much more about it, than he who has only looked upon and felt of it.[53]

Ultimately, however, Edwards's concept of "a sense of the heart" is little more useful than Augustine's complete reliance on the intuitive powers of his reader. Edwards is rigidly confined to the faculty language. All the "taste" metaphors imaginable do not obviate the fact that "heart" is a simple synonym for will-affections, a disjunctive structural unit.

No scholar has made a serious attempt to rescue Edwards from his quandary. To Roback and Fay, of course, Edwards is in no dilemma; he fits neatly into the traditional faculty mold. This view, however, is very superficial; it fails completely to appreciate Edwards's idiosyncratic use of the concepts of faculty psychology. Historians who are more familiar with Edwards have concluded that his vision of a unified mind does not at all fit the faculty mold. What mold, then, does the unified view of Edwards fit?

Does Edwards represent a situation in which the language of psychology is devoid of concepts which might be used to explicate Edwards's ideas? Or is the present psychological situation a function of historians' failure to notice that Edwards is part of a select but old tradition in psychology, and that a relatively more precise and suitable language now exists to describe that tradition of psychological thought? The latter is more likely.[54] Even the convoluted, metaphorical brilliance of Perry Miller fails to shed any light on the topic:

In Edwards' "sense of the heart" there is nothing transcendental; it is rather a sensuous apprehension of the total situation. And what makes an idea in the total situation important for man, as the idea taken alone can never be, what makes it in that context something more than an inert impression on passive clay, is man's apprehension that for him it augurs good or evil. It is, in short, something to be saluted by the emotions as well as by the intellect.[55]

Miller, and this is true of the other historians, says nothing that Edwards himself does not say. What is meant to be explanation is only paraphrase.

Human Nature: Proactive, Reactive, or Both?

In 1949 Perry Miller, though hardly a mathematician, derived an equation which cast Edwards's scholarship into a state of immediate confusion and controversy. Among the many remarkable contentions in his "intellectual" biography of Edwards, Miller claimed that, psychologically speaking, Edwards equals Locke.

The mind of Edwards . . . was trained by the doctrine of New England, in which it had always been held that man is passive in the reception of grace and that he is bound to sin if he tries to earn salvation by his own efforts or on his own terms. Was it not precisely here that the new metaphysics and the old theology, the modern psychology and the ancient regeneration, came together in an exhilarating union? The whole reach of the vision unfolded before Edwards as he read Locke's innocent observation that simple ideas, "when offered to the mind, the understanding can no more refuse to have, not alter when they are imprinted, nor blot them out and make new ones itself, than a mirror can refuse, alter, or obliterate the images or ideas which of the objects set before it do therein produce."

The empirical passivity became for Edwards, in the context of eighteenth-century New England, not an invitation to lethargy, but a program of action.[56]

Miller was a historical missionary who spent much of his career trying to convince his readers that the religious thinking of Colonial New England is "modern" rather than "medieval." Thus Miller holds that much of the thinking of the seventeenth-century New England theologians can be traced to Renaissance Neoplatonism and that Jonathan Edwards, the greatest Puritan, derived his world view from Newton and his psychological views from Locke, "the father of modern psychology."[57] There is a sense in which Miller is justified in asserting that Locke is the father of modern psychology. Locke's central doctrine, his description of human nature presented in the *Essay,* is that of a passive, reactive creature who merely responds to impinging stimulation. The mind, to Locke, is like a sheet of "white paper" which is written upon by "EXPERIENCE."[58] The "simple ideas" were said to be products of the incoming sensations.[59] In some respects, to be sure, a strict "tabula rasa," associational interpretation of Locke is a caricature of his thought.[60] Yet it was this view of the mind that passed from Locke to the later British empiricists (or associationists), to Wundt, and into the early psychological laboratories of Germany and America.

In part, William James dedicated his opus to demonstrating the superficiality of the " 'associationist' schools" who

> seek common elements in the *divers* mental facts rather than a common agent behind them [such as a "faculty"], and to explain them constructively by the various forms of arrangement of these elements, as one explains houses by stones and bricks.[61]

Clearly, James chose not to conceive of human nature as an inert cognitive "house."

Where did Edwards stand on this crucial issue? On the one hand is a group of scholars who follow Miller's assertion that "he [Edwards] adopted the sensational psychology with a consistency that outdoes the modern behaviorist."[62] Faust and Johnson, for example, maintain that neither the "will" nor the "understanding" described by Edwards is capable of initiating any sort of physical or mental activity. While the imposition of the discrete faculty constructs upon Edwards's system is erroneous (see previous section), their intent is clear. They wish to prove that Edwards followed Locke in asserting the passivity of psychological processes. They maintain that Edwards held, with Locke, that the mind is moved by the strongest motive:

> Edwards was obviously anxious to exclude any notion of independent activity on the part of the will. As he saw it, the will was purely passive.[63]

Moreover,

> . . . in Edwards' view the understanding, dependent as it was upon the senses—
> natural and supernatural—, was purely passive.[64]

Thus a verbal picture is painted of a person whose actions in the world and whose perception of it are totally a function of external events.

Much of the case for the Edwards-Locke psychological equation rests upon Edwards's adoption of some Lockean terminology. Most importantly, Edwards sometimes referred to the presence of the divine and supernatural light of the Holy Spirit as a "new simple idea."

For instance:

> I say, if God produces something thus new in a mind, that is a perceiving, thinking, conscious thing; then doubtless something entirely new is felt, or perceived, or thought; or which is the same thing, there is some new sensation or perception of the mind which is entirely of a new sort, and which could be produced by no exalting, varying or compounding of that kind of perceptions or sensations which the mind had before; or there is what some metaphysicians call *a new simple idea*. (Italics mine)[65]

To Locke, a "new simple idea" represented the culmination of a passive process, and it is assumed that Edwards adopted Locke's essential meaning along with the terminology. Thus Edwards is said to have conceived of the conversion experience as a completely passive reception of the Spirit. Although the topic is still a matter of some conjecture, it seems clear that Edwards viewed the faith-act as the prototype of all human perceptual acts rather than as an experience which required a unique "supernatural" sense.[66] The proponents of the Edwards-Locke equation may therefore defend the position that Edwards was, in all essential respects, a Lockean who merely happened to focus his attention on a particular kind of perceptual act, the conversion experience.

No one would deny Edwards's emphasis on human beings as reactive passive creatures. In the Calvinist scheme of things people do not have the wherewithal to save themselves. "God . . . holds you over the pit of hell," Edwards preached in the bone-rattling sermon for which he is best known, "and yet it is nothing but His hand that holds you from falling into the fire every moment."[67] It is obvious that a psychological doctrine which emphasized human passivity, such as Locke's, would hold tremendous appeal to a Calvinist predestinarian like Edwards. Yet, perhaps surprisingly, a number of scholars see in Edwards a somewhat muted emphasis on human active perceptual abilities in addition to the obvious Lockean passivity. Although they have experienced great difficulty in expressing the precise manner in which Edwards conceived of human nature as both active and reactive, each of these commentators rejects the view that Edwards's psychology can be reduced to that of Locke.

Commentary on the thought of Edwards has gone through a number of phases. During his own lifetime his contemporaries seemed most interested in his emphasis on emotional religion. Later, from 1770 to 1850, many theologians argued over how to counter Edwards's formidable defense of determinism. Around the turn of the twentieth century, interest centered on the origins of Edwards's early "idealism," especially upon whether or not he had read Berkeley. At approximately the same time, in 1889, A. V. G. Allen offered the first, and in many respects still the most successful, attempt to describe Edwards's psychological views.[68] According to Allen,

> What we call psychology was to him [Edwards] an unknown science, and yet no modern psychologist could have laid more stress upon the importance of observing the different phases of human experience. In this study, his conception of inspiration or revelation enabled him to move with perfect freedom. The same spirit which clarified the vision of apostles or prophets was now illuminating the minds of the common people with a divine supernatural light.[69]

This statement was made the year before the appearance of James's watershed *Principles,* before "psychology" began to be equated, by most educated persons, with the experimental endeavors of the German Wundt and his American disciples. Allen himself, like Edwards, could "move with perfect freedom" in conceiving a system of psychology ("the different phases of human experience") existing within and augmenting a large theological superstructure ("his conception of inspiration or revelation").

Allen was, of course, aware of Locke's influence upon Edwards, but he minimized its importance. The commentary of Allen was written long before Perry Miller had formally stated the Edwards-Locke psychological equation.

> The intellectual impulse came from the philosophy of Locke, whose *Essay on the Human Understanding* Edwards read when he was but fourteen years old. The impression it left upon his mind was a deep and abiding one. But even in his early adherence to the sensational philosophy he was still himself, independent, accepting or rejecting in accordance with an inward dictum which sprang from the depth of his being. Locke was after all the occasion rather than the inspiring cause of his intellectual activity. Had he read Descartes instead, he might have reached the same conclusion.[70]

This is a remarkable contention when one considers that the Lockean tabula rasa and Cartesian innate ideas are usually placed at opposite poles of the psychological continuum.[71]

Although Allen's conception of psychology is vague, it is clear that he saw in Edwards's psychological system a view of man which included far more than a passive Lockean lump of clay. In each of its two phases the conversion experience was said to consist of both *re*action to the divine light *and* self-initiated action on the part of the convert. Allen calls Edwards's first phase "the tragic element in the process" or "the realization of an awful danger and the importance of speedy escape."[72] Allen contends that Edwards's view of this stage of awakened consciousness "appeared like a great struggle with some hostile power, as of a serpent disturbed or enraged."[73] A struggle is hardly a passive reception of anything; it connotes activity of the most vigorous sort. Not only must the devil be actively discouraged, but the Spirit must be actively encouraged. In the second stage of awakening, one's own impotence and a need for divine mediation must be perceived. The struggling convert's eventual regeneration is, of course, dependent on God's merciful infusion of his Spirit; in that respect, the convert is passive. Yet God treads only where he is made welcome. As Allen reads Edwards, "we get a confused picture in which the consciousness of sin in the sight of God leads the sufferer in various ways to seek relief."[74]

The "confused picture" derived from Edwards by Allen demonstrates remarkable honesty as well as insight. Allen, and many others, have been bewildered by Edwards's apparent attempt to show that people are both proactive and reactive in the act of faith, that they are and are not instrumental in their own conversions. Edwards did not state his case clearly and neither have his commentators.

Allen wrote in 1889 and, in a sense, his task was relatively easy. He did not have to contend with Perry Miller and the Edwards-Locke equation. Arguing with Perry Miller can be very difficult and frustrating indeed.[75] Recently, Miller's Edwards-Lock psychological equation has begun to be qualified, most importantly by Claude A. Smith.[76] It is Smith's purpose to "advance the discussion of Edwards' relation to the thought of Locke a step beyond the treatment accorded it by Perry Miller" by showing that "Edwards was forced to go beyond Locke's analysis, in order to do full justice to the richness of his experience."[77] In Smith's view, Edwards saw the mind as considerably more than a tabula rasa; it had active as well as passive powers. It was obvious to Edwards, according to Smith, that neither our perception of the natural nor the supernatural is a function of random glances. There are, as Edwards put it, "rules of harmony and regularity" that may be observed in all perceptual acts.[78] In other words, perception is selective. Likewise, Conrad Cherry, who finds the sources of Edwards's psychology in Solomon Stoddard and Augustine as well as Locke, describes Edwards's concept of perception rather cryptically as "active—receiving."[79]

Did Edwards follow Locke all the way or didn't he? Those who agree with Miller say that he did and that Edwards thus conceived of people as simple, passive creatures, waiting patiently to be written upon by the pen of God directly, or indirectly by the constituents of God's universe. For those who have sought to qualify the Edwards-Locke psychological equation, either before or after it was formally written, the task of characterizing Edwards's psychology is not so easy. It is one thing to say that Edwards went beyond Locke, but quite another to explain where, exactly, he went. The problem is very similar to that faced by those who characterize Edwards's view of the mind as a rational-emotive unity. In each case, attempts to explain Edwards's view of man have resulted in redundant paraphrase. Allen maintains that "needs" are related to the perceptual "struggle," Smith talks of "rules" that govern the process, and Cherry speaks paradoxically of "active receiving." The complexity of Edwards's psychological thought requires that his view of the mind be characterized as a rational-emotive unity and as both proactive and reactive. But this is speaking in riddles. What is needed is a believable psychological model that will incorporate each pair of seeming polar opposites into a coherent scheme. Edwards didn't have one and neither have his commentators. But one is needed to unravel Edwards, the psychological paradox.

The Problem of Interpreting Edwards's Psychology

The problem of describing Edwards's psychological views is indeed a difficult one for those commentators who have failed carefully to construct an appropriate historical scheme of psychology into which Edwards's thought can be inserted. The consensus is that Edwards was not a faculty psychologist who postulated mythical constructs in an effort to explain human behavior. Likewise, there is a rising tide of scholarly opinion which holds that Edwards somehow transcended the traditional proactive-reactive dichotomy and viewed human perception as a process (in Cherry's phrase) of "active-receiving." Much comment on Edwards's psychology has, therefore, resulted in a sterile admiration of his uniqueness. We know that he disagreed with the psychological views of his contemporaries to such an extent that he experienced great difficulty in expressing himself intelligibly. The essence of Edwards's psychology, and most have agreed intuitively that the essence is very profound, must remain a mystery until a model of human behavior is provided which can incorporate the paradoxical Edwardsean concepts into a coherent unity.

One may wonder, in light of all the confusion and ignorance concerning Edwards's psychological system, why anyone would try to *interpret* his psychology. Why, in other words, would a scholar be inclined to try to place Edwards in the overall perspective of the history of psychology and to compare his views with modern, nontheological psychologists. The answer lies somewhere in the confidence, or foolhardiness, of otherwise competent scholars who are blissfully ignorant of the precise nature of Edwards's views and of twentieth-century psychology. They have been free to rely upon their creative imaginations to produce farfetched analogies with little fear of criticism from their colleagues who, like themselves, know little of the ground from which the analogies have been fetched.

Consider Perry Miller. His position as the preeminent Puritan scholar is universally acknowledged and, although his writing was often brash, argumentative, and one-sided, he usually based his arguments on extensive data. In his interpretation of Edwards's psychology, however, Miller extends his claims far beyond what the data, or even the reader's imagination, will allow. In his controversial "intellectual" biography of Edwards, Miller's affection for mysteries takes on an almost pathological intensity. Strangeness is everywhere; Edwards never meant what it seems he meant. Hidden meanings abound.

> So his second publication ["A Divine and Supernatural Light . . .] like his first— and his last—contains an exasperating intimation of something hidden. There is a gift held back, some esoteric divination that the listener must make for himself. Edwards' writing is an immense cryptogram, the passionate oratory of the revival no less than the hard reasoning of the treatise on the will.[80]

Despite this confession of ignorance, however, Miller later can claim that

> . . . though he defeated himself by employing the very term ["faculty"] he repudiated, his thought was tending, as fast as any in the eighteenth century

could, toward conceiving reason itself, or even logic, as an image of tempera-ment; it would have taken him about an hour's reading in William James, and two hours in Freud, to catch up completely.[81]

Miller was fond of comparing Edwards with Kierkegaard, and it appears that, following the dictum of the Dane, Miller himself has taken a "leap of faith." The evaluation of his remarkable claim depends on Miller's (and the reader's) intuitive feel for the nature of psychology and its history, Edwards's psychological views, and those of James and Freud. What is psychology? What did James or Freud say that can be directly compared and contrasted with Edwards's (admittedly crypto-grammatic and therefore not fully comprehensible) psychological theory? These questions have no answers, of course, until the views of each theorist are translated into a common language of the relevant dimensions of human nature, and until the understanding of Edwards's views comes to depend less on faith than on an explicit model.

Miller would have Edwards become a precursor of Jamesian or Freudian psy-chology but, characteristically, he left the detailed investigation of the truth of this assertion to "future research." It is almost certain that some budding scholar will undertake in the future, or perhaps has already begun, to study the Jamesian or Freudian aspects of Edwards's thought. Miller's esoteric vices are often, at the same time, heuristic virtues.

The other significant attempt to interpret Edwards's psychological theory within the context of the history of psychology lies poles apart from Miller's ambiguity. To Joseph Haroutunian, Edwards was no Jamesian or Freudian, but a behaviorist, and unlike Miller, Haroutunian offers a detailed explanation of his interpretation.

A modern rendition of this analysis of Edwards is the study of human behav-ior in terms of "stimulus" and "response." A stimulus is Edwards' "motive," and response is volitional behavior. Such a study is based upon the principle that where there is no stimulus, there is no response; where there is no action, there is no reaction; where there is no cause, there is no effect. The nature of a given stimulus is irrelevant to the fact that it acts as a stimulus. An "S-R bond" may be physical or it may be moral, and in both cases it is a "certain connec-tion" between a "motive" and an act of volition. Edwards' metaphysical princi-ple of necessity is the modern methodological principle that all action is reaction. The excellence of Edwards' thought consists in that he withstood a careless attribution of mental functions to underlying quasi-physical structures or entities (which is also the virtue in behaviorism), *and* did not commit the fallacy of reducing one function into another, the mental and moral into the physical (which is the vice of modern behaviorism as understood by the "vul-gar"). The will is neither a "faculty," nor an uproar in the cells of a muscle or a gland. Volition is not *caused* by the will, because there is no will to cause such an act.[82]

This is an extremely complex statement and it requires careful examination. First it is asserted that Edwards is a behaviorist. Why? Because of his ruthless hard determinism: "where there is no cause, there is no effect." Clearly, Haroutunian equates behaviorism and determinism. Perhaps, in 1932 when Haroutunian wrote, behaviorism was so dominant in America that he could not see, for instance, that Freud, surely no behaviorist, was also holding that all effects have causes. The chief difference between behaviorists and most other more cognitively oriented psychologists is not relative adherence to hard determinism. The widest gulf separating behaviorists and other scientific psychologists concerns reductionism. Behaviorists have always been hesitant to speculate upon or postulate the existence of definable mental operations.[83] Observable behavior, they claim, is the object of their analysis. Many psychologists, of course, including Freudians, functionalists, and Gestaltists, have objected to this stimulus-response psychology; i.e., that the mind is not a fit topic for respectable scientific research. E. C. Tolman expressed the principal objection to S-R behaviorism very cogently back in the thirties.[84] Of course, all behavioral events are caused, he readily admitted; every response has a stimulus. But this simple S-R level of analysis, though convenient, is too simple. The organism effectively intervenes between stimulus and response. The observable response, to Tolman, is a function not only of some specifiable, stimulus complex, but also of an individual's assumptions, expectations, and purposes concerning the stimuli. Tolman, and other cognitive psychologists, believe that responses are constructed within the organism based upon the information present in the stimuli *and* upon what the organism is looking for.

Cognitive psychologists, then, may be characterized by their willingness to speculate about mental functioning while behaviorists tend to view the organism as empty-headed. Certainly, in this context, Edwards is no behaviorist, in spite of his uncompromising determinism. Indeed, much of the secondary commentary on Edwards consists in trying to restate his voluminous, bewildering attempts to explicate the mental functioning which occurs during the conversion experience. In groping for a contemporary label for Edwards's psychological views, Haroutunian picked the wrong one. Edwards simply lacked the reductionistic mentality that would permit classifying him as an eighteenth-century behaviorist. After all, Edwards's first serious philosophical endeavor, undertaken while a young teenager, was entitled *Notes on the Mind*.[85] The idealistic metaphysics contained in this early work would provide nothing but profound embarrassment to an aspiring behaviorist.

Haroutunian's faulty conception of modern psychology leads him directly to contradict himself in a curious manner. Edwards, he states, "did not commit the fallacy of reducing . . . the mental and moral into the physical." Therefore, Edwards is not a reductionist. It is obvious to Haroutunian, an excellent ecclesiastical historian, that Edwards's tracts and pamphlets are packed with discussions of mental and moral "faculties," regardless of what he might have meant by the term. Edwards, the S-R behaviorist, therefore, is no behaviorist at all. He does not concentrate strictly, or even primarily, upon "the physical," or what modern behaviorists call "observables." Haroutunian, in effect, offers a sound interpretation of Edwards as a cognitive psychologist, while maintaining all along that he is a behaviorist.

Summary and Conclusions

The study of the psychological thought of American Puritanism and of its most important expositor, Jonathan Edwards, has suffered from diverse historiographical misdemeanors and from Edwards's own linguistic complexities. For historians of psychology, Edwards's fate is that of Plato, Aquinas, and all other thinkers whose books Boring failed to find on the shelves in Wundt's laboratory: intriguing and profound though the works may be, they are irrelevant to the Event, the founding of experimental psychology. Some students of American history have treated Edwards as if he were no more than a fire-and-brimstone preacher, a manipulator of sweating colonial lunatics. Others, holding with H. L. Mencken that a Puritan is simply a person who fears that somewhere, someone may be happy, have been unable sufficiently to shed their anti-Puritan biases and to appreciate, therefore, the intellectual drama that often lay beneath the apparently cadaverous Puritan exterior. Still others have tried to demonstrate that Edwards was an enthusiastic assimilator of and contributor to profound traditions in Western intellectual life. Yet, because of timidity and lack of interest in psychology they have been unable to unravel Edwards's psychological thought. Finally, Edwards himself, trapped in the language of faculty psychology but possessed with a vision of something else, is teeming with paradoxes and apparent contradictions.[86] He has made scholarly life difficult for his interpreters.

The rectification of this situation requires, clearly, that scholarship on Edwards's psychology be preceded by some interest and sophistication in the history of psychology and by immersion in the works of Edwards and his commentators.[87] The careful, historian will discover in the writings of Edwards and many other Puritans a cutting edge, an intensity that is altogether lacking in the work of many psychological thinkers. These Puritans are no mere speculators; because their psychology was rooted in a broader conception of their communion with a personal and terrible Calvinist God, the means of life and death became for them in part psychological. One need hardly be a Calvinist (or perhaps one cannot be) to experience the exhilaration of reading the psychology of persons for whom a conception of psychology had moment-to-moment significance. The presentist is confronted with the challenge of explaining what, if anything, the psychology of Edwards and his fellow Puritans had to do with the psychology of James and beyond. "There is a gap therein," James himself said in a similar context, "but no mere gap. It is a gap that is intensely active."[88] (One may be intense without being prolific.)[89] In recent years scholars have found Puritan origins of the American Mind, Revolution, Self and a dozen other attributes. Is it possible that there are also Puritan (i.e., American) origins of American psychology?

NOTES TO THE SUPPLEMENT

1. See Edwin G. Boring, *A History of Experimental Psychology*, 2d ed. (New York: Appleton-Century-Crofts, 1950), chapters 14 and 16, for Boring's influential assessment of the importance of Fechner and Wundt.
2. See Boring, *History*, chapter 2.

3. William James, *Principles of Psychology*, 2 vols. (New York: Holt, 1890). James's *Principles*, for example, is cited in nearly every "introduction to psychology" while James's American predecessors are cited in none.

4. Of course, scholars have long recognized James's Yankee-Calvinist heritage as well. After all, his grandfather was a self-made Presbyterian millionaire, his father a self-styled transcendentalist; James himself was a self-effacing, unhappily schismatic youth, attracted to his father's tendency to philosophize but haunted by his grandfather's Calvinist conscience. Thus, though New England was in his marrow, the psychology of New England was not. How, one might facetiously ask, can this be? The answer, implicit in the research on James's psychology (also facetious) is that there is no "New England Psychology." This review essay is in part an attempt to refute this.

5. Of the recent general histories of psychology, only two give more than the merest mention of American psychological thought before James and the importation of the "new psychology" in the 1880s: Virginia Sexton and Hendryk Misiak, *History of Psychology: An Overview* (New York: Grune and Stratton, 1966) and Gardner Murphy and Joseph K. Kovach, *Historical Introduction to Modern Psychology*, 3d ed. (New York: Harcourt Brace Jovanovich, 1972). Each devotes approximately two pages to American psychology, 1630–1880. One may occasionally find an article or book in which persons in the early, pre-Jamesian period are discussed; cf. Ernest Harms, "America's First Major Psychologist: Laurens Perseus Hickok," *Journal of the History of the Behavioral Sciences* 8 (1972): 120–23, and Gregory A. Kimble and Laurence C. Perlmuter, "The Problem of Volition," *Psychological Review* 77 (1970): 361–84. The latter discusses at length one Joseph Buchanan of Kentucky. Yet in nearly all such research the few psychological thinkers deemed worthy of discussion are treated as oddballs, unfortunate to have endured American psychology's "glacial age."

6. I owe the phrase "indigenous American Psychology" to Rand B. Evans. He first used it, I believe, at a symposium on that topic at the meeting of the Cheiron Society, Plattsburgh, N.Y., 1973.

7. A number of historians have contended that some sort of psychological system lay at the core of Edwards's thought; cf. Alan Heimert, *Religion and the American Mind: From the Great Awakening to the Revolution* (Cambridge, Mass.: Harvard University Press, 1966), and "Introduction" to Alan Heimert and Perry Miller, eds., *The Great Awakening* (New York: Bobbs-Merrill, 1967). See also the "Introduction" of Clarence Faust and Thomas Johnson to their *Jonathan Edwards: Representative Selections* (New York: Hill & Wang, 1962).

8. See Boring, *History*, pp. 396–410, for an analysis of the difference between Wundt and Külpe.

9. J. R. Trumbull, *History of Northampton* (Northampton, Mass: Forbes Library, 1898), provides a detailed account of this controversy; see also Ola Elizabeth Winslow, *Jonathan Edwards* (New York: Macmillan, 1940), pp. 241–67. Robert Lowell sees the controversy this way:

> Yet people were spiders
>
> in your moment of glory,
> at the Great Awakening—"alas, how many
> in this very meeting house are more than likely
> to remember my discourse in hell!"
>
> The meeting house remembered!
> You stood on stilts in the air,
> but you fell from your parish.
> "All rising is by a winding stair."

(From "Jonathan Edwards in Western Massachusetts," in *For the Union Dead* [New York: Farrar, Straus & Giroux, 1956].)

10. Boring, *History*, p. 316.

11. Preface to the first edition of the *History* (New York: Appleton-Century-Crofts, 1929).

12. Boring, *History*, p. 343.

13. Quoted in Alexander V. G. Allen, *Jonathan Edwards* (Boston: Houghton Mifflin, 1889), p. vi.

14. On Edwards and the fundamentalist tradition, consult William Warren Sweet, *Revivalism in America* (New York: Scribner, 1944) and Bernard W. Weisberger, *They Gathered at the River* (Boston: Little, Brown, 1958). Perry Miller fills in the gaps between Edwards and the transcendental movement in "From Edwards to Emerson," in *Errand into the Wilderness* (New York: Harper & Row, 1964), pp. 184–203. The connection between Edwards's "New Light" theology, preaching, and the American Revolution is explored in Heimert, *Religion*.

15. The classic treatment of the origins and fate of Edwards's theology is Joseph Haroutunian, *Piety versus Moralism: The Passing of the New England Theology* (New York: Harper & Row, 1963) (1932). For another account consult Frank Hugh Foster, *A Genetic History of the New England Theology*. (Chicago: University of Chicago Press, 1907).

16. This is the so-called tragic aspect of Edwards. In general, this view of Edwards acknowledges

his powerful intellectual gifts but regrets the alleged time worn, dead issues to which he addressed himself. Edwards, it is held, yearned to re-create a medieval Bible commonwealth when he might have used his extraordinary gifts to promote the importation to America of the European Enlightenment. Expressions of this view may be found in Peter Gay, *A Loss of Mastery: Puritan Historians in Colonial New England* (Berkeley, Calif.: University of California Press, 1966) and Vernon L. Parrington, *The Colonial Mind* (New York: Harcourt, Brace 1927).

17. See expecially his *The New England Mind: The Seventeenth Century* (Boston: Beacon, 1961) (1939).

18. *A History of American Psychology* (New York: Collier, 1964).

19. *American Psychology before William James* (New Brunswick, N.J.: Rutgers University Press, 1939).

20. Herbert W. Schneider, *The Puritan Mind* (Ann Arbor. Mich.: University of Michigan Press, 1958), pp. 3–7.

21. See Arthur O. Lovejoy, *The Great Chain of Being* (Cambridge, Mass.: Harvard University Press, 1936) for the definitive summary of the medieval world view which was inherited by the New England Puritans.

22. Miller, *Seventeenth Century*, pp. 239–79.

23. Ibid., p. 239.

24. See J. Rodney Fulcher, "Puritans and the Passions: The Faculty Psychology in American Puritanism," *Journal of the History of the Behavioral Sciences* 9 (1973): 123–39, for an account of the scholastic origins of seventeenth century Puritan psychological views. Fulcher's article provides a good entry in the complex and utterly odd psychology of the Puritans in the seventeenth century. He is, I believe, more knowledgeable about psychology and certainly less convoluted than Miller.

25. Miller, *Seventeenth Century*, p. 280.

26. Miller probably derived his implicit view of psychology directly from George S. Brett's *History of Psychology*, 3 vols. (London: Allen and Unwin, 1912–21). Miller's chapter "The Nature of Man" contains more references to Brett than to any other secondary source. In any case, judging Miller by his sources is difficult. George Selement has suggested that Miller was neither as reliable nor as erudite as he often boasted; see "Perry Miller: A Note on His Sources in *The New England Mind: The Seventeenth Century*," *William and Mary Quarterly* 31 (1974): 453–64.

27. Miller, *Seventeenth Century*, p. 245.

28. Ibid., p. 287.

29. Ibid., p. 267.

30. Cf. my own response to Miller's innuendoes about an alleged "unconscious" conflict between Increase Mather (1639–1723) and Solomon Stoddard (1643–1729) in the late seventeenth and early eighteenth centuries: James G. Blight, "Solomon Stoddard's *Safety of Appearing* and the Dissolution of the Puritan Faculty Psychology," *Journal of the History of the Behavioral Sciences* 10 (1974): 238–50. The usual interpretation of the antipathy between these two patriarchs involves their differing views over church polity, with Mather characterized as the old, hard-line Bostonian and Stoddard as the rebellious frontiersman who was willing to let almost anyone join his Northampton congregation. Miller contended that the conflict went deeper, down to the frightening (to Mather), irrational conception of human nature sketched in Stoddard's treatise, *The Safety of Appearing* (1687). In my view, much of the evidence supports Miller's interpretation, and Miller's view at least makes Edwards's psychology a trifle more explicable. For Edwards, like James, is often thought to have been an American (by birth) who, after taking an overdose of European controversy, i.e., (James = Darwin; Edwards = Locke), became a cosmopolitan expositor of "Western Culture." If, on the other hand, the germ of Edwards's psychology can be seen in Stoddard, his grandfather and predecessor in the Northampton pulpit, then perhaps historians should begin to investigate the relationship between, say, frontier conditions such as existed in Northampton and psychological thought in America. Edwards, solitary genius though he was, stood on the shoulders of others. Some of them, surely, were on his side of the Atlantic.

31. One of Miller's most brilliant and controversial students is Alan Heimert. In *Religion*, Heimert, like Miller, often prefers to record and interpret what he feels historical figures "meant" rather than what they said. This approach strikes some historians as a perversion of historiography, and one critic's evaluation of Heimert might easily be applied to Miller, his mentor:

The world he offers us has been constructed by reading beyond the lines of what men said; and what he finds beyond the lines is so far beyond, so wrenched from the content, and so at odds with empirical evidence, that his world, to this reviewer at least, partakes more of fantasy than of history.

From Edmund S. Morgan, review of *Religion* by Alan Heimert, *William and Mary Quarterly* 24 (1967): 259.

32. The rejection of this view began with Kenneth B. Murdock's *Increase Mather: Foremost American Puritan* (Cambridge, Mass.: Harvard University Press, 1925), continued through the many volumes of Samuel Eliot Morison, and culminated in Miller. See Edmund S. Morgan, "The Historians of Early New England," in Ray Allen Billington, ed., *The Reinterpretation of Early American History* (New York: Norton, 1968), pp. 41–63.

33. Roback, in his *History*, selects most of his information about Puritan psychology from the secondary accounts of Samuel Eliot Morison.

34. Roback, *History*, p. 35.

35. Roback also uses this implicit argument against contemporary neo-scholastic psychology in America (*History*, pp. 424–46). It is remarkable that he apparently saw no kinship between Puritan psychology and neo-scholasticism. Both, of course, are saturated with a Thomistic faculty psychology.

36. Roback, *History*, pp. 36–37.

37. Ibid., pp. 38–39

38. Fay, *American Psychology*.

39. Ibid., p. 6.

40. Ibid., p. 169.

41. Roback, *History*, pp. 46–47.

42. Fay, *American Psychology*, p. 43.

43. See Norman S. Fiering, "Will and Intellect in the New England Mind," *William and Mary Quarterly* 24 (1972): 515–58. This is a valuable article. Among its many useful analyses are a comparison of the psychological views of Edwards and Augustine and a blunt chastisement of Fay for completely misunderstanding Edwards. Yet Fiering, like many other commentators, also fails, I think, to grasp completely the subtlety of Edwards's psychological syntheses. It is Fiering's contention that Edwards (and Augustine) merely emphasized will (and emotions) while others, from Aquinas to Edwards's archenemy, Charles Chauncy of Harvard, emphasized intellect.

44. Those who would agree that Edwards avoided a scholastic dichotomization of the mind include Perry Miller, *Jonathan Edwards* (New York: Sloane, 1949) and "Jonathan Edwards on a Sense of the Heart," *Harvard Theological Review* 41 (1948): 123–45; Douglas J. Elwood, *the Philosophical Theology of Jonathan Edwards* (New York: Columbia University Press, 1960); Roland Delattre, *Beauty and Sensibility in the Thought of Jonathan Edwards* (New Haven, Conn.: Yale University Press, 1968); Conrad Cherry, *The Theology of Jonathan Edwards* (New York: Doubleday-Anchor, 1966); Faust & Johnson, *Selections;* Heimert, *Religion,* and "Introduction"; Haroutunian, *Piety versus Moralism;* Paul Conkin, *Puritans and Pragmatists* (New York: Dodd, Mead, 1968); and John E. Smith, "Editor's Introduction" to Edwards's *Treatise on the Religious Affections* (New Haven, Conn.: Yale University Press, 1959).

45. Cherry, *Theology*, pp. 12–13.

46. Ibid., p. 14.

47. The issue concerning the sources of Edwards is a large and complex one. Those who view his sources as biblical or ecclesiastical generally see Edwards as a medieval man, inhabiting a world of devils and angels, saints and sinners. Others, especially Perry Miller, believe that Edwards's greatest debt is to Locke and Newton. The "medievalist" viewpoint is forcefully advanced by Vincent Tomas, "The Modernity of Jonathan Edwards," *New England Quarterly* 25 (1952): 60–84. The "modernist" interpretation is in Miller, *Jonathan Edwards*.

48. Peter van Mastricht, *A Treatise on Regeneration*. Extracted and translated from the *Theologia Theoretico-Practica* (New Haven, Conn., 1770).

49. Augustine *Ennarationes in Psalmos, CXVIII, Sermones XVIII* 3; quoted in Elwood, *Philosophical Theology*, p. 113.

50. John Locke, *An Essay concerning Human Understanding*, 2 vols., ed. A. C. Fraser (New York: Dover, 1959), II, xxi, 17. (1690).

51. Ibid., II, xxi, 6.

52. Elwood, *Philosophical Theology*, p. 114.

53. Jonathan Edwards, *A Treatise concerning the Religious Affections*, ed., John E. Smith (New Haven, Conn.: Yale University Press, 1959), p. 272. (1746)

54. I have elsewhere suggested a number of contemporary salves for Edwards's wounded psychology. See the "Summary and Conclusions" below for pertinent references and a brief but uninhibited plunge into psycho-historical speculation.

55. Miller, "Sense of the Heart," p. 127.

56. Miller, *Jonathan Edwards*, p. 57.

57. Ibid., p. 72.

58. Locke, *Essay*, II, i, 2.

59. Ibid., II, xxxiii.

60. Locke's chapter on the association of ideas was not added to the *Essay* until 1700, in the fourth edition; thus it may be treated, as Robert I. Watson puts it, merely "as an appendix to the rest of his thinking" (*The Great Psychologists: From Aristotle to Freud*, 3d ed. [Philadelphia: Lippincott, 1971], pp. 190–91). And, of course, Locke had a great deal to say about the manner in which the mind actively constructs complex ideas; cf. *Essay*, II, xxii, 2, and II, xiii. Edwards, however, seems to have extracted from Locke only the latter's passive sensationalism.

61. James, *Principles*, 1: 1.

62. Miller, "Sense of the Heart," p. 124.

63. Faust and Johnson, *Selections*, p. xlvi.

64. Ibid., p. xlvii.

65. Edwards, *Affections*, p. 205.

66. Some scholars, however, believe that the conversion experience, in Edwards's view, involved a perceptual process which is qualitatively different from that used in mundane perception. Some hold the opposite view, that Edwards saw no qualitative differences in the operation of the mind in supernatural and natural perception. The former viewpoint is expressed in Paul Helm, "John Locke and Jonathan Edwards: A Reconsideration," *Journal of the History of Philosophy* 8 (1969): 51–61; the latter view may be found in Cherry, *Theology*, pp. 27–33.

67. Jonathan Edwards, "Sinners in the Hands of an Angry God"; a sermon preached at Enfield, Conn., July 8, 1741; in S. E. Dwight, ed., *The Works of President Edwards*, 10 vols. (New York: Cargill, 1830), 7: 163–77.

68. Allen, *Jonathan Edwards*.

69. Ibid., p. 144. The phrase "divine supernatural light" is borrowed by Allen from Edwards's sermon "A Divine Supernatural Light, Immediately Imparted to the Soul by the Spirit of God, Shown to be both a Scriptural and Rational Doctrine"; a sermon preached at Northampton, Mass., 1734 (Dwight, ed., *Works*, 6: 171–88). In this remarkable sermon Edwards first made public the psychological ruminations which were to consume his attention for the rest of his life. Most of his ideas are present in the sermon, though in highly condensed form, including his determinism, his notion of "a sense of the heart," and an outline of the mental mechanics of the conversion experience. The "Divine Light" sermon, written by a thirty-one-year-old frontier pastor, is, without question, one of the most extraordinary documents in the history of American psychology.

70. Allen, *Jonathan Edwards*, p. 5.

71. Cf. Watson, *Great Psychologists* (3d ed.), pp. 155–58 and pp. 186–87, and Richard Lowry, *The Evolution of Psychological Theory: 1650 to the Present* (Chicago: Aldine, 1971), pp. 5–23. Perry Miller also speaks of the "Lockean victory over innate ideas" ("Sense of the Heart," p. 125).

72. Allen, *Jonathan Edwards*, pp. 144–45.

73. Ibid., p. 145.

74. Ibid., p. 146.

75. In what may be the most balanced evaluation of Miller yet published, Peter Gay *(A Loss of Mastery)* openly concedes Miller's greatness as a historian while lamenting his tendency to overwrite, and his "overly fertile" mind. Yet Miller's brashness, his bullish approach to writing, and his often indiscriminate ejaculation of ideas onto the printed page were, perhaps, necessary. He, more than anyone else, revived Puritan scholarship and, in the process, gave it many new directions.

76. Claude A. Smith, "Jonathan Edwards and the Way of Ideas," *Harvard Theological Review* 59 (1966): 153–73. See also the following for a reassessment, in other contexts, of the relationship between Edwards and Locke: Leon Howard, ed., *"The Mind" of Jonathan Edwards: A Reconstructed Text* (Berkeley, Calif.: University of California Press, 1963); Edward H. Davidson, "From Locke to Edwards," *Journal of the History of Ideas* 24 (1963): 355–72, and *Jonathan Edwards: The Narrative of a Puritan Mind* (Boston: Houghton Mifflin, 1966); Paul Helm, "Locke and Edwards," in Helm, ed., *Treatise on Grace and Other Writings* (Cambridge: Clarke, 1971).

77. Smith, "Way of Ideas," p. 154.

78. Jonathan Edwards, "Notes on the Mind" (No. 1), in Harvey G. Townsend, ed., *The Philosophy of Jonathan Edwards from His Private Notebooks* (Eugene, Oreg.: University of Oregon Press, 1955), p. 26 (1716–20).

79. Cherry, *Theology*, p. 19.

80. Miller, *Jonathan Edwards*, p. 50–51.

81. Ibid., p. 183.

82. Haroutunian, *Piety Versus Moralism*, pp. 225–26.

83. Jerry A. Fodor's remarkably concise (for Fodor) summary of the essence of the "Skinner-Chomsky debate" brings the reader straight to the issue of reductionism.

. . . the disagreement between Chomsky and Skinner is *not* about whether verbal behavior is caused (they both assume that it is . . .) . . . On the contrary, what Skinner tried to show is that learning a language is learning the stimulus conditions upon discriminated responses . . . . What Chomsky argued is that learning a language is not learning S-R connections, hence that . . . One cannot, therefore infer from the premise that verbalizations are caused to the conclusion that verbalizations are responses. (Italics Fodor's)

From *The Language of Thought* (New York: Crowell, 1975), p 102.

84. Edward C. Tolman, *Purposive Behavior in Animals and Men* (New York: Century, 1932).

85. In Townsend, *Philosophy,* pp. 21–73.

86. Perry Miller has summarized this traditional (some would say medieval) aspect of Edwards's intellect:

Edwards drew each verse in the Bible for an object in experience, drew from it the baldest, most obvious doctrine, reasoned it out, and applied it in the Standard Puritan form . . . . He was an artist working in a tradition and for him the tradition was sufficient.

From *Jonathan Edwards,* p. 43.

87. I have tried to establish some small oases of coherence around Edwards, Solomon Stoddard (an important predecessor), and Asa Burton, whose *Essay* is a kind of culmination of the "New England Theology" (and psychology) championed by Edwards. See "Solomon Stoddard" (ref. in note 30); "The Psychological Theory of Jonathan Edwards" (Paper read at the annual meeting of the American Psychological Association, Montreal, 1973); "Jonathan Edwards' psychology of Conversion" (Paper read at the annual meeting of the Cheiron Society, Durham, N.H., 1974); "Introduction" to Asa Burton, *Essays on Some of the First Principles of Metaphysics, Ethics and Theology* (Albany, N.Y.: Scholar's Fascimiles and Reprints, 1973) (1824). These papers, however, are only the first, halting steps toward a systematic consideration of Edwards's psychology.

88. James, *Principles,* 1: 251.

89. I have sketched an outline of the relationship between the psychologies of Edwards and James in "From Jonathan Edwards to William James: A Sketch of a Psychological Journey," chapter 6 of my unpublished doctoral dissertation, "Gracious Discoveries: Toward an Understanding of Jonathan Edwards' Psychological Theory, and an Assessment of His Place in the History of American Psychology" (University of New Hampshire, 1974).

David Jayne Hill:
Between the Old and the New Psychology

Lehigh University

Introduction

In his life, David Jayne Hill (1850–1932) played many professional and personal roles: college teacher, preacher, author, president of Bucknell University,[1] president of the University of Rochester,[2] a politician and a diplomat,[3] and, importantly, a grandfather. The introduction to Hill's unpublished autobiography is entitled "To My Grandchildren," and the title preceding the table of contents reads "Confidences of a Grandfather."[4]

In the present context Hill is of particular interest as a psychologist and, more specifically, as a teacher of psychology, author, and thinker. Among his book-length publications, two are of direct relevance: his 1888 textbook, *The Elements of Psychology*,[5] with psychology viewed as "the systematized knowledge of the facts of consciousness" (as the unknown owner of my copy of Hill's *Elements* wrote on the frontispiece), and his 1893 *Genetic Philosophy*,[6] with chapters on the genesis of consciousness, feeling, thought, and will (pp. 100–231).

Hill was a "part-time psychologist" in that academic psychology occupied his attention for a limited period of his life (ca. 1879–96), and even at this time he had heavy concurrent responsibilities, including administrative and professional duties as university president, teacher of other subjects than psychology, and author.

On the title page of his autobiography, Hill identified himself as "Educator, Diplomatist, Historian." When he died, in his eighty-second year, the *Rochester Alumni Review* carried an obituary notice in which Hill was described as "president of the University of Rochester from 1888 to 1896, trustee since the latter date, distinguished diplomat, historian and authority on international law."[7]

Hill's involvement in psychology was no longer a part of the man's professional

121

David Jayne Hill

"image" and the author of the obituary notice can hardly be blamed for beginning at the start of Hill's career at the University of Rochester. Only in a broader perspective does the fact that Hill became professor psychology of the University at Lewisburg in 1881 acquire historical significance. It appears that his was the first professorship of psychology in the United States, even though his title read "professor of psychology and ethics."

General Chronological Framework

We are concerned here with four contiguous segments of Hill's life: his under-graduate studies at the University at Lewisburg (1870–74), service on the staff of the university (1874–79), presidency of the University at Lewisburg (1879–88), and presidency of the University of Rochester (1889–96), preceded by a sabbatical year spent in Europe (1888–89). The milestones in his career during this time are as follows:

1850 Born on 10 June in Plainfield, New Jersey.
1870 Entered the University at Lewisburg (renamed Bucknell University in 1886), Lewisburg, Pennsylvania.
1874 Graduated from the University at Lewisburg. Became a staff member.
1879 Was elected President of the University at Lewisburg.
1888 Was elected President of the University of Rochester, Rochester, New York. Published *The Elements of Psychology*.
1889 Assumed the Presidency of the University of Rochester.
1893 Published *Genetic Philosophy*.
1896 Resigned from the Presidency of the University of Rochester.

The years between Hill's resignation from the University of Rochester and his death in 1932 were devoted to writing and to politics. Since they have no bearing on our topic, they are not considered here. Hill died on 2 March 1932.

The University at Lewisburg (Bucknell)

1. Learning at Lewisburg

Hill's College Years

The official transcript of the courses Hill took at Lewisburg shows the pattern of those years, with "Composition" and "Declamation" carried as the fourth and fifth courses through all the terms.

Year	1st Term	2nd Term	3rd Term
1870–71, Freshman	Xenophon Virgil Geometry	Xenophon Livy Geometry	Odyssey Rhetoric Algebra

1871–72, Sophomore	Cicero, De senectute Trigonometry Chemistry, etc.	Iliad Anal. Geometry Chemistry, etc.	Horace Surveying Geology, etc.
1872–73, Junior	Sophocles Nat. Philosophy Logic	Tacitus Nat. Philosophy Rhetoric	German Astronomy Political Economy
1873–74, Senior	Cicero, De officiis Mental Philosophy French	Demosthenes Mental Philosophy Moral Philosophy	Juvenal Moral Philosophy Butler's *Apology*

In the first term of the Junior year the abbreviation "Phys." (for Physics) is penciled in under "Natural Philosophy."

We see that Hill's curriculum of courses at the University at Lewisburg was heavy on Latin (seven terms) and Greek (six terms) but also included an introduction to German and French. He had two terms of Rhetoric, a field in which he later excelled as a practitioner and a textbook writer. He had a more than cursory exposure to mathematics and geometry (algebra, two terms of geometry, trigonometry, analytical geometry, surveying) and to the natural sciences (astronomy, two terms of physics [Natural Philosophy], two terms of chemistry, geology) while the "social sciences" were represented by a term of Political Economy. He had two terms of Mental Philosophy, two of Moral Philosophy, and a term of the inescapable exercise in the argumentative defense of Christianity, centered on Butler's *Apology*.[8]

The small college at Lewisburg gave Hill an excellent preparation for his years of self-initiated "continuing education."

We know what courses Hill took but we do not know how well he did in individual subjects. To prevent any "intrusion into privacy," the Bucknell University registrar, 100 years later, carefully cut out from the transcript those parts in which the grades were reported.

The University Catalogue attests that on 24 June 1874, "on examination," Hill was awarded the degree of the Bachelor of Arts. The printed Order of Exercises for the twenty-fourth Commencement of the University at Lewisburg tells us that David Jayne Hill appeared twice on the program: he presented, early in the program, what was apparently a brief comment on the theme of "Nemesis" and, more importantly, the valedictory address.

Earning the A.M.

A few words should be added about the master's degree, Hill's highest "earned" academic degree (as contrasted with the honorary Doctorate of letters, LL.D.). The procedure is specified in the University Catalogues. The entry in the catalogue for the academic year 1871–72 reads: "The degree of A.M. is conferred on every graduate from the Classical Department, of three years' standing who meanwhile shall have sustained a good moral character and pursued professional or other studies; and who shall make application for the degree, personally or by letter, at least one day previous to commencement."[9] These were generous conditions, all around.

In the year 1877–78 we find Hill registered as "Master of Arts—In course." It appears that he was awarded the A.M. at the end of that academic year, since in the 1878–79 catalogue his name is given as "David J. Hill, A.M."

2. Teaching at Lewisburg

The University at Lewisburg had three divisions ("departments"). Their distinct functions are specified on the front page of the April 1880 issue of the *College Herald*.[10] The College offered three curricula—classical, scientific, and eclectic; the Academy (for men) provided "thorough preparation for college, teaching, or business"; and the Institute afforded "to young ladies the advantages of a college." In fact, the ladies of the Institute attended some of the college courses.

During the first academic year after graduation, Hill served as a tutor. In the subsequent four years his academic title pointed to rhetoric as Hill's central area of responsibility for teaching, with "and librarian" being attached to his title during his first five years of service as a member of the college teaching staff. However, the University Catalogues, though not always very informative, indicate that in the years 1875–78 Hill gave to the Junior class a course of lectures, held every second week, on English Literature and Criticism. In 1877–78 he served also as instructor in Greek at the University Academy, where the following year he taught both Greek and rhetoric.

We are much better informed about Hill's academic duties during the years of his presidency at Lewisburg. The information is summarized below.

Year	1st Term	2nd Term	3rd Term
1879–80	Intellectual Philosophy	Intellectual Philosophy Political Economy & Constitutional Law	Butler's *Apology* Moral Philosophy
1880–81	Psychology	Psychology	Political Economy & Constitutional Law Ethics
1881–82		Psychology	Political Economy & Constitutional Law Ethics
1882–83	Psychology	Anthropology	Ethics
1883–84	Psychology	Anthropology	Economics Ethics

1884–85	Psychology	Anthropology	Ethics
			Economics & Politics
1887–88	Psychology	Anthropology	Ethics

During the years 1879–88 all of his courses were given to the college seniors, at times joined by the fourth-year students of the university's nondegree branch for women, the Institute. At times he taught "Elements of Rhetoric" and "Science of Rhetoric" at the Institute, as well as other courses, as required in case of an emergency.

In 1879–80 (and perhaps in later years as well), Hill gave in the College a "Course of Special Lectures," held once a week, on topics dealing with the history of philosophy, natural theology, and the evidences of Christianity.

Our principal concern is with Hill's teaching of psychology. He began to teach a course entitled "Psychology" in the first term of the academic year 1880–81, while still wearing the hat of a professor of metaphysics and moral philosophy. In 1881 his academic title changed to professor of psychology and ethics.

In 1880–81 he taught psychology, to seniors, in both the first and second terms. In subsequent years the course was taught for one term only, usually the first term. Beginning in 1882–83, psychology was followed by a course in anthropology. Ethics was reserved for the third term and was usually offered together with political economy and constitutional law, economics, or economics and politics.

In Hill's days there were no formal course evaluations by students. Consequently, an entry in the *University Mirror,* a student monthly of the University at Lewisburg, is a particularly welcome piece of information. It reads:

> The Senior class of the College is to be congratulated for the pleasure and benefit it is deriving from the subject of Psychology. Heretofore, classes made use of the text-book alone, which is now done away with, and a series of lectures on the subject is given by the President. No translation of difficult and abstruse sentences from Porter[12] is now needed . . . the concise language and clear expression of the professor (D. J. Hill) make what is considered the most difficult study in the whole course [i.e., the college curriculum] an interesting and fascinating subject.[11]

3. Presidency at Lewisburg

In the present account we are not concerned with Hill as university president. Briefly, it may be said that although his administrative performance was not troublefree at either Lewisburg or the University of Rochester, the Lewisburg students did not wish Hill to leave. An editorial published in the *University Mirror* in June 1888 is outspoken on this issue:

> From the New York Tribune and other sources we learn that Bucknell's President is among those most favorably mentioned as the probable successor of Dr. Anderson as President of the University of Rochester. While we thank our Rochester friends for the compliment which they pay to our honored President

and University, and while we give them credit for the keen eye to business which they show in recognizing the merits of Dr. Hill as a college president, yet we can not but owe them a grudge for any attempt to entice Dr. Hill from his post of duty here.[13]

In the end, Bucknell lost out and the University of Rochester gained a new president.

Before assuming his duties at Rochester, Hill spent a sabbatical year in Europe (1888–89). With Berlin as his base, he visited German universities and numerous professors. By chance he met the psychologist G. S. Hall, who was in Germany before taking over the presidency of Clark University. The meeting led to joint travel to Italy, Crete, Athens, and the universities of Switzerland, but little is known about the professional impact on Hill of this encounter.[14]

The University of Rochester

The period of Hill's association with the University of Rochester is shorter (1888–96) and the chronology is simpler than that pertaining to his stay at the University at Lewisburg (Bucknell). Throughout, his title was President of the University of Rochester and also Burbank Professor of Intellectual and Moral Philosophy.

Psychology retained a significant place among Hill's courses. During his first year of teaching at the University of Rochester, Hill offered a course in psychology during the first term and ethics in the second term. As at Bucknell, these courses were for college seniors. Psychology was a stiff course, with five hours a week and "written dissertations, on especially assigned themes, from each member of the class" (Annual Catalogue for 1889–90, p. 29).[15]

During the following year the pattern was established that was to prevail, with minor changes, during Hill's Rochester years. He taught "Elementary Psychology" during the first term and introduced a new course, "Physiological Psychology," in the third term. The latter, three-hour course was reduced to two hours per week in 1892–93, only to be increased to five hours the following year.

In the Annual Catalogue for 1890–91, p. 63, the course on elementary psychology is described as "including a study of the phenomena of intellect, sensibility and will, with constant application to the development of the mind in the process of education, and the psychological origin of philosophical problems." Hill's *Elements of Psychology* was used as the textbook.

The course on physiological psychology was outlined as "including an account of working hypotheses, methods, experimentation and general results. The method of presentation is as far as possible illustrative, with a large amount of reading upon selected topics (Wundt, *Physiologische Psychologie;*[16] Sergi, *Psychologie physiologique;*[17] Ladd, *Elements of Physiological Psychology;*[18] Schwalbe, *Anatomie der Sinnesorgane;*[19] Edinger, *Nervöse Centralorgane*)."[20] How would today's Rochester seniors react to a course syllabus in which the majority of assigned readings were in German, with some French added for good measure?

Two other, innovative aspects of Hill's activities as teacher of psychology must be mentioned: the undergraduate honor studies, initiated in 1890–91, and a graduate course on "Advanced Psychology," introduced in 1895–96.

The topics of the honor studies varied substantially from year to year. In 1890–91 two areas were covered: recent French psychology (Richet, *Essais de psychologie générale;*[21] Rabier, *Psychologie*),[22] and recent German psychology (Volkmann, *Lehrbuch der Psychologie*).[23] The same offerings were repeated in 1891–92 and 1892–93. In 1893–94 the topics were American psychology (James, *The Principles of Psychology*)[24] and French psychology (Paulhan, *Activité mentale*).[25] In 1894–95, and again in 1895–96, the honor studies covered three areas; American psychology (with James's *Principles* as the text), French psychology (Fouillée, *La Psychologie des idées-forces*),[26] and recent German psychology (Külpe, *Grundriss der Psychologie*).[27]

The materials for the honor studies were well chosen and represented a truly contemporary psychology. By no means was this an old-fashioned, "backwater" fare. Hill seems to have put to good use his sabbatical leave of 1888–89, preceding his assumption of the duties of president of the university in the fall of 1889.

The graduate course entitled "Advanced Psychology" was characterized as follows in the 1895–96 Annual Catalogue (p. 94): "A detailed examination of the phenomena of mental life, with an interpretation from the scientific point of view. The program followed will be the order of study indicated in Külpe's *Grundriss der Psychologie*[28] which will form the basis of the course, supplemented by constant reference to corresponding treatment in the works of Wundt, James, Sully, and Ladd."[29]

The reference in the course description to "the scientific point of view" deserves emphasis. It is reinforced by placing the works of Wilhelm Wundt, the "founding father" of experimental psychology as a discipline in its own right, at the head of the sources to be studied, in conjunction with Külpe's *Grundriss*.

After Hill had left the university, the pattern of the courses on psychology remained for a time the same, except that Hill's *Elements* was apparently replaced by another textbook. In any case, the catalogue description of "Elementary Psychology" for 1897–98 does not refer to Hill's *Elements* as the textbook. The "Advanced Psychology" shifted to James's *Principles of Psychology,* and the supplementary sources were not specified but described as "other standard treatises" (1898–99).

Thinking and Writing

This section might also be called "Teaching and Writing." Hill's principal psychological opus, his *Elements of Psychology,* was born in the context of his course on psychology at the University at Lewisburg (Bucknell) in the 1880s.

1. Hill's Publications

The National Union Catalog registers 125 entries under "Hill, David Jayne, 1850–1932."[30] A number of the entries represent new editions or reprintings, and some are essentially privately printed pamphlets and lecture notes. During his time at Lewisburg and Rochester, nine books appeared under D. J. Hill's signature:

1877 (repr. 1882, 1883, 1884, 1885) *The Science of Rhetoric.*
1878 (new eds. 1884, 1893, 1896) *The Elements of Rhetoric and Composition.*
1879 *Washington Irving,* vol. 1 of *American Authors.*
1879 *William Cullen Bryant,* vol. 2 of *American Authors.*
1883 *The Elements of Logic.*
1885 *The Principles and Fallacies of Socialism* (New York: John W. Lovell Co., no. 533, Lovell Library).
1888 *The Elements of Psychology.*
1888 (repr. 1894) *The Social Influence of Christianity, with Special Reference to Contemporary Problems* (Boston: Silver, Burdett and Co.).
1893 *Genetic Philosophy* (New York: Macmillan & Co.).

Unless noted otherwise, the books were published by Sheldon and Co., New York and Chicago. The fourth edition of *The Elements of Rhetoric and Composition,"* Hill's very popular "textbook for schools and colleges," was published in New York by Butler, Sheldon and Co., apparently in 1899. The fifth and last edition came out in 1906 under the imprint of the American Book Company, as did (in 1905) the sixth printing of Hill's first book, *The Science of Rhetoric.*

Parkman lists twelve other books by D. J. Hill, published between 1905 and 1925 and dealing with diplomacy, foreign policy, and politics.[31] In addition, some eighty "articles, pamphlets and addresses" are listed (pp. 260–66), the majority of which appeared after Hill resigned from the presidency of the University of Rochester.

Hill's *Lecture Notes on Economics and Politics* appeared in 1884 as a privately printed publication and were followed in 1885 by his *Lecture Notes on Anthropology.*[32] While this "homegrown" printed matter does not add significantly to Hill's scholarly bibliography, the *Lectures* document his broad interest in the sciences of man. Hill must have found these teaching and learning aids useful, since he continued the practice after he moved to the University of Rochester, where he had his lecture notes on ethics printed for the senior class.[33]

2. The Elements of Psychology

Hill's *Elements of Psychology* was designed as item no. 4 in the commercially highly successful series published by Sheldon and Co., of New York and Chicago, designated by the publisher as "President Hill's Text-Books." The series was not continued beyond number 4, probably owing to Hill's retirement from academe.

Puzzling Circumstances of the Birth of the "Elements"

The date on which the preface to the *Elements* was signed (p. v), 1 January 1886, is clearly misleading, since there are references (e.g., on pp. 307, 356) to

G. T. Ladd's *Physiological Psychology,* published in 1887. In addition, two versions of the title page seem to have existed. An early unsigned book review in Bucknell University's *Mirror* was published in February 1888, well before Hill's resignation from the presidency of Bucknell University.[34] Yet my copy of the book identifies the author as "President of the University of Rochester," and J. W. Fay, in *American Psychology before William James,* referred to the *Elements* as "a textbook by David Jayne Hill, then President of the University of Rochester."[35]

In the *Mirror* review of February 1888, the author is clearly identified as "David J. Hill, LL.D., President of Bucknell University." This review attests that the book was not only written but also published during Hill's presidency at Lewisburg, unless the reviewer used page proofs to prepare the review.

Content

Hill distinguished "three elemental phenomena of the soul": knowing, feeling, and acting ("volition"). Accordingly, the three parts of the book deal with three "elemental powers of the soul": intellect, sensibility, and will. Hill is careful to point out that "These powers are possessed by the same being and are exercised at the same time, so that, nothwithstanding its variety of capabilities, we must believe in the unity of the soul" (p. 8).

The term "intellect" is interpreted broadly. It covers four "classes of knowledge": (1) "presentative knowledge," consciousness, sensation (Hill's sense-perception), perception (Hill's sense-interpretation); (2) "representative knowledge," association, memory, imagination, and fantasy (including dreams and hallucinations); (3) "elaborative knowledge," conception, judgment, reasoning; (4) "constitutive knowledge," dealing with the categories of being, cause, space, and time.

Part 2, on sensibility, covers sensations ("simple sentience," appetite) and sentiments (emotion, desire, affection). "Simple sentience" refers to "feelings," particularly feelings of pleasure and pain, not to the functions of special senses, treated in Part 1. The "natural appetites" encompass hunger, thirst, suffocation, weariness, restlessness, and sexual passion.

In Part 3, the first chapter deals with involuntary actions (motor mechanism, instinctive action, and acquired action, including habits and language), while the second chapter is devoted to voluntary action ("solicitation," in the sense of "invitation to action," deliberation, and volition).

Each of the three parts closes with a section on "development": the development of intellect, of sensibility, and of will. These closing sections serve in part as vehicles for the "Summaries of Results." The developmental aspects are taken up at greater length in the 1893 volume on *Genetic Philosophy.*

Documentation

The lists of references appended to the individual sections of the book indicate clearly that the author was familiar with the literature of the field, including the most recent writings. Unfortunately, Hill does not indicate the year in which the books he cites were published, although this information is available for journal citations.

Between History and Philosophy

Throughout the book there are historical notes, at times extensive, for example, in reference to "self-consciousness" (pp. 15–19), vision, especially color-blindness (pp. 38–39), psychophysics (pp. 60–61), mind-body relation (pp. 63–65), or laws of association (pp. 70–72). In the section on the nature of concepts ("universals") the presentation of the topic under the headings of realism, nominalism, conceptualism, and relationism (pp. 141–46) is essentially historical, or more precisely, historico-philosophical, as is the discussion of the doctrine of the categories (pp. 157–58) or of the validity of reasoning (p. 162). To present-day readers, much of the section on reasoning would belong to logic rather than psychology, and much of the section on "constitutive knowledge", dealing with the concepts of being, cause, space, and time, would be regarded as metaphysics.

Between Philosophy and Science

Hill is not consistent in his view of the relation of psychology to philosophy. Traditionally—and Hill is steeped in the tradition of the Scottish "common sense" philosophy, in particular—psychological topics were discussed in the context of philosophy under the rubric of "intellectual philosophy," "mental philosophy," or "mental science." In his introduction (p. 1), Hill's view is "modern": "The term 'Psychology' has now come into general use to designate this department of study, having superseded the older and less precise designations." But these are labels. What about the substance, the "nature" of psychology?

In the preface (p. v), Hill notes that substantial information has been provided in the text about the contributions of important thinkers and writers: "The book thus serves as an introduction to the history of philosophy as well as to philosophy itself." A few pages later, in the introduction (p. 1), Hill's attitude changes dramatically: "It [psychology] is a science, not a philosophy, because it possesses the character of definite and positive knowledge derived from observation, not that of theory and speculation."

This viewpoint is expressed again in reference to the considerations of the "Relation of Soul and Body" (p. 62): "The relation between the conscious self, or soul, and the organic system, or body, is not known directly by either internal or external observation. The doctrine of their connection is theoretical, and, as such, does not belong to Psychology as a science."

Disregarding this dictum, however, Hill goes on to discuss the philosophical doctrines. He clearly favors the "dualistic realism" of the Scottish philosophers, from the time of Thomas Reid (1710–96) onward.

Hill's "bi-focal image" of psychology is symbolized clearly in the last pages of the book. While the closing section of the text is devoted to "The Immortality of the Soul," sober but supernaturalistic ("The Power that gave us being can give us also immortality," p. 372), the appendix contains twenty-three diagrams, most of which deal with the anatomy of the nervous system, the special senses, and the musculature.

Between the "Old" and the "New" Psychology

The framework and the foundations of the *Elements* is that of the Scottish, primarily Hamiltonian, mental philosophy.[36] Hill favors Sir William Hamilton's (1788–1856) threefold division of the human faculties as against the twofold scheme of the "intellectual powers" and the "active" powers, advocated by an earlier Scottish philosopher, Thomas Reid.

There is much in Hill's treatment that is old-fashioned. But there is also awareness, attested by the opening sentence of the preface (p. iii), that "although the scientific method has been only recently applied to psychological investigation, it has produced a reconstruction of the sciences relating to the nature of man."

Hill's terminological preferences would strike a present-day reader as strange and his perception of trends in word usage as puzzling. Having defined psychology as "the science of the soul, or conscious self," he writes: "The word 'soul' is . . . now more generally employed than 'mind,' which more strictly denotes the intellectual, or knowing power of the soul. The adjective 'psychical' has also largely taken the place of the more popular word 'mental' in the later and more scientific discussions" (p. 1). If these were, in fact, the changes taking place at Hill's time, they were reversed in more recent times.

To Hill, as to the majority of his contemporaries, the distinctively psychological method "consists in the analysis of consciousness, or of the interior knowing self and its states." Nevertheless, he registers the arguments against introspection brought forth by Auguste Comte (1797–1857), a French thinker, and Henry Maudsley (1834–1918), an English physiologist. More importantly, he discusses (not always approvingly) such developments as Johannes Müller's (1801–58) doctrine of the specific energy of nerves (p. 31), David Ferrier's (1843–1928) studies on the localization of special functions in the brain (p. 27), E. H. Weber's (1795–1878) two-point cutaneous thresholds (p. 34), and theories of color vision (p. 38). There is a tendency to stress the gap between "sense-impression" and "sense-knowledge," and Hill rejoices in cumulating the statements made by outstanding nineteenth-century physicists (John Tyndall), biologists (T. H. Huxley), and physiologists (Du Bois-Reymond), stressing, as did Tyndall, that "the passage from the physics of the brain to the corresponding facts of consciousness is *unthinkable*" (p. 40). Having discussed Hermann Lotze's theory of local signs and their role in the development of space perception, Hill the philosopher comments: "While these genetic hypotheses may serve to show how a knowledge of actual position is acquired by the soul, they do not remove our belief in the soul's original power of space-intuition" (p. 51).

Hill also reports studies on the speed of transmission of excitation through the nerves (p. 59), individual differences in reaction time to sensory stimuli (p. 60), observations ["alleged results," in Hill's phrasing] in the area of psychophysics (p. 60), Wilhelm Wundt's (1832–1920) concept of apperception (p. 61), Francis Galton's (1822–1911) studies of individual differences in the vividness of images (p. 85), William B. Carpenter's (1813–85), *Mental Physiology*)[37] theory of "unconscious cerebration" (p. 94), and H. A. Taine's (1828–93, *On Intelligence*)[38] physiological interpretation of memory (p. 104).

For readers interested in the time required for the acts of recognition and reproduction, Hill refers (p. 106) to specific pages in T. A. Ribot's *German Psychology of Today*,[39] Galton's *Inquiries into Human Faculty*,[40] and "an article by an American psychologist, G. Stanley Hall [1844–1924], in *Mind* for January, 1886." For "rhythm" the reader is referred to Dewey's *Psychology*, of the same vintage.[41]

Galton's *Hereditary Genius*[42] and Ribot's *Heredity*[43] are cited in the section on "The Inheritance of Intellect" (p. 218), and Charles Darwin's *Expression of the Emotions in Man and Animals*[44] is noted in the discussion of feelings, a topic characterized as "the least developed department of Psychology" and "this long-neglected province of the soul" (p. 224). Among the references (p. 240) we find also Bain's *The Emotions and the Will*[45] and his papers published in *Mind* in April and October 1884. Bain's *The Senses and the Intellect*[46] serves as a source of a theory that "states of pleasure are concomitant with an *increase;* and states of pain with an *abatement* of some, or all, vital functions" (p. 232). Darwin's views on expression of emotions are presented in detail (pp. 252, 258), as is William James's theory of "What is an emotion," published in the April 1884 issue of *Mind* (p. 254). Hill registers Edmund Gurney's critique of James's article that appeared in *Mind* in July 1884, and adds critical comments of his own, as he does in many other instances in citing the writings of other authors. For "a very full account of the emotional psychology of small children", Hill recommends (p. 278) Bernard Pérez's *The First Three Years of Childhood*,[47] but he notes a "tendency to read theories into the observed facts, many of which, without doubt, admit two or more explanations," and adds: "The dangers of inference here are similar to those in the allied realm of interpreting animal feelings" (p. 278). This comment very likely has its roots in F. M. Müller's *Science of Thought*[48] from which Hill quotes at some length, beginning with the colorful statement, "If there is a danger from Menagerie Psychology, there is still greater danger from Nursery Psychology."

Hill's call for cautious judgment is repeated in his treatment of "Habitual Expression" (p. 307). On the positive side, "Habitual feelings produce habitual expressions. The face and figure reveal the dominant feelings of the soul, and thus become indexes of the inner life. There is, therefore, a foundation for a science and art of *physiognomy*." However, Hill adds, "there is a wide opportunity for erroneous judgment in the interpretation of the character through the expression."

In discussing instincts, Hill makes use of George J. Romanes's *Mental Evolution in Animals*,[49] noting approvingly that Romanes "criticizes very minutely" the earlier writers on the subject. Hill accepts Romanes's definition of instinct as "reflex action into which there is imported the element of consciousness" and adds a sentence that would not be acceptable to the next generation of psychologists (p. 319): "All these discussions tend to show what chaos naturalists would make of Psychology if they followed a strictly objective method, without any appeal to consciousness."

In the treatment of hypnosis, Hill does not fail to cite G. S. Hall's contributions, including Hall's article on "Reaction-time in the hypnotic states," published in volume 8 (1883) of *Mind,* and notes that H. Bernheim provides "a full account of the results and the theory of hypnotic therapeutics in *De la suggestion.*"[50]

Hill acknowledges that "language is the instrument of thinking" (p. 334) and that in silent thinking in words ("intracranial speech"), "even when no outside signs such as movements of lips are given, it is probable that the internal parts of the linguistic machinery are at work." Yet he insists that "Reason is the *precondition* of rational speech" (p. 335). For the location of the speech center he refers (p. 335) to Ferrier's outstanding *Functions of the Brain.*[51] On the other hand, in the *Elements of Psychology* the traditional body-soul dualism prevails: "cerebral action is but the servant of the soul" (p. 95). Here we see clearly Hill's vacillation between traditional, philosophical psychology and the scientific study of psychological processes and their physiological foundations.

Image in the Mirror

A review of the *Elements* that appeared in the *Mirror,* a monthly publication of an Association of the Students of Bucknell University, could hardly be expected to offer a truly objective, critical assessment of the president's new book.[52] Nevertheless, the review is not without interest. Furthermore, it seems to have been the only contemporary review of the book. The *American Journal of Psychology,* founded by G. S. Hall in 1887 as the first American journal to be devoted to psychology, had just begun to appear.

The *Mirror* review begins (p. 57) by drawing the reader's attention to "the extraordinary activity, during the past few years, in the production of books relating to the nature of the mind and its activities." This was quite true. If one considers the books published within two years before and after Hill's *Elements of Psychology,* using Fay's bibliography,[53] the list is impressive:

1886	J. McCosh	*Psychology, The Cognitive Powers*
1886	B. P. Bowne	*Introduction to Psychological Theory*
1886	J. Dewey	*Psychology*
1887	G. T. Ladd	*Elements of Physiological Psychology*
1887	J. McCosh	*Psychology, The Motive Powers*
1888	D. J. Hill	*The Elements of Psychology*
1889	J. M. Baldwin	*Handbook of Psychology, vol. I: Senses and Intellect*
1889	E. C. Hewett	*Elements of Psychology*
1890	W. James	*The Principles of Psychology*

The reviewer ascribes this "mushroom growth" to two factors: (1) the increased interest among educators in the subject of psychology ("Never before in the history of education has there been so strong and wide a demand for works treating of the nature of the mind and its culture, as at present time"); (2) "The application of the scientific method to psychological investigation has necessitated a restatement of its principles."

The reviewer justly praises the book's "internal arrangements." There is a detailed table of contents at the beginning of the book, and an extensive subject-and-name index is appended. The individual units of text are short and clear in structure. Important terms are printed in large type, while materials intended for more advanced or more interested students are presented in a smaller type. Clearly, this is a textbook written by an experienced teacher, and the reviewer believed that it would be welcomed by both instructors and students. The reviewer records the practices of the time: "The student of a science needs a book in which he can prepare a lesson for the recitation in the classroom" and notes that "most books in psychology are deficient in this respect."

The reviewer had good words to say for the literary merits of the book. As to the system, he stresses the influence of Sir William Hamilton, the Scottish philosopher. Apparently Hamilton was the source of Hill's ideas concerning the basic structure of the human faculties. Hill himself notes (p. 8) that it was Hamilton "who divided the soul into (1) 'intellect,' (2) 'sensibility,' and (3) 'will'—the very same pattern that Hill follows. Similarly, there are only minor terminological differences between Hamilton's division of the phenomena of consciousness into "cognitions," "feelings," and "conations," and Hill's division of the "elemental phenomena of the soul" (p. 7) into "knowledge," "feeling," and "volition."

Finally, the reviewer notes that every section of the textbook concludes by considering the relation of psychology to education. In his judgment, teachers and parents will regard these paragraphs as the "gems of the book."

There is one point made in the review that American psychologists, brought up in the tradition of behavioral (though not necessarily behaviorist) psychology, will read with disbelief. Approving that Hill, in his treatment of the will, adhered to the introspective approach, the reviewer complains—in 1888—that "psychologists too often make only bodily manifestations the basis of their conclusions" (p. 58).

The Popularity of the Book

The Elements of Psychology constituted the fourth volume of Sheldon and Company's series "President Hill's Text-Books." *The Elements of Psychology,* limited to one edition, was less popular than the volumes on rhetoric.

The use of Hill's *Elements of Psychology* in American colleges is difficult to ascertain. However, in the *14th Annual Report of the President* of The Johns Hopkins University, George H. Emmott (asssociate professor of logic and ethics) cites it in the section dealing with Courses of Instruction, 1888–89, in the area of "Logic, Ethics, and Psychology": "During the second term Psychology was taught by Drs. E. C. Sanford and W. H. Brunham on the basis of Hill's *Psychology.* The work consisted of frequent recitations with practical lectures on such subjects as mental hygiene, memory, attention, association of ideas, feelings, and will, together with the most surely demonstrable facts in experimental Psychology."[54] Although Hill's *Elements of Psychology* clearly was not a textbook of rigorously experimental psychology, it was considered to be compatible with the experimental approach.

3. Genetic Philosophy

Genetic Philosophy was the fruit of Hill's effort to arrive at a philosophical synthesis, with "development" (genesis) as the key to the secrets of matter, life, mind, morality, religion, and the relation of the sciences to the progress of human thought. The part of the book concerned with the mind consists of chapters on the genesis of consciousness and of the three categories of psychological phenomena (feeling, thought, and will). In the section on "The Genesis of Consciousness," Hill considered the age-old problem of the relationship between "mind" and "matter."

The Genetic Method

In Hill's view, the "genetic" approach calls for the study of continuous processes, of the "phases of becoming." It aims at "unifying the aspects of being by tracing them through their various phases of change" (p. 14), at "referring every fact to its place in the series to which it belongs" (ibid.). What are the specific implications of this method for psychology?

The Genetic Approach in Hill's "Elements"

The developmental approach, stressed in *Genetic Philosophy,* was not a novel feature of Hill's psychological thought. In *The Elements of Psychology* all three parts, dealing with the "elemental powers of the soul," close with summary sections on the development of intellect (especially pp. 215–16), the development of sensibility (pp. 305–6), and the development of will (pp. 368–69). There is a difference, however, in the treatment of consciousness, which is accorded a substantial, separate chapter in *Genetic Philosophy* (pp. 100–134) but is treated briefly in the *Elements* (pp. 14–23) as one of the topics under the rubric of "Intellect."

In the *Elements* (p. 214), the "processes of knowing" are presented in what is viewed as a developmental sequence in "the progressive unfolding of the knowing power": "Sense-presentation, association of ideas, reproduction of ideas, recognition of ideas, recombination of ideas, formation of abstract ideas, judgment and reasoning are possible only as each preceding state furnishes the materials for each successive process in the development of intellectual activity" (p. 214).

To the question of whether "Intellect is gradually evolved from something that is not Intellect" (p. 215), specifically from "mere sensations" and their associations, Hill's answer is no. We must "consider its growth as the progressive manifestation of a peculiar power already latent in the soul." This view might be labeled, by analogy to the use of the term in biology, as a "preformationist theory" of the development of intellect.

In the section on "Sensibility," the presentation of different categories of "feelings" proceeds from the lower, "physical" feelings, including appetites (as "incentives to action") to the higher forms, the sentiments or "psychical feelings," such as emotions and desires. The development of sentiments is tied to intellectual growth. "The sentiments are not possible until the Intellect has a stock of ideas of which these higher forms of feeling are accompaniments" (p. 305).

"Will" is defined as "a power of the soul to direct its own activity toward ends of its own choosing" (p. 367). While both involuntary actions (reflexes, ideo-motor actions, instincts, habits) and voluntary actions are discussed, the two categories are treated as separate classes of phenomena, not as a single developmental sequence. On the other hand, the four forms of volition (attention, assent, choice, and execution) are viewed as successive stages of voluntary action.

Hill stresses that "Will, like Intelligence and Sensibility, is a primary and underived faculty" (p. 368) and that "it can not be derived from anything that is not Will" (p. 369).

Genetic Psychology in Hill's Genetic Philosophy

In *Genetic Philosophy* Hill deals with the genesis of consciousness (pp. 100–134), feeling (pp. 135–62), thought (pp. 173–201), and volition (pp. 202–31). In order to understand Hill's ideas on the genesis of consciousness, we need to familiarize ourselves with his parallelistic "model": "as parts of the brain are developed and adapted to specific uses, the correlated psychic manifestations, although not identical either with their substance or their activities, are also developed and adapted in a corresponding manner." Alfred Binet's observations, reported in his work on *The Psychic Life of Microorganisms*,[55] strengthened Hill's belief that even living cells are not "wholly devoid of psychic life" (p. 112). In the multicellular organism it is the cells of the nervous system that "have assumed and discharge the functions with which psychic phenomena are associated" (p. 117).

To Hill (p. 128), cosciousness is a complex phenomenon, not a simple state. Man is a microcosm in which the world around him mirrors itself. Different forms of energy—light, sound, impact—stimulate different sensory organs and the information is carried by afferent ("incarrying," in Hill's terminology) nerves to specific centers in the brain. The genesis of consciousness is the outcome of the pooling of "the psychic aspects of a great many cerebral cells unified through the organic unity of an organized brain" (p. 129). Hill wishes to make the point clear to the reader: "The whole significance of a nervous system consists in this, that it focuses energy in such a manner that its psychic concomitants acquire unity" (p. 129).

The chapter on the genesis of feeling opens by portraying pleasure and pain as "the psychic concomitants of organic process of development and deterioration," of advance and retreat in the adaptations of life (p. 135). Hill relates pleasure to stimulation of organs that is in harmony with their capacities, whereas pain is the result of an excessive excitation of a single organ or group of organs.

More interesting is Hill's theory centered on the role of rhythm of activities—the alternation of action and repose—in the genesis of the feelings of pleasure and pain: "All continued action becomes painful, and pleasure is conditioned upon change" (p. 138). This is clearly so when we deal with muscular activities. Hill points out, further, that "free muscular motion is accompanied with augmented pleasure when it becomes rhythmical; that is, when its variety is restrained by a pervading order which gives it unity, as in dance" (p. 139).

In more general terms Hill attempts to deal with the "sensuous elements of aesthetic pleasure" by "reducing them all to the integration and harmonization of variety with the fundamental unity of nervous rhythm" (p. 157). He examines a wide range of esthetic experiences in the areas of music, poetry (with its rhythmic components), and visual arts offering the pleasure of light, color, form, and proportion, in which the "distinct apprehension of variety in unity in the presentation of the sense . . . is carried into the realm of ideas by the operation of imagination, . . . or combining faculty" (pp. 158–59).

In discussing the genesis of thought, Hill distinguishes two categories of thought: (1) original, "presentative," perceptual, and (2) derivative, "symbolic," conceptual. The direct "presentations" (perceptions), and their equivalents in memory, are considered to be common to man and to animals. Man is not limited, however, to perceptual images: "The concepts, . . . elaborated from these elements of perception and memory, are formations of higher order, not images, but *sums* of relations" (p. 175).

Concepts are, typically, symbolized by spoken or written words. Thus "language becomes the instrument of conceptual thought" (p. 177). In this sense, Hill is ready to define conceptual thought as "intracranial speech" (p. 185). Yet he is careful to point out that "every sense, although with various degrees of excellence, may furnish a system of symbols serving the purpose of conceptual thought" (p. 187). Thus, in a broader sense, thought is a manipulation of symbols—a "symbolic activity" (p. 194). To Hill, "thought is primarily a refined reflex [reflection] of the external world" (p. 179) and the most potent impulse to thinking is "the desire to find the means of accomplishing our ends" (p. 180).

Hill's chapter on the "Will" is more philosophical than genetic and psychological. The line of development is seen as going from pleasure as a motive for action and pain as a deterrent, to "rational self-direction" (p. 227). In the process of development, man's sensibility becomes more intellectual ("cerebral") and less sensual. In Hill's words, "Such a line of development is essentially a progressive embodiment of reason in sentient life" (p. 220). When the awareness of duty becomes an effective "telic factor in volition," then "the true law of the will is not to follow the direction of least resistance but the line of greatest resistance" (p. 225).

Critical Assessment: Book Reviews

Hill's *Genetic Philosophy* was fairly widely reviewed. Parkman[56] registers seven book reviews published in 1893 and 1894, accidentally leaving out C. S. Peirce's brief but caustic account published in the *Nation* in 1894.[57] Peirce addresses himself, very critically, to Hill's incorrect reference to astronomical theory (more specifically, to the discovery of the planet Neptune) but he assures us that "there are plenty of other proofs of Dr. Hill's incompetence to treat of his subject." Peirce adds: "It is a pity, because the title of the book and those of several chapters are decidedly appetizing." The chapters that would have been "appetizing" to psychologists were the ones that we have just been discussing, since psychology responded vigorously and positively to Darwin's ideas about the evolution of man, phylogenetic as well as ontogenetic.

Surprisingly, the review of the book in the *American Journal of Psychology* emphasizes the philosophical rather than the psychological issues.[58] The reviewer concludes: "The trouble with a 'genetic philosophy' is apt to be that, as long as it is genetic, it is not philosophy, and as soon as it becomes philosophical, it becomes uncritical and superficial" (p. 310). The psychological considerations are limited to Hill's view of the genesis of a personal being as consisting "in the concentration and unification of preexisting isolated, unconscious psychic elements . . . into a conscious individual" (*Genetic Philosophy,* p. 128). To this the reviewer responds: "What these unconscious psychic elements are, or how he knows that they exist at all, or how the organic unity of the brain can turn them into a consciousness, the author does not explain" (p. 310).

Comment

In contrast to *The Elements of Psychology,* provided with copious references to the literature, the psychological section of *Genetic Philosophy* contains only a handful of references in a text of 131 pages. There are no references at all in the chapter on "The Genesis of Thought" (pp. 173–201).

Two works by Italian anthropologists, dealing directly with the topic of "psychogenesis," are cited. The first is P. Siciliani's *Psychogénie moderne,*[59] which is cited (pp. 112–13) in support of Hill's criticism of Herbert Spencer's "synthetic psychology," which endeavored to reconstruct the evolution of the mind starting with reflex activities. The second, *L'Origine dei fenomeni psichici,* by G. Sergi,[60] sustains a "functionalist" thesis, sympathetic to Hill, that "consciousness is a means of protection to a living organism" (p. 206).

The terminology used in the text is sometimes confusing for a present-day reader. For instance, Hill uses the term *neurosis* as equivalent to "organic phenomena" (activity of the nervous system), and *psychosis* designates mental phenomena (p. 101). Only when a reader can translate these terms into more familiar ones will he read with understanding Hill's statement that "While it may be said that every psychosis [i.e., mental activity] is accompanied by a correlated neurosis [neural activity], it can not be maintained that every neural change is attended with consciousness" (p. 102).

4. From Dualism toward Monism

We shall endeavor to trace the development of Hill's views on the mind-body problem from his extensive review, in 1881, of a part of G. H. Lewes's *Problems of Life and Mind,*[61] through his *Elements of Psychology* (1888), to his *Genetic Philosophy* of 1893, in which he touched repeatedly on this issue.

Hill's Critique of the View of G. H. Lewes

Hill points out that his purpose in reviewing Lewes's book is "to state and criticize its assumptions and its inferences" (p. 1), and he rejects Lewes's fundamental thesis that "our psychical [read: mental] activity is the expression of the action of the external medium on the organism and the reaction of the organism."[62]

We shall not pursue Hill's argumentation but cannot resist asking: If one could trace in full the history of Hill's "scientific monism," formulated in *Genetic Philosophy,* would the thread not lead back eventually to G. H. Lewes?

The Dualisms of "The Elements of Psychology"

In the *Elements,* Hill's position on the issue of mind-body relations is that of "dualistic realism":

> Dualistic Realism . . . rests upon the clear apprehensions of the soul by Self-consciousness and of the body by Sense-perception as two modes being so unconvertible in thought and antithetical in attributes that we are obliged to regard them as *two* different, but real, substances, whose relation is established in the psychophysical unity of our being, but in a manner unknown to us. (p. 63).

This is the position held by the Scottish school of "common sense," initiated by Thomas Reid in the 1700s and still flourishing in America in Hill's days, where James McCosh, president of Princeton University, and Noah Porter, president of Yale University, were the standard-bearers of Scottish mental philosophy. The fourth edition of Porter's *Human Intellect*[63] came out almost simultaneously with Hill's *Elements.*

Hill praises Dualistic Realism for having "the advantage of adherence to facts and the rejection of arbitrary or mystical hypotheses"; he adds that "It also avoids a metaphysical, or abstract, conception of either mind or matter, rather regarding both as concrete realities" (*Elements,* p. 64).

Later on, Hill states confidently that activity of the mind is *always* accompanied by activity of the brain and that "states of brain at all times affect and sometimes determine states of mind" (p. 89). He stresses that brain and intellect develop together: "As the brain of a child grows, Intellect increases; when the brain is injured or diseased, the functions of the Intellect are impeded, when health is restored to the brain, the vigor of Intellect is regained" (p. 216).

Nevertheless, Hill does point out that the parallelism is not absolute and should not be interpreted as a causal relationship: "The parallelism is not closer than that between the fine workmanship and superior tools,—which certainly does not prove that the tools do the work" (p. 217).

The traditional dualism of body and soul retains the upper hand: "cerebral action is but a servant of the soul" (p. 95).

Hill's Response to C. L. Morgan's Concept of "Metakinesis"

G. S. Lewes had stimulated Hill but had not convinced him. Much more influential was Hill's later intellectual encounter with C. L. Morgan, the author of *Animal Life and Intelligence* (1890)[64] and originator of the theory of "metakinesis." Morgan is introduced to the readers of *Genetic Philosophy* as "a scientific writer of highly accredited authority, Professor Lloyd Morgan, of Bristol" (p. 126). His views are cited by Hill *in extenso* (pp. 126–27). Morgan uses the term *kinesis* and *kinetic* for physical phenomena (including those we call physiological phenomena), interpretable in terms of known forms of energy.[65] He refers to psychological phenomena, closely associated with the activity of the nerve centers in the brain, as "metakinetic"; the term *metakinesis* designates all psychological phenomena. According to Morgan's monistic hypothesis: "When the kinetic manifestations assume the form of the molecular processes in the brain, the metakinetic manifestations assume the form of human consciousness."

Morgan notes that "all matter is not conscious, because consciousness is the metakinetic concomitant of a highly specialized order of kinesis." Phrased in the evolutionary framework, "parallel to the evolution of organic and neural kinesis there has been an evolution of metakinetic manifestations culminating in conscious thought."

In *Genetic Philosophy* Hill rejects the traditional dualism of mind and matter, and stresses their "real unity" (p. 363). To him, the ancient dualism "consists in the abstraction of the concretely coexisting qualities from their real unity and regarding them as if they were separately real. One of these is 'consciousness,' which is floated off and hypostasised as 'mind'; the other is the 'objects-of-consciousness,' which are hypostasised as 'matter.'" Hill's monism stresses the unity of conscious mind and the living body, a "concrete unity" that presents a "double appearance" (p. 364). The progression from traditional dualism via dualistic realism to "monistic realism" (p. 129) is an expression of Hill's search for a "realistic" view of the world.

Hill's concrete unity is a unity of two "modes of experience": "If we seek in our experience for the unity of both the psychic and the physical elements, we seem to find it in the concrete experience of 'will,' which is logical and dynamical at the same time, 'mind' as conscious direction of energy, 'matter' as energy directed and working material changes." (p. 363).

In addressing himself to "objections to monism," Hill elaborates the idea of will as the "concrete experience of energy consciously exercised": "In this there is the complete concrete unity of 'mind' as percipient and of 'matter' as operant. One and the same being at the same time knows and acts. Here, then, is a conscious being modifying objects" (p. 365).

Hill protects himself against possible accusations of materialism by asking a rhetorical question, "Why not say that the unity is found in 'matter'?", and by answering that this would be a "one-sided identification," a "putting of a part in place of the whole" (p. 364). To Hill, "The materialistic view, that matter becomes conscious without containing psychic elements, is an assumption without proof and without logical consistency" (p. 129).

Sympathetic to N. S. Shaler's concept *(The Interpretation of Nature)*[66] of the "soul-bearing capacity of matter" (p. 132), Hill postulates the presence of both physical and mental ("psychic") properties throughout the animal world, down to the "universal organic unit," the living cell.

Hill's monism remains dualistic in its essence: "The genesis of a personal being consists, then, not in the transmutation of physical forces into psychic states . . . but in the concentration and unification of preëxisting elements, which in their isolation are unconscious, into a conscious individual" (p. 128). Hill's emphasis on the concrete unity of man was a step in the right direction, but it remains light years away from the current view of psychology as the study of the activities of organisms that develop through genetically controlled maturation and through interaction with the sociocultural environment. It is in *this sense* that mental activities of the human organism can *not* be viewed as a "mere function of the nervous system," a "direct product of the brain." The concept of genuine "psychogenesis" remains foreign to Hill.

Applying Psychology

In Hill's time there existed no "applied psychology" in the modern sense, although phrenology partly fulfilled that function in America.[67] Yet, in the preface to his *Elements of Psychology* (p. v), Hill points out that "special pains have been taken to apply the principles of Psychology to the practical problems of Education, in the hope that the value of the book might thus be enhanced for those who contemplate teaching as a profession."

Hill returns to the relation of psychology to education in the introduction (pp. 3–4), where he makes two related points: first, the theory of teaching begins in psychology ("Whoever understands the science of the soul possesses the fundamental principles of the science of education"), and second, the study of psychology is essential to a preparation for teaching ("Pedagogics is, in reality, little more than applied Psychology") although "experience alone can furnish the corresponding art."

Concern with the implication of psychological concepts for education is present throughout Hill's textbook in the form of special sections at the ends of chapters dealing with self-consciousness (p. 23), sense perception (p. 65), association (p. 80), fantasy (p. 89), memory (p. 111), imagination (p. 139), concept formation (p. 168), judging ("the process of asserting agreement or disagreement of the differences between ideas," p. 159), reasoning (p. 169), sensation (p. 238), appetite (p. 247), emotion (p. 274, with special reference to the training of children, treatment of the learner, the influences of the environment and of instruction, and the effect of practice), desire (p. 289), affection (p. 301), motor mechanisms (p. 317), instinct (p. 323), habit (p. 337), motivation ("solicitation," p. 345), deliberation (concerning ends, means, and timing of an action, p. 354), and volition (p. 364).

Hill endeavored to "apply the principles of Psychology" in a variety of practical contexts. In what may have been his first formal publication, he used the principles of psychology in analyzing the conflict between the disciplinarian and the utilitarian philosophies of education.[68] Whereas the disciplinarians "think of education as a mere preparation for any kind of intellectual labors," the utilitarians stress that acquisition of knowledge that is "directly tributary to the practical purposes in life." The disciplinarian theory is based on a particular view of the nature of man's mind. Specifically, it is "the outgrowth of a metaphysical analysis of the powers and modes of action of the human mind. It proceeds upon the postulate that a discriminating, organizing, creative faculty is more valuable than a mass of data without the power of emphasizing it for high ends."

What term could have a more "applied" flavor than *efficiency,* used prominently in Hill's address to the students of the Crozer Seminary in 1884?[69] True, notes Hill, the productivity of the great artists, poets, and composers is an unsolved problem; the secret of genius "is hidden from critical analysis in the penetralia of human personality" (p. 47). And yet, Hill goes on, it is not emancipated from the laws of the human mind that pertain to knowing, feeling, and acting: "Possibly it consists largely in a clearer apprehension of those laws, either because of a larger endowment of native intuition, or because of a more patient and steadfast gaze into the luminous spaces whence inspiration comes" (ibid.).

Hill's central point is that, for the theologians, "general study is the *conditio sine qua non* of all successful special study" (p. 48), and he spells out the implications to a minister's efficiency as a man, as a pastor, and as a preacher.

In a substantial pamphlet, of unknown vintage, Hill addresses himself to the ability to perform—the "executive faculty" in man—without referring to a particular occupational setting.[70] In the psychological parts of the essay, followed by philosophical analysis of the "probable relation between the forces within and the forces without," the author approaches the topic from two points of view: "that of subjective analysis, summarizing the facts that lie open to consciousness," and "that of objective observation, bringing into recognition the facts of physics and physiology that bear upon man's activity" (p. 2). More concretely, the second approach includes "an examination of the organic mechanism through which our acts are executed, and the consideration of habit, instinct, cerebration and sleep" (p. 10). The treatment closely resembles the discussion of the relevant topics and the terminology found in Hill's *Elements of Psychology.*

Synopsis

The present account is an exploration of one facet of Hill's manifold activities, that concerning psychology. J. W. Fay, author of *American Psychology before William James,*[71] has some good words for Hill's *Elements* but classifies it unequivocally: "The year 1886 marks the definite end of the old psychology. After the last expiring glow, a tiny but luminous flicker was emitted by 'The Elements of Psychology,' a textbook by David Jayne Hill."[72]

This tends to put Hill summarily, and, we believe, unfairly in the category of "old psychology." To us, he is a figure marking the transition between the old and the new. As a college teacher, he replaced the approach calling for student recitations by one using vivid lectures. During Hill's presidency at Lewisburg, a distinct change in terminology occurred. While the 1879–80 catalogue of the university still referred to "Mental Philosophy," the course Hill taught from 1880–81 to 1887–88 was labeled "Psychology."

More importantly, in terms of the national (and international) scene, while Hill began his teaching career at Lewisburg in 1879–80 as professor of metaphysics and moral philosophy, from the fall of 1881 onward his academic title was professor of psychology and ethics. This was apparently the earliest professorship of psychology in the United States.

Hill continued to be innovative in teaching when he came to the University of Rochester in 1889. He not only added a course on "Physiological Psychology," and later (in 1895) a graduate course on "Advanced psychology," but also offered honor courses in which students were introduced to contemporary European and American psychology. Hill's *Genetic Philosophy,* in which substantial attention was given to psychology, appeared in print in 1893.

Hill's resignation from the presidency of the University of Rochester, in 1896, marks the end of his involvement in academic psychology. The period of his active concern with psychology coincided with profound changes in the psychological scene, in America and in Europe, symbolized by the establishment of Wilhelm Wundt's research laboratory in Leipzig (usually dated as the fall semester of 1879).

As R. I. Watson reminds us, "Before the 1880s, there were in the United States only two major psychological traditions—phrenology and Scottish mental philosophy." Between 1880 and 1895, psychology in the United States "was transformed in a dramatic fashion. By 1895 there were twenty-four psychology laboratories, three journals, and a flourishing scientific society, many of whose members were full-time psychologists. Only fifteen years before, none of this existed. The new psychology had obviously arrived."[73]

Hill did not play an active role in these developments, but he was aware of them. In his writings and, even more, in his teaching, especially in his honor courses and his graduate course on advanced psychology, he familiarized the students with the best of contemporary psychological thought.

ACKNOWLEDGMENTS

I wish to thank Mrs. Barbara Winslow for making readily available the materials held in the archives of Bucknell University. Effective use of the archival treasures relevant to the life and work of David Jayne Hill was greatly facilitated by Mr. Karl Kabelac, librarian in the Department of Rare Books, Manuscripts and Archives of the University of Rochester Library. Mrs. Eunice Brožek shared in the labors of distilling the essential information from a large volume of potentially useful printed, typed, and handwritten material, and the final manuscript was typed by Margaret Maria (Brožek) Caliandro.

NOTES

1. J. Orin Olifant, *The Rise of Bucknell University* (New York: Appleton-Century-Crofts, 1965), sp. chap. 6, "Reorganization and Revival," pp. 137–63. The chapter covers the events from D. J. iill's election to the presidency of the University at Lewisburg to his resignation in July 1888.

2. Arthur J. May, *A History of the University of Rochester, 1850–1962* (Rochester, N.Y.: University f Rochester, 1977), "The Hill Decade," pp. 91–112.

3. Aubrey Parkman, *David Jayne Hill and the Problem of World Peace* (Lewisburg, Pa.: Bucknell niversity Press, 1975).

4. David Jayne Hill, "As It Seemed to Me: Confidences Regarding the Inner and Outer Phases of a 'aried Life," Alternate title: "Confidences of a Grandfather." Hill Collection, the Archives, Bucknell Iniversity Library. An unpublished autobiography ending with Hill's resignation from the presidency f the University of Rochester in 1896.

5. David Jayne Hill, *The Elements of Psychology* (New York and Chicago: Sheldon and Co., 1888).

6. David Jayne Hill, *Genetic Philosophy* (New York and London: Macmillan and Co., 1893).

7. "David Jayne Hill" (an obituary notice), *Rochester Alumni Review* 10 (March 1932): 69.

8. In D. J. Hill's times, the short term *"Apology"* was used widely to designate Joseph Butler's *The nalogy of Religion, Natural and Revealed, to the Constitution and Course of Nature* (London: ames, John and Paul Knapton, 1736). It was one of the most popular books of Christian apologetics in he English language.
Among the many reprintings of the work are those by J. B. Lippincott in Philadelphia (1870) and by Iarper and Brothers in New York (1872).

9. *Twenty-second Annual Catalogue of Officers and Students in the University at Lewisburg, Penn-ylvania, 1871–1872* (Lewisburg, Pa.: Printed for the University), p. 20.

10. "The University at Lewisburg," *College Herald* 10, no. 4 (April 1880).

11. Anonymous paragraph in the *University Mirror* (October 1882), p. 8.

12. Probably a reference to *The Human Intellect, with an Introduction upon Psychology and the ioul* (New York: Scribner, 1868, and later editions; 4th ed., 1887) by Noah Porter, president of Yale Jniversity and a major exponent of Scottish mental philosophy in the United States.

13. "Editorial," *University Mirror* (June 1888), p. 117.

14. Parkman, *David Jayne Hill*, p. 35.

15. Annual Catalogue of the Officers and Students of the University of Rochester. Published by the Jniversity. The specific volumes, cited in the text, are identified by year.

16. Wilhelm Wundt, *Grundzüge der physiologischen Psychologie* (Leipzig: Engelmann), 1st ed., in ! vols., 1873–74; 2d ed., 1880; 3d ed., 1887.

17. Giuseppe Sergi, *La psychologie physiologique* (Paris: Alcan, 1888). Trans. from the Italian.

18. George Trumbull Ladd, *Elements of Physiological Psychology* (New York: C. Scribner's Sons, 887). There were frequent later editions.

19. Gustav Albert Schwalbe, *Lehrbuch der Anatomie der Sinnesorgane* (Erlangen: Besold, 1883).

20. Ludwig Edinger, *Zwölf Vorlesungen über den Bau der nervösen Centralorgane* (Leipzig: Vogel), 2d ed., 1889; 3d ed., 1892.

21. Charles R. Richet, *Essais de psychologie générale* (Paris: Alcan, 1887), 2d ed., 1891.

22. Élie Rabier, *Leçons de philosophie*, 4th ed., P. 1. Psychologie (Paris: Hachette, 1893).

23. Wilhelm Volkmann, *Lehrbuch der Psychologie vom Standpunkte der Realismus und nach genetischer Methode*, 3d. ed. of the *Grundriss der Psychologie*, ed. by C. S. Cornelius (Cöthen: Schulze, 1884–85).

24. William James, *The Principles of Psychology* (New York: Holt, 1890).

25. Frédéric Paulhan, *Activité mentale et les éléments de l'esprit* (Paris: Alcan, 1889).

26. Alfred Fouillée, *La psychologie des idées-forces* (Paris: Alcan, 1893).

27. Oswald Külpe, *Grundriss der Psychologie* (Leipzig: Engelmann, 1893).

28. Ibid.

29. Annual Catalogue . . . of the University of Rochester; William James, *The Principles of Psychol-ogy;* James Sully, *Outlines of Psychology* (New York: Appleton, 1885 and later eds.; 1st ed., London, 884); G. T. Ladd, *Elements of Physiological Psychology*.

30. Library of Congress and American Library Association, comps., *The National Union Catalog, Pre-1956 Imprints*, vol. 245, items NH 0367518-0367643, "Hill, David Jayne, 1850–1932" (London: Mansell, 1973).

31. Parkman, *David Jayne Hill*, p. 260.

32. David Jayne Hill, *Lecture Notes on Economics and Politics* (Lewisburg, Pa.: The University, 1884), 76 pp.; idem, *Lecture Notes on Anthropology* (Lewisburg, Pa.: The University, 1885), 92 pp.

33. David Jayne Hill, *Lecture Notes on Ethics* (Rochester, N.Y.: Printed for the senior class, 1891). 62 pp.

34. "A New Book," [Bucknell] *University Mirror* 7, no. 5 (February 1888): 57–58.

35. Jay Wharton Fay, *American Psychology before William James* (New Brunswick, N.J.: Rutgers University Press, 1939), p. 167.

36. Sir William Hamilton is the author of *Lectures on Metaphysics and Logic*, ed. by H. L. Manse and John Veitch (Edinburgh and London: Blackwood, 1859–60, and later editions, including New York: Sheldon, 1878, 1880).

37. William B. Carpenter, *Principles of Mental Physiology* (New York: Appleton, 1864, and later editions, incl. 1883, 1886).

38. Hippolyte A. Taine, *On Intelligence* (New York: Holt, 1884). Trans. from the French.

39. Théodule A. Ribot, *German Psychology of Today, the Empirical School* (New York: C. Scribner's Sons, 1886). Trans. from the 2d French ed.

40. Francis Galton, *Inquiries into the Human Faculty and Its Development* (New York: Macmillan, 1883; also 1885).

41. John Dewey, *Psychology* (New York: Harper, 1886).

42. Francis Galton, *Hereditary Genius: An Inquiry into Its Laws and Consequences* (New York: Appleton, 1870; rev. ed., 1884).

43. Théodule A. Ribot, *Heredity: A Psychological Study of its Phenomena, Laws, Causes, and Consequences* (New York: Appleton, 1875; also 1884). Trans. from the French.

44. Charles Darwin, *The Expression of the Emotions in Man and Animals* (New York: Appleton, 1873).

45. Alexander Bain, *The Emotions and the Will* (New York: Appleton, 1867; 3d ed., 1876 and 1886; first London ed., 1859).

46. Alexander Bain, *The Senses and the Intellect* (New York: Appleton, 3d ed. 1874, 1879, 1883, 1885; first London ed., 1855).

47. Bernard Pérez, *The First Three Years of Childhood*, ed. and trans. from French by A. M. Christie (London: Sonnenschein & Co., 1885; 1st French ed., 1878).

48. Friedrich Max Müller, *Science of Thought* (New York: C. Scribner's Sons, 1887; reprint ed., New York: AMS Press, 1978).

49. George J. Romanes, *Mental Evolution in Animals* (New York: Appleton, 1884).

50. Hippolyte Bernheim, *De la suggestion et de ses applications à la thérapeutique* (Paris: Doin, 1886).

51. Sir David Ferrier, *The Functions of the Brain* (New York: G. P. Putnam's Sons, 1876; 2d ed., 1886).

52. "A New Book," [Bucknell] *University Mirror* 7, no. 5 (February 1888): 57–58.

53. Fay, *American Psychology before William James*, pp. 225–26.

54. *Fourteenth Annual Report of the President* (Baltimore, Md.: Johns Hopkins University, 1889), pp. 60–61.

55. Alfred Binet, *The Psychic Life of Microorganisms: A Study in Experimental Psychology* (Chicago: Open Court, 1882, 1889, and later editions). Trans. from the French.

56. Parkman, *David Jayne Hill*, p. 266.

57. (C. S. Peirce), book review of D. J. Hill's "Genetic Philosophy," *Nation* 58 (1894): 278.

58. H. A. A. Review of D. J. Hill's "Genetic Philosophy," *American Journal of Psychology* 6 (1893): 309–10.

59. Pietro Siciliani, *Prolegomènes à la psychogénie moderne* (Paris: Baillière, 1880). Trans. from the Italian.

60. Giuseppe Sergi, *L'origine dei fenomeni psichici e il loro significato biologico* (Milan: Dunnbard, 1885).

61. George Henry Lewes, *Problems of Life and Mind*, 3d ser. (Boston: Houghton, Osgood and Co., 1880). Of special relevance for Hill's purposes was problem 2, "Mind as a Function of the Organism."

62. David Jayne Hill, "Organization and personality," a review of *Problems of Life and Mind* by G. H. Lewes (Third Series), *Baptist Review* 3 (January–March 1881): 1–17.

63. Noah Porter, *The Human Intellect*, 4th ed., 1887.

64. C. Lloyd Morgan, *Animal Life and Intelligence* (Boston: Ginn & Co., 1891).

65. Ibid., p. 467.

66. Nathaniel Southgate Shaler, *The Interpretation of Nature* (Boston and New York: Houghton Mifflin, 1893).

67. Johann Kaspar Spurzheim, *Phrenology; or, The Doctrine of the Human Mind* (Philadelphia: Lippincott, 1825). O. S. Fowler, *Human Science of Phrenology* (Philadelphia: National Publishing, 1873).

68. D(avid) J(ayne) H(ill), "The elective system," *College Herald* 5, no. 8 (February 1875): 57–58.

69. David Jayne Hill, "The relation of general study to ministerial efficiency," *University Mirror* (Univ. at Lewisburg) 3, no. 4 (January 1884): 47–55.

70. David Jayne Hill, *The Executive Faculty in Man*. A privately printed pamphlet, with no place or date shown. 25 pp. It is not registered by Aubrey Parkman, *David Jayne Hill,* in his list of "Articles, Pamphlets and Addresses of David Jayne Hill," pp. 260–66.

71. Fay, *American Psychology before William James,* p. 167.

72. The date refers to the work of James McCosh (president of Princeton University from 1870 to 1892), *Psychology: The Cognitive Powers* (New York: Scribner, 1886), followed by the second volume, *The Motive Powers* (Scribner, 1887).

William James's Psychology of Will: Its Revolutionary Impact on American Psychology

WILLIAM R. WOODWARD

University of New Hampshire

But the whole modern impact of James' luminous contribution is in danger of being deflected to this one metaphysical issue, the issue of the meaning of freedom, while his rich, beautiful, and very modern conception of how the will actually operates has been almost forgotten. I believe that to an empirically oriented historian of psychology, and in particular one who is interested in contemporary research, there are very few ideas as fundamental and valuable as the full working conception that James developed regarding the nature of voluntary processes.[1]

In 1971, Gardner Murphy emphasized the central importance of William James's psychology of will to the development of American experimental and clinical psychology. Yet the implication of a 1960 symposium, "Whatever happened to Will in American Psychology?" is that the term disappeared in this century.[2] A problem is posed herewith for the historian of psychology. The fact is that the term *will* did virtually disappear; certainly textbooks no longer lead up to a discussion of will, volition, or character, as did those of James, Baldwin, and Ladd. New terms such as *purposive behaviorism* and *existential therapy* should remind us, however, that the problem of accounting for voluntary action remains just as central as it always has been. Disciplinary boundaries and specialty knowledge need not be allowed to obscure the basic, underlying identity of issues as fundamental as the *psychological* explanation of freedom. History records that William James's psychology of will was prominently referred to by the founders of modern American psychology until at least 1910. Since then, his formulation has received a continuing, though often overlooked, development in a broad spectrum of fields of psychology

William James's Psychology of Will

William James (1842–1910) was in the midst of a personal "crisis of will" when he wrote to his father in 1869 that he was convinced of the universal sway of determinism. A year later, in 1870, having read Charles Renouvier's *Psychologie rationelle,* he asserted that his first act of free will would be to believe in free will itself.[3] James's vacillation between scientific determinism and existential choice was typical of the New Psychology of the late nineteenth century, with moral philosophy and physiological psychology as its dual heritage. The problem of reconciling free will and determinism found its sharpest expression in the consideration of will in relation to reflex neurology.

During the years 1870 to 1890, James wove his theory of will from five major strands, which will be separately considered in the first part of this chapter: habit and ideo-motor action, fiat as inhibition and consent, interested attention, a refutation of feelings of innervation, and a functional reinterpretation of the Meynert scheme. He maintained the "moral" element of choice by fiat and interest, while severely restricting choice to the "feeling of effort" in holding one idea in attention. The vast majority of actions did not require such effort, being automatic or ideo-motor in nature. Thus, James argued paradoxically that will is a relation among ideas, yet most actions are reflexive. By 1890 the theory was a connecting theme throughout the *Principles of Psychology,* combining a critique of the "structuralist" assumption that the association of ideas parallels the association of reflexes with a proposal for a "functionalist" interaction of ideas and reflexes.

The complexity of James's theory is mirrored in the divergent responses to it, as treated in the second part of this chapter. Beyond his negative critique of the prevailing theories of automatic action and will, James provided a positive program for the further investigation of a wide range of problems, from attention through the production of movement. In the two decades after the *Principles* few psychological theoreticians would leave his statement unacknowledged. In present-day terms, he addressed issues of habit-formation, drive, and imitation as they came to be known in learning, motivation, and cognitive psychology. In addition, the concepts of functional autonomy, attitude, and moral therapy became important in the fields of personality, social psychlogy, and psychotherapy. This essay examines the origin, the development, and the echoes of William James's psychology of will.

Habit and Ideo-Motor Action

As a young man in the 1870s, William James sought to assuage doubts raised by the "scientific naturalism" of his day.[4] His search for a consistent moral philosophy was common to many Victorian scientists and men of letters. Among the scientists, many held an outmoded dualism in which will controlled automatic action. For example, William B. Carpenter's *Principles of Human Physiology* was the textbook for the first course James taught in 1872.[5] James was both impressed and dissatisfied with Carpenter's defense of psychological causation against the physical causation upheld by proponents of the Human Automaton Theory, such as Herbert Spencer, William B. Clifford, and Thomas H. Huxley.[6]

James adopted Carpenter's conception of ideo-motor action for the more automatic side of volitional activity, while reserving Renouvier and Hermann Lotze for guides on the more voluntary aspects. In James's words, "whenever movement follows *unhesitatingly and immediately* the notion of it in the mind we have ideo-motor action."[7] In piano playing, for example, habits are formed which are ideo-motor in nature: they simplify the movements required, and they diminish the conscious attention with which our acts are performed (Figure 1). Thus, letting

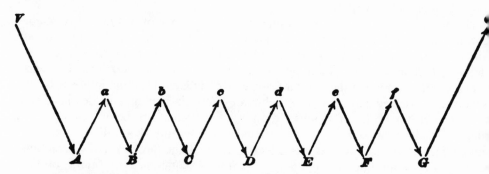

Figure 1. Piano-playing habit as ideo-motor action, with volition V *leading to ideational effect* G' *via sensations* a *through* f *and muscular contractions* A *through* G. (*From William James,* Principles of Psychology, 2 vols. [*New York: Henry Holt & Co., 1890*], *1: 116.*)

V = the volition, and A, B, C, D, E, F, and G, the habitual chain of muscular contractions in touching the keyboard, while a, b, c, d, e, and f are their respective sensations of sight, sound, and kinesthesis, we see that a volition sets off a reflex chain ending in movement G, which gives rise to the ideational effect, G'.[8] Numerous ethical maxims were derived from this ideo-motor model, such as that we ought "to make our nervous system our ally instead of our enemy" and "to seize the very first opportunity to act on every resolution that [we] make."[9]

James's favorite example was the experience which he says convinced him of the phenomenon.[10] He was lying in bed on a freezing morning, torn between getting up in a cold room and remaining in a warm bed. Suddenly he realized that he had made the choice and was in the process of dressing. Once the inhibiting idea of staying in bed disappeared, the other idea gave rise to action.

James's appropriation of the concept of ideo-motor action as the basis for volition was theoretically significant in that it did not directly involve pleasure or pain. The stimulus initiating the action was the "idea of the end" of getting up, the so-called "anticipatory image," bereft of hedonistic feelings. In James's theory of emotion, which is exactly parallel to his theory of will, the sight of the bear precipitates our running away. This ideo-motor event is followed by the afferent flux of nervous impulses perceived as fear.[11]

Fiat as Inhibition and Consent

Second only to ideo-motor action in the conceptual development of James's psychology of will was the concept of fiat, or consent. When James first introduced courses on physiological psychology in Harvard's Department of Philosophy (with a graduate course in 1875–76 and an undergraduate one in 1876–77), he went beyond Carpenter's ideo-motor theory by drawing upon Renouvier's suggestion of fiat as effortful consent.[12] Fiat meant literally "let it be"—an expression of voluntary submission to a course of action involuntarily carried out.

In 1875 James's textbook was Herbert Spencer's *Principles of Psychology,* in the second edition of 1871, with its philosophy that determinism prevails from the lowest inorganic forces to the highest forms of human reasoning.[13] James formulated the theme of his course as a challenge to Spencer's thesis: "Can actions accompanied by intelligence be conceived under the form of reflex action?"[14] Although he answered in the affirmative, and thus subsumed will under the reflex conception of consciousness, he held out against universal determinism in the mental realm.

James was unwilling to capitulate to the "Automaton Theory" of Herbert Spencer, and he drew from Renouvier his chief argument against it.[15] Spencer had affirmed that conscious life is predetermined by physical evolution. James applauded his consistent adherence to a single factor, the association of ideas, in mental evolution. Against this doctrine, wrote Renouvier, the "reinforcement" of one idea and the "inhibition" of another precipitates an "act." This constitutes a decision for the future, a new beginning.[16]

To James, this was the crack in the door of determinism that allowed for will. Will is that degree of intensity, unknown beforehand, in which one series of phenomena "excludes other series which were previously possible."[17] To the sailor lying exhausted on the deck, and facing the necessity of manning the pumps, it is the fiat which says "let it be the reality"—whereupon he saves the ship.[18] To the insomniac counting sheep, or to the person in the dentist's chair facing pain, the decision to ignore distracting thoughts requires not a muscular effort but a mental one exactly proportionate to the discomfort or pain. "To sustain a representation, to think, is what requires the effort, and is the true moral act."[19] The fiat, then, is the mental act of consent which clears the way for ideo-motor action by inhibiting antagonistic impulses. Consciousness may be reflex in nature, as the ideo-motor action of ideas, and yet amenable to voluntary inhibition.[20]

Subjective Interest and Attention

Thus, in James's view, will is largely determined by the reflex character of ideo-motor action. Yet it is instrumental in the making of a choice. In brief, "the stable survival of one representation is called a volition."[21] Notice the allusion to survival. As mentioned above, James's textbook during the middle 1870s was Spencer's *Principles of Psychology,* with its evolutionary assumption that mind is a product of matter through "correspondence" or "adjustment of inner to outer relations."[22] Examples included the reactions of the polyp, the storing of food by an animal, and even the astronomical observations of a human—in each case those reactions survive which benefit the organism, and those die which are useless.[23]

The link between psychological and biological evolution came through the feelings. In Spencer's words,

> . . . those races of beings only can have survived in which, on the average agreeable or desired feelings went along with activities conducive to the maintenance of life, while disagreeable and habitually-avoided feelings went along with activities directly or indirectly destructive of life; and there must ever have been, other things equal, the most numerous and long-continued survival among the races in which these adjustments of feelings to actions were the best tending ever to bring about perfect adjustment.[24]

James attacked Spencer's proclamation of determinism for being teleological despite the pretence of "correspondence." Thus, for Spencer, pleasure was the feeling which we try to obtain, and pain the feeling we try to avoid—a crude unacknowledged teleology that left no room for moderation, choice, or will. In his 1878 "Remarks on Spencer's Definition of Mind as Correspondence," James accused Spencer of confusing external teleology with internal teleology. In this case the polyp and the human may well exemplify external purposes of survival in some behaviors, yet the mind may have other internal ideal ends than feelings of pleasure or pain and of survival. Mind "not only serves a final purpose, but brings a final purpose—posits, declares it."[25] James concluded that Spencer's hedonism ignores the subjective interests by which we "adjust." Wrote James: "How much of our life is occupied with this better or worse?"[26] To laugh, to cry, to act on behalf of a neighbor—each involved judgments of the ideal beyond mere judgments of fact.

This became James's critique of pleasure and pain in his chapter on will in 1890. Impulsive ideas start our actions, pleasures and pains modify and guide them, and interests select them. From Hermann Lotze he took the crucial idea, penciled into the flyleaf of his copy of the *Medizinische Psychologie* during 1867–68, of "emotions due to bodily reverberation, #438."[27] The "springs of action" for James included the entire spectrum of behavior: "I do not breathe for the pleasure of the breathing, but simply find that I am breathing. . . . Who will pretend that when he idly fingers his knife-handle at the table, it is for the sake of any pleasure it gives him, or pain which he thereby avoids."[28] Broader than pleasure and pain theory yet subsuming it, was the concept of interest whereby some ideas survive in consciousness and others disappear.

James's theory of will is thus thoroughly purposive, and yet ideo-motor action seemed quite deterministic. This raises the question how he joined the two apparently contradictory theoretical components. It is now clear that interest linked automatic action with choice through attention. Summing up in his penultimate chapter in 1890, James wrote in 1890 that "this is what we have seen in instinct, in emotion, in common ideo-motor action, in hypnotic suggestion, in morbid impul sion, and *voluntas invita*—the impelling idea is simply the one which compels attention."[29] This leads finally to the foundation of existential choice: "effort of attention is thus the essential phenomenon of will."[30] Already spelled out in his 1880 essay was the "feeling of effort" which, in the context of interested attention, is a commitment of one's whole self to action: "it is action in the line of greatest resistance."[31] His formula was "moral motive *per se* < Sensual motive," while 'Moral motive + Effort > Sensual motive." James was careful to point out that this should not be construed to mean that effort was an outgoing "force" of muscular feelings meeting external resistance: "the moral effort is not transitive between the inner and outer worlds, but is put forth upon the inner world alone. Its point of application is the idea."[32]

Feelings of Innervation Refuted on Empirical Grounds

All of the preceding strands of James' psychology of will—ideo-motor action, fiat, interest, attention—were developed prior to his contract with Holt for a textbook of psychology in 1878, when he was thirty-six years old. His essay on effort, which would become the chapter on will, was published two years later. It was, therefore, one of the first installments of a twenty-eight-chapter work. Its position as chapter 26 indicates that James had the idea of the whole in mind when he began to write the *Principles of Psychology*.

In both versions of the account of will, dated 1880 and 1890, James opened with a broadside attack on the prevailing theory of innervation. This doctrine, derived by Wilhelm Wundt from the local sign theory of spatial perception, stated that feelings of ocular movement provide an index of location in three dimensions. Wundt's account of volitional action meant that even paralyzed patients can have the feeling of innervation despite inability to move a lamed muscle or limb.[33] In both cases, involving eye and limb, a feeling of effort and direction *precedes* the movement.

Alexander Bain held a theory similar to James's, though the emphasis was slightly different. For Bain, movement was primary. He drew directly upon Johannes Müller, who referred to the spontaneous discharge of the "nervous principle" from the motor areas of the cerebrum to the motor fibers of the spinal cord.[34] For example, a bird singing for the first time connects a blind exertion of volition with the effect produced by its laryngeal muscles. Bain commented that "Müller's application of the term 'voluntary' to the initial movements . . . is not strictly correct; these movements are but one term of the couple that makes up an act of volition; both a feeling and a movement are necessary parts of every such act."[35] This qualification is important, for it is precisely the point where a feedback mechanism replaced the mentalist assumption that feelings precede movements. Indeed, James took exception to both Wundt and Helmholtz on the basis of an argument similar to Bain's.

So universal was the assumption that feelings guide movements in volition that England's foremost physiologist, Hughlings Jackson, uncritically adopted from Spencer the introspective evidence of their existence. Jackson's student, David Ferrier, challenged this view in his *Functions of the Brain* in 1874.[36] His criticism was directed toward Wundt's claim that paralytic patients feel innervation in their limbs even though they cannot move them. Ferrier suspected that the alleged feeling of effort was due to an afferent rather than an efferent nervous discharge, noting that "it is necessary, however, to exclude movements altogether before such an explanation (as Wundt's) can be adopted."[37]

William James seized upon Ferrier's critique of Wundt and Bain, and Jackson, as falling into line with his own afferent ideo-motor theory of will. He quoted verbatim Ferrier's simple experiment with the finger. Extend your right arm and hold your forefinger so as to fire a trigger; without even moving the finger, a feeling of effort becomes noticeable. Then hold the trigger finger as before, relax and breathe rhythmically. Now you will recognize that the feeling of effort was due to the constriction of the chest and tightening of the glottis muscles, which are afferent and not efferent sensations. Concluded Ferrier: "when these active efforts are withheld no consciousness of effort ever arises."[38] Will, according to James, involved the effects of movement, in addition to ideo-motor action and interest.

To these remarks of Ferrier's I have nothing to add. Anyone may verify them, and they prove conclusively that the consciousness of muscular exertion, being impossible without movement *effected somewhere,* must be an afferent and not an efferent sensation, a consequence and not an antecedent of the movement itself. An idea of the amount of muscular exertion requisite to perform a certain movement can consequently be nothing other than an anticipatory image of the movement's sensible effects.[39]

The key to this critique of traditional volitional theory is found in the pragmatic criterion of meaning which Charles Peirce had enunciated in 1878.

Consider what effects, which might conceivably have practical bearings, we conceive the object of our conception to have. Then, our conception of those effects is the whole of our conception of the object.[40]

James was simply applying this criterion to the definition of will.

James argued that the most reputable of authorities, Hermann von Helmholtz, had been led astray on a similar point of introspection. He quoted Helmholtz's account of a patient unable to rotate his eye to the right side because the external rectus muscle or its nerve was paralyzed. Helmholtz explained that, though the will produced no effects, we believe it to have been operative because of our feelings of innervation: "we feel then what impulse of the will, and how strong a one, we apply to turn our eye into a given position."[41] James wrote exultantly:

Beautiful and clear as this reasoning seems to be, it is based on an incomplete inventory of the afferent data. The writers have all omitted to consider what is going on in the *other eye.*[42]

He invoked Ewald Hering's experiments, showing that the innervation of the two eyes is single, in support of his own rebuttal.[43] The idea of the sympathetic movement *(Mitbewegung)* of the two eyes came from Lotze.[44] James's explanation was simply that if the left eye, which is covered during Helmholtz's experiment, were observed it would be shown to follow the sweep of the visual field even though the right eye came to an abrupt halt. The movement of the field is caused by the *afferent* feelings of muscular exertion from the sound left eye rather than the *efferent* feelings of motor innervation to the paralyzed right eye.

This simple but profound insight, that volition selects its afferent effects, became the conceptual foundation of behaviorism. Peirce and James introduced a principle of effect, if we may call it that, which was much broader than the hedonism of the traditional law of effect.[45] It was really the evolutionary principle that survival of the fittest applies to the behavioral and mental realms together. This devastating critique of both British associationism and German Herbartianism prepared the way for the acquisition of behavior to replace the association of ideas.

The Meynert Scheme Revised: A "Functionalist" Critique of the Association of Ideas

A physiological model was added by James to his theory of will in 1890. A tour de force of original speculative physiology, the model was reworked subsequently by Ladd, Baldwin, Thorndike, Dewey, Woodworth, Angell, Cannon, Calkins, G. Allport, Mead, F. Allport, Prince, and Putnam—leaders in the movement from James's "science of mental life" into the modern subfields of psychology.

In a section called "The Education of the Hemispheres" in chapter 2, "Functions of the Brain," James set out to correct the scheme of the Austrian anatomist, Theodor Meynert, widely cited by physiologists as the standard account of brain function. Meynert ascribed a "supernumerary surface" of projection to the cortex. In other words, association centers in the brain were thought to connect as a "telephone switchboard" to reflex movements localized in centers below.[46] James illustrated this traditional model with the example of the child and the flame (Figure 2). Grasping and reflex withdrawal of the finger leaves a linkage of associated ideas of sight-movement-pain-movement in the cortex. According to James, the problem with the Meynert scheme was that it depicted the cortex as a tabula rasa for the association of ideas of sensation and movement, and the lower brain as a mere reflex machine. James argued that "the lower centres are more spontaneous, and the higher spheres are more automatic, than the Meynert scheme allows."[47] James proposed to account for the psychogenesis of habits and even reasoning in a way which would make the action of the higher centers more automatic or reflexlike and the lower ones more "intelligent" or adaptive. In chapter 26 on "Will," he termed this "The Education of the Will." Although explicitly couched in the current jargon of physiology, as before with the child-flame case, the logic of this "education," or learning, conformed to his principle of effect. The three hypotheses he put forward were: (1) the paths all run from sensory cells *(S)* to motor cells *(M)* and via motor pathways to muscles; (2) each discharge tends to drain the cells lying behind, and this path *(P)* will tend to carry off activity in the same direction; and (3) the muscle contraction having occurred, it excites a secondary sensory or kinesthetic cell *(K)* which gives rise along con-

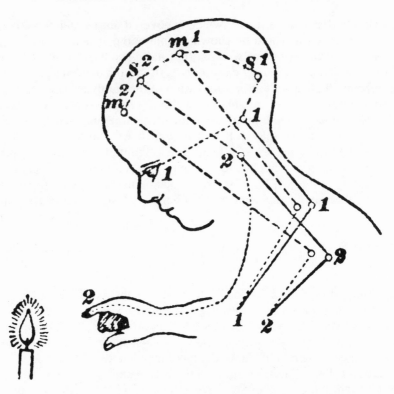

Figure 2. The child and flame example of the Meynert scheme: "The dotted lines stand for afferent paths between the centres, the entire lines for efferent paths." (From William James, Principles of Psychology, *2 vols. [New York: Henry Holt & Co., 1890], 1: 25.)*

nate path *(p)* to an anticipatory image *(Effektsbild)* enabling subsequent reactions to the idea rather than the primitive object itself.[48]

James noted that the kinesthetic cell *(K)* may be thought of as the source of an afferent sensation, whether of sight, sound, touch, or kinesthesis (Figure 3):

> K thus gets excited directly by S *before* it gets excited by the incoming current from the muscle; or, translated into psychic terms: *when a sensation has once produced a movement in us, the next time we have the sensation, it tends to suggest the idea of the movement, even before the movement occurs.*[49]

Here is the crucial transition from reflex to learning, or in James's language, from an idea as effect to an idea as cause: "Here then, we have the answer to our original question of how a sensory process which, the first time it occurred, was the effect of a movement, can later figure as the movement's cause."

James then offered the example of learning to recite the alphabet—*A, B, C, D.* Imitation would occur through hearing the sound, followed by motor discharge in the brain and the resulting laryngeal movement. The three hypotheses above would account for the so-called "motor circle" of repeating *A,* then *B,* then *C,* and so on. How then would we anticipate *B, C,* and *D,* reflexively? Here James introduced a fourth hypothesis: the serially concatenated movements require a successive discharging of sensory and motor cells (Figure 4). Two important assumptions were required: (1) the first discharge is inhibited from recurring by the second discharge, because the undischarged cell is a "stronger drainer" of current. Moreover, (2) a "connate path" (*p*→) is worn between *S* and *K,* parallel to the path between *S* and *M,* such that subsequent sensations produce the idea of the movement in *K* before the actual movement in *M.* The psychological fact is that we *do* escape from the "primitive motor circle" of repeating one letter, or touching the flame, and on subsequent occasions we have learned from experience.

Thus, concatenated sequences of reflexes have been shown to constitute the basis of impulsive, or ideo-motor, thought and action. Beyond this, the feeling of effort involved in the fiat is based upon the hypothetical physiological mechanisms of inhibition and forward conduction, or nerve conduction in a single direction. The afferent kinesthetic cue—the anticipatory image—becomes both the result of movement and the cue of volition. Centers of pleasure and pain were ruled out, although feelings of pleasure might accompany the increase of a current, and

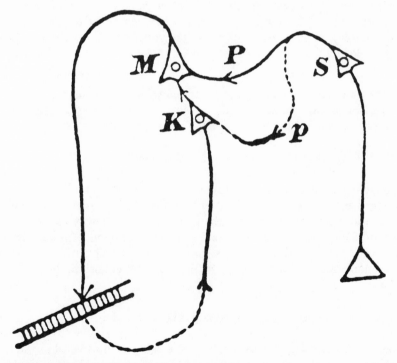

Figure 3. Education of the will depicted by the "motor circle," with the connate path (p) providing an anticipatory image (in kinesthetic cell K) which suggests the idea of a movement (in motor cell M) even before a movement occurs. (From William James, Principles of Psychology, *2 vols. [New York: Henry Holt & Co., 1890], 2: 585.)*

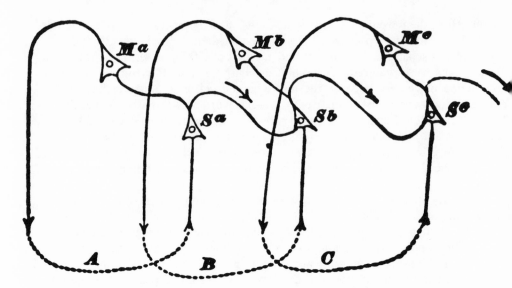

Figure 4. Learning the alphabet, the idea of letter A *leading to* B *and* C *through the discharge of sensory* (S^a) *and motor* (M^a) *nervous paths. This "motor circle" is connected to the next* (S^b, M^b) *by the forward conduction of the anticipatory image. Repetition is prevented by inhibition of the previous "motor circle." (From William James,* Principles of Psychology, *2 vols. [New York: Henry Holt & Co., 1890], 2: 588.)*

displeasure the dampening. James typically ended with a mechanism *plus* mental effort. Mechanism prevails in the nervous currents, while "the soul . . . selects . . . not as an 'epiphenomenon,' but as something from the play gets moral support."[50]

The Impact on American Psychology

James's psychology of will, as portrayed above, consolidated aspects of his chapters on the functions of the brain, attention, association, spatial perception, emotion and will. It is not surprising, then, that its impact was felt in a wide spectrum of subfields in psychology. The following discussion will consider the specific use which was made of James's formulations of will during the period from its first enunciation in 1879 through its more distant echoes in the twentieth century.

Physiological Psychology: G. T. Ladd

The initial reception of James's psychology of will lay in the area of physiological psychology. An early spokesman at Yale University was George Trumbull Ladd (1842–1921), who endorsed, but later qualified his endorsement of, the "peripheral" theory of James.

In his 1887 *Elements of Physiological Psychology,* Ladd reiterated both of James's examples of the "peripheral" origin of the feeling of effort.[51] The example of cocking the trigger finger, as proposed by David Ferrier, and that of moving the one eye of a person paralyzed in the other eye, as noted by Helmholtz, were both cited as evidence against Wundt's theory of the "central" innervation of will. The terms peripheral and central were Ladd's, and they signify that he chose to interpret the debate in physiological terms. It is significant that he overlooked the subtle play of selective attention and interest in volition. Mental and physical processes were different orders of explanation in his psychophysical parallelism. Yet he wrote that James's view "has by far the most in its favor,"[52] because it represented two conceptions close to his own—will as mental activity and as ideo-motor action:

> The activity of which we are directly conscious under the term "to will" is a purely psychical activity; it is marked by no transition of force from the spiritual realm to the material molecules of the nervous structure. The feeling of effort, which seems to us to accompany the active putting forth of will, is itself a resultant of mixed sensations that have a peripheral origin. The whole descrip-. tion of such transactions of voluntary motion as are constantly occurring—for example, when we rise to close the window, take the pen in hand to write, etc.—is as follows: We desire to have something done; mental images of the bodily motions and positions involved in this doing arise in the mind; the fiat of will goes forth in adopting one of them, and *willing* it, as we say; an order of nature which has correlated this fiat with certain cerebral changes, but of which we know nothing whatever directly, and little through the most searching investigations of science, runs its course, and the transaction which we have ideated and willed takes place. The mind can represent the ideas in consciousness, and issue the fiat of will; it can do nothing more. . . . The mind has no native or acquired knowledge of the different ideo-motor areas of the cerebrum[53]

The key to Ladd's hearty endorsement of James may well stem from their common source, Hermann Lotze, whose lecture outlines Ladd had translated and whom Ladd cited in the passage above as follows: "This view of the subject has been repeatedly enforced by Lotze; see, especially, the *Microcosmus*, i, pp. 283 ff. Edinburgh, 1885."

In 1890, however, William James's *Principles of Psychology* appeared with its stunning critique of the Meynert scheme and its proposal of a physiological model for "the education of the hemispheres" underlying the fiat of will. Ladd wrote a critical review in 1892, in which he referred disparagingly to James's phrase "blank unmediated correspondence" between physical and mental processes.[54] James replied that this criticism represented his views "rather unfairly."[55] Ladd's differences came out more plainly in his *Psychology: Descriptive and Explanatory* in 1894. Evidently, he felt that James had vastly undervalued the "active consciousness."[56] But he was well aware of the other point of view:

> It is doubtful whether there are any experimental means of deciding beyond question how far our so-called "feeling of effort" is determined by centrally initiated and outgoing motor processes. The negative answer to the question is given by writers like Ferrier, James, Münsterberg, G. E. Müller, and others; the affirmative is maintained by Bain, Wundt, Beaunis, Preyer, and many more. We have already ranged ourselves with the latter authorities.[57]

Ladd revealed, by his resistance to the afferent or "peripheral" theory, his commitment to psychological causality à la Wundt.[58] His biographer commented:

> The power of will to direct attention was one of several "indubitable facts" of Ladd's psychology. It was indubitable in 1887, but it was even less open to doubt by the time he wrote his *Psychology: Descriptive and Explanatory.*[59]

Ladd's commitment to a sharp dualism of mind and body led him to reify will versus reflex action. He was unable to accept the radical shift implied in the sensationalistic (in today's terms, phenomenological) theory of will proposed by James, wherein the voluntary effort was limited to fiat and interested attention, and the rest was due to automatic action.[60]

Cognitive Development: J. M. Baldwin

James Mark Baldwin (1861–1934), by comparison, not only adopted James's argument for an afferent theory of will but developed an analogous theory of cognitive development. When he published volume 1 of his *Handbook of Psychology* in 1889, he did not cite James's essay on the feeling of effort.[61] He was then still an adherent of the traditional theory of feelings of efferent innervation. Like Wundt and Ladd, Baldwin believed that feelings and attention are guides to action: "In voluntary attention we find the first exhibition of will."[62] By 1891 in volume 2, though, Baldwin had dismissed outgoing "feelings of expenditure."[63] Now he favored the alternative theory of the feelings of activity as "incoming muscular feelings:"[64]

> In this position, the text is in substantial agreement with James (2, p. 561) except that he uses the expression "muscular effort" to designate the sensational content of muscular volition, which is not consistent with the use of the same term "effort" to designate volition itself in the case of attention. The effort is exactly the same in the two cases: in one case it is exercised about "muscular feelings," in the other, about "intellectual feelings." In the one case, the object is a motor intuition, in the other a logical relation: the form, the effort, is the same. Hence it is not true that "muscular effort consists of all those peripheral feelings to which a muscular 'exertion' may give rise" (James, *loc. cit.,* 2, 562 note). It consists of these, plus voluntary attention (effort), plus the muscular sensations peculiar to voluntary attention.[65]

Baldwin clearly differentiated two kinds of effort: (1) effort of the fiat in attending to an idea or end, and (2) effort of the muscles as pleasure or pain. Thus he resolved an ambiguity in James's theory between feeling of effort as attention and as afferent sensation by giving them separate designations—"ideal volition" and "muscular volition."

An example from an infant (probably his own daughter) made this clearer. In her "first acts of volition," a "concentration of [her] attention" upon any object led to a "muscular discharge" while she was "quite unconscious of [her] muscles."[66] He agreed with James that "we begin by pursuing an object," since the infant's appetites which were at first directed to "objects which satisfy," her bottle and milk, were later superseded by "the pleasure of eating."[67] Pleasure and pain, contrary to the claim of Bain for their primitive nature, are slow to develop:

Bain makes (2), above, the starting point. Pleasure must be associated with a muscular movement, and the muscular movement pursued for the sake of the pleasure; this, he says, is the birth of volition. To him the mere idea (1, above), with no associated pleasure or pain, has no motive influence whatever. He is directly refuted by observations of imitative suggestion in childhood."[68]

Coming immediately after his discussion of James's chapter on will, this passage shows that Baldwin was reworking a conception derived from him.

Like James, Baldwin was tremendously impressed by the evidence of suggestion and ideo-motor action stemming from it. Imitation was the paradigm case of "motor consciousness." Baldwin also referred to this phenomenon as "the law of nervous dynamogenesis, i.e., that every state of consciousness tends to realize itself in an appropriate muscular movement."[69] He took the term "dynamogenesis" from the hypnosis literature, where it is found in the writings of Alfred Binet, and from a similar conception in Lotze.[70] His diagram, however, the so-called "motor square," was directly adapted from James's "motor circle" in the chapter on "The Functions of the Brain" (Figures 5a, b, c).[71] The lower "reflex circuit" is shown by dark lines in each diagram. The actions of decorticate frogs and pigeons were ascribed by Baldwin to the Law of Habit, since they were possible without consciousness. The higher "voluntary circuit" of the organism

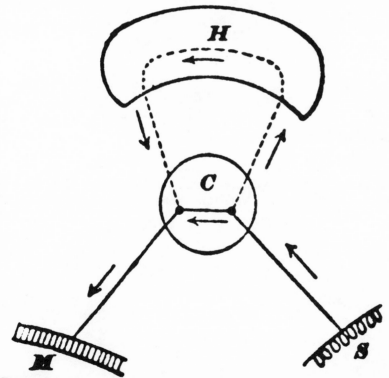

Figure 5a. Motor circle, with hemispheric loopline. S = sense organ, C = central nervous system, M = muscle, H = hemispheres. (From William James, Principles of Psychology, 2 vols. [New York: Henry Holt & Co., 1890], 1: 21.)

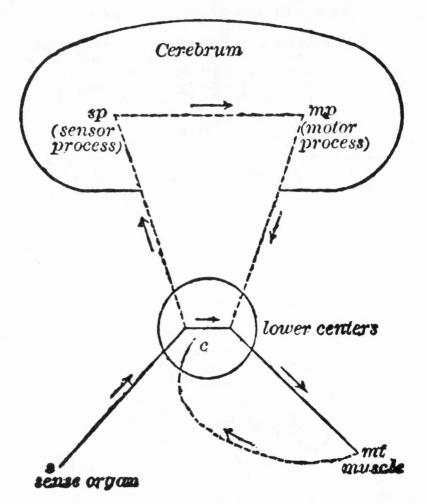

Figure 5b. Motor square, with cortical voluntary circuit. s, c, mt = *reflex circuit;* s, c, sp, mp, c, mt = *voluntary circuit. (From James Mark Baldwin, Handbook of Psychology, 2 vols. [New York: Henry Holt & Co., 1894 [1891], 2: 42.)*

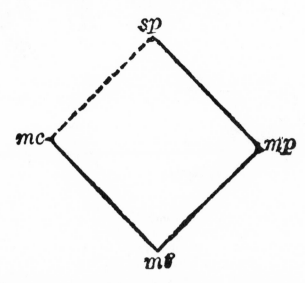

Figure 5c. Motor square, simplified. sp, mp, mt = *reflex circuit;* mc = *voluntary element. (From James Mark Baldwin,* Handbook of Psychology, *2 vols. [New York: Henry Holt & Co., 1894 [1891]], 2: 42.)*

with its cortex intact was indicated by a dotted line. Baldwin ascribed voluntary actions to the Law of Accommodation, since they involved a revival of consciousness through voluntary control, or "what we know as Interest."[72] In brief, Baldwin took over the concepts of habit and interest (renamed accommodation) from James. He combined them into a Lamarckian Law of Inheritance which referred to the learning experiences of the individual of the species.

In the 1895 *Mental Development of the Child,* Baldwin adopted the familiar child-flame diagram from James (Figures 6a, b):

> The kinesthetic centre empties into a lower motor centre in some such way as that described by James, along the diagonal lines, *mc, mp,* in the 'motor square' diagram given above.[73]

Baldwin explained that "the two processes *v* and *v'* flow together in the old channel *v, mp* fixed by association."[74] This mechanism of habit formation was of course derived from James's "motor circle." Pushing James's theory further, however, Baldwin then proposed not only an associationist mechanism but also a cognitive-developmental explanation of how new responses are generated. Where James relied on inhibition and forward conduction, Baldwin introduced "persistent imitation," the "try-try-again" experience of infants following sights, sounds, and movements."[75] For example, his own child went from reflexive to volitional activity when she copied freehand the figure her father gave her—instead of merely tracing it. Having detected differences between what she saw and what she produced with her hand, she then made an "effort" to adjust her imitation to the "copy."[76]

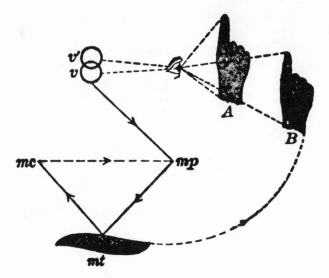

Figure 6a. Motor square, simple imitation. v, v' = *visual seat;* mp = *motor seat;* mt = *muscle moved;* mc = *muscle sense seat;* A = *'copy' imitated;* B = imitation made. (From James Mark Baldwin,* Mental Development of the Child and the Race *[New York: Macmillan Co., 1915 [1895]], p. 356.*

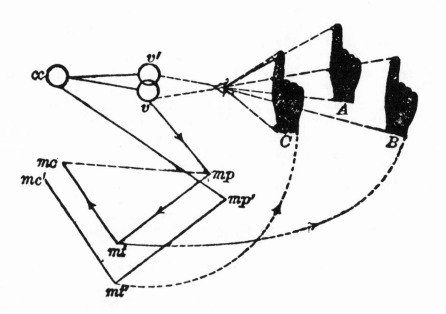

Figure 6b. "Motor square, persistent imitation with effort. C = *successful imitation;* cc = *coordinating center, either local or purely functional. Other letters same as Fig. 6a, with the added circuit* cc, mp', mt', mc'. *The processes at* v *and* v' *do not flow together in the old channel,* v, mp, *but are coordinated at* cc *in a new reaction* mp', mt', *which includes all the elements of the 'copy'* (A) *and more. The useless elements then fall away because they are useless and the successful effort is established." (From James Mark Baldwin,* Mental Development of the Child *and the Race [New York: Macmillan Co., 1915 [1894]], p. 358.)*

The significance of Baldwin's cognitive-developmental mechanism in relation to James's is that it built upon the "remote stimuli" of memory as opposed to the "immediate stimuli" of observation.[77] Baldwin was more explicit than James in emphasizing the developmental aspect of "imitation:"

> The theory that all voluntary movements are led up to by spontaneous reactions which result in pleasure or pain, and then get repeated only because of their hedonic result, will not hold water for an instant in the presence of the phenomena of imitation. . . . In cases of imitation there is more than association as such. The movements initiated are new, as combinations. . . . For this reason, as was said above, I believe that in persistent imitation we have the skeleton process of volition; . . . . A child imitates automatically a sound he hears—one case; and then, remembering it but not hearing it, wills to make it—a second case.[78]

Here, Baldwin cited Alfred Binet's exposition of James's view and then related it to his own conception of a spiral development of the "life plan" through successive "suggestions" from the environment and adaptations of the child to it through accommodation and assimilation.[79] This is the historical link from James's conception of the circular reflex to Jean Piaget's theory of cognitive development, whereby a child moves through a process of "equilibration" to a higher stage of adapted thought and action.[80]

Attention and Volition: John Dewey and J. F. Angell

Two founders of "Functionalism," John Dewey (1859–1952) and James Rowland Angell (1869–1949), also drew directly upon James as well as upon Baldwin. In 1896, John Dewey announced in "The Reflex Arc Concept in Psychology:"

> The older dualism between sensation and idea is repeated in the current dualism of peripheral and central structures and functions; the older dualism of body and soul finds a distinct echo in the current dualism of stimulus and response.[81]

Certainly Ladd was implicated by this charge of dualism. Dewey proposed his alternative formulation in direct reference to James:

> Let us take, for our example, the familiar child-flame instance (James, *Psychology*, Vol. I, p. 25). The ordinary interpretation would say the sensation of light is a stimulus to the grasping as a response, the burn resulting is a stimulus to withdrawing the hand as response and so on. . . . Upon analysis we find that we begin not with a sensory stimulus, but with a *sensori-motor coordination* [italics added], the optical-ocular, and that in a certain sense it is the movement which is primary, and the sensation which is secondary . . . In other words, the real beginning is with the act of seeing; it is looking, and not a sensation of light.[82]

Coordination was a new term; it deemphasized the dichotomy of fiat and ideo-motor action, highlighting the feedback loop. Even Baldwin came under criticism here. Dewey cited his three elements of reactive consciousness, e.g., the stimulus of sound, the attention involuntarily drawn, and the muscular reaction—for taking insufficient account of attention:

Professor Baldwin, in the passage quoted, has inverted the real order as between his first and second elements. We do not have first a sound and then activity of *attention* [italics added], unless sound is taken as mere nervous shock or physical event, not as conscious value. The conscious sensation of sound depends upon the motor response having already taken place; or, in terms of the previous statement (if stimulus is used as a conscious fact, and not as a mere physical event) it is the motor response or *attention* [italics added] which constitutes that, which finally becomes the stimulus to another act.[83]

This shift of emphasis onto "attention" underlay Dewey's functionalist criticism of "the controversy between the Wundtian 'apperceptionists' and their opponents. Each has a *disjectum membrum* of the same organic whole, whichever is selected being an arbitrary matter of personal taste."[84]

This functional orientation had already inspired Dewey's protégés, James Rowland Angell and Addison W. Moore, to a critique of the Wundtian reaction-time literature in 1896.[85] Reaction time was the method of measuring volition as the difference between the simple reaction time and the complex one involving a disjunctive choice. In a controversy with Edwin B. Titchener, Baldwin had showed that individual differences between the sensory and motor type of reaction could account for this difference.[86] Angell and Moore explained that subjects actually progressed from the sensory to the motor form of reaction. They acknowledged Dewey and George H. Mead "for suggestions without which the following interpretation would not have been reached."[87] Their notion of a functional "coordination" combined aspects from both predecessors: Wundt's view that volition time was reduced to habit time through practice, and Baldwin's view that this reduction depended upon the individual's stock of "coordinations, instinctive and acquired." Angell and Moore had demonstrated that, "in a word, the time question is not a case of a 'sensory' vs. a 'motor' reaction, but of *a sensori-motor less habitual vs. a sensori-motor more habitual*."[88]

The replacement of the reflex arc concept by the more flexible conception of habit and attention was consistent with the subtle mechanism of volition which James had proposed. By 1904, when Angell published his *Psychology*, the two chapters on volition and one on character and will were no longer direct commentaries on James.[89] Yet the mechanism of cortical association and serially-coordinated movements was directly derived from him (Figures 7a, b, c). In one passage, the reworking of James's conception is especially clear:

James employs a useful pair of terms in calling those ideas of movement which originate in the part of the body moved, "resident," designating all other ideas which arise from the consequences of the movement, "remote." It must be added, however, that in practice the severance of the two from one another is in most persons by no means so complete as his description implies.[90]

Taking James's example of learning to play the piano, he explained that playing a scale the first time requires both sensory and motor control—both visual and tactual-kinesthetic images are held in conscious attention. Later on, consciousness disappears as the coordination of remote interests takes over, e.g., recollection of the melody rather than reading the notes. Angell thus clearly distinguished

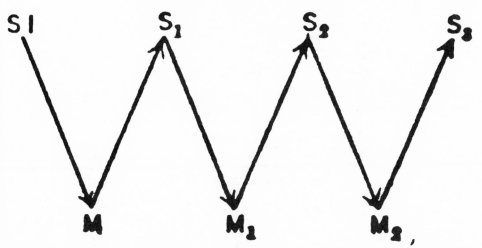

Figure 7a. Habit, or habitual coordination. S = sensation, M = movement. (From James Rowland Angell, Psychology. An Introductory Study of the Structure and Function of Human Consciousness, *4th ed., rev. [New York: Henry Holt and Co., 1908 [1904]], p. 72.)*

and then recombined the essential elements of James's theory of volition—the habit, interest, and anticipatory cues. At the same time, he also incorporated Baldwin's persistent imitation and Thorndike's trial and error formulations of learning into his own theory of the transition from random to controlled movements by accidental success, elimination of useless movements, and ideational control. Thorndike's theory, as will be seen below, also had distinct roots in James's theory.

Learning: E. L. Thorndike

Edward Lee Thorndike (1874–1949) was a graduate student of James in the mid-1890's who first became known for his contributions to comparative psychology and animal learning. In 1898 his dissertation on association in animal intelligence gave indirect recognition to James's model of volition.[91] It provided the point of departure for Thorndike's critique of the associationist tradition represented by Lloyd Morgan, the leading British comparative psychologist.

Lloyd Morgan had written that to the chick the sight of a ladybird beetle suggests a nasty taste. "It has been assumed," wrote Thorndike, "that the association was *an association of ideas*."[92] After documenting this assumption in Morgan's writings, he explained that in his view "the impulse is the *sine qua non* of the association."[93] By impulse, he meant "the consciousness accompanying a muscular innervation."[94] Thus, the cat who is "put through the proper movement" of pulling a latch to escape from Thorndike's orange-crate puzzle-box would not actually feel the impulse.[95] By contrast, the cat who discovered the way to escape would associate the sight of the box with the impulse it had experienced: "The groundwork of animal associations is not the association of *ideas*, but the associa-

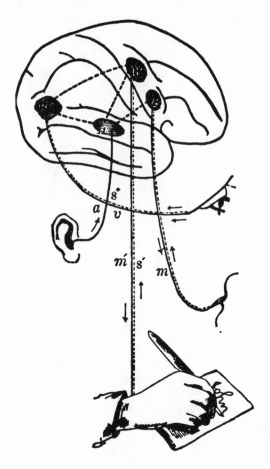

Figure 7b. Sensori-motor coordination, involving cortical association centers.
A = *auditory center,* V = *visual center,* W = *writing center,* E = *speech center,*
a = *auditory nerve,* v = *visual motor nerve,* s = *visual sensory nerve,* m = *mouth nerve,* m' = *muscle motor nerve,* s' = *muscle sensory nerve. (Identical*
figure from William James, Principles of Psychology, *2 vols. [New York: Henry*
Holt & Co., 1890], 1: 57, and from James Rowland Angell, Psychology. An
Introductory Study of the Structure and Function of Human Consciousness, *4th*
ed., rev. [New York: Henry Holt and Co., 1908 [1904]], p. 47.)

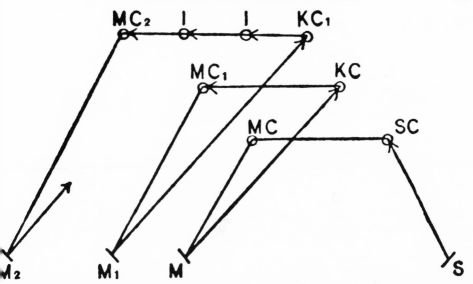

Figure 7c. "A series of coordinated movements. S = sense organ, SC = sensory cortical center, MC = muscle motor center, KC = kinaesthetic sensory center, MC_1 = another muscle motor center innervating M_1, which in turn produces the kinaesthetic sensory impulse reported at KC_1, etc." I, I = "ideas or images whose brain processes may be interpolated anywhere throughout such series, discharging into the motor center MC_2, thus originating a fresh series of movement and kinaesthetic sensations." (From James Rowland Angell, Psychology. An Introductory Study of the Structure and Function of Human Consciousness, 4th ed., rev. [New York: Henry Holt & Co., 1908 [1904]], p. 56.)

tion of idea or sense-impression with *impulse*."[96] Certainly this bears comparison with James's emphatic statement: "*There is no a priori calling up of one 'idea' by another; the only a priori couplings are of ideas with movements.*"[97]

Thorndike did not cite the "Will" chapter in 1898, though his concept of impulse is comparable to ideo-motor action. He did mention James's "Reasoning" chapter: "Professor James made the simple but brilliant criticism [of G. J. Romanes] that all a recept really means *is a tendency to react in a certain way.*"[98] Like James, Thorndike was also relying upon a physiological model underlying behavior:

My statement of what has been the course of development along this line is derived from observation of animals' behavior and Professor James's theory of the nature of and presumable brain processes going with the abstractions and conceptions of human consciousness.[99]

Finally, Thorndike's hedonism may owe a debt to James's afferent theory rather than to Wundt's efferent one:

There is no pleasure along with the association. The pleasure does not come until after the association is done and gone."[100]

However, these are only speculations as to influence.

By 1905, though, Thorndike had become more explicit in his recognition of James. He wrote in his *Elements of Psychology:*

> To Professor James I owe the common debt of all psychologists due for the genius which has been our inspiration and the scholarship which has been our guide. The obligation is patent in every chapter. Indeed, the best service I wish for this book is that it may introduce its readers to that masterpiece of thought and expression, the *Principles of Psychology.*[101]

He was also specifically conversant with James's critique of efferent feelings of innervation:

> By feelings of innervation are meant feelings directly due to the passage of the nervous impulse to efferent neurons and through them to muscles. It is very doubtful whether any feelings are so caused. They certainly are not essential to the execution of a purposely made movement.[102]

By 1905 Thorndike had clearly distinguished the anticipatory cue as "any mental state whatever" from the result of a movement, the pleasure or pain. Moreover, Thorndike's earliest statement of the laws of exercise and effect bears a striking resemblance to the education of the will in James. James had written in 1890:

> How is a fresh path ever formed? All paths are paths of discharge, and the discharge always takes place in the direction of least resistance . . . If mechanical activities in a cell, as they increase, give *pleasure* [italics added], they seem to increase all the more rapidly for that fact; if they give *displeasure* [italics added], the displeasure seems to dampen the activities. . . . *The result is a new-formed 'path' which path will deepen itself more and more every time it is used* [italics in James].[103]

Thorndike reformulated this in 1905 as a "Law of Acquired Connections," which

> includes the action of two factors, frequency and pleasurable result. It might be stated in a compound form as follows: (1) *The line of least resistance is, other things being equal, that resulting in the greatest satisfaction to the animal; and* (2) *the line of least resistance is, other things being equal, that oftenest traversed by the nervous impulse.* We may call (1) the *Law of Effect,* and (2) the *Law of Habit.*[104]

Nor can it be said that Thorndike ignored the role of interest and attention in James's theory of volition. Posing the question why a boy attends to his spelling lesson rather than to the parade outside, he answered that "some feel satisfaction only in the directly pleasurable . . . whereas others feel satisfaction in the prospects of far off benefits."[105] James had similarly characterized the healthy will by objective and subjective teleology, i.e., by "feelings or ideas of pleasure or pain" and "ideas of remoter objects": the latter, more abstract purposes "prevail, when they ever do prevail, *with effort.*"[106] While it may be that Thorndike came to be known for his archetypal associationism and hedonism, his early position was closely modeled on James's theory of will.[107] The fact that Thorndike had sought during the period 1902 to 1905 to induce James to accept his collaboration on a revision of the *Principles of Psychology* suggests that Thorndike, at least, saw a kinship in their fundamental conceptions.

Motivation: R. S. Woodworth

Motivation would appear to be the central legacy of James's theory of volition. However, the emergence of this research topic actually occurred somewhat later than the topics treated so far. An early spokesman was Robert Sessions Woodworth (1869–1962) who spent two years at Harvard under William James and Josiah Royce, from 1895 to 1897, before completing a dissertation under James McKeen Cattell at Columbia on "The Accuracy of Voluntary Movement" in 1899.[108]

The career of Woodworth is illustrative of the gradual emergence of the modern problem area of motivation from issues encountered in the study of the more classical topics. In his dissertation, in which use was made of psychophysical methods to determine constant errors in carrying out movements, Woodworth concluded that these errors are due to "sensations of movement" rather than to feeling of innervation of kinesthetic images. Here he adopted the afferent, or feedback, interpretation of James as against the efferent one. He cited this passage from James's chapter on "The Perception of Space":

> The attempt to ascribe our ideas of motion to a purely "intellectual" origin fails, not only before these empirical facts, but also before the logical difficulty advanced by James (*Principles,* 2: 171) that "we can only infer that which we already generically know in some more direct fashion." Unless we had some direct means of perceiving movement, no congeries of sensations of position would ever suggest the idea of movement to us.[109]

In a 1906 paper on "The Cause of Voluntary Movement," Woodworth excluded kinesthetic images as the conditions for volition and proposed a "total set of the nervous system" which included habits and sensations of movement.[110] Now Woodworth quoted from James's chapter on "Will":

> It is not so much a 'supply of ideas of the various movements that are possible' as a knowledge of the various effects that can be produced, that is 'the first prerequisite of the voluntary life.' The kinesthetic image must be given up. . . ."[111]

Woodworth's argument was very close to James's, and he adopted James's terminology of remote sensations, present in consciousness as the "fringe," and resident sensations, as the thought of some particular change to be effected.

In his systematic works, Woodworth became a perennial critic of instinct and reflex doctrines which did not allow for modifiability. His *Dynamic Psychology* in 1918 took issue with mentalist doctrines as well:

> But if the extreme behaviorist errs by wishing to exclude from psychology a legitimate method and object of study, the extreme introspectionist, who would exclude the study of behavior by objective methods, is equally at fault.[112]

The common-sense view which he espoused was termed *dynamics,* in reference to the dynamic relation of mental processes to behavior. The key term was *drive,* which was distinguished from reflex by the simple fact that it continues after the initial stimulation. "Drive" replaced the circular reflex (James), persistent imitation (Baldwin), and sensorimotor coordination (Dewey, Angell), with a hypothetical internal state which contributes to the external stimulation. Woodworth drew upon the distinction of another teacher, Charles S. Sherrington, to further define drive as (1) a preparatory reaction, such as stalking a prey and (2) a consummatory reaction, such as devouring it.[113]

Woodworth did not cite James conspicuously in the chapter on "Will" in his textbook, *Psychology: A Study of Mental Life,* in 1921.[114] He did refer the student to James's "Hypnosis" chapter, however, and to the "Volition" chapter in William McDougall's *Social Psychology* of 1908.[115] Both sources are popularizations of the basic physiological mechanism of association by contiguity, as Ladd and Woodworth recognized in 1911.[116] Moreover, it would be difficult to deny the Jamesian tenor of Woodworth's discussion of ideo-motor action, of will as the overcoming of obstruction through effort, and of the development of voluntary control. Indeed, it helps us to understand better the common themes in this diffuse field when we compare James's concepts of anticipatory cue, subjective interest, and ideo-motor action with Woodworth's concepts of preparatory reaction, the drive state, and the consummatory reaction. Woodworth also extended James's conception of a conflict of ideas, or motives, to subsume Freud's concept of repression. Thus, the contribution of Woodworth was to translate the outdated dichotomy of automatic action and effort in which he was schooled under James into the mainstream vocabulary of "drive," "motive," "cue function," "selection and control," and "reinforcing function." The field of motivation came into being when these concepts were both operationally defined and put to experimental test.

Emotions: W. B. Cannon

The history of the study of emotions in the first quarter of the twentieth century was dominated by a physiological challenge to James's afferent theory. Beginning in 1900, Charles S. Sherrington (1857–1952) set out to address the theories of James, Carl Georg Lange, and Giuseppe Sergi that vascular changes and neural events precede the emotional states. He summarized this work in 1906, writing that "to obtain some test of his view is not difficult by experiment."[117] His initial experiments in 1900 were conducted on seven young dogs in whom the spinal and vagal nerves had been sectioned. Judging from the facial expressions of the dogs, no disturbances in "emotional character" could be detected; they continued to experience "joy," "anger," "displeasure," and "fear." Thus, emotions did not seem to come from the periphery, since the sections excluded this possibility.[118] In 1904, in collaboration with Robert S. Woodworth, he elicited "pseudaffective reflexes" in decerebrate cats whose brain-stems had been truncated at the level of the midbrain.[119] Here, in effect, he had demonstrated that the "neural machinery" for emotional expression was located below the midbrain. However, the conclusion he drew was that the basis of the emotions is cerebral: "when the expression occurs, it may be assumed that, had the brain been present, the feeling would have occurred."[120] In reply to James, he wrote:

> In view of these general considerations and the above experiments, we may with James accept visceral and organic sensations and the memories and associations of them as contributory to primitive emotions, but we must regard them as reinforcing rather than initiating the psychosis.[121]

The fact that the "psychosis," or emotional state, was followed by "visceral and organic sensations" thus returned the psychology of the emotions to a facsimile of the efferent theory of "feelings of innervation" which James had refuted.

In 1914, another prominent physiologist, Walter B. Cannon (1871–1945), concentrated on vascular changes as the source of afferent sensations. A former undergraduate student of James's during the 1890s, Cannon mentioned his teacher, in connection with Darwin and William McDougall, for his explanation of emotions in evolutionary terms of the survival of serviceable reactions.[122] He showed experimentally, by allowing a dog to bark at a cat in confinement, that fear, rage, and pain are accompanied by a discharge of adrenalin into the blood:

> The most significant feature of these bodily reactions to pain and to emotion-provoking objects is that they are of the nature of reflexes, they are not willed movements, indeed they are often distressingly beyond the control of the will. . . . [123]

Neither the hormone adrenalin, however, nor the reflexive autonomic nervous discharges which released its secretion, could account for the diversity of the emotions.

> We do not "feel sorry because we cry," as James contended, but we cry because we are sorry or overjoyed or violently angry or full of tender affection—when any one of these diverse emotional states is present—there are nervous discharges by sympathetic channels to various viscera, including the lachrymal glands. In terror and rage and intense elation, for example, the responses in the viscera seem too uniform to offer a satisfactory means of distinguishing states which, in man at least, are very different in subjective quality.[124]

Notwithstanding this physiological evidence, J. R. Angell in 1916 still defended the James-Lange theory on two grounds: (1) Angell maintained that Sherrington had proven neither that visceral sensation plays no part in emotion nor that emotion precedes its expression; (2) in reference to Cannon, he admitted that the visceral excitement may be similar but the diversity resides in the differences of tone of the skeletal muscles.[125]

A compromise settlement, in essence, was offered in the 1920s. Summing up over a decade of research in 1927, Cannon published "The James-Lange Theory of Emotions: A Critical Examination and an Alternative Theory."[126] He defended five points against the James-Lange theory: Sherrington's transection of the spinal cord and vagus nerve leading to the viscera, his own evidence of the similarity of visceral changes, the insensitivity of visceral structures, the slowness of onset of visceral changes, and the fact that artificial induction of visceral changes does not produce emotions. His main positive contribution was to announce a theoretical corrective to James:

> The section in James' discussion, headed "No Special Brain Centres for Emotion" must be modified in the light of this accumulated information. The cortex at one end of the nerve paths as a reflex surface and the peripheral organs at the other end as a source of return impulses make too simple an arrangement.[127]

Following Cannon's suggestion that the emotions originated in the thalamus, Philip Bard performed ablations of various parts of the brain-stem after removing the cerebral hemispheres of fifty cats.[128] He succeeded in locating the source of the emotions in the diencephalon (in the hypothalamus) while the neural organization of emotional expressions was located in the midbrain or below (Figure 8). The

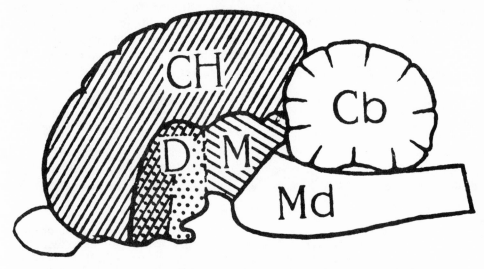

Figure 8. Subcortical regions responsible for emotional activity of decorticate cats. CH = cerebral hemispheres, D = diencephalon (indicated by dots), M = mesencephalon (mid-brain), Md = medulla oblongata, CB = cerebellum. The cross-hatching, from right downward to left, marks the portion of the brain which can be removed without interfering with the expression of rage. (From Philip Bard, "Emotion: I. The Neuro-Humoral Basis of Emotional Reactions," Chap. 12 in Carl Murchison, ed., The Foundations of Experimental Psychology *[Worcester, Mass.: Clark University Press, 1929], p. 472.)*

source was in fact neither central nor peripheral, but in between. The Cannon-Bard compromise view was that emotional tone is provided by the hypothalamus, while the coordination of bodily expressions of emotions is governed by the midbrain. The cortex preserves inhibitory control over these lower centers, as seen by the sham rage and pseudaffective reflexes consequent upon its removal. Recalling that James also postulated an inhibitory role for the cortex, the characterization of his theories of emotion and will as "peripheral" by the physiological tradition does not do them justice.

Personality: Mary W. Calkins and Gordon Allport

Two founders of the psychology of personality, Mary Whiton Calkins (1863–1930) and Gordon Allport (1897–1967), were great admirers of James. While it would not be appropriate to derive their personality theories exclusively from him, it will prove instructive to consider the aspects of James's theory of will which they did incorporate.

Calkins described herself as a "psychological personalist" in contradistinction to such "biological personalists" as William McDougall, Wilhelm Stern, G. F. Stout, and James R. Angell.[129] For them the basic unit was the "embodied self," whereas for her it was "the strictly psychological conception of the self-which-has-a-body."[130] She was trained by William James in the 1880s to value the introspective method above all others, and in her interpretation of James's position on emotion and volition she avoided confusing the actual experience with the analysis of it. Will, for instance, is experienced as active, emotion as passive; both are derived from habits, yet they are experienced as mental "dispositions" which function in relation to others.[131]

On the one hand, she gave qualified endorsement to James's view that bodily movements and brain changes precede the emotion:

Modern psychologists, led by William James and by the Danish physiologist, Conrad [sic] Lange, have successfully combatted this traditional theory of emotional expressions. In so doing, they have, however, sometimes fallen into an opposite error and have, first, treated the bodily changes as entire, and not merely partial, bodily conditions of emotion; and then, second, they have defined emotion as nothing more than this consciousness of bodily changes.[132]

On the other hand, she elaborated his theory of will, as an active subordinating of others to oneself, in contrast to her theory of faith, as submission of oneself to others. Her theory of belief also drew upon James's chapter on "Will":

So James says that the "quality of reality is a relation to our life. It means our adoption of things, our caring for them, our standing by them." And with a similar suggestion, Baldwin speaks of our 'personal endorsement' of reality.[133]

Calkins thus followed the side of James's volitional theory which emphasized the relation between ideas—not as atomistic units, nor as physiological processes, but rather as "the self, immediately experienced."

Modern psychology has quite correctly rid itself of the metaphysicians' self—the self often inferred to be free, responsible, and immoral [sic]—and has thereupon naively supposed that it has thus cut itself off from the self. But the self of psychology has no one of these inferred characters: it is the self, immediately experienced, directly realized, in recognition, in sympathy, in vanity, in assertiveness, and indeed in all experiencing.[134]

Will, faith, and belief were integral to Calkins's theory of self. Her view of personality is alive today in the existential writers, in ego psychology, and above all, in the personality theory of Gordon Allport.

Gordon Allport's basic admiration for James, and a characteristic which they share, are revealed in the 1943 essay "The Productive Paradoxes of William James."[135] Allport's three concepts of personality belong to the Jamesian tradition: traits, functional autonomy, and a unifying philosophy of life.[136] Like Calkins, who was a critic of atomistic doctrines of self, he resisted attempts to found a science of personality solely on doctrines of what he termed "specificity," referring to factor analytic traits and transfer of training skills.[137] He wrote that "it was the teaching of William James and Ed. L. Thorndike that led to a conception of conduct largely in terms of habit."[138] Although primarily remembered today for the endorsement of a trait theory in the 1930s and an existential-phenomenological theory of personal lives in the 1960s,[139] Allport actually joined together these paradoxical extremes throughout his career—very much in the spirit of William James. In fact, the hierarchical levels of integration in personality which Allport illustrated by his familiar diagram would equally serve for James (Figure 9):[140]

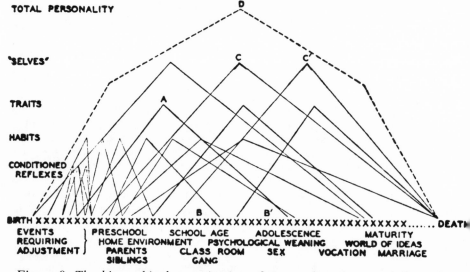

Figure 9. The hierarchical organization of personality. A = an independent, dissociated system, B = infantilism, or immature level of development for age, B' = maturity corresponding to age, C, C' = multiple selves or personalities, D = the unity of personality. (From Gordon Allport, Personality: A Psychological Interpretation *[New York: Henry Holt & Co., 1937], p. 141.)*

He even acknowledged both extremes, selves and reflexes, in James: "The prototype for conceptions of this sort [hierarchical definitions of personality] is to be found in James' classic treatment of the four levels of the Self. . . . To James, as to the modern specificists, the faculties should have been analyzed into smaller, sensori-motor, elements."[141]

The volitional center of Allport's conception of personality was "functional autonomy," and it too was informed by Jamesian insights:

William James taught a curious doctrine that has been a matter for incredulous amusement ever since, the doctrine of the *transitoriness of instincts*. According to this theory—not so quaint as sometimes thought—an instinct appears but once in lifetime, whereupon it promptly disappears through its transformation into habits. If there *are* instincts this is no doubt their fate, for no instinct can retain its motivational force unimpaired after it has been absorbed and recast under the transforming influence of learning. Such is the reasoning of James, and such is the logic of functional autonomy.[142]

Functional autonomy was exemplified by the longing of the sailor for the sea after it has ceased to provide financial gain, and by the neurotic symptoms and peak experiences which persist in the absence of further reward. Defined as a "contemporaneous system of motivation," functional autonomy included learned behaviors which continue on their own such as "circular reflexes," "sentiments," "interests," and "life plans." Each of these terms used by Allport echoed the language of James. This is not accidental. The reason lies in their shared dynamic conception of will, constructed theoretically upon reflexes and traits, yet amenable to a phenomenological life-history description. Their historical contexts were different; James corrected the reflex tradition with flexible habits, while Allport modified the trait tradition with common traits and values. But each gave due recognition to the experienced, concrete reality of the individual life.

Social Psychology: G. H. Mead

In this century social psychology has taken on aspects of both behaviorism and Gestalt psychology. "Roles" are socially learned through modelling and imitation, while "group processes" involve the self in a social field. These two basic aspects of modern social psychology were formulated by Mead and Floyd Allport in response to the critiques of the reflex arc by James and Dewey.

George Herbert Mead (1863–1931) studied with James and Josiah Royce at Harvard in the 1880s, and his first paper was called "A Theory of Emotions from the Physiological Standpoint" in 1895.[143] As he began to formulate his social psychology in 1909, he remained interested in emotions because they stood for a key issue: "either they are elements—mainly preparatory—beginnings of acts—social acts, i.e, actions and reactions which arise under stimulation of other individuals, such as clenching the fists, grinding the teeth, assuming an attitude of defense—or else they are regarded as outflows of nervous energy which sluice off the nervous excitement or reinforce and prepare indirectly for action."[144] Intrinsic to this proposal that "gestures" are social stimuli for others was a functional reinterpretation of the reflex arc.

Mead was immensely impressed by John Dewey's article on the reflex arc in 1896, and he was by then a colleague of Dewey at the University of Chicago. A clue to the significance of the "social act" is conveyed in another early paper in 1900, where he used the child-flame example to illustrate its four steps: (a) a problem which persists and cannot be ignored, (2) an advance toward a solution by means of a habitual reaction, (3) the control or inhibition of this reaction indicated by the hesitation of the child's finger, and (4) the "moral struggle" in the choice of a reaction, revealing "the identification of the self with one set of tendencies to the exclusion of others."[145] Mead was here extending Dewey's functional conception into a theory of social process. Yet in 1903, it was still couched in terms of a critique of Wundt's feelings of effort—the very same foil against which James had written almost twenty-five years before: "This real crux of the situation is to be found in the feelings of activity. Are they reduced to simple sensations of motion and effort, or may the activity appear directly, without representation?"[146] Mead argued against Wundt, and James Mark Baldwin, that they committed the psychologist's fallacy of mistaking the analysis of an action into feelings of conscious effort for the "immediate act." This act need not be conscious, either as Wundt's "apperception" or Baldwin's "imitative introjection." Rather, action involves coordination of an "impulse" "instinct," or "sentiment" with reference to other persons: "Thus the distinction between the act and the conditions of the act does not appear."[147]

The debt of Mead to James is thus primarily an indirect one through Dewey, Baldwin, Royce, and William McDougall. He gave explicit recognition to these men in a revealing essay in 1909, "Social Psychology as Counterpart to Physiological Psychology."[148] The conception of a social act came from Dewey's "sensori-motor coordination," construing the stimulus as a social object. The conception of "instinct," which McDougall had taken in large part from James and adapted to his own theory of volition, was modified in the following manner by Mead. A social instinct, such as gregariousness or parenting, both "implies a certain type of stimulus to which the organism is attuned" and "represents the group of responses for which such an instinct is responsible."[149] Here was the seed of social behaviorism, the expression of the social act in terms of S and R. "Imitation," which Baldwin had developed from James's circular reaction, was extended by Mead from the individual to the group; for example, the child uttering "da-da-da" does so in response to a social stimulus, a parent's voice, "without there being any justification for the assumption that the process is one of imitation."[150] The actual origin of imitation, according to Mead, is social. He corrected Josiah Royce's concept of "imitation" preceding "social consciousness" with the opposite assertion: "social consciousness" is the presupposition of "imitation."[151] In other words, if and when a self becomes aware of another doing something, then it may engage in a similar action.

Instead of a concatenated series of reflexes, as in James's theory of volition, Mead proposed a "theory of social stimulation and response" in which "the conduct of one form is a stimulus to another to a certain act, and . . . this act again becomes a stimulus at first to a certain reaction, and so on in ceaseless interaction."[152] The fault of James's theory he explained thus:

> In Professor James's treatise the self is brilliantly dealt with in a chapter by itself. Within that chapter we see that, as a self, it is completely knit into a social consciousness, that the diameter of the self waxes and wanes with the field of social activity, but what the value of this nature of the self is for the cognitive and emotional phases of consciousness we do not discover.[153]

In fact, Mead's program for social psychology may be expressed as a connecting of James's theory of self with James's theory of volition and emotion. The "social self" which acts with reference to others was the essence of Mead's reformulation of self into a group process in 1913,[154] while the gestures, sounds, and language, as well as the implicit speech of thinking, constituted his "attitudes." This went well beyond James's theory of the afferent feeling in volition and emotion, but the logic of response preceding feeling was identical. Finally, the mechanism by which we take on the attitude of others and play the "role" of another self as our own—as in the child thinking about his conduct in terms of what his parents would say was right and wrong—became the important connecting link between social stimulus and behavioral response. Again, the extension to "social consciousness" was original, but the mechanism is strongly reminiscent of James's "anticipatory image" and "connate path": *"when a sensation has once produced a movement in us, the next time we have the sensation, it tends to suggest the idea of the movement, even before the movement occurs."*[155]

Although Mead's influence was ultimately felt more in sociology, his transitional importance for social behaviorism was acknowledged in Floyd Allport's *Social Psychology* in 1924. Allport considered the reflex arc to be "the functional unit of behavior."[156] He brought James's conception of the "circular reflex" up to date with a discussion of the autonomic nervous system, as well as the central nervous system. Yet he continued to employ the diagrams and terminology of "the chain reflex" and "the circular reflex," while adding the conditioned reflex.[157] Citing Mead, he was quite clear about the extension of these concepts to social behavior:

> The reader should distinguish clearly between circular behavior and the circular reflex (p. 39). The former requires two or more individuals; the latter is completed in the nervous system of a single individual.[158]

Allport illustrated circular behavior with the example of ordinary conversation, "each party thereto being stimulated to utterance by the response which his former remark has aroused in his interlocutor." He took this example, and another one involving the provoking of one individual to hostility by another through threats, from Mead's 1912 essay on "The Mechanism of Social Consciousness":

> This succession of reactions Professor Mead has aptly termed a "conversation of attitudes."[159]

Then he made Mead's mechanism explicit with diagrams of linear, circular, and conditioned social behavior. In each diagram, the receptor *(r)* of one individual *(I)* is stimulated to a response (Rsp *I*) by the action of another individual (Figures 10a, b). Social stimulation may be either direct or contributory. A direct stimulus, as when food (F) is eaten in isolation, is contrasted to a contributory stimulus, such as the guests at a dinner party (Figure 10c). Contributory stimulation may become circular, rather than linear, if the response of one individual contributes to the response of another individual (Figure 10d). For example, in a fire, *(F)*, one individual (I_1) sees another (I_2) running, and this makes him run faster.[160]

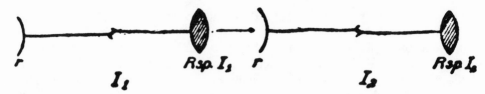

Figure 10a. Linear social behavior. I₁ and I₂ = reflex arcs of two individuals, Rsp I₁ and Rsp II₂ = responses of the respective individuals, r = receptors. (The response of the first individual serves as a stimulus to the second.) The arrow indicates the direction in which the social response is operative. (From Floyd Henry Allport, Social Psychology *[Boston: Houghton Mifflin Co., 1924], p. 149.)*

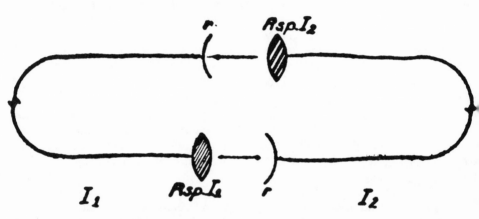

Figure 10b. Circular social behavior. Same caption as Figure 10a. The response of each individual serves as a stimulus to the other. (From Floyd Henry Allport, Social Psychology *[Boston: Houghton Mifflin Co., 1924], p. 150.)*

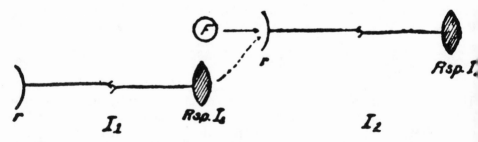

Figure 10c. Contributory social stimulation in linear social behavior. Same caption as Figures 10a and 10b, with Resp. I₁ = social stimulus, F = non-social stimulus of food. A social stimulus contributes to the effect of a non-social one. (From Floyd Henry Allport, Social Psychology *[Boston: Houghton Mifflin Co., 1924], p. 151.)*

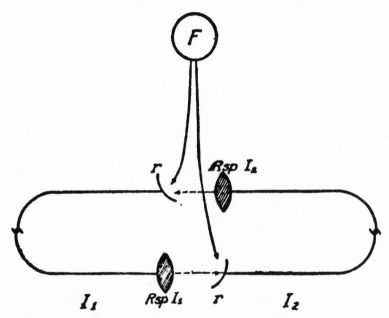

Figure 10d. Contributory social stimulation in circular social behavior. Same caption as Figures 10a, 10b, and 10c, with Rsp. I₁ and Rsp. I₂ = contributory social stimulus, F = non-social stimulus of fire. Two individuals each respond to a non-social stimulus, but each also serves as a contributory social stimulus to the other and increases the reaction by circular reinforcement. (From Floyd Henry Allport, Social Psychology *[Boston: Houghton Mifflin Co., 1924], p. 152.)*

Abnormal Psychology: Morton Prince, Boris Sidis, and J. J. Putnam

The reception of abnormal psychology in America has been much studied.[161] The personal and intellectual role of William James in this reception, while frequently mentioned, remains to be established in terms of the continuity of ideas. In keeping with the thesis of this chapter that his psychology of will was influential, the work of the "Boston School" of psychotherapy—comprising Morton Prince, Josiah Royce, Hugo Münsterberg, Boris Sidis, James Jackson Putnam, and James himself—will be examined.

James developed his theory of will in relation to abnormal phenomena. Ideomotor action was based on Carpenter's account of hypnotic action, and the healthy will was contrasted to the explosive will and the obstructed will of Ribot's *Diseases of the Will* and T. S. Clouston's *Clinical Lectures on Mental Diseases.* In 1889, James favorably reviewed the dissociation theory of Pierre Janet, recognizing that "psychological automatism" was a characteristic of the self dissociated from a personality—either through artificial or natural causes.[162] As if to emphasize the future importance of the abnormal, he placed his "Hypnotism" chapter after the "Will" chapter and next to last in the *Principles.* In it he joined his theories of self, or multiple selves, and of will, as based on habits and interests. In his *Varieties of Religious Experience* in 1902, he wrote: "To say that a man is "converted" means, in these terms, that religious ideas, previously peripheral in his consciousness, now take a central place, and that religious aims form the habitual centre of his energy."[163] The mechanism of attention to another self in the conversion experience thus comprised the basis of James's own dissociation theory. Its three facets—associated movements, dissociated selves, and moral education—were separately developed by three younger contemporaries, respectively.

Graduating from Harvard College in 1875, Morton Prince (1854–1929) won the Boylston Prize for an essay on "The Nature of Mind and Human Automatism," which he published ten years later, in 1885.[164] Turning his medical practice from diseases of the nose and throat to diseases of the mind sometime afterwards, he reviewed the hypnosis literature—including James's recent essay review of Janet—at a meeting attended by James, Josiah Royce, and James Jackson Putnam in March 1890.[165] By December of that year, he had presented a theory of "association neuroses" to account for hysterical conversion reactions.[166] For example, Prince described the case of a little girl who had continued to walk on the ball of her foot due to a sprained knee one and a half years after it was healed. He diagramed the situation as an inhibition of the extensor muscles and an excitation of the flexor muscles (Figure 11).

Two features of Prince's description, the centripetal muscular feelings and the associative connection which produced the neurosis, are similar to James's theory:

> The slightest motion, that is to say, the slightest centripetal impression, from the joint due to change of position, excited not only the sensory centres of muscular sense and pain, but the motor centres as well. By constant repetition these centres became physiologically associated together. . . . The automatic process having become once established, it continues as an independent neurosis after the original exciting cause has ceased to exist.[167]

The technique of the reeducation of the will may also have been suggested by James. Prince simply taught the girl to relax the inhibited muscles while lying on her back and kicking. In one important respect, however, Prince came to differ with James's notion of a subconscious self: "No evidence has thus far been brought forward that there is such a large doubling of normal minds; and even in hysterical minds, though the theory may well be true, it still lacks, as does that of Sidis, experimental verification."[168]

Boris Sidis (1867–1923) was a younger psychologist, who did experimental work under James's auspices at the Harvard Psychological Laboratory during the 1890s. In 1897, James wrote an introduction to Sidis's book, *The Psychology of Suggestion* in which he gave only a somewhat qualified assent to Sidis's theory that suggestion accounted for a splitting off of consciousness through physiological inhibition. Sidis had written:

> Physiologically, hypnosis *is an inhibition of the inhibitory centres.* . . . Psychologically, *hypnosis is the split-off, disaggregated, organic, reflex consciousness pure and simple.*[169]

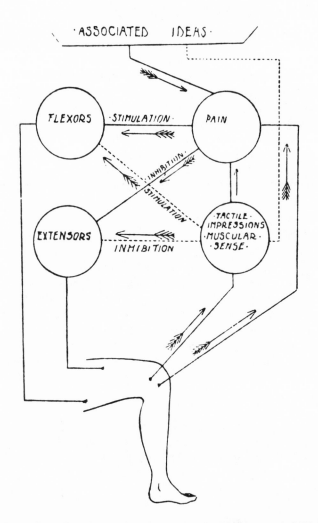

Figure 11. Little girl with association neurosis. Voluntary inhibition of extensor muscles due to pain following a local foot injury. Involuntary or automatic associ-ation of this muscular inhibition with pain and sensory centers of muscular sense. Neurosis continues after local cause of pain has subsided. (From Morton Prince, "Association Neuroses: A Study of Hysterical Joint Affections, Neurasthenia and Allied Forms of Neuro-Mimesis," Journal of Nervous and Mental Disease *18 (1890): 270, reprinted in Nathan G. Hale, Jr.,* Morton Prince. Psychotherapy and Multiple Personality: Selected Essays *[Cambridge, Mass.: Harvard University Press, 1975], p. 73.)*

In short, the volitional consciousness is dissociated from the reflex one through inhibition. This was a somewhat one-sided rendition of James. Sidis noted that this view had been enunciated by Rudolf Heidenhain and Hugo Moll, and he found it implicit in the strictly psychological theory of Hippolyte Bernheim. He discovered it explicitly stated by Edmund Gurney: "The heart of the problem (of hypnosis) . . . lies not in *consciousness,* but in *will.*"[170] However, he was clearly influenced primarily by his teachers at Harvard. He referred to James and Royce in terms which indicate that both shared a supervisory role in his research.[171] His appreciation of help from Hugo Münsterberg (1863–1916), a later proponent of a physiological theory of the subconscious, is another important link with James.[172] For Münsterberg's 1888 *Die Willenshandlung* had been prominently cited by James, both in his critique of the Meynert scheme and his refutation of feelings of innervation.[173] So impressed was James with Münsterberg that he had brought him to Harvard to take over his psychological laboratory.

Ironically, it was James's older friend since medical school, James Jackson Putnam (1846–1921), who did fullest justice to his psychology of "moral therapy." Late in his distinguished career as a neurologist, Putnam turned to a more psychological explanation of nervous disorders.[174] Following the lead of Pierre Janet and Morton Prince, Putnam defined mental health as an equilibrium of conscious and subconscious factors. The "subconscious" was understood by him in terms of the split-off habit patterns and mental associations. In this Putnam was only taking over Prince's version of James. However, his therapeutic method involved more than retraining habits, as it had for Prince. He encouraged his patients to reconceptualize their views of themselves and to act as if they had hope and confidence.[175] He argued that physicians needed training in psychology and even philosophy. Putnam's close friend James was an example of the kind of cure he recommended, and Putnam expressed this clearly in his necrology in 1910.[176] By 1915, having supported psychoanalysis and corresponded with Freud for over a decade, Putnam finally communicated his reservations about Freud's theory of instincts: "the choice of motives, whether voluntarily or instinctively made, must depend in the final analysis on the standards arrived at through education, the true function of which consists in leading to the discovery of deeper and deeper relationships between the outside world and the inner life."[177] The teaching of James in regard to the role of interest, and the direction of will by attention to ideas, is implied here. An optimism and faith in human nature to cure itself through education was the crucial difference between the outlooks of the Boston School and the followers of Freud.

Overview

James's influence has been acknowledged by psychologists, but the reasons for this acknowledgment are seldom stated. Was it James's personality, or his pragmatic philosophy, or his moral fervor, or his picturesque style, that endeared him to posterity?

Gardner Murphy has suggested that James's working conception of volition was his most central contribution to psychology. This working conception has been found to contain five main ingredients, and all five have proven important in the psychology of this century. A brief review of the impact of these themes may suggest an answer to the question of James's popularity among psychologists.

First, habit and ideo-motor action were the mainstays of his theory. He re-worked the concept of reflex from physiology and the concept of ideo-motor action from hypnosis in such a way that they became plastic, subject to modification. Similarly, the field of animal learning which was initiated by James's student Thorndike relied on the change of habits through use and disuse, the so-called law of exercise. In the field of personality, Mary Calkins, another student of James, referred to mental "dispositions" in a manner similar to James's "habits"— as the experience of emotion and will in relation to others. Habit was also central to Morton Prince's conceptualization of the "association neurosis," which was established by the associative connection of pain and feelings of movement, and which was cured by establishing a new connection without pain.

Second, fiat as inhibition and consent, rather than inhibition and excitation, was an original aspect of his theory. Renouvier's grasp of the French clinical tradition, as well as Kantian philosophy, led to this subtle solution to the problem of action. The personality functions as a whole and is immediately experienced, as Calkins emphasized; it becomes functionally autonomous, as Gordon Allport phrased it. The only opportunity for change is to either redirect our habits or to let them be. Freedom is strictly limited to the inhibition of and consent to existing actions.

Third, attention acquired a distinctly functional interpretation through James's concept of interest. Much broader than Spencer's hedonism of pleasure and pain, interests were conceived by James as the remote and resident stimuli of action. Their functional significance was soon recognized by Dewey, who replaced the reflex-arc concept with a sensori-motor coordination involving attention. Angell followed Dewey with his critique of the reaction-time literature based not upon the attention to a single stimulus but attention over a period of time, i.e., on the basis of a reduction in reaction time through acquired, or coordinated habits. Woodworth developed James's concept of attention further into a theory of moti-vation based upon selection and control. Finally, Mead's "social act" by which a response is attuned to a social stimulus became a sociological version of James's concept of interest.

Fourth, mentalism, in which outgoing feelings of innervation provided intro-spective evidence of will, was rejected. In its place, James drew upon Peirce's definition of ideas in terms of their effects. This novel theoretical orientation was adopted by Dewey, Angell, and Mead—all of whom belonged at one time or another to the Chicago Functional School, which emphasized the instrumental effect of actions on the environment. For slightly different reasons, Thorndike was opposed to mentalism and adopted the concept of impulsive acts, and ulti-mately trial and error responses, to combat the mentalistic attribution of ideas to animals by Lloyd Morgan. Certainly behaviorism was an extension, and in some ways an unfortunate exaggeration, of the revolutionary insight from the evolution-ary tradition that ideas, like physical characteristics, are selected according to their effects. The law of effect, which was originally put forward in a physiological form by Thorndike, later achieved general acceptance as the empirical law of effect, or the principle of reinforcement.

Fifth, the Meynert scheme, which dominated physiological psychology in the latter nineteenth century, was radically revised by James. He substituted a functional version of it, which accounted for the modification of experience through a hypothetical physiological mechanism, the so-called "motor circle." Though resisted by Ladd on grounds of being materialistic, it was enthusiastically embraced by Baldwin for his theory of mental development and renamed the "motor square." Dewey made use of the familiar child-flame example to convey the essential logic of instrumentalism. Angell used James's model as the physiological mechanism underlying attention and volition, and Thorndike extended it into his two laws of learning. Holt later repeated it as late as 1931. The circle was also implicit in the concept of drive formulated by Woodworth and the functional autonomy of Allport. It achieved lasting notoriety through James's theory of emotions, which was caricatured as a peripheral theory and replaced by a central one through the research of Cannon and Bard in the 1920s.

Conclusion

In the present account, an endeavour was made to tie together several hitherto disconnected conclusions about the contribution of William James to modern psychology.

(1) From the context of the rise of American philosophy, Bruce Kuklick noted in 1977: "Although he [James] began work on *Principles of Psychology* in 1878, much of his published work from then until 1890 expanded and developed his ideas on the will."[178] Certainly will proved to be an organizing theme for the conceptual development of James's *Principles*.

(2) Writing in 1967 and 1970 about learning and motivation, Gregory Kimble compared James's theory of volition to the principles of classical and operant conditioning.[179] In this chapter the origin of behaviorism was traced not only to Thorndike's laws of exercise and effect, but to the implications of the feedback conception which permeated subsequent theories of motivation, emotion, personality, attention, cognition, and social and abnormal psychology.

(3) During the past two decades, it has become almost commonplace to refer to James as an existentialist or a proto-phenomenologist; Rollo May, Hans Linschoten, Herbert Spiegelberg, Aron Gurwitsch, Bruce Wilshire, and Richard Stevens may be mentioned.[180] The existential core of James's theory of will is in the selective role of fiat as it directed ideo-motor action. It can be seen that scholars approaching James from widely divergent vantage points have all converged upon his theory of will—but unfortunately without elucidating its debt to previous theories or the nature of its reception and further development.

In fact, James schooled himself in nineteenth-century physiological psychology. His psychology of the voluntary processes was developed through a critique of Bain, Helmholtz, Wundt, Spencer, Carpenter, and Meynert—the very men from whom he borrowed his concepts of habit, feelings of movement or innervaion, interest, and ideo-motor action. Their association psychology was grounded n reflex physiology, cerebral localization of "associative centers," and the associ- tion of ideas.[181] The laws of the connection of brain states A and B became the aws of the association of the corresponding ideas, a and b in this psychophysical aarallelism. On this argument, the last brain state and the last idea in a series of uch parallel events would determine the action. This last mental state was termed he "feeling of effort," or the introspective equivalent of will.

James's positive program for the study of the volitional processes introduced explanation in place of description. In "A Plea for Psychology as a Natural Sci- nce," James criticized the foregoing program of research as "tedious"—"tedious aot as really hard things like physics and chemistry, are tedious, but tedious as the hrowing of feathers hour after hour is tedious."[182] By natural science, he meant hat

the real thing to aim at is a *causal* account; and I must say that that appears to lie (provisionally at least) in the region of the laws as yet unknown of the connection of the mind with the body. There is *the* subject for a "science" of psychology![183]

ames shifted the "feeling of effort" conceptually from the cause of action to the esult of action, drawing this "behavioral" aspect of will from the physiologist, David Ferrier, and to a lesser extent from Hermann Lotze, Carl Stumpf, and Ewald Hering. His functional redefinition of will involved the holding of the results of prior action in attention, through fiat or consent, on the basis of a set of interests. He derived this "existential" aspect of will chiefly from Renouvier. His complete psychology of will thus involved a feedback loop of three parts: ideo- motor action, the effects of this action, and the fiat of will which selected among hese effects.[184]

The impact of this program was revolutionary in that it provided a conceptual oundation for the New Psychology in America. The concepts of "sensori-motor coordination," "motor square," "law of effect," "drive," "disposition," "social acts," and "human motives," covering the major subfields of psychology, testify .o the broad scope of this foundation. The common factor was the replacement of a parallelistic associationism by functional interaction. The consensus of the gen- eration after James, and on up to about 1920, was that both behavior and con- sciousness belong to causal explanation. Thus, it may be said without exaggeration that behaviorism and phenomenology, as they have come to typify the poles within psychological theory, were held together by a "productive oaradox" in James's theory of will.[185]

ACKNOWLEDGMENTS

I am grateful to Ronald E. Shor, David E. Leary, William M. Baum, Richard High, Laurence D. Smith, and Ernest R. Hilgard for discussions relating to specific points. Critical comments leading to revision were also provided by John C. Burnham, Brian Mackenzie, John Mills, Franz Samelson, and Robert

Wozniak. Especially helpful stylistic and conceptual clarification was contrib
uted by George Haslerud and Josef Brožek.

NOTES

1. Gardner Murphy, "William James on the Will," *Journal of the History of the Behavioral Science*
7 (1971): 254.
2. The Symposium "Whatever Happened to the Will in American Psychology?" was cosponsore
by Divisions 1 and 26 at the Annual Convention of the American Psychological Association in Sa
Francisco, Cal., 31 August 1968. Papers subsequently published included: James E. Royce, S.J.
"Historical Aspects of Free Choice," *Journal of the History of the Behavioral Sciences* 6 (1970): 48–51
Albin R. Gilbert, "Whatever Happened to the Will in American Psychology?" ibid., pp. 52–58; Orl
Strunk, Jr., "Values Move Will: the Problem of Conceptualization," ibid., pp. 59–63.
3. Ralph B. Perry, *The Thought and Character of William James*, 2 vols. (Boston: Little, Brown &
Co., 1935), 1: 654–58.
4. James was not alone. See Frank M. Turner, *Between Science and Religion. The Reaction t
Scientific Naturalism in Late Victorian England* (New Haven, Conn.: Yale University Press, 1974)
Turner deals specifically with Henry Sidgwick, Alfred Russel Wallace, Frederic W. H. Myers, George
John Romanes, Samuel Butler, and James Ward. "Moral philosophy" spanned both ethical philosophy
and social science. W. R. Sorley and Henry Sidgwick wrote under "ethics" in James Mark Baldwin's
Dictionary of Philosophy and Psychology, 3 vols. (New York: Macmillan, 1901), 1: 346, that "the
terms ethics, moral science, and moral philosophy are used almost synonomously." James Mark
Baldwin, ibid., 2: 106, defined "moral sciences" as "those branches of inquiry which deal with min
and conduct, as opposed to matter and life . . . history, political economy, law, and statistics, as well as
psychology, anthropology, and ethics." For these persons, their classical training in philosophy as wel
as their varied exposure to such recent scientific developments as medical hypnosis, evolution, and
experimental psychology, raised anew the fundamental question of responsibility for one's actions—
which was the problem of sin in a naturalistic guise.
5. William B. Carpenter, *Principles of Human Physiology*, ed. Henry Power (Philadelphia: H. C
Lea, 1876, lst ed. 1852). The course was "Natural History 2. Comparative Anatomy and Physiology o
Vertebrates." Carpenter's chapter on somnambulism construed ideo-motor action in the hypnotic
trance state as automatic action with the will suspended (chap. 13, sec. 6). This crude interactionist
view was expanded into a subsequent book, *Principles of Mental Physiology*, 4th ed. (London and
New York: D. Appleton and Co., 1876), from which James taught in 1879–80. This was the academic
year in which he composed his essay on "The Feeling of Effort" (see note 10) which was later rewritten
as the chapter on "Will" in the *Principles of Psychology* (see note 7). The defense of moral causation is
found in Carpenter, *Mental Physiology*, 1876, pp. vii–xlix. William James's initial criticism of feelings
as efficacious in "moral" causation dates from his medical student days in 1869, as he acknowledged in
a footnote to chap. 5, "The Automaton-Theory," *Principles of Psychology*, 1: 130–31.
6. "Psychological causation" as the explanation of human activities has been distinguished from
"physical causation" as the explanation of occurrences by Theodore Mischel, "Wundt and the Conceptual Foundations of Psychology," *Philosophy and Phenomenological Research* 31 (1970): 7. The issue
for proponents of the New Psychology came down to dualism versus monism, since exponents of
psychological causation would not rule out physical causation, while the reverse exclusion did occur
under the impetus of arguments for the universal determination of matter and mind according to
evolutionary and energetic principles. Actually, among psychologists, both types of causation were
frequently entertained. For example, mental events such as sensing, feeling, and willing might be
described in terms of psychological elements (ideas) or physical elements (reflexes). The issue under
debate was (1) whether mind and body required two disparate types of causation, and, if so,
(2) whether these could be reconciled. As Mischel mentions, volition was the type for psychological as
opposed to physical causation since it deals with goals, values, etc., as well as reflexive activity.
7. On Renouvier and Lotze, see notes 11, 15, and 28 below. William James, *Principles of Psychology*,
2 vols. (New York: Henry Holt & Co., 1890), 2: 522, chap. 26, "Will."
8. Ibid., 1: 122, chap. 5, "Habit." A subtle but crucial theoretical point about this diagram is that one
idea (*V*, or volition) begins the chain and other ideas (*G'*, or ideational effects) follow it. In fact, ideo-
motor action is always followed by feelings of effort which become "anticipatory cues" for the subsequent action. This is stated most clearly in James's functional critique of the Meynert scheme (see
below). Notice too, that James used the terms idea, feeling, and sensation interchangeably in many

cases. Hence, any of these terms could stand as *V* or *G'*. For example, the kinesthetic feeling and auditory sensation of having played a note on the piano would represent both the ideational effect and the anticipatory cue for the next performance of this action.

9. Ibid., 1: 124.

10. Ibid., 2: 525. Also, William James, "The Feeling of Effort," *Anniversary Memoirs of the Boston Society of Natural History,* (1880), pp. 1–32, reprinted in *Collected Essays and Reviews,* ed. Ralph B. Perry (New York: Russell and Russell, 1969; reissued from London: Longmans, Green and Co., 1920), p. 184. Hereafter, *CER* will indicate this volume.

11. James, *Principles* 2: 449–50, chap. 25, "The Emotions." The basic mechanism of "anticipatory image" and automatic action, followed by afferent feeling or sensation, is set forth in Herman Lotze, *Medizinische Psychologie, oder Physiologie der Seele* (Leipzig: Weidmann, 1852), pp. 287–325, bk. 2, chap. 3, "On Movements and Drives," from which James took several quotations.

12. Sheldon Stern, "William James and the New Psychology," in Paul Buck, ed., *Social Sciences at Harvard: 1860–1920* (Cambridge, Mass.: Harvard University Press, 1965), pp. 182–85.

13. Herbert Spencer, *Principles of Psychology,* 2 vols. (New York: D. Appleton & Co., 1876, reprint of second ed. 1871, revised from 1st ed., 1855), *in toto.* Cf. Stern, "William James and the New Psychology," p. 186.

14. Stern, "William James and the New Psychology," p. 183.

15. William James, "Bain and Renouvier," Review of Alexander Bain, *The Emotions and the Will,* 3d ed. (New York: D. Appleton, 1876), and Charles Renouvier, *Essais de critique générale, Premier essai: Traité de logique générale; Deuxième essai: Traité de psychologie rationelle,* 2d ed., 5 vols., (Paris: Bureau de la Critique philosophique, 1875), *Nation* 22 (1876): 367–69, reprinted in James, *CER,* pp. 26–35.

16. Cf. Perry, *James,* 1: 658, chap. 41, "James and Renouvier: Early Correspondence."

17. James, "Bain and Renouvier," *CER,* p. 31.

18. James, "The Feeling of Effort," in *CER,* p. 198.

19. Ibid., p. 200.

20. James, *Principles,* 2: 526.

21. James, "Bain and Renouvier," *CER,* p. 31.

22. Spencer, *Psychology,* 1: 291–394, Part 3, General Synthesis. Cited in James, "Remarks on Spencer's Definition of Mind as Correspondence," *Journal of Speculative Philosophy* 12 (1878): 1–18; reprinted in *CER,* pp. 43–68, quotations from p. 44.

23. James, "Spencer's Definition," *CER,* pp. 44, 49. The examples are taken from Spencer, *Psychology,* 1: 409–10, Part 4, Special Synthesis.

24. Spencer, *Psychology,* 1: 280. Cf. a recent discussion of "the new hedonism" of Spencer by Robert C. Bolles, *Theory of Motivation* (New York: Harper & Row, 1967), p. 42.

25. James, "Spencer's Definition," *CER,* p. 64.

26. Ibid., p. 45.

27. Perry, *James,* 2: 89.

28. James, *Principles,* 2: 553. James relied on Lotze for his critique of hedonism. For example, Lotze had described the three components of a drive as (1) the physical or mental events which stimulate the nerves, (2) the feeling of harmonic or contradictory combination of mental states as pain or pleasure, and (3) the ideas of an attainable goal. Lotze pointed out that the feelings would simply perseverate without any outlet "if experience had not taught us which means are available for them, or in which satisfactory exit they can be transferred. As soon as these ideas of an attainable goal crop up in memory, the excited movement occurs as if oriented toward this goal and approaching it, the inhibited [movement] held back from it, and the feeling of a situation has transformed itself into the pleasant or unpleasant feeling of a movement which leads us to a beneficial or painful endpoint. Desire and aversion, which possess no clear resolution, are nothing else but such feelings of being driven, not however, drives in the sense of a driving force." Lotze, *Psychologie,* pp. 297–98. Translation mine.

29. James, *Principles,* 2: 559.

30. Ibid., 2: 562. James comes to grips most tenaciously with the knotty problem of deterministic "effects" and purposive "effort" in his chap. 11, "Attention," For example, he discusses "the effects of attention," pp. 424–25, and "is voluntary attention a resultant or a force?" pp. 447–48.

31. James, "The Feeling of Effort," *CER,* p. 211.

32. Ibid., p. 216. It is the freedom in this limited aspect of James's overall psychology of volition which has provided the focus of James's "moral philosophy." The best recent account is John K. Roth, ed., with intro., *The Moral Philosophy of William James* (New York: Thomas Y. Crowell Co., 1969), pp. 1–18. Cf. Lewis R. Rambo, "The Strenuous Life: William James' Normative Vision of the Human" (Ph.D. diss., University of Chicago, 1975).

33. Wilhelm Wundt, *Vorlesungen über die Menschen- und Tierseele* (Leipzig: L. Voss, 1863),

p. 222. Cited in James, "Feeling of Effort," *CER*, p. 163, and *Principles*, 2: 503. Cf. William R
Woodward, "From Association to Gestalt: The Fate of Hermann Lotze's Theory of Spatial Percep
tion, 1846–1920," *Isis* 69 (1978): 572–82.

34. Johannes Müller, *Elements of Physiology*, trans. William Baley, 2 vols. (London: Printed fo
Taylor and Walton, 1842), 2: 936–37, cited in Alexander Bain, *The Senses and the Intellect*, 3d ed
(New York: D. Appleton, 1868, 1st ed. 1855), p. 296. Cf. Mary Mosher Flesher, "The Role of Müller'
Elements of Physiology in Pre-Darwinian England, or From Bell to Bain," (Unpublished MS, Lehigh
University, Department of History). Communications from Brian Mackenzie and Kurt Danziger also
led me to this interpretation.

35. Bain, *Senses*, note 34, p. 299. Cf. Richard High, "Bain and American Functionalism" (Pape
presented at APA Convention, Sept. 1976).

36. David Ferrier, *The Functions of the Brain* (New York: G. P. Putnam's Sons, 1886, 1st ed. 1874)
The book was dedicated to Hughlings Jackson.

37. Ibid., American 1st edition, p. 222, quoted in James, "The Feeling of Effort," *CER*, p. 164.

38. Ibid., p. 244, quoted in James, *CER*, p. 167.

39. James, *CER*, pp. 167–68.

40. Charles Sanders Peirce, "How to Make Our Ideas Clear," In *Collected Papers of Charle
Sanders Peirce*, eds. Charles Hartshorne and Paul Weiss, 6 vols. (Cambridge: Harvard University
Press, 1960 [1931–35], 5: 248–271. Ralph Barton Perry has remarked that this essay marks the officia
beginning of the movement of pragmatism. See Perry, *James*, 2: 410.
In 1898 James observed in reference to this essay that "to attain perfect clearness in our thoughts o
an object, then, we need only consider what effects of a conceivably practical kind the object may
involve—what sensations we are to expect from it, and what reactions we must prepare. Our concep
tion of these effects, then, is for us the whole of our conception of the object, so far as that conception
has positive significance at all." In James, "Philosophical Conceptions and Practical Results," *Univer
sity Chronical* (Berkeley, Calif.), September 1898, reprinted in *CER*, pp. 410–11.

41. Hermann von Helmholtz, *Handbuch der physiologischen Optik*, 3 vols. (Leipzig: L. Voss, 1856
1860, 1866, 3 vols. bound as one in 1866), p. 600. In Helmholtz's experiment, the subject sweeps hi
eyes across a field of vision from left to right. Helmholtz ascribed this illusion to the feeling o
innervation.

42. James, "Feeling of Effort," *CER*, p. 172.

43. Ewald Hering, *Beiträge zur Physiologie*, 5 monographs (Leipzig: W. Engelmann, 1861–64)
citation of monograph 5, "Die Lehre vom binoculären Sehen," in James, "Feeling of Effort," *CER*
p. 173.

44. Lotze, *Psychologie*, pp. 322–23.

45. Cf. H. L. Hollingworth, "Effect and Affect in Learning," *Psychological Review* 38 (1931): 153-
59: "The outstanding mystery in the psychology of learning is of course the so-called 'law of effect.'
Part of the mystery arises from that ambiguity of the law which leads to confusion between 'effect' and
'affect.' As often stated, and as expressed in Bain's early formula, it is *affects*—agreeableness and
disagreeableness, pleasure and pain—that are responsible for the result. Pleasure reinforces the ac
that led to it; annoyance tends to eliminate the act producing it. On this basis the law should be called
the 'law of affect.' . . . As we have intimated, however, another form of the statement is possible, in
which it is the effect or result, rather than the *affect* or feeling-tone that accomplishes the trick. This i
in fact the form that Thorndike gives the law in his more guarded statements; it is the 'state of affairs
resulting in satisfaction, not the satisfaction itself, that is given the credit." The law of effect, thus
defined, is comparable to the principle of effect expressed by Peirce and James. Compare the discus
sion of Thorndike's Law of Effect in the section on "Learning" below.

46. James, *Principles*, 1: 26, chap. 2, "The Functions of the Brain," pp. 24–27, 72–80.

47. James, *Principles*, 1: 72.

48. Ibid., 2: 582–88. The translation "memory image" is also employed by James, ibid., 2: 586.

49. Ibid., 2: 585–86.

50. Ibid., 2: 584.

51. George Trumbull Ladd, *Elements of Physiological Psychology* (New York: Charles Scribner's
Sons, 1887), pp. 523–31.

52. Ibid., p. 504.

53. Ibid., p. 529.

54. George Trumbull Ladd, "Psychology as so-called 'Natural Science,'" *Philosophical Review*
(1892): 24–53.

55. William James, "A Plea for Psychology as a 'Natural Science,'" *Philosophical Review* 1 (1892)
54–59.

56. George Trumbull Ladd, *Psychology: Descriptive and Explanatory* (New York: Charles Scribner's Sons, 1894), p. 221.

57. Ibid., p. 221

58. Cf. Mischel, "Wundt and the Conceptual Foundations," p. 7.

59. Eugene S. Mills, *George Trumbull Ladd; Pioneer American Psychologist* (Cleveland, Ohio: The ress of Case Western Reserve University, 1969), p. 140.

60. Hans Linschoten, *On the Way Toward a Phenomenological Psychology: The Psychology of Villiam James* (Pittsburgh, Pa.: Duquesne University Press, 1968), passim, provides a standard henomenological interpretation of James.

61. James Mark Baldwin, *Handbook of Psychology*, vol. 1, *Senses and Intellect*, 2d ed. (New York: lenry Holt and Co., 1890 [1889]).

62. Ibid., p. 72.

63. Ibid., vol. 2, *Feeling and Will*, 2d ed. (New York: Henry Holt and Co., 1894 [1891]).

64. Ibid., pp. 286–94. Note that he refers to James's theory as "the association or effect theory" and Vundt's theory as "the spiritual theory" of reflex attention. He concludes that "whatever ground may e found subsequently for such an active executive self, we find no such ground here," i.e., in "motor onsciousness" of cases of attending to a loud sound and the like. Cf. his judicious discussion of the heory of innervation, pp. 348–50.

65. Ibid., p. 343.

66. Ibid.

67. Ibid., p. 327: "The subject is ably discussed by James, loc. cit., II, pp. 549–59: see also the eferences he gives on p. 558."

68. Ibid., p. 344.

69. Ibid., p. 281.

70. Cf. Alfred Binet, *Alterations of Personality*, trans. Helen Green Baldwin, with notes and a reface by J. Mark Baldwin (New York: D. Appleton and Co., 1896), chap. 6, pp. 155–88, using the erm "dynamographic." With regard to Lotze, Baldwin wrote (pp. 35–46): "There are only two ways to econcile these positions, provided they are well taken. We may hold with Lotze[1] [Note 1. *Microcosus*, bk. II, chap. v. Para. 5–6. A view for which James has some fondness, loc. cit., II, pp. 576 and 84] that consciousness is dynamic; that it adds to the energy of the system by modifying muscular eactions through volition, at the same time that, by its inhibitions and efforts to control other reacions, it suppresses energy; and that the additions and subtractions neutralize each other in the long un. This preserves both the dynamic value of consciousness, and the proper balance of the nervous ystem in relation to its environment.

"Or we may hold that consciousness enters as an apparently new principle which develops by laws f its own, but which develops apace with nervous integration: that the reason of their concomitance, f their mutual dependence, lies hidden; there are no analogies in nature by which to explain it."

71. Baldwin, *Feeling and Will*, p. 42. Cf. James, *Principles*, 2: 14–27, 74–80. Diagram is on pp. 20, 5.

72. Baldwin, *Feeling and Will*, p. 49.

73. James Mark Baldwin, *Mental Development of the Child and the Race. Methods and Processes* New York: Macmillan Company, 1915 [1895]), pp. 356–57, citing James, *Principles*, 2: 582. The actual iagram is most similar to James, *Principles*, 1: 25.

74. Ibid., p. 358.

75. Ibid., p. 355.

76. Ibid., p. 84. Cf. pp. 361–64 for other examples.

77. Cf. James, *Principles*, 1: 20 and 2: 521, 586.

78. Baldwin, *Mental Development*, pp. 362–63.

79. Ibid., pp. 203–4 on accommodation, pp. 291–92 on assimilation, pp. 363–66 on life plan, citing Binet, *Alterations*, pp. 156–57. Cf. John Broughton and John Freeman-Moir, eds., *The Cognitive Developmental Psychology of James Mark Baldwin: Current Theory and Research in Genetic Epistemology* (New York: Ablex Pres, in press.)

80. William R. Woodward, "Young Piaget Revisited: From the Grasp of Consciousness to Décalage," *Genetic Psychology Monographs* 99 (1979): 131–61. Cf. Jean Piaget, *The Origins of Intelligence in Children*, tr. M. Cook. (New York: International Universities Press, 1952 [1936]).

81. John Dewey, "The Reflex Arc Concept in Psychology," *Psychological Review* 3 (1896): 357–58.

82. Ibid., p. 358.

83. Ibid., pp. 362–63. Dewey quoted from Baldwin, *Feeling and Will*, p. 60.

84. Ibid., p. 361

85. James Rowland Angell and Addison W. Moore, "Studies from the Psychological Laboratory of

192 EXPLORATIONS IN THE HISTORY OF PSYCHOLOGY

the University of Chicago. 1. Reaction-time: A Study in Attention and Habit," *Psychological Review* 3 (1896): 245–58.

86. Edwin G. Boring, *A History of Experimental Psychology* (New York: Appleton-Century-Crofts, 1929), pp. 413–14.

87. Angel and Moore, "Studies," p. 252.

88. Ibid., p. 258.

89. James Rowland Angell, *Psychology. An Introductory Study of the Structure and Function of Human Consciousness*, 4th ed., rev. (New York: Henry Holt and Co., 1908 [1904]).

90. Ibid., p. 402.

91. Edward Lee Thorndike, "Animal Intelligence: An Experimental Study of the Associative Process," *Psychological Monographs* 2, no. 41 (1898): 1–109; reprinted in Edward L. Thorndike, *Animal Intelligence*. (New York: Hafner Publishing Co., 1965 [1911]). Quotations are from the later edition.

92. Ibid., p. 99. Thorndike cited Lloyd Morgan, *Introduction to Comparative Psychology* (London: Walter Scott Publishing Co., 1894), pp. 90–91.

93. Ibid., p. 102.

94. Ibid., p. 37.

95. Ibid., p. 105.

96. Ibid., p. 106.

97. James, *Principles*, 2: 581.

98. Thorndike, *Animal Intelligence*. p. 120. Cf. James, *Principles*, 2: 327–28, 349–53. James wrote, for example, "that a dog will perceive whether you have kicked him by accident or by design, and behave accordingly. The character inferred by him, the particular mental state in you, however, it be represented in his mind—it is represented probably by a 'recept' (p. 327) or set of practical tendencies, rather than by a definite concept or idea . . ." (p. 350). He referred to George John Romanes, *Mental Evolution in Man* (London: Kegan, Paul, Trench, 1889) pp. 68–80, 197–98, 353, 396.

99. Thorndike, *Animal Intelligence*, p. 121.

100. Ibid., p. 148.

101. Edward L. Thorndike, *The Elements of Psychology*, 2d ed. (New York: A. G. Seiler, 1907 [1905]), p. ix.

102. Ibid., p. 282. Thorndike continued: "Nearly all writiers on psychology seem sure that some special sort of feeling is a necessary element of purposive action; that really *any mental state whatever may be the antecedent of an intentional act*. . . . Professor James, who maintains that 'whether or no there be anything else in the mind at the moment when we consciously will a certain act, a mental conception made up of these sensations (of the movement's results) . . . must be there,' (*Principles*, 2: 492) gives illustrations which prove precisely that the antecedent to a movement need never have been its result" (p. 283).

103. James, *Principles*, 2: 581, 584.

104. Thorndike, *Elements*, p. 166. See note 45 above.

105. Ibid., p. 312.

106. Compare the section above on "Subjective Interest and Attention." James, *Principles*, 2: 536.

107. Professor Ernest R. Hilgard (personal communication, 16 August 1979) has pointed out to me that Thorndike opposed the concept of ideo-motor action in his 1913 Presidential address to the American Psychological Association. The substance of Thorndike's critique is misleading, however. He is attacking mentalistic explanation by ideas, *not* the logical argument that action is guided by the effects of previous action. The latter feedback mechanism derives from James. Cf. Edward L. Thorndike, "Ideo Motor Action," *Psychological Review* 20 (1913): 91–106, reprinted in Ernest R. Hilgard, ed., *American Psychology in Historical Perspective* (Washington, D.C.: American Psychological Association, 1978).

108. Robert S. Woodworth, "The Accuracy of Voluntary Movement," *Psychological Review*, Monograph Supplements, vol. 3, no. 3, (1899): 1–114. It should be noted that Woodworth and Thorndike were friends at the time they were studying under James, and that this was the heyday of influence of the *Principles*. In his autobiography, Woodworth noted that Thorndike encouraged him to pursue the new field of "motivology." Through their joint work on transfer of training, they were instrumental in founding the field of human learning. Both demonstrated a knack in their dissertations for choosing a quantifiable dependent measure; this was consistent with James's methodological requirement that ideas must be measured by their effects.

109. Ibid., p. 109.

110. Robert S. Woodworth, "The Cause of a Voluntary Movement," *Studies in Philosophy and Psychology by Former Students of Charles Edward Garman*, 1906, pp. 351–92, reprinted in *Psychological Issues: Selected Papers of Robert S. Woodworth* (New York: Columbia University Press, 1939), pp. 29–60.

111. Ibid., pp. 47–48. Quoting James, *Principles,* 2: 488.

112. Robert S. Woodworth, *Dynamic Psychology* (New York: Columbia University Press, 1918), p. 34.

113. Ibid., p. 40.

114. Robert S. Woodworth, Psychology: A Study of Mental Life (New York: Henry Holt and Co., 1929 [1921]), pp. 523–51.

115. Ibid., p. 551.

116. George Trumbull Ladd and Robert Sessions Woodworth, *Elements of Physiological Psychology,* 2d ed. (New York: Charles Scribner's Sons, 1911), p. 618.

117. Charles S. Sherrington, *The Integrative Action of the Nervous System* (New York: Arno Press, 1973 [N.Y.: Charles Scribner's Sons, 1906; reprinted, ed., Cambridge: at the University Press, 1948]), p. 260.

118. Charles S. Sherrington, "Experiments on the Value of Vascular and Visceral Factors for the Genesis of Emotion," *Proceedings of the Royal Society* 66 (1900): 397.

119. Robert S. Woodworth and Charles S. Sherrington, "A Pseudaffective Reflex and its Spinal Path," *Journal of Physiology* 31 (1904): 234.

120. Sherrington, *Integrative Action,* p. 253.

121. Ibid., p. 268. Cf. Judith P. Swazey, *Reflexes and Motor Integration: Sherrington's Concept of Reflex Action* (Cambridge, Mass.: Harvard University Press, 1969), pp. 149–50.

122. Walter B. Cannon, "The Interrelations of Emotions as Suggested by Recent Physiological Researches," *American Journal of Psychology* 25 (1914): 264.

123. Ibid., p. 263.

124. Ibid., p. 280. Reprinted in Walter B. Cannon, *Bodily Changes in Pain, Hunger, Fear, and Rage* (New York: D. Appleton and Co., 1925 [1915]), p. 280 [*sic*]).

125. James R. Angell, "A Reconsideration of James's Theory of Emotion in the Light of Recent Criticisms," *Psychological Review* 23 (1916): 259–60.

126. Walter B. Cannon, "The James-Lange Theory of Emotions: A Critical Examination and an Alternative Theory," *American Journal of Psychology* 39 (1927): 106–24.

127. Ibid., p. 118.

128. Philip Bard, "Emotion: I. The Neuro-Humoral Basis of Emotional Reactions," Chap. 12 in Carl Murchison, ed., *The Foundations of Experimental Psychology* (Worcester, Mass.: Clark University Press, 1929), pp. 449–87.

129. Mary Whiton Calkins, autobiographical essay, in Carl Murchison, ed., *History of Psychology in Autobiography,* vol. 1 (Worcester, Mass.: Clark University Press, 1930), p. 44.

130. Ibid., pp. 49–50. Cf. Mary Whiton Calkins, "Is the Self a Body or Has It a Body?" *Journal of Philosophy* 5 (1908): 12–20.

131. Ibid., pp. 48–49. Cf. Mary Whiton Calkins, *A First Book in Psychology* (New York: Macmillan, 1916 [1909]), pp. 282–83 on emotion, pp. 226–27 on will.

132. Mary Whiton Calkins, *An Introduction to Psychology* (New York: Macmillan, 1908 [1901]), pp. 296–97.

133. Ibid., p. 312, quoting James, *Principles,* 2: 569.

134. Calkins, autobiography, note 129, p. 54.

135. Gordon Allport, "The Productive Paradoxes of William James," *Psychological Review* 50 (1943): 95–120.

136. Richard P. High and William R. Woodward, "William James and Gordon Allport: Parallels in their Maturing Conceptions of Self and Personality," in Robert Rieber and Kurt Salzinger, eds., *Psychology: Theoretical and Historical Perspectives* (New York: Academic Press, 1980).

137. Gordon Allport, *Personality: A Psychological Interpretation* (New York: Henry Holt & Co., 1937), chap. 9, "The Search for Elements," and chap. 10, "The Theory of Identical Elements," pp. 235–85.

138. Ibid., p. 249.

139. "The Concept of Self," from Gordon Allport, *Becoming* (New Haven, Conn.: Yale University Press, 1955), and "Personal Dispositions," from Gordon Allport, *Pattern and Growth in Personality* (New York: Holt, Rinehart and Winston, 1965), are excerpted by Salvatore R. Maddi, ed., *Perspectives on Personality: A Comparative Approach* (Boston: Little, Brown and Co., 1971), pp. 307–28.

140. Allport, *Personality,* p. 141.

141. Ibid., pp. 45, 82.

142. Ibid., p. 194.

143. Andrew J. Reck, ed. with intro., *Selected Writings, George Herbert Mead* (Indianapolis, Ind.: Bobbs-Merrill, 1964), p. xiii. See George H. Mead, "A Theory of Emotions from the Physiological Standpoint," *Psychological Review* 2 (1895): 162–64.

144. George H. Mead, "What Social Objects Must Psychology Presuppose?" *Journal of Philosophy, Psychology and Scientific Methods* 7 (1910): 174–80; reprinted in Reck, *Selected Writings*, p. 109.

145. George H. Mead, "Suggestions toward a Theory of the Philosophic Disciplines," *Philosophical Review* 9 (1900): 1–17; reprinted in Reck, *Selected Writings*, pp. 6–24.

146. George H. Mead, "The Definition of the Psychical," *The Decennial Publications of the University of Chicago*, "First Series," III (Chicago: University of Chicago Press, 1903), pp. 77–78, 92–112; reprinted in Reck, *Selected Writings*, pp. 25–59, quotation from p. 43.

147. Ibid., pp. 49–50.

148. George H. Mead, "Social Psychology as Counterpart to Physiological Psychology," *Psychological Bulletin* 6 (1909) 401–8; reprinted in Reck, *Selected Writings*, pp. 95–104.

149. Ibid., p. 98. Cf. William McDougall, *An Introduction to Social Psychology*, 3d ed. (Boston: John W. Luce & Co., 1920), pp. 45–89.

150. Ibid., p. 100. Cf. Baldwin, *Mental Development*. Gordon Allport noted that "Mead (1934) saw clearly the implications of Baldwin's ejective stage. It helps to explain how the individual comes to take the role of other people. We do more than imitate. We perceive what the other is doing (through ejective imitation), but we also perceive our own response to it. What occurs is an interweaving process. Each act is the resultant both of our role assumption and of our self-perceptions. . . . Mead's theory of socialization is not exclusively 'imitationist'; yet his point of departure lies in the doctrine as expounded by Baldwin." "The Historical Background of Modern Social Psychology," in Gardner Lindzey, ed., *Handbook of Social Psychology*, vol. 1 (Cambridge, Mass.: Addison-Wesley Publishing Co., 1954), p. 22.

151. Ibid., p. 100. Cf. Josiah Royce, *Outlines of Psychology: An Elementary Treatise with Some Practical Applications* (New York: Macmillan Co., 1903), chap. 12, pp. 274–98.

152. Ibid., p. 101.

153. Mead, "Social Psychology as Counterpart . . . ," p. 96.

154. George H. Mead, "The Social Self," *The Journal of Philosophy, Psychology, and Scientific Methods* 10 (1913): 374–380; reprinted in Reck, *Selected Writings*, pp. 142–49.

155. James, *Principles*, 2: 586. Cf. p. 17 above.

156. Floyd Henry Allport, *Social Psychology* (Boston: Houghton Mifflin Co., 1924), p. 19.

157. Ibid., pp. 36–41. Cf. William R. Woodward, "The 'Discovery' of Social Behaviorism and Social Learning Theory," *American Psychologist* 37 (1982): 396–410.

158. Ibid., p. 149.

159. Ibid. Cf. George H. Mead, "The Mechanism of Social Consciousness," *Journal of Philosophy, Psychology and Scientific Methods* 9 (1912): 401–6; reprinted in Reck, *Selected Writings*, pp. 134–41.

160. Ibid., pp. 149–52.

161. John Chynoweth Burnham, *Psychoanalysis and American Medicine. 1894–1918: Medicine, Science and Culture* (New York: International Universities Press, 1967); Nathan G. Hale, Jr., *Freud in America: The Beginnings of Psychoanalysis in the United States, 1876–1917* (New York: Oxford University Press, 1971).

162. William James, "The Hidden Self," *Scribner's Magazine* 7 (1890): 361–73.

163. William James, *The Varieties of Religious Experience* (New York: Longmans, Green and Co., 1923 –1902]), p. 196.

164. Otto Marx, "Morton Prince and the Dissociation of a Personality," *Journal of the History of the Behavioral Sciences* 7 (1970): 121–22.

165. Morton Prince, "Some of the Revelations of Hypnotism," *Boston Medical and Surgical Journal* 122 (1890): 463–67, 475–76, 493–95; reprinted in Nathan G. Hale, Jr., *Morton Prince. Psychotherapy and Multiple Personality: Selected Essays* (Cambridge, Mass.: Harvard University Press, 1975), pp. 37–60.

166. Morton Prince, "Association Neuroses: A Study of Hysterical Joint Affections, Neurasthenia and Allied Forms of Neuro-Mimesis," *Journal of Nervous and Mental Disease* 18 (1890): 257–82; reprinted in Hale, *Morton Prince*, pp. 61–82.

167. Ibid., p. 72–73.

168. Morton Prince, *The Dissociation of a Personality* (London: Longmans, Green and Co., 1905), p. 352.

169. Boris Sidis, *The Psychology of Suggestion* (New York: D. Appleton and Co., 1898), pp. 69–70.

170. Ibid., p. 71.

171. Ibid., pp. 85, 143–47, 189–200, 282.

172. Ibid., p. 36: "Thanks to the advice of Prof. H. Münsterberg, I was enabled to continue my research further and penetrate deeper into one of the most obscure, most mysterious, but also most promising regions of human nature."

173. James, *Principles*, 1: 77; 2: 505.

174. Nathan G. Hale, Jr., ed. with intro., *James Jackson Putnam and Psychoanalysis* (Cambridge, Mass.: Harvard University Press, 1971), pp. 12–14.

175. James J. Putnam, "A Consideration of Mental Therapeutics as Employed by Special Students of the Subject," *Boston Medical and Surgical Journal* 151 (1904): 181.

176. James J. Putnam, "William James," *Atlantic Monthly* 106 (1910): 839. Cf. Hale, *James Jackson Putnam*, p. 47.

177. James Jackson Putnam, *Human Motives* (Boston: Little, Brown and Co., 1915), p. 174.

178. Bruce Kuklick, *The Rise of American Philosophy: Cambridge, Massachusetts, 1860–1930* (New Haven, Conn.: Yale University Press, 1977), p. 165.

179. Gregory A. Kimble, "The Concept of Reflex and the Problem of Volition," in *Foundations of Conditioning and Learning* (New York: Appleton-Century-Crofts, 1967); Gregory A. Kimble and Lawrence C. Perlmuter, "The Problem of Volition," *Psychological Review* 77 (1970): 361–84.

180. Rollo May, ed., *Existential Psychology* (New York: Random House, 1960); Hans Linschoten, *On the Way;* Herbert Spiegelberg, *The Phenomenological Movement*, 2 vols. (The Hague: Martinus Nijhoff, 1965); Aron Gurwitsch, *The Field of Consciousness* (Pittsburgh, Pa.: Duquesne University Press, 1964); Bruce Wilshire, *William James and Phenomenology* (Bloomington, 2nd.: University of Indiana Press, 1968); Richard Stevens, *James and Husserl: The Foundation of Meaning* (The Hague: Martinus Nijhoff, 1974).

181. Cf. Roger Smith, "The Background of Physiological Psychology in Natural Philosophy," *History of Science* 11 (1973): 75–123.

182. James, *CER*, p. 343. Cf. William R. Woodward, "Introduction," *Essays in Psychology. The Works of William James* (Cambridge: Harvard University Press 1983).

183. William James to James Ward, 1 November 1982, quoted in Perry, *James*, 2: 96.

184. D. C. Philips, "James, Dewey and the Reflex Arc," *Journal of the History of Ideas* 32 (1971): 555–68. Cf. John C. Malone, Jr., "William James and B. F. Skinner: Behaviorism, Reinforcement, and Interest," *Behaviorism* 3 (1975): 140–50.

185. Cf. T. W. Wann, *Behaviorism and Phenomenology: Contrasting Bases for Modern Psychology*. Chicago: The University of Chicago Press, 1964; Allport, "Productive Paradoxes"; High and Woodward, "James and Allport."

Pioneer Psychology Laboratories in Clinical Settings

JOHN A. POPPLESTONE AND
MARION WHITE McPHERSON

University of Akron

University Laboratories: A Preamble

Toward the end of the nineteenth century the noun *psychology* began to be combined with such adjectives as *new* and *physiological*. These modifiers were variously defined but they shared the implications of moving psychology away from a speculative and rhetorical basis to an empirical framework, from traditional rationalism to techniques of experimentation. Psychology—like chemistry, physiology, and physics—had been around, at least in the form of an argument (with occasional excursions into experimentation or demonstration) for centuries, but the move from the gentleman amateur scientist to the trained researcher was delayed until the nineteenth century.

Consideration of the reasons for this timing is beyond the scope of this particular discussion. Yet relegating the precursors of experimentation to another occasion does not nullify their influence, and one of the antecedents, society's approbation of technology, had so much direct influence on the pioneer laboratories that at least some attention must be given to it.

During the nineteenth century a pervasive conviction developed that the machine improved matters. Western Europe had seen life—as compared with the Middle Ages—become longer, more comfortable, and richer. Even spiritual experiences could be intensified, as when the organ was used during the Mass or trumpets played at the Elevation of the Host.[1] In this milieu, endorsements of procedures that relied on equipment were inevitable, and the psychology laboratory and its appurtenances came to be honored prior to actual use.

At the same time psychology was plagued with doubts about its scientific credentials, and when these doubts were combined with the positive orientation toward instrumentation two practices developed: the acquisition of as much apparatus as possible and the flaunting of the laboratory as evidence of worthy membership in the fraternity of science. In this monograph attention will be given both to the reputation and to the character of early psychology laboratories. Again and again there will emerge a theme of discrepancy between affirmation and accomplishment.

One requisite for understanding the development of pioneer laboratories is the appreciation that they were distinct from contemporary models. The referents of the word *laboratory* in early accounts may merely be an adaptation of an attic, a basement, a kitchen, or even a cabinet under the stairs.[2] Boring designates Stumpf's cigar box filled with a collection of tuning forks as "an acoustic 'laboratory.'"[3]

Titchener, in his presidential address to the Sigma Xi Chapter at Cornell University, described the chemist Berzelius (1779–1848) as "pottering about among the sauce-pans and dish-cloths of his kitchen,—for that was his only laboratory,— very much, I have no doubt, to the disturbance of the household economy, but very much to the advantage of science. . . ."[4]

Austerity disappeared, and the purpose of this monograph is to depict some of these changes between the 1890s and the first ten to twelve years of the twentieth century. This era was one in which the schools of structuralism and functionalism were dominant, and each was perceived as a framework adequate for the explanation of the total field of psychology. The beginning date marks a period in which excitement about the inaugural laboratories was accompanied with enthusiasm for increasing their number and influence. The terminal date was selected because it marks the beginning of changes that would lead to impressive alterations in psychology laboratories and to an apportionment of subject matter into specialty areas. The forces of the behaviorist explosion were aggregating, and specialized technologies were appearing in industrial contexts, in educational settings, and in patient care.

1. Growth of Academic Laboratories

The founding dates for several laboratories have been published by Krohn, Delabarre, Buchner, and Miner, and by the *Committee on the Academic Status of Psychology*.[5] The data in these articles are complemented by the responses of 141 institutions to a questionnaire, distributed by Garvey in 1929, that solicited information about the founding of laboratories.[6] Thus two types of "facts" are available: those based on information obtained by participants on the scene at the time of founding and those drawn from recollections and/or records. These two sources drew samples from different populations and thereby assured discrepancies. Although there is variation in the dates in which particular laboratories are reputed to have been established, there is also some concurrence. The various articles agree that there was a rapid expansion in the number of laboratories at a positively accelerated rate, at least up to the turn of the century. Furthermore, the total number of facilities reported to be established at various intervals is not markedly different.

Following is a list of the years of publication for various authors, the number of laboratories each estimated, and the number Garvey reports:

Publication Date	Author	No. of Laboratories estimated by	
		Author	Garvey
1891	Krohn	15	14
1894	Delabarre	27	29
1903	Buchner	40	51
1904	Miner	54	52
1914	Committee	88	76

In a paper written in 1950, Harper indicated that forty-seven research facilities were founded between 1875 and the end of the century in the following locations: twenty-five in the United States, ten in Germany, two each in England and France, and eight scattered among eight countries.[7] The fact that 53 percent of this count was in the United States underscores an unusually strong attraction in America to laboratory psychology.

The laboratories were designed for three purposes: demonstration, drill, and research. The demonstration facility did not involve any investigative goals or procedures but was actually a teaching aid, that is, equipment was immediately at hand to demonstrate points made in a lecture. This was typically a part of the introductory course, and students were provided with visual evidence of psychology's status as a science.[8]

Titchener's development of the demonstration laboratory is legendary.[9] His lectures in introductory psychology were theatrical performances augmented by faculty attendance and equipment displays. Friedline was convinced that he practiced them word for word and gesture for gesture.[10] Boring sympathized deeply with all who were on hand when demonstrations deviated from plans.[11]

The drill laboratory was also an instructional tool, but it did adhere more closely than the demonstrations to current conceptions of a laboratory format. Groups of students using simple, inexpensive apparatus carried out procedures that were familiar to and well recognized by the faculty. These exercises were offered both as a way of learning about the scientific method and of acquiring some substantive psychological information. The former mission brought about deliberations concerning appropriate course content.[12] Although these laboratories were on occasion criticized (Wolfe, 1895;[13] French, 1898)[14] they were also praised. Since they involved entire classes they provided space and personnel to support budget requests.

The third form of the laboratory was that of a research facility with the attendant qualities of innovation, uniqueness, and generation of knowledge. The growth of the discipline at large was the product in good measure of the achievements within the research installations, and the sophistication they developed shaped events in demonstration and in drill enterprises.

The archetype for the research laboratory was at Leipzig where specific areas were set apart for different types of investigation. The apparatus for haptics was in the haptics room, the dark room was used for experiments requiring special lighting, and the time room contained the chronoscopes. This facility and the work in it has been described comprehensively, e.g., by Cattell[15] and Stratton.[16] Although Leipzig was an impressive resource it was not consistently copied, either because of ideological disinclination or lack of institutional support of space, budget, and faculty.

Laboratories were frequently considered important enough to merit published accounts of floor plans, budget, and equipment. For example, Baldwin printed the floor plan of the installation at the University of Toronto,[17] and Titchener publicized the layout at Cornell.[18] Martin printed the floor plans of the laboratory at Leland Stanford Jr. University, [19] and Münsterberg reported those at Harvard University.[20]

2. Equipment

The laboratory could be of any size, and in 1893 Sanford calculated the cost of a fully equipped resource as between four and five thousand dollars. He also advised:

> If a starvation appropriation is all that is to be had, the most satisfactory pieces would probably be: a sonometer and a few tuning forks for audition, a color-mixer and Wheatstone stereoscope for vision (the latter home made), and a stop watch for time measurements.[21]

During the same year Münsterberg published a list of the apparatus at Harvard University. He warned readers that because of the very recent formation of the laboratory this register was provisional and then enumerated 240 items. The accurate sum is indeterminate but larger than 240 because many of the entries referred to various items. For example,

151. Five hand-stereoscopes
199. Large and finely graded thermometers, six ordinary thermometers[22]

The inventory of Cornell University in 1899–1900 consists of 373 entries. Many of these are multiple but some of them are not functional in research operations. For example,

59. Etched portrait of Charles Darwin
61. Bust of Aristotle[23]

Whipple's *Manual of Mental and Physical Tests* (Simpler Processes)[24] enumerates fifty-five "Special Appliances" and thirty-nine "General Appliances and Materials"[24]. There are many sketches including a vernier caliper, head calipers, wet spirometer, Smedley dynamometer, stop watch, metronome, kymograph, Marey tambour, Mosso ergograph as modified by Lombard, tapping-board, tracing-board, telegraph sounder and key, steadiness tester, trial frame, Verhoeff's astigmatic chart, Maddox multiple rod, Stevens's stenopaic lens, apparatus for the discrimination of grays, apparatus for brightness discrimination, pressure-pain balance, Jastrow's improved esthesiometer, needle esthesiometer, and disc tachistoscope.

Practically all laboratories owned models and diagrams of the total brain, of each hemisphere, of each lobe as well as of the eye and ear. There were also color mixers, visual illusions, sonometers, spectroscopes, pneumographs, sphygmographs, Quincke tubes, olfactometers, tonometers, chronographs, control hammers, and stereoscopes.

Many of these pieces came in various models and some with different names, for example, stroboscope, or zoötrope; perimeter, or campimeter. Chronoscopes, for example, were variously identified as Bergström, Ewald, Hipp, Münsterberg, and Sanford. Apparatus for measuring color blindness was developed by Dvorine, Hering, Holmgren, and an adaptation of Holmgren's wools was devised by Galton. Hearing was studied by means of tuning forks (manual, electric, and magnetic), acoumeters (both Politzer and Lehmann), audiometers, Galton whistles, Appunn's lamellae, tone variators, Helmholtz resonators, steel cylinders, labial pipes, and the chord siren.

In addition to these pieces which could be used repeatedly there were many items that were consumed: smoke paper for kymographs, chemicals, graph paper, marking fluids, and even kerosene for the illuminator projectors. Paper items were particularly numerous: geometric figures, letters, dots, targets, colored squares, line drawings of illusions.

The hardware was devised both by commercial enterprises and by individual psychologists. Some of the latter were drawn to equipment, adept at inventing and prolific in output. Cattell, Sanford, and Whipple each fall into this category. Their contributions were increased significantly by a large number of researchers who made or modified one, or a few, instruments, for example, Delabarre, Jastrow, Münsterberg, Pillsbury, and Titchener.

The enthusiasm of the profession for equipment is illustrated by a meeting of the New York Academy of Science that was held on 27–28 December 1906. This was organized not as a paper-reading session but for the purpose of providing individual scientists in various disciplines with an opportunity to share information about methods and apparatus and to disply new inventions.[25]

Equipment manufacturers were numerous. Münsterberg[26] recommended seventy companies and a count of these identified 74 percent as European and 26 percent as American. The conspicuous European names included Edelmann, Koenig, Kohl, Petzold, Verdin, and Zimmermann. The domestic list includes the Milton Bradley Company, Clay and Torbensen, Meyrowitz Brothers, and James W. Queen.

European dominance was soon to be dissipated, and as early as 1904 Miner boasted that America excelled Europe in equipment and had done so for a period of ten years.[27] Stoelting was probably the most important manufacturer in this country, and when the company's founder, Christian H. Stoelting, died in 1943 his contributions to the science were acknowledged in a necrology in the *American Journal of Psychology*. This tribute, by an unidentified author, makes reference to Stoelting's vigilance about equipment needs, his effectiveness in meeting them, and his surpassing European productivity.

"It was largely through his unselfish service and patient skill that America succeeded Germany as a source of apparatus and equipment for the laboratories of psychology."[28]

3. Support

Laboratory hypertrophy was not univeral, and inhibiting forces were at work. The latter were so strong that both The Johns Hopkins University[29] and the University of Minnesota[30]—two schools that would come to have important laboratories—allowed their first departments to vanish for a period of time.

The frustrations occasioned by the lack of laboratory support were acknowledged, sometimes in terms that connoted resignation and retreat from pretension. Sanford explained the need for compromise:

The laboratory must occupy such rooms as are free for it. As a younger member in the family of sciences, psychology must be content with the outgrown clothes of its elders.[31]

Titchener complained about limitations:

I do not know that any psychologist has hitherto succeeded in persuading his university to provide him with a special building, constructed after his own designs . . . . everywhere, indeed, psychology has come late to the feast, and been obliged to content itself with what it can get.[32]

Miner also laments:

In spite of the constant increase in equipment, the directors of the best laboratories are seriously embarrassed in trying to meet the demands made upon them for instruction in experimental work. The opening of tempting fields of investigation has to be postponed until the needs of the present courses are met.[33]

Ruckmich perceived psychology to be in a competitively unfavorable position and was convinced that this was due to the initial costs of procuring equipment and staff: ". . . the *per capita* expenditure for psychology, a laboratory science, is about equal to that of philosophy, not a laboratory science. Adequate laboratories have not been everywhere provided."[34]

4. Two Steps Forward, One Step Back

In spite of lags in growth there was a great deal of activity within the laboratories. This contrasted with a retreat from experimentation by some directors who began to display more verbal than actual allegiance to research. James imported Münsterberg from Germany to become the director of the Harvard Laboratory and, following this appointment, James returned to work in philosophy. Boring observed, "He believed in the laboratory, but he did not like it."[35]

Stevens talks about three giants:

The line of descent from Wundt to Titchener to Boring was more than direct, it resembled successive incarnations: . . . Titchener interpreted Wundt. . . . Boring, ever fascinated by the phenomenon of Titchener, interpreted him. . . . All three became laboratory directors who did not themselves experiment. . . .[36]

In eulogizing his master, Pillsbury commented on both dedication and reticence on the part of Titchener:

He was full of enthusiasm for the laboratory and all that went with it. From the first year at Cornell he began to gather apparatus and plan new pieces for the investigations of his students. It must be said that he was not especially gifted on the mechanical side and later rather looked down on too great intimacy with the designing of apparatus as worthy only of a mechanic. Still he believed in the possession of apparatus and in its use.[37]

Boring, the director of the Harvard Laboratory for 25 years, characterized his master in a manner similar to that of Pillsbury:

Titchener always seemed to be such a sympathetic experimentalist. I wonder about this now because we never saw him much in the laboratory. But the way he would tenderly unscrew a screw with affection for every knurl in the handle always made you feel that the apparatus was a lovely, tender, and sweet thing.[38]

In 1888, when G. Stanley Hall accepted the presidency of Clark University, he offered Edmund C. Sanford an instructorship. In 1892 that appointment was changed to director of the laboratory and Hall occupied himself with other matters.[39] Watson noted that Hall's last publication "within the conventional limits of experimental psychology" was as early as 1887.[40]

Fernberger recalls Hall's early interest and competence in the laboratory:

During his later life Dr. Hall was not known as an experimentalist. But during my time at Clark University I never thought of preparing an experimental study for publication without first going to Dr. Hall's house and talking over my problem and my results and their possible interpretation. And Dr. Hall never failed to understand the technical difficulties. . . .[41]

Titchener hints that Hall may have regretted his retreat:

. . . sometimes, in his later years, he spoke a little wistfully of the laboratory, almost as if he wished himself again in the field that he had so often decried as narrow and overtilled.[42]

5. The Laboratory and Scientific Psychology

The disaffection on the part of a few directors failed to slow down the growth of experimental psychology, faced with identifying its subject matter as well as developing and refining methodology. The literature of the period contrasts with the later sanitized accounts of what was going on and discloses amorphous ideas concerning the nature of the discipline. The subject matter was not clearly specified. There was question as to whether or not psychic phenomena should be included. The boundaries between psychology and such fields as anthropology, neurology, physiology, phonetics, child development and the study of deviant behavior were unsettled.

The reaction within the field of psychology to the issues of what to include was generally that of incorporating, and most alternatives were endorsed by at least a few individuals. This served to spread the subject matter of psychology over a wide spectrum. Both separatism and conflict were in force. Titchener was a structuralist, Dewey was a functionalist. The houses were disjunctive. Titchener would not admit James, applied psychology, and the unconscious. Watson would jettison the mind. Angell rejected mental elements. James ejected psychophysics. Münsterberg and Hall were both disdained because of their excursions into the practical.

The laboratory has been assigned a major role in the transformation of psychology into a science, but this ascription is probably appropriate only during the formative era. As the proponents of various stances refined their arguments they also modified ideas about the kinds of information they desired from the laboratory. Thus, as the discipline matured, the laboratory did not fashion it as much as the particular concepts determined various research programs. Differences in emphasis emerged. For example, as early as 1904 Miner described the heterogeneity of American psychology:

> The trends of thought which prevail among graduate students at present suggest that those who are fundamentally interested in philosophy gravitate to Harvard; those seeking primarily the scientific attitude find Columbia congenial; Cornell is the best university to place the student in touch with the historical development of experimental work and of systematic psychology; Clark is most widely known for its pedagogical interest in the science; Princeton for the biological interpretations of Professor J. Mark Baldwin; Yale for training courses in psychological measurement; and Pennsylvania for the introduction of extended experimental work into its sophomore introductory course in psychology.[43]

6. To Introspect or Not to Introspect

Whatever the favored theory, laboratory personnel were confronted with the problem of introspection. Recent literature (for example, Murphy and Kovach, 1972[44] and Robinson, 1976[45]) implies that introspection was the dominant method of the era, but the literature of the period discloses that neither the role nor the method of introspection was monolithic and its importance to research is equivocal. Both the defenders and the critics of the procedure were vocal, and Bakan has characterized the writing on this topic as "anguished," a term that can be faulted only for its mildness.[46] Introspection meant different things to different people, and matters were even more densely clouded by unevenness in appreciation of the procedures. Some perceived introspection as a panacea, whereas others perceived it as an anathema.

Boring asserted that "introspection is generally acknowledged to be, if not the most important, at least one of the fundamental methods of psychology."[47]

Pillsbury noted that of the dissertations directed by Titchener "all are treated primarily as exercises in controlled introspection."[48]

The critics of introspection were at work prior to the 1913 manifesto by Watson: "Introspection forms no essential part of its methods. . . ."[49] For example, Stratton in 1908 remarked that it was a "peculiar and solitary method of getting at the facts of mind." He concluded that the "results of self-observation consequently seem to be personal and 'subjective,' and lacking in that universality which is the pride of chemistry and physics."[50]

The influence of both outspoken critics and ardent defenders was sharpened by some individuals who managed to treat the topic inconsistently. James indexed the term, used it, but failed to define it.[51] Sanford's *Course in Experimental Psychology,* published in 1898, contained segments originally written in 1893, 1894, and 1896.[52] The index to the 435 pages of the text does not include the term although Sanford had sanctioned introspection in an 1892 paper.[53]

One of Scripture's references (1896) to introspection might be characterized as surreptitious. He enumerated five laboratory courses but deferred any reference to introspection until the description of the highest-level course and then commented merely, "Participants in this course are either investigators or assistants. For assistants the object is such a training in accurate introspection . . . as is desirable for the general psychologist."[54]

In another publication Scripture (1897) observed that introspection was adequate for analysis but that it also distorted because it emphasized a fragment rather than the whole. He was forthright about the duality: "Thus on the question of the validity of introspection we have granted to both parties the main contention—namely, that it is a valid method, and that it is in a degree erroneous."[55]

At least two writers managed to characterize the method as a basic in need of substantiation. Angell referred to introspection as "the fundamental psychological method" but added that it should be used in conjunction with "immediate objective observation of other individuals."[56]

Calkins identified "the method which distinguishes psychology . . . introspection." But she did not let it stand alone; "The verification of our introspection is best secured by an important *subsidiary* method shared by psychology with many of the physical sciences—the method of experiment."[57] (Italics ours.)

The instructions as to how to introspect ran the gamut from the recondite procedures advocated by Titchener through hazy references to personal experiences that were in some instances vivid, even traumatic, and in others fleeting and near threshold. In some research designs introspection involved the mere designation of a sensation as present or absent. On occasion introspections were in the form of written retrospections, not distinct from recall. In some experiments only thoroughly trained observers were used. Other investigations were based on people who had had practically no training. In still others the results from both trained and untrained observers were combined.

The pattern was much less diffuse at Cornell University, where carefully prescribed introspection was in command. Heidbreder had commented on Titchener's "insistent demand for thoroughness,"[58] and this is exemplified in Friedline's notes written during the sessions with Titchener in which he supervised her dissertation, "The Discrimination of Cutaneous Patterns below the Two-Point Limen":

> Have Mr. Bishop look over the apparatus every Saturday. . . . Get Dr. Boring to help. . . . I would suggest adding to the instructions "Be passive, let the experience claim your attention. . . ."[59]

Selected fragments of Titchener's own statements in the public ledger disclose his veneration of introspection:
In 1901:

> But introspection cannot be learned from books. If one is a born psychologist, it may be learned from the experience of ordinary life; and learned the more quickly, if this experience is supplemented by reading and by listening to lectures. . . . Once gained, it is never lost: one can no more forget how to introspect than one can forget how to walk or swim.[60]

In 1905:

> How, indeed, shall we call a man a psychologist who deliberately turns his back upon the one psychological method, in the one field to which that method directly applies? There is no excuse in psychology, for the neglect of introspection, save the one—and that must be demonstrated—that introspection is impossible.[61]

In 1908:

> . . . the psychological attitude, the introspective habit, which so grows on one with time and experience that . . . one can no more help psychologising than one can help breathing.[62]

In 1912:

> There are specific differences of introspective procedure, but all the forms show a generic likeness; introspection always presupposes the point of view of descriptive psychology, and the introspective methods thus do us the same service in the psychologising that 'observation and experiment' do in natural science.[63]

7. Laboratories in Action

The literature which relates the pioneer laboratory activity is, as in the case of the activity itself, widespread. American psychologists were quick to produce in hard covers. The more familiar books, under the date of first edition, included: James M. Baldwin, *Handbook of Psychology,* I & II, *Mental Development in the Child and the Race,* and *The Story of the Mind;*[64] William James, *Principles of Psychology,* 2 volumes;[65] George T. Ladd, *Elements of Physiological Psychology* and *Psychology, Descriptive and Explanatory;*[66] Edward W. Scripture, *Thinking, Feeling, Doing* and *The New Psychology;*[67] and Edward B. Titchener, *Outline of*

Psychology, A Primer of Psychology, and *Lectures on the Elementary Psychology of Feeling and Attention.*[68]

It is paradoxical, but laboratory manuals were not as plentiful as textbooks. A few handbooks did exist and the better known ones were: Edmund C. Sanford, *A Course in Experimental Psychology;*[69] Edward B. Titchener, *Experimental Psychology: A Manual of Laboratory Practice,* Volume I, *Qualitative Experiments* Part I, *Student's Manual,* Part II, *Instructor's Manual* Volume II, *Quantitative Experiments* Part I *Student's Manual,* Part II, *Instructor's Manual;*[70] Guy M. Whipple, *Manual of Mental and Physical Tests;*[71] and Lightner Witmer, *Analytical Psychology.*[72]

These texts discussed theory, reported details of the subject matter of psychology, particularly sensations, perception, illusions, memory, and movement, with references to both effort and fatigue. Sense organs and neural anatomy were described and illustrated. Both photographs and sketches of equipment were abundant. The psychophysical methods, as well as instructions for handling quantitative results, were discussed at some length.

Walker indicates that as early as 1896 ten or twelve universities in America were probably offering courses in statistics and in three institutions—Clark, Pennsylvania, and Yale—the instruction was provided in the psychology department. She designates Cattel and Titchener as the prime movers in orienting psychology toward statistics.[73]

Research results were reported both in texts and in journals. The latter were plentiful and there was space for dissertations. Complaints about a dearth of publication outlets were essentially nonexistent; rather, the pattern for the era was one of publishing the same article in more than one journal. Professional periodicals, for example, *Nature* and *Science,* were already in existence at the time of the psychology laboratory expansion and they opened their pages to psychologists. Other periodicals accepted papers in psychology as well as in other fields, for example, the *Journal of Comparative Neurology and Psychology* and the *Journal of Philosophy, Psychology and Scientific Methods.*

Periodicals intended primarily for the dissemination of research in psychology came into being with rapidity. G. Stanley Hall established the *American Journal of Psychology,* 1887, and the *Pedagogical Seminary,* 1891. James McKeen Cattell and James M. Baldwin added the *Psychological Index,* 1894, *Psychological Monographs,* 1894, the *Psychological Review,* 1894, and the *Psychological Bulletin,* 1904. Morton Prince started publishing the *Journal of Abnormal Psychology* in 1906.

Reading samples of this pioneer literature discloses that the articles were lengthy but frequently lacking in perspective and filled with minutiae often undifferentiated as to importance. There was no standard organizational format, and procedural items might be deferred to the discussion section. There were no uniform standards for style and the editing was casual. There were criticisms about this neglect,[74] but citations continued to be omitted, inconsistent, and/or incomplete. Misspellings are present and arithmetical errors are noticeable. Reading the literature is, in spite of these shortcomings, informative and gratifying in that many of the raw events within the laboratory are exposed. The coverage is incomplete and the sequence blurred, but specific activities can be grasped.

Much more accuracy and care were accorded the equipment than the research procedures. Authors made remarks about the necessity of experimental controls and then proceeded to violate their own recommendations by failing to regulate. There are inconsistencies in sample size, heterogeneity of sample composition, neglect of response criteria, trials scheduled as much for the convenience of personnel as for the demands of the design, changes in method introduced at various stages of an experiment, and incomparable variables treated as if they were comparable.

These crudities are typically embedded in expressions of enthusiasm for research. On occasion investigators become so enthralled that they print data acknowledged to be barely relevant and at times the impression is gained that laboratory data have enough intrinsic merit to stand without additional support.

Action outweighed caution and the evidence is overabundant that during the era of the pioneer laboratories the practice of the scientific method varied from orderly to capricious. The ideals of the laboratory procedures were different from the realities, but the match was closest in hardware. These observations about the academic laboratories will be particularized in a chronicle of some of the detailed events in laboratories located in settings devoted to the care of psychotic and of intellectually retarded patients.

Psychological Research in Psychiatric Settings

The first two psychology research laboratories to be developed in clinical contexts in the United States were established in the 1890s. One was in the Minnesota School for Feeble-Minded at Fairbault in 1896, and the other in 1895 was in the New York Pathological Institute in New York City, a nonresidential facility devoted to the study of psychosis.[75] The events in each of these installations developed along paths sufficiently disparate to mandate separate discussions of them. The investigations conducted with psychotics resembled those in academic settings, and this similarity directed our discussion first to these facilities.

The early ventures into experimentation in psychiatric settings were frequently merely brief flourishes, but this discontinuity is generally overlooked. Histories of the period tend to report the founding of psychology laboratories but to omit discussions of their dissolution.[76] This incompleteness not only fosters a false sense of continuity but also implies more influence on the part of psychology than the discipline probably exerted. Shakow is one of the few who has called attention to the relative unimportance of psychology. He commented explicitly on the lack of support for the adage that psychology is the basic science for psychiatry.[77]

The image of significance is not merely a by-product of the writing of history but was fostered by individuals who were not trained in psychology but were highly visible participants in its business, if not its substance. Among the early contributors in the United States to the psychological study and care of psychotics were Edward Cowles, August Hoch, William Noyes, and Adolf Meyer—all physicians. A remark or two about the career of each of them will illustrate their activity on the psychological scene. Hoch published in the *Psychological Bulletin*,[78] Cowles studied under G. Stanley Hall and published information about the *American Journal of Psychology* among psychiatrists.[79] Noyes and Cowles probably attended the meeting at which the American Psychological Association was planned.[80]

Adolf Meyer may have contributed more than anyone to the illusion of a dominant psychology. He was highly conspicuous on the psychological scene, even though his early interests were in pathology and only later did they spread to psychiatry. He lectured to Clark University graduate students from 1897 to 1902 and replaced G. Stanley Hall as demonstrator in the clinics at the Worcester State Hospital. Meyer also held editorial responsibilities for the *Psychological Bulletin*. Further, he was on the staff of two facilities that were the site of pioneer psychology laboratories—the Illinois Eastern Hospital for the Insane in Kankakee and the New York Pathological Institute. In the former he was assigned quarters for a pathological laboratory in the clock tower of the Centre Building and was given the apparatus that had made up the German display at the World's Columbian Exposition, Chicago, 1893. The New York Pathological Institute had a history of productivity at the time Meyer joined the staff.

In contrast to the prevalent views, Meyer opposed a distinction between clinical and research facilities. At Worcester State Hospital he resisted separating these two functions with such force that a special laboratory building was not constructed as long as he was at the hospital. Meyer agreed to accept the directorship of the laboratory in the New York Pathological Institute only if it were moved to a location adjacent to a residential facility, in this instance Ward's Island.[81] Meyer was an exception.

Laboratory work not dramatically different from that undertaken in universities was underway in some psychiatric hospitals, although there were problems when patients were used because they were not trained observers and on occasion were refractory. These drawbacks were balanced, to some degree at least, by the pertinence of such procedures as the recording of autonomic activity and reaction time measurements.

Formal psychological research in psychoses gradually declined. One of the many factors contributing to this weakening was the development and acceptance of psychoanalysis, a school that degraded ego psychology and advocated a non-laboratory method. One event which signified that psychoanalysis established a stronghold in this country was the Clark Conference of 1909. This date serves as an appropriate mark of the fading of the laboratory era of research on psychoses, a period that started in 1895 at the New York Pathological Institute.

The roster of research psychologists active in laboratory investigations of psychiatric disorders between 1895 and 1910 is limited to four: Boris Sidis, William Krohn, Shepherd I. Franz, and Frederic L. Wells. This group is astonishingly small. Furthermore, none of these men were active during the entire period. Krohn worked in a hospital laboratory for only two years and published no research during that time. Wells did not start until 1906, only four years prior to the end of the era. Franz was also relatively a latecomer, but by the close of the period he had six years' experience in clinical settings. Sidis was active in research at both the beginning and end of the interval, but he did not publish any experimental papers between 1898 and 1908.

In spite of the restricted tenure, these psychologists generated an impressive amount of research, and their papers will be reviewed in enough depth to allow scrutiny of the actual practices of the period.

This probing of experimental procedures included a checking of the accuracy of computations whenever the figures that researchers had used were printed. It was undertaken in order to gain some idea of the level of accuracy when investigators functioned within the rigid framework of arithmetic. Pervasive but generally minor mistakes were found and are reported in this monograph, even though an authoritative tally of errors is blocked by the impossibility of distinguishing between mistakes in printing and in calculating. Whatever the true count may be, the disclosure of even a few inaccuracies in arithmetic raises questions about how much cursoriness may permeate the less structured experimental procedures. The carelessness that has been found is reported as one means of depicting the realities of the early laboratories; the goal is not censure, but rather that of providing evidence that precision came only gradually to scientific psychology.

1. Institutional Personnel

The laboratory in the New York Pathological Institute was founded under the directorship of Ira Van Gieson,[82] a histologist-neurologist, for the purpose of developing knowledge that would be of assistance to the New York State Hospital system. It was located in a Manhattan office building, physically removed from the demands of patient care. Van Gieson was relatively uninterested in clinical matters but was highly motivated to work toward "a correlation of sciences." In 1896 he asked Boris Sidis to represent psychology in this endeavor.

B. Sidis

Boris Sidis (1867–1923) received an A.B. in 1894 and a Ph.D. in 1897 from Harvard University.[83] Sidis expressed appreciation to Münsterberg for allowing him the use of the laboratory,[84] but Münsterberg was not on the thesis committee. It was composed (in the order of signature) of G. H. Palmer, William James, E. B. Delabarre, and Josiah Royce. The title of the dissertation was "The Psychology of Suggestion," but the formal authority for the topic was philosophy. George Herbert Palmer joined the faculty in 1889 and at the time of Sidis's degree was Alford Professor of Natural Religion, Moral Philosophy, and Civil Polity.[85]

During much of his career Sidis was concerned with suggestibility, dissociation, and the subconscious, with incidental excursions into psychic phenomena. Hypnosis was a favored method, and he formulated a concept of hypnoidal states. These topics put him on the fringes of the psychology of the day, but his writing documents a familiarity with, and a reliance on, conventional concepts. Sidis appears to have been quite comfortable with his psychological universe, but he did comment that a study restricted to consciousness produces results which "though remarkable for their thoroughness are after all of a rather trivial nature."[86]

Sidis was adept in the management of equipment. Zubin and Zubin comment on the abundance of instruments in the early laboratory at the institute and indicate that Sidis was the dominant figure in the technical aspects of the research which he conducted jointly with Van Gieson. In 1898 they published research devoted to substantiating postulations about neural energy. Their explanations were untestable.[87]

William Alanson White also comments on Sidis's involvement with equipment. White's first meeting with Sidis took place when an administrator led him unannounced into the laboratory at the Institute at a time when Sidis was thoroughly engrossed in making some recordings. The intruder soon realized that Sidis could use another hand and without speaking White began to assist him, a contact that initiated both a friendship and collaborative research.[88]

Sidis's first singly authored work, "The Psychology of Suggestion," appeared in book form in 1898. This contains thesis data as well as protocols collected at the New York Pathological Institute. In the custom of the day Sidis used the word experiment rather than trial and thus was able to report that he conducted more than 8,000 experiments. The narration occasionally falls short of clarifying what actually transpired. There is a failure to identify subjects and the method of selecting them. The reader is generally spared knowledge of the frequency of trials, the intervals separating them as well as the conditions under which they took place.

The research itself encompassed an array of problems, including comparison of normal pneumographic and sphygmographic tracings with those procured under hypnotically induced states. The data that are presented are illustrative rather than comprehensive, and there are reprintings of a few smoked kymographic sheets. These provide a striking contrast between the complete and the incomplete in that the reproductions are annotated merely as "after pleasure," "ammonia," and "more."[89]

The mass of the research on suggestion did not call for much equipment but involved the presentation of a series of stimuli (letters, digits, geometric forms, colors, etc.) at a regulated rate and so arranged that within each sequence a single variable was emphasized, for example, repeating one stimulus three times in a trial. At the end of each trial the subjects were asked to record any associations. The frequency with which the recorded items resembled the featured variable was used as a measure of the amount of suggestion. Thus, in 300 experiments a recurrent stimulus was noted in 53 associations. Sidis converted this 53/300 ratio into a "suggestibility factor" for repetition of 17.6 percent.

The project on suggestion also included a study of subliminal stimulation as well as calculations of the percentages in which both orders and ideas contiguous with orders characterized associations. Sidis compared results obtained from normal and from patients, but he was cautious about drawing conclusions and invoked mathematical strategies to rule out the influence of chance.

This text is the only publication of Sidis that contains quantified material. allows twenty-three recalculations. Minor mistakes were found in two instance with one error amounting to 0.1 and one value that is accurately 7.67 percent being reported as 6.41 percent. These mistakes are inconsequential in that interpretations would not have varied had the correct figures been used.

Sidis published an invited address before the American Medico-Psychological Association in 1899. This did not include systematic data but was an attempt to point out the mutual advantages of cooperation to both psychology and medicine. Sidis endeavored to reassure physicians that psychologists were scientists. He informed them that the field was no longer preoccupied with "ideal philosophical wisdom" but was turning in favor of the "pathways of concrete sciences."[90]

Van Gieson refused to develop a program directly relevant to patient management, and this led to conflict with the State Commission in Lunacy and to his departure in 1901.[91] Sidis also left the New York Pathological Institute. This marked the beginning of a prolonged interruption in psychological work in that laboratory. In 1910, nine years later, August Hoch enticed Frederic L. Wells to accept an appointment, but he remained only a few months. Other psychologists were in residence during brief intervals, but continuity was deferred until Carney Landis came in 1930, a date far beyond the scope of this paper.[92]

Sidis became director of the Psychopathic Hospital and Psychopathological Laboratory of the New York Infirmary for Women and Children. While there he published, in two installments, a discourse on hallucinations for which he drew heavily on a structuralist analysis of perception.[93] In 1906 he expanded his writings on hallucinations by analyzing their relationship to hypnosis. He offered some anecdotal evidence and concluded that there are no hypnotically induced hallucinations.[94]

In 1904 Sidis entered medical school and his later career was concentrated in, but not confined to, psychiatry. He continued to conduct research,[95] and maintained a psychopathological laboratory probably in the Sidis Psychotherapeutic Institute in Portsmouth, New Hampshire.[96] Sidis was prolific, and it is neither practical nor necessary to review the entire bibliography. It is filled with duplicate publications and frequent revisions.

In 1908 Sidis wrote two articles on sensory elements in perception and in hallucinations.[97] In that same year three papers on sleep were completed.[98] These included speculations about the neurological bases of sleep, reports of variations in thresholds, observations and measurements of some motor components, as well as comparisons of the relationship between hypnoidal states and sleep. The publication of these data was quite delayed inasmuch as they had been procured under Walter B. Cannon's auspices in the physiological laboratory at Harvard Medical School and in the laboratory of the Pathological Institute. Observations were made on frogs, guinea pigs, cats, dogs, children, and adults.

In 1909 there were two articles in which Sidis advocated the therapeutic use of hypnoidal states. He was convinced that these alterations of consciousness are more tractable than hypnotic conditions.[99]

Three research papers conclude Sidis's work during the time span covered in this monograph.[100] These were studies of galvanic deflections and were carried out with the assistance of two collaborators. The purpose was to make certain that galvanic action was the result of psycho-physiological processes. In order to assure this the apparatus was subjected to various tests concerning, for example, the time lag in recording. Precautions were taken against mechanical and physiological artifacts, for example changes in resistance at the electrodes were avoided by coating the wrist, the area of electrode attachment, with shellac. Splints were applied to reduce the probability of muscular contractions. The results are presented in columns that list the centimeters of displacement of the galvanometer. As in the case of the dissertation, all this detail is accompanied by notations about the stimuli that are erratic and vague. For example, "difficult calculation," "pinch," "imagines pleasant experience," "burn with lighted cigarette (very painful)."[101]

There is no information about trial schedules, the pattern of stimulation, or the conditions surrounding the observations, and the identity of the subjects is very vague. The authors conclude that ideational processes do not activate a galvanometer but that intense affect and sensory stimulation do cause displacements. After a complicated series of manipulations of the equipment and a number of recordings from animal tissue, Sidis and a co-author, Louis Nelson, conclude that the meter action is due to electromotive forces generated by psycho-physiological events.

Dunlap[102] was to dispute this conclusion but, whether correct or incorrect, Sidis earned a firm position in the line of descent of the modern research and clinical registering of the physiological components of responses. Sidis's involvement with the dominant theories of the day was too attenuated to allow him to influence the doctrines then popular in academia, but his investigations of the subconscious and of hypnosis helped to promote both to the status of valid subject matter.

The second psychology laboratory established in a psychiatric setting, but the first within an institution for psychotics, was founded under the directorship of William Otterbein Krohn (1868–1927) at the Illinois Eastern Hospital for the Insane at Kankakee, Illinois on 1 September 1897. This enterprise was the second in that institution in that it followed the facility for research in pathology, the State Psychopathic Institute, that Adolf Meyer had directed between 1893 and 1896.[103]

W. O. Krohn

Krohn received a B.A. from Western (later Leander Clark) College in Toledo, Iowa, in 1887 and a Ph.D. from Yale in 1889. The dissertation, philosophical in nature, was entitled "The Ethics of Modern Pessimism." Immediately after the doctorate Krohn was appointed head of the Department of Philosophy, Psychology, and Ethics at Adelbert College and Cleveland College for Women of Western Reserve University and served in this post from 1889–1891. He then turned his attention to experimental psychology and visited eleven European research installations. During this nine-month period of travel he enrolled as a graduate student at both Berlin and Freiburg universities.[104] Krohn's interest in hardware was apparently keen and he wrote three accounts of equipment in American and European laboratories.[105]

Upon returning to the United States in 1892 Krohn was a senior fellow in psychology at Clark University for six months. He then joined the faculty of the University of Illinois—in 1892 in the Department of Psychology and Pedagogy and in 1893 in the Department of Psychology.[106] The laboratory at the University of Illinois was founded by Krohn with the first piece of equipment installed on 10 January 1893.[107]

In 1893 Krohn reviewed the literature on pseudo-chromesthesia, "the association of colors with words, letters, and sounds." He struggled diligently to find an explanation for the phenomena and in doing so he dealt with such beliefs as "women, who as a class can hardly be called *introspective;* at least they are less so than men but they are more observant."[108] (Italics Krohn's.) He finally concluded that central processes were the determiners.

In 1893 Krohn's sole paper reporting systematic research data was published, "An Experimental Study of Simultaneous Stimulations of the Sense of Touch." This research was carried out at Clark University, not in the laboratory which he established, and it utilized apparatus that had been devised with the help of E. C. Sanford. It consisted of bellows that activated ten tambours, each of which thrust a cork forward and when positioned ½″ from the skin generated a separate touch stimulus. The subjects were blindfolded and provided with a board on which to fix their teeth so as to stand perfectly still.

The care that went into devising this equipment appears not to have been transferred to the neurological components of the study. The author fails to offer a rationale for the stimulus configurations that he used, and little success has been encountered in attempts to infer what the reasoning may have been. For example, in a test labeled "On line through navel and bilateral" the following points on the skin were touched:

Right hip over joint
Left hip over joint
4 inches to right of navel
4 inches to left of navel
3 inches to left of small of back
3 inches to right of small of back
Great toe of left foot

Readers are not enlightened about various procedures. Apparently the stimulus patterns were rotated, but probably not regularly.

Flexibility is apparent in the account of the pretrial preparations, with "any kind of combinations or any sort of group of spots being used to determine the general dermal sensitivity of the subject. . . ."[109]

Numerous conclusions were reached, for example, the joints and the ventral portion of the body were shown to be the areas most sensitive to touch, and localization was found to be more accurate on the right than on the left side of the body. Krohn enumerated four different kinds of localization errors, indicated that attention played a role, and concluded that practice resulted in improvement. He discussed dermal after-images, bilateral asymmetry and various allied topics, and promised that research on simultaneous stimulation would be followed by a study of successive stimulation. This commitment was not fulfilled.

This paper is the only one of Krohn's that allows checking of arithmetical accuracy. Errors were found in two out of nineteen instances. In both instances the errors were inconsequential, merely 0.3.

The next paper was a brief report of increases in difference limen for touch in an arm immobilized by injury.[110] These observations were made on a single patient.

Krohn's experiences at Clark University with the Child-Study movement may have had a more enduring effect than did his exposure to formal research. He was enthusiastic about G. Stanley Hall and referred to him as "that Nestor of Child-Study in America."[111] Krohn founded the Illinois Association for Child-Study[112] and edited the *Transactions of the Illinois Child-Study Society,* as well as the *Child-Study Monthly.*[113]

In 1895 he wrote three articles for the latter. These provided directions for appraisal of the sensory integrity of imbeciles, a blank for recording the results of psychological examinations of individual children, and a plea for the "training" of beneficial habits in school children in order to alleviate the strain of attending school.[114] In 1897 he expounded in *Charities Review* on the applications of child study to defective children.[115]

In 1897 Krohn accepted a position as psychologist at the Illinois Eastern Hospital for the Insane where he again founded a laboratory. The announcement of the establishing of this facility was acknowledged by commendations from William James, T. Wesley Mills, and George T. Ladd. Felicitations were also received from abroad, specifically from Kraepelin, Krafft-Ebing, Ziehen, and Sergi. The equipment was described as "infinitely delicate, modern, scientific."[116]

The laboratory was served by *The Psychiater,* a quarterly edited by the superintendent of the hospital and designed to report experimentation carried out at the hospital. A paper by Krohn, "Laboratory Psychology as Applied to the Study of Insanity," was published in Volume 1, probably in 1898. This was an explanation of how brass instrument psychology could, by virtue of its objective methods assist psychiatry, particularly in differential diagnosis. Krohn devised a method for conducting clinical examinations that included twelve areas, for example sensory perversions, memory disorders, disorders of volition, and disturbances in the association of ideas. The recommendations were for standard laboratory methods and demanded the use of such equipment as Verdin's esthesiometer and Elb's muscle-sense apparatus.

Krohn foresaw no problems in working with the patients and, quite the opposite, he was optimistic about their cooperation:
"The array of apparatus before him is regarded by the patient as an expression of especial interest in his case and he is more than simply willing to act as a subject for special investigation. . . . Occasionally a patient with acute mania becomes intractable but a little tact soon rights matters with him."[117]

Krohn left the Illinois Eastern Hospital for the Insane in 1899, entered the medical school at Northwestern University in 1902, and obtained an M.D. in 1905. The biographical sketches of Krohn do not account for his activities between the departure from the Kankakee institution and admission to medical school. After graduation he practiced medicine in Chicago.

Krohn's departure from the hospital appears to have brought about the closing of the laboratory, at least no research in psychology has been found from that facility during the period under consideration. The first, and apparently only, issue of *The Psychiater* contained, in addition to Krohn's article, three other papers, each written by a member of the hospital medical staff and none reporting results of systematic research.[119] Thus, the psychology laboratory at the Illinois Eastern Hospital for the Insane might be awarded first prize in a competition for the maximal structure with minimal function. There was space, equipment, a journal, an experienced investigator, and practically no published research.

Krohn spawned textbooks. In 1894 he published *Practical Lessons in Psychology,* a text intended for teachers and providing information about such topics as the senses, attention, habit formation, associations, memory, and reasoning. The book was reprinted in 1895 and again in 1896. Markedly more successful than the treatise on psychology was a series of books on hygiene and physiology written for school children. There were several revisions of *First Book in Hygiene, First Book in Physiology and Hygiene, Graded Lessons in Hygiene,* and *Graded Lessons in Physiology and Hygiene.* The dates of original publication and revisions ranged from 1902 through 1923. The books were printed by various houses, including the William O. Krohn Company.[120]

Krohn coauthored a book on forensic psychiatry[121] and came to public attention when he testified at the Leopold and Loeb trial and was censured, even ridiculed, by Darrow.[122] This experience is reported to have left him so ill at ease that he indulged in a bit of escapism. He traveled to Borneo and wrote an account of the Dyaks and Malays of Dutch Borneo. It was published in 1927, the year of his death.[123]

Krohn shares with G. Stanley Hall the distinction of having founded two laboratories, but he failed to labor intensively in either of them and his involvement in psychology was diverted from experimentation. His main thrust seems to have been in the promotion of the field as a laboratory science and as a disseminator of knowledge about child development. In this sense his imprint is more in the area of public relations than in substance.

Contacts with Hall at The Johns Hopkins University motivated Edward Cowles, Superintendent of the McLean Hospital, to include psychology in the research laboratory he was planning.[124] Some historians assign this facility primacy among hospital laboratories because it came into being in 1889, seven years before the installation at the New York Pathological Institute. This is not justified, because there was no one on the staff who was fully trained in psychology until 1904, when Shepherd I. Franz accepted a position there.[125] This appointment of a bonafide psychologist places the McLean laboratory in third place in the order of founding, but in first place in terms of institutions in which the psychology laboratory was maintained without interruption.

Between 1889 and 1904 a limited amount of research involving some psychological techniques was carried out by physicians at the hospital, but the nature of the experimental enterprise was amorphous. Hall wrote that the purpose was "to combine neurological studies in the departments of psychiatry and physiological psychology, and their relations with anatomical and chemical pathology, etc."[126]

In 1896 the McLean hospital was moved from Somerville to Waverley, enlarged, and the buildings separated, a dispersion that became feasible because of the advent of the telephone. A new laboratory was included in this expansion, but once again a statement of purpose defies comprehension:

> This room is for the special work in physiological psychology, and is equipped with apparatus for psychophysic experiments, and the clinical application of instruments of precision in neurological diagnosis.[127]

In 1891 Wiliam Noyes, a member of the medical staff, fashioned a counting device for a chronoscope. In 1892 he published a study of the knee-jerk under varied auditory stimulation, in one patient, selected because of a long history of apathy that was interpreted as a willingness to cooperate. The data consisted of kymographic tracings of patellar reflexes, supplemented by a few plethysmographic records from the arm and the leg.[128] The results were discussed in a neurological frame of reference. Noyes's alignment with psychology appears to have been quite tenuous and he preferred clinical work to research. He left McLean to accept a position at the Massachusetts Hospital for Dipsomaniacs and Inebriates.[129]

In 1893 Cowles appointed August Hoch, a physician, as both psychologist and pathologist in the laboratory. Cowles also arranged for Hoch a two-year European trip. This included a sojourn with Wundt, Mosso, and Kraepelin. In 1904 Hoch published in the *Psychological Bulletin* a review of research on such topics as span of apprehension for senseless syllables, association, memory, reaction time, and motor processes in mental patients. The only American paper which he cited is one of his own, an ergograph study published in the *Journal of Nervous and Mental Diseases* in 1901.[130]

As in the case of Noyes, Hoch's commitment to psychology was transient, and as his career continued his orientation became distinctly psychoanalytical.[131] By 1907 he had strayed far enough away from brass instrument psychology to write "The Psychogenic Factors in the Development of Psychosis." This was also published in the *Psychological Bulletin* and in it Hoch suggests that searching for the causes of disease in mental events might be as fruitful as searching for them in brain disorders.[132]

S. I. Franz

Shepherd Ivory Franz (1874–1933) met Edward Cowles in 1903 when they were both lecturing at Dartmouth Medical School. The latter was convinced that fatigue was an important component of both excitement and depression but was experiencing difficulty in aligning the diverse symptoms with his knowledge of neurophysiology.[133] Franz, who had already investigated some variables related to fatigue,[134] was invited to outline a research program. Franz complied, Cowles procured funding for three years, and in 1904 Franz joined the staff of the Laboratory of Pathological Physiology of the McLean Hospital.

Franz was educated at Columbia University and was awarded the doctorate in 1899. Structuralism was not in the center of his interests, but he did spend a semester at Leipzig. The trip seems to have produced exposure rather than indoctrination. His dissertation, on visual afterimages yielded three publications,[135] as well as a firm decision not to do any more work in this area because of a self-rating as "only slightly visual minded."[136]

The first part of the afterimage research, published four years prior to the doctorate, was an attempt to ascertain the response limens for afterimages, using apparatus that had been designed by Cattell. Franz conducted nearly 3,000 "experiments" using himself and three additional observers and was able to specify the time, area, and intensity of a kerosene light that was required to induce an afterimage in 75 percent of the exposures. Franz reports specifics about the equipment, such as the absorbing power of the ground glass in the aperture and the frequency with which the wick was trimmed. The duration of both trials and intertrial intervals was regulated. The distance of the participants from the stimulus was uniform, as was the time for dark adaptation. Franz states that the only variable over which he was unable to gain control was a fixation point.

The paper offers evidence that data collection per se was important in that some results are printed even though they were obtained at a brightness level that was not comparable with the bulk of the data. Franz acknowledged the disjunctiveness but nevertheless devotes an entire table to the figures.

The complete dissertation, published as a monograph in 1899, reported the threshold data, as well as information about latency, duration, fluctuations, color changes, spatial relations, and retinal transfer. The dissertation concludes with a six-page review of research on afterimages.

There is an interesting pattern in the write-up in that the material on threshold latency and duration is reported with about the same degree of completeness, but the treatment of later topics takes on the form more of a commentary than of an experimental report. For example, the account of the fluctuation research includes some unquantified results and very limited information about the circumstances under which they were collected. The section on spatial relations contains a description of equipment but merely illustrates the results and furnishes no conclusive support for the generalization, that "most of the results, however, seem negative."

There is at least one additional instance in which conviction overpowers confirmation:

While the grouping and averaging of these diverse figures cannot be well justified, I have done so because, in a general way, the figures of the averages seem to show what ordinarily would be expected.[137]

Franz's dissertation is the only publication that allows opportunities to check calculations. There are forty-five such instances and Franz was in error in three of them. As in the case of Sidis and Krohn the mistakes are minor (range from 0.2 to 0.75) and noteworthy only because they demonstrate the pervasiveness of at least some inaccuracy.

Franz coauthored two papers during his predoctoral days. One was an investigation of the variables in reading that induced visual fatigue, a phenomenon that was believed to contribute to the increasing prevalence of myopia and astigmatism. The authors explored such factors as the size of the type, space between letters and lines, and intensity and quality of the illumination as well as the quality of the paper. There is an inconsistency in interpretation:

> We conclude that the size of the type is the all important condition of visual fatigue. . . . Very low intensities, less than from 3 to 10 candle-meters, are sources of even greater fatigue than small type. . . .[138]

The second paper, published in the same journal and placed immediately after the first, is entitled "The Accuracy of Observation and of Recollection in School Children." Students were asked to answer such diverse questions as the nature of the weather two weeks previously, the number of years that had elapsed since George Washington's death, and the number of feet from the schoolhouse door to the street. The authors dutifully report the result and appropriately disavow interpretation:

> The questions are so complex in themselves, all including observation, with errors of judgment, and memory with its errors, that no general conclusion can be drawn.[139]

Franz described his second work on fatigue as "largely a destructive critique of the methods hitherto used."[140] On a more constructive note he proposed various refinements in the construction of instruments, but the paper is more a treatise on mechanics than on psychology.

Franz's next publication was the first of the training-extirpation studies that would bring him fame. The inaugural experiment was concerned with cats' acquisition and retention of a learned response before and after excision of both frontal lobes. The results suggested that the loss of tissue induced changes. In order to increase the likelihood that this was actually a function of the frontal lobes he carried out additional operations, including the inactivation, in sequence, of the parietal and frontal areas, as well as the excision of both parietal areas. The anatomical modifications were monitored at autopsy.

This caution did not extend to all other aspects of the investigation. There was no control of the age or preoperative physical condition of the animals. The intervals between acquisition and surgery, as well as between surgery and retention tests, varied. The hours of food deprivation were not specified, and "the speed together with the elimination of random movements determined for me when the habit was learned."[141]

The data consisted of the amount of time an unspecified number of cats required to escape from boxes "similar to those used by Thorndike." Solving the puzzle boxes indicated to Franz that a simple association had been formed between a motor response and a food reward.

Franz concluded that the removal of both frontal lobes resulted in the elimination of a recently acquired habit. However, it could be relearned. He observed

ut did not systematically examine, the retention of such older habits as alertness
o mice and rubbing against people.

"Observations on the Functions of the Association Areas (Cerebrum) in Mon-
eys" was read before the Section on Pathology and Physiology of the American
Medical Association at the 1906 Annual Meeting. The paper included a literature
eview, a report of prior surgical interventions in cats, and a preview of similar
work with monkeys.[142] The latter research was published in 1907, and in this the
monkeys were confronted with two associations to be learned: to turn a button 90°
in order to open a food box attached to the cage, and to go through a sequence of
ctions that involved jumping onto two bars, up into a box, up and then down
hort ladders and finally, lifting a lid. The design was essentially the same as that
f the first study and the conclusions can be characterized more as refinements
han as corrections of those of the first investigations.[143]

Franz's research on psychoses began, in 1905, with study of simple and choice
eaction times to sound of a severely depressed patient. It was undertaken in
rder to supplement, and if possible to clarify, occasional observations of prolon-
ations more marked in simple than in choice reactions. The Hipp chronoscope,
egulated by a fall hammer, was used, and the experimental procedures appeared
o be routine with the exception of the discarding of reactions "only when there
was evidence that the subject had not reacted in a perfectly normal manner."[144]
here is no explanation as to why "perfectly normal" should be requisite in a
tudy of pathology.

In 1905, Franz and G. V. Hamilton published "The Effects of Exercise upon the
Retardation in Conditions of Depression." In this paper research is given
herapeutic power:

> The more accurate methods available in the laboratory . . . offer more tangible
> evidence of the values of the various curative methods. Moreover, it reassures
> the patient in that he believes something is being done for him.[145]

There were two series of trials designed to indicate whether passive exercise
vibration) or active exercise modified response limens for pain and touch, simple
nd choice reaction times, rapidity and accuracy of movement, and reading speed.
n the first series a patient was mechanically vibrated at various points along the
pine. Touch and pain thresholds were then measured at 27 different anatomical
oints and then the patient was required to tap on a sheet of paper for 30 seconds,
uccessively draw a line 20 times and, during latter trials, to read 100 figures.
hese procedures were carried out on successive days for two weeks, or with no
ore than one day intervening between the trials. Then, for undisclosed reasons,
e trials were stopped, then resumed for eleven days on a nearly daily basis and
uspended for the same period just prior to one final session. The latter, however,
as apparently not the last, since a footnote reported some additional results
btained "after the MSS. was sent to the *Journal*."[146] The patient was disturbed
n three days and the figures for those trials were discarded.

In the second series, numerous measurements were made after periods of rest
nd after walking. Data were obtained for six days from the subject who par-

ticipated in the first series, as well as for four days from a second male patient. The former was forty-four years of age and the latter sixty-seven, a discrepancy that brought with it extraneous differences in the effect of exercise.

The authors concluded that the response limens for both pain and pressure were higher than among normals, that mechanical vibration lowered both thresholds and increased rapidity of movement, and that moderate exercise accelerated the speed of mental processes. The changes were perceived as warrants to prescribe both active and passive exercise.

Franz's next paper was the first in a long series of therapeutic attempts. This was an account of the retraining of an aphasic and was undertaken both to treat and to probe the issue of whether the reinstatment of speech was the result of functional recovery of neural pathways or the formation of new ones.[147] Franz decided, somewhat tentatively, in favor of the latter.

In 1906 Franz, as Sidis and Krohn had done, discussed the relationship between psychology and psychiatry.[148] In this article he brought up the matter of patients and introspection. He volunteered that while many were not able to introspect others were competent candidates because, as a result of their discomfort, they were sensitized to their own experiences. Franz decided that it was proper to select those who were able to cooperate because such choices were not basically different from the selection process in a normal sample. This endorsement was presented in a convincing manner, but Franz rarely included introspection in the designs he formulated.

Franz's next investigation illustrates the uninhibited movement between psychology and neurology that was typical of the period. The paper is entitled "The Time of Some Mental Processes in the Retardation and Excitement of Insanity," but the observations were made to find out "to what part or parts of the nervous system may we refer the increased and the decreased psychomotor activity usually found in depressed-maniacal insanity."[149] Measurements were made of simple and choice reaction times as well as of the speed of tapping, reading, adding and discriminating letters and colors. In selecting tasks Franz looked for simple ones that might be used on the wards.

In spite of the avoidance of heavy equipment the Hipp chronoscope was used for timing. All subjects were right-handed, and in measuring simple reaction time only this hand was used. This variable, however, appears to be the only subject related one that was regulated, and the choice of participants practically mocks rigorous control. For example, there is a statement that both education and practice contribute to reading competency, yet "the patients who were used . . . did not vary very much in their average of intelligence, and possibly not much in their reading practice."[150]

The design called for three clinically distinct subsamples, each with an N of two: normal, retarded, and excited. The *normal* group consisted of Franz and a *patient* who had been hospitalized for seven years but "at the time of the laboratory experiments he was practically well. . . ." The members of the depressed group were twenty-one and sixty-five years of age, respectively. The diagnosis of one of the excited patients was in dispute in that there was a question of manic vs. general paresis. Franz noted, "If . . . it happens that he is found to be paretic, the results of the experiments would not be affected, because at the time the tests were made he was undoubtedly in an excited, maniacal condition without dementia."[151]

Franz observed that excited patients were not consistently faster than normals or depressed patients and was led to conclude that excitement involved an increase in motor diffuseness rather than in motor ability. He speculated that retardation involved a "lowering of . . . irritability."[152]

In 1907 Franz became Professor of Physiology at George Washington University and Psychologist at the Government Hospital for the Insane in Washington, D.C. The latter appointment involved him in the inauguration of a psychology research laboratory that had been proposed by Superintendent William Alanson White. The latter gave the laboratory three charges: to devise a practical method for examining the mental status of patients, to stimulate interest among the medical staff in research, and to provide facilities for experimentation.[153] Arrangements were made for Ph.D. candidates in psychology at George Washington University to work in the hospital laboratory.[154] There was also a publication outlet, *Government Hospital for the Insane—Bulletins.*

The laboratory consisted of five separate rooms and contained an elaborate array of equipment borrowed from the United States Bureau of Education. The apparatus had been accumulated by Arthur MacDonald, an anthropologist, who had studied at numerous universities including Harvard, Leipzig, and Berlin.[155] White's inventory of the equipment contains 144 entries, a minimal count because several of the entries are multiple, for example, three oval hand dynamometers and seven algometers.[156]

As might be expected Franz's first papers after the move to Washington were based on ventures prior to the move. First, there was a lengthy presentation of an unsuccessful attempt to distinguish in the case of a McLean patient the cause of a migraine as either fatigue or a metabolic, sensory, or vasomotor disturbance.[157] The second was a description of a soundproof room in Zwaardemaker's laboratory in Utrecht.[158]

By 1909 Franz was beginning to broaden his interests beyond instrumentation and physiology to an appreciation of the patient's viewpoint.

From many careful and oft-repeated introspections of normal individuals we know that every presentation is interpreted, perceived, or apperceived only in the light of all our past experiences. . . . It is this functional interrelationship that gives us the means of understanding and of curing many of the cases of the functional type of insanity.[159]

This interest was pursued in a program of research on association that was initiated by a joint study with William Alanson White.[160] The project was intended to find out if irregularities in associations are valid cues to affective reactions. Normal adults were shown strong or attention-commanding stimuli and asked to associate to a list of words, and to try to conceal what they had witnessed. The researchers then tried to identify those individuals who had had particular experiences. They encountered both successes and failures, and interpreted the former as evidence that associations are indicative of differing experiences. They also welcomed the failures as indicators of the necessity of having a considerable amount of information, if misinterpretations are to be avoided.

A second paper on association appeared shortly after this joint study, and it was the last one to be issued during the period covered by this monograph. Franz waved a banner of superiority of psychology:

> The elaborate methods of registration employed in association experiments by the professional psychologist are too complex, too unwieldy, and at the same time *too accurate* for the purposes for which the results of similar experiments on psychiatric cases are obtained. The latter, we well know, are observers unskilled in a psychological sense. . . . [161] [Italics ours]

Ives observed that differences between Franz and White, his superior on the hospital staff but his junior author, developed and she points to a reduction in the amount of attention given to the laboratory in White's Annual Reports. Franz does not deal with the matter, except perhaps indirectly when he complains about "a volcanic rise of psychoanalytic belief."[162] White shared Sidis's enthusiasm for the subconscious and dynamics. Franz did not.

In 1924 Franz resigned from St. Elizabeth's Hospital, formerly the Government Hospital for the Insane. After Franz's departure the laboratory continued, but the growth was not as marked in research as it was in patient care and in staff training

In 1924 Franz joined the faculty of the University of California at Los Angeles where he also served as chief of the Psychological and Education Clinic of Children's Hospital in Hollywood, California. He remained there until 1933, the year of his death.

Franz's career was a distinguished one. He was editor of the *Psychological Bulletin,* 1912–24, of the *Psychological Monographs,* 1924–27, and associate editor of the *Journal of General Psychology,* 1927–33. He was president of the American Psychological Association in 1920. He was a fellow of the American Medical Association and in 1915 was awarded an honorary M.D. degree by George Washington University.[163] Franz was an avid investigator throughout his professional life. The bibliography approximates one-hundred entries.[164]

At the end of the laboratory era of psychological research on psychoses Franz was *a* leader in instrumentation and *the* leader in neuropsychology. He was the first psychologist who continued for an extended period of time to study psychopathology, and by virtue of this persistence he became one of the distinguished ancestors of modern apparatus and neuropsychological theory, diagnosis and treatment.

F. L. Wells

When Franz resigned from McLean Hospital he was asked to name a successor He nominated Frederic Lyman Wells (1884–1964) who, in 1907, accepted the post of assistant in Pathological Psychology.[165] Because of this succession the McLean laboratory became the first psychiatric institution to maintain continuity of personnel in psychology. Wells received an A.B. from Columbia University in 1902 an M.A. in 1904, and a Ph.D. in 1906. He remained on the McLean staff until 1921 with the tenure interrupted by a brief interlude in 1910–11 when he was at the New York Psychiatric Institute and Columbia University and by military service in 1917–8.[166]

In the first three years after the doctorate Wells published twelve papers. The first was the dissertation, ". . . Perception of Linguistic Sounds." In this research trisyllabic nonsense syllables were dictated and the subjects' written reproductions of them were compared with the actual stimuli. Tallies were made of the sounds that were erroneously perceived. Wells's introduction is exceedingly interesting in that he acknowledges that spoken speech consists of intrinsically variable stimuli and that a listener has a tendency to hear what is expected and to "make sense and not nonsense out of what he hears."[167]

Wells appears to have been eager to try out his professional skills in new areas. In 1906 he applied a ranking technique to the heretofore strictly subjective area of literary standards.[168] He also began, in 1906, a search for a measure of intellectual efficiency. Wells was convinced that such a test must consist of a task that could be scored for accuracy, and he perceived reading with its "absolutely controlled associations" as meeting these criteria. He ranked six individuals "according to their degree of objective intellectual performance" and measured the speed of reading aloud passages of varying content. Wells concluded that high speed and low variability are characteristic of intellectual efficiency, but there are "striking individual exceptions."[169]

Even after beginning to work in a psychiatric hospital, Wells continued to investigate topics extraneous to psychopathology. In 1907 a paper in the technology of testing appeared. Specifically, it dealt with three varieties of problems in addition, examples, for Wells, of different "arithmetical associations."[170] The next publication was a second application of psychological procedures to literature, in this instance, literary merit.[171]

In *Essays Philosophical and Psychological in Honor of William James,* Wells treats the rankings of fifty souvenir postal cards, differences in colors in twenty-eight pairs of silk cloth, and six weights. These stimuli were selected to provide a continuum from feeling tone or preference through differences in sensation to accuracy. The raters of the cards and colors were ten individuals with varying amounts of training in psychology. Wells then made an excursion, but in a very restricted way, in the direction of psychopathology by having the weights judged by six patients as well as by four normals. He noted that "there is nothing in the results to indicate a distinct species of performance in the abnormal subject as a class."

In the discussion Wells pointed out that the rankings clustered around personal means that were "constant and peculiar to the individuals." He commented that this is analogous to the dissertation finding of "a constant tendency to hear certain sounds rather than others, which differed with the individuals."[172]

Wells's next two articles were on the topic of fatigue.[173] The first was a literature review; in the second, norms for the maximum rate of repeated voluntary movements were compiled in order to have a baseline against which to compare patient data. This study was merely an approach to clinical matters, since patients were not observed. The procedures were conventional laboratory ones, and this is the first investigation conducted by Wells that testifies to an in-depth familiarity with brass instrument technology. The participants were all males and the data, the total number of taps, were organized around eighteen issues, for example, warming up, fatique, and practice considered separately for the left and for the right hand.

In the next article, "Technical Aspects of Experimental Psychopathology," published in a psychiatric journal, Wells, like Sidis, Krohn, and Franz, interpreted scientific psychology to the medical profession.[174] His presentation is sophisticated, detailed, and has an 90-item bibliography. The reassurances about the gains from interdisciplinary cooperation are relegated to citations, and attention is concentrated on a critical appraisal of experimental methods and apparatus. Wells's publications of research based on patients were up to this point limited to one study, but this treatise discloses a penetrating awareness of the literature and of the problems within the laboratory.

Much of the discussion was devoted to the choice of instruments and to the question of what the instruments actually measure. Wells is critical. For example he remarks that "the plethysmograph has not shown itself in any sense of the word a 'psychoscope.'" He notes further:

If we could measure, with any objective validity, sensibility to pain; but we cannot do it, and some of the best known instruments for this purpose are as good examples of precision running amuck as experimental psychology affords

Wells found fault with specific instruments. For example,

The dynamometer . . . is a uniformly unsatisfactory instrument. The most patent objection is the different leverage allowed according to whether the hand is large or small, the fingers short or long. . . . Nor is the calibration always trustworthy; I have seen records all the way from 30 to 70 kilograms made on different instruments by the same individual under similar external conditions.

In another instance.

I have yet to see a key operated by laryngeal action that can be depended upon with voiceless spirants. . . .

Wells complained about the failure to modify apparatus for use with patients and stated that this rigidity was an important reason for a number of studies being based on only a single subject. He made various concrete suggestions and recommended procedures that demanded less cooperation. Thus in measuring steadiness he suggested avoiding the inserting of a stylus in holes in favor of making dots inside circles printed on paper.

Wells lamented the discarding of data and suggested:

The printing of a distribution seldom requires more than two lines, and ought to prove a healthy corrective for the ruthless throwing out of extreme cases which is responsible for so many small m.v.'s, particularly in reaction time work. We often tend to consider low variability as indicating careful experimentation, as is may in physical measurements, but in the present field, it is much more likely to mean a rigid censorship of the results.

This article was followed by an empirical study of a clinical topic, that is, patient fatigue as manifest in tapping. Except for the patient status of the participants the experiment was a duplication of the earlier normative one. The rate of tapping was measured in ten patients with "manic-depressive depression," and all of the averages in the published report were based on these subjects. However, in accord with the prevailing eagerness, Wells printed also the results of two individuals who were not comparable because their depression was complicated by other symptoms. Wells concluded that depressed patients, as compared with normals, are generally slower but that they exhibit other differences from normals, for example, less fatigue and greater rapidity during early trials.[175]

Wells next moved into the perplexities of differential diagnosis, repeating the study of fatigue with subsamples composed of seven manics, six cases of dementia praecox, and five general paretics. He compared the results with those obtained on the previously studied depressed patients as well as on normals. He concluded that motor retardation, which is a symptom of more than one disorder, consists of a generally lowered rate of tapping as well as a rise in the curve at points where normals show a decline.[176]

Wells's last paper during the period under consideration was an expansion of the original normative study of tapping. It involved measuring the rate of ten women and comparing the protocols with those obtained in the original investigation. Various sex differences were discussed, including the finding that women's introspective reports of fatigue agree more with tapping scores than do those of men." The accuracy of this conclusion would be increased if the noun *man* were substituted for *men*, inasmuch as the introspections were confined to those of Wells. Further, the women's accounts were those of a group of nurses, personnel not only untrained in introspection but also generally unfamiliar with the methods of psychological research.[177]

In many respects Wells was a wary, circumspect investigator but he was not free from errors in arithmetic. He was fond of quantifying, and his articles furnish 16 opportunities to check his accuracy. Mistakes were found in 124 instances, or 7 percent. They were concentrated in the dissertation, which reproduced the number of errors made by each subject. There were 77 mistakes in adding these scores, ranging in size from 1 through 17.

The effect of these mistakes on the interpretation is elusive because there are discrepancies between the figures in the text and those in the tables. For example, the text indicates that the largest number of mistakes by a single subject was 1,041, but the tables state 1,134.[178]

The remaining 47 mistakes were scattered among six papers and ranged in size from 0.01 through 3.6 with only six larger than 1. Thus, Wells augments the membership list of careless mathematicians.[179]

The year 1909 is that of the Clark conference, and also a sign of the end of the laboratory era of research in psychoses. Wells was then merely twenty-five years of age, and only 12 items in what would become a 150-item bibliography had been completed. His research in psychopathology was slow to develop, but firm when once established. One element that persisted throughout his career was the awareness of the phenomenon of projection and this was developed as early as the dissertation. And this openness about dynamics was undoubtedly strengthened by his attendance at the Clark Conference. Wells also respected experimentation and for many years wrote about the links between experimental psychology and psychoanalysis.

Wells was chief of the Psychological Laboratory of Boston Psychopathic Hospital from 1921 to 1938. In 1932 he was also appointed assistant professor in the Harvard Medical School and in 1938 he became Psychologist in the Department of Hygiene at Harvard University. He remained in that position until his retirement in 1950. Wells's primary professional identification was with the clinical rather than the academic sphere. He was vice-president of the American Association for Applied Psychology, 1939–40, and twice president of the American Psychopathological Association, 1942–44 and 1946–47.[180]

Shakow points out that toward the end of his life Wells was in a unique position: "Until his death in 1964 he was the last person alive pictured on the famous photograph posed by most of the prominent attendants at the 1909 meeting at Clark University."[181]

2. Academic Personnel

Investigations based on psychotics were not confined to institutional personnel, and at least two experiments by extramural investigators were conducted. These two papers do not vary significantly from those coming from the hospitals.

J. W. Baird

One of these researchers was John Wallace Baird (1869–1919).[182] He received a B.A. from the University of Toronto in 1897 and the next year traveled to Leipzig to study with Wundt. After returning to this country, he was a fellow in psychology at the University of Wisconsin before attending Cornell, where he took the Ph.D. in 1902. He served on the faculty of The Johns Hopkins University, University of Illinois, and Clark University. One of his specialty areas was vision, and in 1906 he compared the color zones of normals with those of hysterics and neurasthenics by means of a set of Hegg discs loaned by Mrs. C. Ladd-Franklin. The minutiae of measuring the color zones are reported, but such variables as age and visual acuity are ignored. One striking aspect of this research is Baird's opening comment that "diminished sensitivity to color is a prominent symptom."[183] This statement is grossly in error.

F. B. Barnes

Florence Berenice Barnes (Mrs. John F. Shepard; ?–1952) also published research based on patients.[184] She obtained an M.A. in psychology from the University

sity of Michigan in 1907[185] and in 1908 published "Some Aspects of Memory in the Insane":

> Our particular problem was to determine the rate of learning and degree of retention as compared with the normal and to study the relative value of "heaped up" vs. divided repetitions and the influence of generative, effectual, and retroactive (rückwirkende) inhibition.[186]

The author commented on the self-centered attitude of many of the patients and indicated that this preoccupation created a barrier to research. In order to minimize this she used the Treffer method of recall for the six to twelve nonsense syllables to be learned. The Treffer method demands only the giving of a second syllable when E offers the first of a pair. This is much simpler than the more frequent demand of an accurate repetition of an entire series. In order to avoid the complications of using apparatus with patients she exposed the nonsense syllables on cards, which she handed to the subjects. Barnes concluded that patients' acquisition rates are much slower than normals', all varieties of inhibition are more pronounced, and "divided" rather than "heaped up" repetitions are more advantageous for the insane than for the sane.

3. An Overview

In many respects the research that took place in psychiatric surroundings resembled the investigative practices in laboratories in the academic context. There has also come to light a profusion of specific examples of less than ideal practices many of which seem to be the result more of carelessness than of ignorance. Certainly the rules of calculation were known. Furthermore, each of the researchers has demonstrated an awareness of the mandate to control. Yet, heterogeneous conditions are acknowledged and then ignored.

There are instances of puzzling polarity, as in the coexistence of the thoroughness of printing kymographic records and vague labeling of stimuli. Essentially irrelevant data are included in articles that furnish examples rather than complete findings. The reports of experiments are lengthy, but often fail to depict what occurred and certainly do not provide enough detail to allow replication.

The use of instruments stands a bit distant from these shortcomings, in that they were generally regulated within the limits of the available technology. Equipment was widely used, adapted, improved, and venerated—with skepticism emerging only in isolated episodes. Franz and Wells (as well as Barnes) simplified some equipment, but these modifications were, however, exceptions.

Introspection was not an important investigative ingredient but residuals of it in the form of qualitative analyses were apparent. Franz was trying to see matters from the patient's point of view and Wells was striving for an understanding of the nature of psychological phenomena.

The work on components intrinsic to the dominant psychology of the period was probably less then the work on tangential matters. Whatever the proportions, the era generated material for historians of learning and neuropathology, child development, test construction, the subconscious, and the mechanism of projection. Historians of psychology, psychiatry, and medicine are provided with grist, inasmuch as informing the medical profession of the potential of scientific psychology for the healing profession was the rule.

Psychological Research in the Context of Mental Deficiency

A. C. Rogers, medical superintendent of the Minnesota School for Idiots and Imbeciles at Fairbault, Minnesota, was enthusiastic about the potential of laboratory psychology for the field of mental deficiency and in 1896 he hired A. R. T. Wylie to serve both as a druggist and a psychologist.[187] This was also the year in which Rogers became the editor of the *Journal of Psycho-Asthenics,* a periodical that replaced the *Proceedings of the Association of Medical Officers of American Institutions for Idiots and Feeble-Minded Persons.*[188]

Rogers was to publish a number of studies conducted in the Minnesota laboratory, but he did not keep the journal subscribers waiting for material from that nascent enterprise, then dependent upon a borrowed Hipp chronoscope.[189] Rather, in the first two volumes he reprinted, as five articles, "Contribution to the Psychology and Pedagogy of Feeble-Minded Children," written by George E. Johnson, a fellow in Pedagogy at Clark University.[190] Johnson collected data from residents of the Massachusetts School for the Feeble-Minded at Waltham, and this research probably constitutes the inaugural application of the laboratory method to mentally defective patients in this country. The results appeared originally as a single paper in *The Pedagogical Seminary* in 1894,[191], a date that moves the inception of formal research back two years prior to the stirrings at Fairbault and four years prior to 1898, the date occasionally reported for the establishing of a research facility at the Minnesota School.[192]

Two additional journals in the field of mental deficiency were established. The earlier of these was the *Training School,* originally a house organ for the New Jersey Training School for Feeble-Minded Boys and Girls. This publication was founded in 1904 but enlarged in 1907 by means of the *Supplement to the Training School,* an addition designed for the printing of experimental results in biochemistry, pathology, and psychology that were expected from the research laboratory that had been founded the previous year. The editor, E. R. Johnstone, was superintendent of the institution and the editorial staff consisted of Henry H. Goddard and Alice F. Morrison, an educator.[193]

The *Psychological Clinic* was inaugurated in 1907 by Lightner Witmer. As in the case of the companion journals, the approach was interdisciplinary, but the psychology laboratory of the University of Pennsylvania was an important source of material, especially in the early years. Although attention was given to emotional disturbances, the first volume bore the subtitle "A Journal for the Study and Treatment of Mental Retardation and Deviation," and the focus was on individuals who were more responsive to therapeutic intervention than the patient featured in the other two publications.[194]

These three journals formed an impressive information network, particularly in view of the fact that it existed outside the mainstream of psychology and psychiatry. Although some research was published in other outlets, the contributors to the *Journal of Psycho-Asthenics,* the *Training School Supplement,* and the *Psychological Clinic* constituted the investigators whose laboratory work with mentally defective patients is reviewed in this part of the present monograph.

The laboratory era of mental deficiency differs from research on psychoses for two reasons: (1) patient ineptitude blocked the effective use of equipment; (2) the merits of brass instruments were quickly challenged and laboratory techniques were displaced when the age-scaling method of intelligence testing was introduced. In 1908 the *Training School* published Goddard's translation of the Binet scale.[195] In 1909 the *Journal of Psycho-Asthenics* printed an article by Goddard in which he suggested that the DeSanctis and/or Binet tests might be used as a basis on which to formulate prognoses.[196] In 1910 this journal published an account of the examination of 400 mentally defective children, as well as a second description of the Binet methods.[197] By 1911–12 publications on the subject had grown into a deluge. For example, a series of five papers appeared, in an uninterrupted sequence, in one volume of the *Psychological Clinic.*[198] Thus, the laboratory era of mental deficiency that began in 1894 with Johnson's experiment ended in 1910–12 with the takeover by mental testing.

This interval was concurrent with, but a bit longer than, the laboratory era of psychological research on psychoses. The psychologists who conducted investigations with intellectually handicapped patients were more numerous than those who reported experimentation on psychoses, yet they remained a small fold readily divisible into three groups. The first consists of only two members—George E. Johnson and A. R. T. Wylie. Both of these men worked assiduously trying to conduct laboratory research on the mentally handicapped, published reports of it, and then defected from the field of psychology. A review of their work highlights some of the vicissitudes of the experimental method when it was applied in the least feasible context.

The second group consists of researchers who were experienced in the laboratory method and who also became involved in the clinical assessment of mental defectives. These people form a bridge between conventional procedures and those used in the management of patients. They are, in the order of the date of the doctorate: Lightner Witmer, Henry H. Goddard, Edmund B. Huey, J. E. Wallace Wallin, and Fred Kuhlmann. A study of their efforts disclose those aspects of experimental psychology that were valued enough to be tried in a new undertaking.

The third group consists of contributors to the publication network who had not been personally attracted to formal experimentation but who were pioneers in mental testing. In a sense these investigators do not belong in a history of brass instrument technology, but limited attention is devoted to them because they could not have escaped familiarity with the hardware of research, although they chose not to work with it. Since preferences are shaped, in part at least, by the practices they are designed to replace, the practices of this group shed some light on laboratory psychology. The members, in the order of publication, are: Naomi Norsworthy, Isabel Lawrence, Leonard P. Ayres, Clara Harrison Town, and Lewis M. Terman.

1. The Laboratory Era

G. E. Johnson

George Ellsworth Johnson (1862–1931) earned an A.B. in 1887 and an A.M. in 1890 from Dartmouth College. He then taught in a high school and also attended Hartford Theological Seminary for a year before enrolling in Clark University. He obtained an A.M. from Clark University in 1895[199] and while a student there compiled an unusually extensive review of the literature on mental deficiency. From this broad spectrum of topics he chose to investigate auditory memory span, the speed and nature of associations, and motor ability. The latter included observing responses to commands to carry out various specific movements, determining the amount of body sway, computing the ratio of speed of shoulder to finger movements, and measuring dexterity. No clearly articulated purpose is offered for conducting this research, but there are hints of a generalized drive to experiment.

Johnson does mention an enigma in each of the three major topics he selected. In memory there is the contrast, previously acknowledged by "Scupture" (E. W. Scripture), between severe impairments that are clinically pervasive and the dramatically superior memory of a few patients. In association there is both relevant and irrelevant content. In the motor sphere there is apparent insensitivity to pain. Johnson believed, and he was probably correct, that he was the pioneer investigator of the motor responses of idiots.

Johnson's literary style is diffuse, but at times it becomes telegraphic and several details are reported only vaguely, if at all. For example, the participants' ages are only sporadically identified. There is an account of the data generated by the administration of a digit span test to seventy-two patients, but no indication is made of the size of a sample that reacted to such orders as "Rise" and "Hold out hands." The reader is all too often forced to make inferences. For example, the ataxiagraph results are labelled simply "cm. by cm."[200]

Johnson's procedures fall clearly within the experimental format in that he takes measurements for all members of a sample, notes the methods used, briefly at least, presents results in tabular form, and tries to formulate some conclusions. This compliance with the experimental method is, as in the case of his peers, less than complete. For example, gross but relevant differences in experience are ignored for a group of thirteen boys who were asked to string beads for a two minute interval. The scores are offered as unqualified measurements of speed even though "most of them had practiced this exercise for one year or more."

The investigative irregularities are compounded by patient idiosyncracies. Johnson endeavored to minimize the attrition by restricting some of the sample to "school cases," but this did not eliminate failures. For example, there was "very general difficulty even among school cases"[201] in grasping the directive to open and close the fingers laterally. Johnson's solution consisted primarily of calling attention to the failures, and disregarding them when summarizing.

Although Johnson's paper was a lengthy one, he printed figures that allowed only five recomputations. Only one error was found. This was a sum of 93.2 that should have been 95.3, a change that would not influence the conclusions.

Johnson's results were both confused and confusing, and the conclusions mirror, more than clarify, the problems. The association times were generally slower than those of normals, but incongruent content was associated very rapidly. Tallying the successes in carrying out voluntary movements sheds little light on why some patients indulge in actions that are normally painful. The perplexity is clearly illustrated in the memory-span results. Johnson recognized the lack of a satisfactory system of classifying the intellectual level of the patients, and this has contributed to the following mixture of data and speculation:

> The feeble-minded fall considerably below normal children in memory-span. But the memory-span is so good in some cases, and the average for the majority is so high, that we are led to conclude that the degree in which the memory-span of feeble-minded children falls below that of normal children is not commensurate with the degree in which the feeble-minded fall below normal children in general intelligence.[202]

In spite of the perplexities, Johnson affirmed faith, which he never substantiated, that the experimental method could be applied to mental deficiency:

> A test which requires any introspection on the part of the subject must be discarded, except in the most intelligent cases, where, of course, the test becomes proportionately less valuable as the subject approaches the normal. But these few tests show that experimental psychology and pedagogy have no impossible field even among idiots.[203]

Johnson's convictions may have been durable, but his loyalty was not. After this program of research he became involved in public school education and at the end of his career was associate professor in the Harvard University Graduate School of Education.[204] He wrote both books and papers in education, and one of the latter was published in volume 3 of the *Psychological Clinic*.[205] Johnson's addition to the stockpile of psychological knowledge remains essentially an exposure of the embarrassments that accrue to attempts to use mentally defective patients as subjects.

A. R. T. Wylie

Many of the obstacles that Johnson struggled against were to be encountered by Arthur Rufus Trego Wylie (1871–1941), who undertook research under the impetus of A. C. Rogers in the spring and summer of 1896 at the Minnesota School for Idiots and Imbeciles. Wylie earned an A.B. from the College of Wooster in 1892, where he had enrolled in all the courses offered in the departments of philosophy and biology. In order to study psychology he spent the academic year of 1892–93 at Harvard University where, in addition to a course in French, he took one with Herbert Nichols and the equivalent of three with Münsterberg. He was awarded an A.B. from Harvard University in 1893.[206]

At that time Wylie aspired to conduct research on the insane, but was unable to secure a position that allowed him to do so. During the academic year following the second baccalaureate he served as Principal of the Central College Academy, Central, Ohio, and also worked toward a doctorate in an innovative program at the College of Wooster. He earned a Ph.D. in philosophy in 1894. The dissertation, philosophical in content, is variously identified as "Implication of Materialism" and "The Implications of Empiricism."[207]

Wylie's career in psychology was deferred for two postdoctoral years and even at the end of that interval, that is, 1896, the initial appointment as pharmacist and psychologist at Fairbault was for less than one year. Information as to where Wylie obtained the requisite skills for a pharmacist is sparse. The available biographical details are incomplete, and one or more of the lapses could easily conceal an opportunity to take a correspondence course or even to attend one of the "cramming schools" available in the 1890s to would-be druggists.[208]

Wylie taught science at Hiawatha Academy, Hiawatha, Kansas, for one or two years, and this responsibility included giving instruction in psychology for at least one year.[209] In 1898 he returned to Fairbault and was provided with space in the hospital wing of the institution, but there may have been some delay before experimentation began. Wylie's own writing states that the "Minnesota laboratories opened in 1899."[210] It was not until 1900 that Rogers reported to the Annual Meeting of the Association of Officers of American Institutions for Idiots and Feeble-Minded Persons that two hundred dollars had been appropriated for laboratory equipment. He also called attention to Wylie's diligence, "working at the experiments ten hours per day, besides his routine work."[211] Once underway, from whatever starting date, Wylie produced research—seven papers published between 1899 and 1904 in the *Journal of Psycho-Asthenics.*[212]

Wylie's investigations were directed toward three comparisons: mental defectives and normals; mental defectives and criminals; and varying levels of mental deficiency. The variables that were assessed included, in the order in which they were published: height, weight, taste, reaction time, touch threshold, pain sensitivity, muscle sense, auditory acuity, visual sense; auditory, visual, and muscular memory spans; muscular steadiness, tactile localization, motor speed or tapping, strength of hand grasp, instincts, and emotions.

This enumeration does not do justice to Wylie's conception of the problems he was investigating, in that he readily translated behavior as it was observed in the laboratory into both neurological phenomena and complex psychological processes. Muscular steadiness was believed to yield information about attention and fatigue. Tactile localization was seen as a measure of attention. Dynamometer readings were perceived as indices of "nerve power," and this was synonymous with will power, but "the strength of the nerve impulses, other things being equal, depends on the strength of the stimulus."[213]

The list of equipment which Wylie used is impressively long. It includes "Hipp's chronoscope" and an electric hammer;[214] Scripture's touch weights, "aethesiometer," "Cattel's" algometer, Galton's whistle, "Appun's Reed," a tone tester, Snellen chart, color wheel;[215] geometric forms, Bradley's colored papers, letters, nonsense syllables, a graduated rod with adjustable stops;[216] Scripture' steadiness apparatus, Sanford arm rest, telegraph key and sounder, metronome, kymograph, and Carroll dynamometer.[217]

The apparatus seems to have been used with care, and Wylie reports numerous details about the handling of the equipment. For example, algometer pressure was increased at a rate of two kilograms per second and applied to a uniform area of the forehead. The dynamometer was calibrated after each use. The rate of presentation of nonsense syllables was regulated by a metronome.

Wylie overlooked the fact that calibrated equipment does not assure response calibration, and he failed at times to specify the criteria for judging reactivity. There is, for example, no information as to the basis of a decision that a difference in weight was perceptible or what established a pain threshold. In the measurement of taste sensitivity Wylie reported that he relied on "any indication of a difference."[218]

Variable or inconsistent stimuli were used on several occasions. For example, the investigation of immediate visual span was conducted with "the more common geometrical forms as well as some irregular ones." Nonsense syllables were devised so as "to get *some* as free from association as possible."[219] (Italics ours.)

Wylie's tactics for minimizing patient fade out occasionally modified the nature of the sample, but the shift was not always recognized. For example, in measuring hearing Wylie tested only the most mature children, but the acuity as measured was interpreted as that of the feeble-minded, not as that of a cooperative subsample. In another instance five of twelve patients were nonresponsive to the reaction time procedures, and the results were again offered as measures of the reaction times of the feeble-minded.

In one instance patient recalcitrance prompted a change of apparatus. Wylie wanted to investigate visual acuity, but inasmuch as many patients could not read letters he abandoned the Snellen chart in favor of a color wheel, which he then used to ascertain difference thresholds for saturation. In other words, patient behavior was sufficiently disruptive to transform a study of acuity into one of saturation, but Wylie gave no indication that he was aware of this, "We conclude that there is a dullness of the visual sense among the feeble-minded."[220]

There are also fluctuations in the number of patients for reasons less obvious than patient malfeasance. For example, the text concerning muscular steadiness indicates that thirty-five boys and thirty-three girls were examined and that three girls were unable to comply, but the table of results for this examination contains scores for forty-six boys and thirty-six girls. In a second instance the author reported an N of thirty but gave only twenty scores.[221]

Wylie asked teacher(s) to assign each individual to one of three levels of general mental ability, designated from most to least efficient as A, B, and C, but no criteria for the rankings are given. Doctrine prescribed an inverse relationship between the severity of mental deficiency and competency, but the data did not always agree. On occasion Wylie managed these discrepancies by ignoring them. He concluded that touch sensitivity varies directly with mental ability even in the face of uneven progression of means. For example, the average weights, in milligrams, which induced a sensation in the right hand in males were for A = 4.3, B = 1.5, C = 6.8 and in the left hand, A = 3.5, B = 2.0, and C = 7.3.

The lack of respect for the data could stem from at least two sources: first, the misalignment between patients' behavior and laboratory methods reduces the credibility of the technique. Secondly, Wylie believed that irregularity was intrinsic to feeble-mindedness. In accord with this conviction he frequently calculated mean variations, and these computations generally disclosed marked dispersion. For example, the mean variation exceeded the mean in three of twelve measures of response lines for touch.[222]

Wylie was convinced that patients were basically antisocial and the paper on instincts has some of the qualities of a character indictment. Yet, he strained to gather empirical evidence. The literature allowed very few comparisons with the data procured in the Minnesota laboratory, but Wylie was able to report that both criminals and the feeble-minded share taste impairments and restricted visual fields.

Wylie published only enough scores to allow ten opportunities to assess his accuracy. In all instances the totals are correct and the only errors are small ones in two subtotals.[223] Thus, Wylie probably should be exonerated from membership in the group of the arithmetically negligent.

Wylie's influence on psychology began to extend from the laboratory into clinical matters. In 1900 the Association of Medical Officers of American Institutions for Idiotic and Feeble-Minded Persons appointed an ad hoc Committee on Psychological Research. This committee, composed of two physicians and Wylie as chair, was charged with the task of devising a form for recording the results of psychological examinations. The plan was to induce all institutions to follow the same procedures so that a data bank could be built. At the 1901 meeting Wylie read a paper, "A Scheme for Psychological Investigation of the Feeble-Minded". The examination blank on which this was to be recorded was printed in the journal.[224] This lengthy record booklet allows space to log numerous variables, including anthropometric measurements, level of scholastic skills, and such psychological data as fears, "illusions," and adequacy of memory. The influence of laboratory procedures, as in Krohn's blank, is apparent in the instructions for examining patients. These include directions to examine touch by means of Scripture's touch weights, pain with either Cattell's or McDonald's algometer, hearing by means of a tuning fork or watch, smell with an olfactometer, and muscle sense by means of weights.

Wylie reported that an adverse political climate was developing in Minnesota.[225] He did not go into detail, but this was about the time all the state hospitals were placed under the jurisdiction of the Minnesota Board of Control.[226] He was granted a fellowship at Clark University for the 1901–2 academic year and during that period he completed a comprehensive review of "The Psychology and Pedagogy of the Blind" and published it in the *Pedagogical Seminary*.[227]

After one year at Worcester, Wylie entered medical school and obtained an M.D. from the University of Minnesota in 1906. Political clouds notwithstanding, he returned to the Minnesota School as a staff physician and held that position until 1910 when he was appointed superintendent of the State Institution for the Feeble-Minded at Grafton, North Dakota. He held that post throughout the remainder of his career.[228]

Wylie's bibliography contains no research papers after he left the Fairbault laboratory, but he did publish research data he had accumulated in the laboratory through 1903. No additional papers in psychology were to emanate from that source until Fred Kuhlmann joined the staff in 1910, a date approximating the beginning of the psychometric influx, with a resultant marked change in research practices.

2. Between the Experimental Laboratory and the Testing Room

At least five psychologists who were experienced in experimental psychology were to move into the field of mental deficiency and into laboratories in clinical settings. The differences in the birthdates of these investigators span only nine years, and these contemporaries will be discussed in the order in which the doctorate was awarded.

L. Witmer

Lightner Witmer (1867–1956), who comes first in this list, is distinct from the other four members of the group in several respects. He was the only one not to have received at least some education at Clark University. He took charge of what had been established as an academic laboratory and transformed it into a clinical facility, and was enough of a heretic to start this change in 1896, the year during which pioneer experimental laboratories were founded in hospital settings.

Lightner Witmer earned an A.B. from the University of Pennsylvania in 1888. He then attended law school for one year before entering graduate school. As early as June 1890 he was appointed assistant in psychology and he completed an M.A. in philosophy in 1891. During this period of study he also taught English in a Philadelphia college preparatory school, an experience that was to contribute significantly to his interest in clinical psychology. Apparently Witmer would have been satisfied to have completed his education at the University of Pennsylvania, but Cattell pressured him to study at Leipzig and even procured some financial support for the venture.[229] This netted him a Ph.D. but, like Franz, he did not become a Wundtian.[230]

Some insight into Witmer's personal assessment of his doctoral education can be gained from a description of his three most influential preceptors. Wundt is included in this list, but is the last to be named, and is referred to in general terms and ones that contrast with the specific acknowledgment of the other two: "Professor Fullerton, from whom I learned the method and value of introspective analysis, Professor Cattell, to whom I owe my first acquaintance with the ideals of the experimental method. . . ."[231]

The date of Witmer's doctorate is not consistently reported. Collins, Misiak and Sexton, Penniman, and Watson concur with the American Psychological Association Directories that the degree was awarded in 1892.[232] Tinker includes Witmer's dissertation in a list of degrees granted by Wundt in 1893.[233] Fernberger, a colleague of Witmer, commented on Tinker's paper and supplemented it in various ways, but made no reference to the 1893 date.[234]

In 1892 Witmer joined the faculty of the University of Pennsylvania as director of the Laboratory of Psychology, a facility that had been founded by Cattell.[235] Even though he occasionally accepted extramural responsibilities, that institution was his headquarters for forty-five years until retirement in 1937. Shortly after going to Pennsylvania he became consultant to the Pennsylvania Training School for Feeble-Minded Children and to the Haddonfield Training School, as well as to a private facility, Miss Marvin's Home School in West Philadelphia.[236] He taught at Bryn Mawr, and Collins states that he established a laboratory at that institution in 1896.[237] Garvey assigns this role to J. H. Leuba and specifies the date as 1898.[238] Collins also credits Witmer with founding a laboratory at Lehigh University in 1903 and as serving in that institution as professor from 1903 to 1905.

Witmer is reported to have asked to do a dissertation on an applied topic, but the request was disallowed[239] and he investigated the aesthetics of asymmetry. The data which he collected were largely introspective, and were supplemented by an analysis of previously unpublished data that Fechner had obtained. Witmer published in three places the work he completed in Wundt's laboratory. A version of it was read at the 1892 meeting of the American Psychological Association,[240] an author abstract appeared in the *Psychological Review* in 1894,[241] and portions were incorporated into *Analytical Psychology*, published in 1902.[242] These items, plus a description of a pendulum Witmer devised for a chronoscope, completed his laboratory officiation.[243]

This retreat from the rituals of research did not dissipate the interest in doctrine. Witmer continued to make use of introspection and early in his career was actively spreading the structuralist word. He addressed three articles on pain to the medical profession and in these exposed the audience to protracted discussions of theory. The arguments do not lend themselves to summary, but the respect for introspection is illustrated by his depicting pain as "a simple unanalyzable mental content . . . a sensation." He asserted that introspective results were compatible with specialized pain tracts in the spinal cord and with pain centers in the brain.[244]

Witmer also dispensed information about psychology in *Pediatrics*. In 1896 he described "Practical Work in Psychology" and offered the opinion that mentally defective children are superior to normal children as research subjects because

> the methods of instruction are simple and the difference in condition at the beginning and end of treatment is more marked than in normal children, so that the relation of result to method is more easily determined.[245]

In the following year Witmer entered the field of education by a twofold step of writing about the role of psychology in education[246] and offering a summer school course in testing, "A Laboratory Course . . . in The Methods and Results of Child Psychology."[247] Featured in this were visits to institutions caring for defectives, the sensory impaired, and young criminals.

Witmer believed that both teachers and clinicians should be taught to introspect. The use of the technique as he taught it involved some distortion of the more typical procedures in that it was to be used in service of the patient rather than of doctrine, was extended from elements to the intricate, and from self-observation to inferences about others. He proclaimed that the more attuned personnel are to their own mental states, particularly in relation to physical movements, the better equipped they are to infer children's private experiences from their overt actions.[248]

Ten years after this endorsement a second appeared:

> Method can only be acquired through individual laboratory work. The student must have presented to him . . . mental phenomena which he can subject to personal observation and introspection. He must be taught . . . especially to distinguish between what is actually before him and what, owing to preconceptions and theories, he thinks ought to be there.[249]

Witmer was also active within his own discipline. In 1896, at the fifth annual meeting of the American Psychological Association, he read a paper in which he declared an intention to investigate psychological phenomena relevant to medicine and to education and to disseminate the results of this research by means of a program of instruction and a Psychological Museum.[250] Collins described the reception accorded Witmer's address: "The only reaction he got from his audience was a slight elevation of the eyebrows on the part of a few of the older members."[251]

Cues that Witmer might turn from the conventional research approach in the direction of practical problems appeared early. First, he tried to write a dissertation around a practical issue. Secondly, he dealt directly with individuals who were retarded in one or more skills. In 1889, while teaching and still a graduate student, he encountered a pupil who had a marked deficiency in English. Witmer labeled this deficit "verbal deafness" and carried out what appears to have been an active program of drill. A grade school teacher sought advice at the University of Pennsylvania Laboratory of Psychology on how to help a fourteen-year-old pupil, "a chronic bad speller." Witmer, unable to find any help in the literature, accepted this vacuum as a challenge, and "with this case, in March 1896, the work of the psychological clinic was begun."[252]

Witmer was taking the lead inasmuch as the date of his formal turning away from the traditional laboratory coincided with the installation of research laboratories in patient facilities in both Minnesota and New York. Ten years after the psychological clinic was established it was supplemented with a hospital school. The university was unable, after the first year, to manage charity patients, but the school served private inpatients for a number of years.[253]

In the clinic Witmer initiated a program of intervention, or to use his term, restoration. Holmes's account of the clinic illustrates the transition from laboratory methods to explicitly clinical work:

> . . . The dynamometer may indicate slight differences in the muscular power of right and left hands and lead to the discovery of slight hemiplegia or to the recollection on the part of the parent of an almost forgotten case of "brain fever" or meningitis. The ergograph reveals weakened muscular power, poor coördination and early fatigue. . . .[254]

Holmes enumerated additional pieces of apparatus that were available: opthalmoscope, esthesiometer, algometer, sphygmograph, and telegraph key. He also noted that photographs were taken and casts were made of faces, hands, teeth, and jaws. Also in use were items that were to become commonplace in clinics, for example, the Binet tests and an adaptation of the Seguin Form Board.

Gertha Williams, a University of Pennsylvania Ph.D., worked in the clinic "not for money but for credit." She recalled in an oral history the honor and care accorded the two Hipp chronoscopes that the clinic owned, ". . . so precious that he [Edwin B. Twitmyer] wouldn't let the cleaning woman in the room."[255]

The availability of this equipment did not modify Witmer's preference for sustained surveillance of gross clinical behavior, and he preferred to see children over an extended period of time rather than adapt to the developing fashion of a brief mental test. He also complained about research paraphernalia. "The greatest laboratories of psychology are the school rooms. No complicated apparatus is required for the investigation of the material to be found there."[256]

By 1909 the disparity between Witmer's laboratory and the more customary academic structure was formally recognized, and Witmer's enterprise was separated from the department of psychology and its budget increased. The director of the Psychological Clinic began to report directly to the university trustees.[257]

Witmer's papers yield meager information about his own experimental habits, but an impression of careful work dominates and even withstands such awkwardness as references to "Sandford" and to "Tichener's."[258] His articles are more concerned with the nature of research and the implications of experimentation than with quantified data. The only figures that allow recomputation are confined to seven sets in the description of the control function of a pendulum and to nine sets in the text. A recalculation of these indicated one minuscule error. Thus, Witmer joins Wylie in barely missing the register of carelessness.

Witmer attempted to bequeath to psychology the use of introspection in clinical work, but there is no evidence that he met with much success in this. His principal heritage, the clinical model, came from outside academic psychology. His statement of gratification when freed from apparatus was a prescient one, and when viewed with the advantage of hindsight, it becomes the first in a series of similar criticisms.

H. H. Goddard

Henry Herbert Goddard (1866–1957) obtained an A.B. in 1887 and in 1889 an A.M. with a major in mathematics from Haverford College. Goddard's education was funded, intermittently at least, by the Society of Friends. His mother was a minister to various parishes, some of them as distant as Europe. When Goddard was nine years of age his father died. Goddard maintained a religious identification throughout life and in his correspondence there are episodic uses of plain speech. Goddard interrupted college for a brief interval to teach in a secondary school, and also pursued this occupation for seven years after obtaining the master's degree. In 1896 he enrolled at Clark University and in 1899 was awarded the doctorate.

He then joined the faculty of the State Teachers College at West Chester, Pennsylvania. He was not content there and wanted access to a laboratory, but was unable to procure a satisfactory, long-term position until 1906. He did serve as acting professor of psychology at Haverford College during the year 1900–1. During the summer of 1904 Meumann allowed him space in the Zürich laboratory where Goddard conducted research on fatigue, but apparently did not publish it.[259]

Goddard's first paper, "Are Drugs Unnecessary to the Cure of Disease?", written while he was at Clark University, is a plea for readers to provide him with accounts of nonmedical cures of illness. The article, published in the *Hypnotic Magazine* in 1897, indicates plans for Hall and Goddard to compile and analyze reports of both successes and failures.[260]

The doctoral dissertation relied in part on the replies to this request. It consisted essentially of a review of both the theory and results reported for various kinds of faith cures. The conclusion was reached that such procedures would not eliminate the need of medical care, but that positive attitudes could prevent and slow down biopathology.[261]

A rather marked shift in subject matter occurs in the third paper, "A New Brain Microtome," published in 1900. This was a description of a piece of apparatus that had been devised by Goddard with considerable assistance from C. F. Hodge.[262]

Goddard's next publication was "Ideals of a Group of German Children". This was a replication of studies carried out by Estelle Darrah-Dyke in Minnesota and California, by Earl Barnes in New Jersey and London, and by Will Chambers in Pennsylvania. Cross-sample comparisons abound.[263]

In 1906 Goddard accepted the directorship of the laboratory at the New Jersey Training School for Feeble-Minded Girls and Boys at Vineland. Some awareness of the forceful and determined nature of the administrative personnel in that institution fosters an understanding of the research that was to be developed in Goddard's name. The founder of the school was the Reverend S. Olin Garrison, who had developed an interest in caring for patients, possibly in response to having two mentally defective siblings. In any event in 1887 he accepted seven patients into his own home in Millville, New Jersey. This operation was very successful, and requests for admission increased. Garrison sought financial support, and B. D. Maxham, a citizen of Vineland, generously offered his own home and forty acres of property. The opening date was 1 March 1888. Garrison promoted the institution assiduously and it thrived. In 1898 Edward R. Johnstone, a man who shared Garrison's zeal for growth and expansion, was asked to join the staff.[264]

Following Garrison's death in 1900 Johnstone became the dominant administrator in the school and retained that authority until retirement in 1944. He was responsible for the founding of the research laboratory and for much of what went on in it. Johnstone's vita lists college enrollment only at the Fort Wayne, Indiana, College of Medicine, 1895–97. There is no record of an earned degree, although he was twice awarded an honorary one—a master's from Princeton in 1923 and a doctorate from Rutgers in 1941. The work experience prior to going to Vineland involved a brief period as "Officer" in a reformatory, four years teaching in public schools, and five years service as teacher and principal of the Indiana School for Feeble-Minded Youth.[265]

At Vineland Johnstone advocated a program of extramural instruction, largely but not exclusively for educators, and was convinced that material for this educational project could be best generated by a research department. In 1906 he requested and gained approval from the board of directors for a research laboratory.

Johnstone was intrigued with the field of child study and he and Goddard met initially at a child study meeting.[266] They liked one another almost immediately, and when Hall recommended Goddard for the directorship there was no hesitancy in making an offer. Goddard disclosed that he was unusually naive in his youth and accustomed to taking "things as they came."[267] Johnstone had a strong drive to manage, and Goddard was certainly not to get much direction from his professional colleagues.

The research precedents were minimal, and when reminiscing Goddard's only literature reference is to Wylie.[268] Sanford reminded him of Johnson's work, advised him to consult with Witmer, and suggested starting the project with an investigation of the expression of emotion and instincts.[269] Hall suggested research on vocabulary development, automatisms, dress, nutrition, taste, and smell.[270] Meyer cautioned him against piling up a hoard of seemingly scientific tests.[271]

Goddard kept a diary in which he recorded, on a nearly daily basis, many of his activities in the Vineland laboratory, as well as various ideas concerning research and the use of equipment. There are approximately 260 entries ranging in date from 17 September 1906 through 24 June 1907. The log, disclosing many more problems than solutions, was apparently maintained, in part at least, for Johnstone's review and on occasion questions are directed specifically to him. Johnstone initialed practically every entry and frequently added words of approbation. The latter were often applied to entries noting work on apparatus, making extramural contacts, and observing individual patients.[272]

Johnstone made the laboratory possible and took pride in it, but he did not allow it a voice:

Our Laboratory personnel, even to the Director, have no executive authority in the institution . . . The Laboratory may recommend, but has no authority to enforce its recommendation.[273]

Goddard's struggles are clearly exemplified in a few excerpts from the diary:

Tuesday 25. The more I study these children the more I feel that their power of attention is likely to be our crucial test. I think we can measure this.

Wed 26 We ought to keep a record of the barometer and the weather and a record of children's activity and dispositions. . . .

Thursday 11. . . . some of our expected results will fail us but it does seem as tho in virgin soil like this something must bear fruit.

Monday 2, 4. As soon as I get an electro-magnet shall have the ergograph complete. Also apparatus for testing the rapidity of tapping. This is used to test will power. Child taps on an electric key at his natural rate. The taps are recorded on drum & counted. He is told to tap as fast as he can. A f.m. child has not the will power to increase his rate very much. I think perhaps this too may be sufficiently significant to serve in classification.

Thurs. 8 Called on Franz at McLean for an hour. He says make haste slowly: it took him a year to understand his problem.

Monday Dec. 3. . . . has highly exaggerated knee jerk. Is this characteristic of hydrocephalus? It indicates a weakened cortex. . . . His hand trembled greatly and yet he managed to hit most of the spots in the coördination test.

Tues 2 Worked on the records. It takes a vast amount of time to count taps, etc.

Wed 17 Dr. Sanford . . . was much pleased with the work. . . . His opinion is that we will get results sooner and surer if I spend more of my time observing the children in their environment and less in putting them thru tests. He says observe first and then test in accordance with the problems suggested by watching them.

The journal referred to various pieces of equipment. They are presented with the names and in the order in which they are noted:

two electric bells made into "signal magnets"
seconds marker
tapping apparatus
moving picture machine
plethysmograph
pneumograph
spirometer
ergograph
metronome
finger grip
automatograph
scales
brass drum
capillary pens
muscular memory test
guillotine for cutting brain
hack saw blade
Petrie dishes
Quincke tubes
apparatus to test winking reflex
apparatus to test eye and hand coordination
dynamometer
target
chronoscope
tambours
machine to test trembling of hand
sense tests
form board
esthesiometer
lantern slide equipment
algometer

ataxiagraph
yard sticks
microtome

In 1907 Goddard was provided with both an assistant psychologist and a part-time clerk. Thus, at hand were the ingedients requisite for research productivity: laboratory space, apparatus, an energetic, motivated director, assistants, and a publication outlet, the *Training School Supplement,* that was expecting copy. As in the case of the Illinois Eastern Hospital for the Insane, this combination of assets failed to yield fruit. During the first two years after the founding, four narrative articles appeared[274] and merely two reports of empirical results, in both instances data on number concepts.[275]

In contrast to Krohn, Goddard stayed with the scene of frustrations. In a description of the research program for 1907 he stated that he had been trying out Naomi Norsworthy's recently published tests, even though they "are not very well adapted to our children." He listed thirty-seven different measurements that he was attempting to make. He complained:

> . . . many children cannot be taught to blow the Spirometer at all. . . . A boy frightened at an insignificant thing so that it took six men to hold him could not squeeze a pound on the Dynamometer tho he clearly understood what was wanted.[276]

The discouragement was strong:

> After two years my work was so poor, I had accomplished so little that I went abroad to see if I could not get some ideas. I came back with the Binet tests. . . .[277]

This payoff must have exceeded all expectations. The Binet procedures offered a means of dealing with, even quantifying, ineffective behavior. To make matters even more gratifying, the breakthrough was in an area strongly approved by the supervisor because it could contribute to patient classification and promote the institution.

This metamorphosis of failure into success did not result in an immediate abandoning of the brass instruments. There was enough faith in them to assign them some criterion validity, and as late as 1910 Goddard reported that he had started to compare mental ages with results obtained with the ergograph, ataxiagraph, and formboard. This approach was however, very shortlived and no further attention is given to laboratory instruments.[278]

Goddard was candid about the reasons:

> . . . feeble minded children cannot do these psychophysical tests. They have not the attention to make the discriminations. I think it would be exceedingly interesting and valuable if we could use them. However, for diagnosis we do not need them, since the Binet tests are proving to be marvelous [*sic*] accurate.[279]

From 1908 through 1910 there were four papers dealing with the mental age scales.[280] In 1910 Goddard introduced the term *moron* at the Annual Meeting of the renamed American Association for the Study of the Feebleminded, and in 1911 "The Menace of the Feeble-Minded" was printed in *Pediatrics*.[281] Goddard's stellar career in psychometrics and in mental deficiency was under way.

Goddard's papers provide sixty opportunities to scrutinize precision in calculation. Errors were found in fourteen instances or 23 percent. These were mistakes in addition and they ranged from 1 through 5 for sums varying from 2 through 63. Carelessness was still in vogue.

This review of Goddard's professional activities to the end of the laboratory era of mental deficiency indicates that the laboratory interests of his early postdoctoral years became more of an embarrassment than an asset in a clinical setting. He was to become one of the leaders in mental deficiency, and his contributions to posterity were derived from that field rather than from the psychology characteristic of the pioneer laboratories.

E. B. Huey

Edmund Burke Huey (1870–1913) obtained an A.B. from Lafayette College at Easton, Pennsylvania, in 1895. After two years of teaching Latin at the Harry Hillman Academy in Wilkes-Barre, Pennsylvania, he enrolled at Clark University where he obtained a Ph.D. in 1899, merely one month after his colleague and close friend, Goddard, obtained his degree.[282]

Huey's doctoral dissertation dealt with the nature of the reading process, but included such practical issues as how to increase the speed of reading, reduce fatigue, and explore how reading induces such "direful consequences" as myopia. Huey's project was elaborate and was published in three parts. It included studying alterations in speed and extent of reading when the first and last parts of words are removed, as well as comparing the speed of reading horizontal and vertical material. He secured introspective reports of associations prompted both by isolated words and by words in context, but rejected introspections concerning fixation points in reading because they were "untrustworthy."[283] Huey was skeptical about the validity of gross clinical observations of eye movements and he devised an ingenious apparatus for recording them. Hodge and Delabarre both contributed to the design of this equipment. The experimental procedures appear to be well controlled, but the maximum amount of effort and care was devoted to the hardware.

Huey published *The Psychology and Pedagogy of Reading* in 1908. This book was reprinted as late as 1968. This volume was his last contribution to the field of reading, and no explanation of his loss of interest has been found.[284]

The reports of the dissertation are the only research papers that contain numerical data. In these three articles there are 187 instances in which figures can be recalculated. Errors were found in eleven cases, or nearly 6 percent, and these ranged from 0.01 through 2.70, with only five in excess of 0.10.

Huey's initial postdoctoral position was at the State Normal School in Moorhead, Minnesota. He remained there until 1901 when he went to Europe for a year. During this sojourn he visited Javal, a French oculist who had provided him with literature relevant to the dissertation, and with Erdmann, a German psychologist who was also interested in the study of reading.

Upon returning to the United States, Huey taught genetic (developmental) psychology at a "normal college" in Miami, Ohio, during the academic year 1902–3. He then returned to Clark University for one year as "honorary fellow." During that interval he developed friendships with Fred Kuhlmann, and Lewis M. Terman. From 1904 to 1908 Huey was professor of psychology and education at the University of Western Pennsylvania, the forerunner of the University of Pittsburgh. He is reputed to have assembled a two-room experimental laboratory in that institution.[285] Garvey questions the identity of the founder, but offers the name of J. H. White and makes no reference to Huey.[286]

In 1908 Huey returned to Paris, where he observed Janet at work and also came to know Binet.[287] He attended the meeting of the Sixth International Congress at Geneva and published an account of the proceedings.[288]

In 1909 Huey became director of the newly founded Department of Clinical Psychology at the Illinois Asylum for Feeble Minded Children at Lincoln, Illinois. This was established by H. G. Hardt, the superintendent, and it was the second psychological facility in a state owned hospital, but it was patterned after the pioneer department in a private institution, that is, the New Jersey Training School for Feeble-Minded Girls and Boys.[289] The choice of the term *department* instead of *laboratory* may well mirror a shift from a program of formal research to one of patient assessment. It was a bipartite operation: Huey worked on standard laboratory measurements and also administered mental tests. He "demonstrated the Binet MA tests in the research laboratory" at Lincoln during the 1910 Annual Meeting of The American Association for the Study of the Feeble-Minded, the gathering at which Goddard introduced the term *moron*.[290]

In an address to the Brainard Medical Association at Bloomington, Illinois, Huey, while asserting that the use of introspection had added important information about mental elements, added the qualifying remark, "But after all, we know very little about what all these do together in enabling a given individual to get along in the circumstances of his life." He then suggested ways in which he believed the field could become more sophisticated and made a direct reference to functionalism: "It will be a functional psychology."[291]

In 1910 Huey published in the Journal of Educational Psychology a translation of the 1908 Binet scale. He was entranced by the method for a variety of reasons, including its convenience. He comments, in the same vein as Witmer, about the freedom from laboratory equipment: "The testing psychologist may carry everything needed in a very small hand case."[292]

In 1910 he also discussed the merits of the Binet examinations in the *Journal of Psycho-Asthenics*. Embedded in this recommendation is explicit censure of doctrine: "Theoretical psychology goes on after its own gods, but as for us we are here to serve men." He also reiterated, "A clinical psychology is ever a functional psychology."[293]

Huey declined an offer by Stanford University to fill the position occasioned by Bergström's death and recommended Terman for the job,[294] but in 1911 he was persuaded to leave Illinois. He was succeeded there by George Ordahl, a psychologist who obtained a Ph.D. from Clark University in 1908.[295] At the time of Huey's departure, diagnosis was gaining in importance and the laboratory productivity from the institution, by then renamed the Lincoln State School and Colony, declined.

In 1911 Huey, with the encouragement of both E. F. Buchner and Adolf Meyer, moved to The Johns Hopkins University to serve both as a lecturer in psychology and as an assistant in psychiatry at the Phipps Clinic.[296] In 1912 he published a review of the clinical examination of thirty-five "border cases,"[297] as well as a paper, "The Present Status of the Binet Tests."[298] The bibliography ends with an article on the education of mental defectives published in 1913, the date of Huey's premature death.[299]

What would have been Huey's principal contribution was obliterated, six months prior to his demise, by a fire which destroyed the manuscript of a book on clinical psychology that he had been working on for a period of ten years. What he did bequeath to psychology was an endorsement of a functional approach to psychological research, as well as a sanction of simple methods of observation. His legacy to the field of reading is sufficiently impressive to justify a 1968 reprinting of the text first published in 1908.

J. E. W. Wallin

John Edward Wallace Wallin (1876–1969) received an A.B. degree from Augustana College, Rock Island, Illinois in 1897 and went directly to Yale University, where he took courses both in philosophy and in psychology. The master's degree was awarded to him in 1899 and the doctorate in 1901, with Scripture supervising the dissertation, "Researches on the Rhythm of Speech."[300]

Wallin states that because of Scripture's absence from campus he was personally responsible for editing the dissertation. Scripture advised him to reduce the length by half. Either this command was not carried out or an insufficient reduction was ordered because a 142-page monograph remains, wordy and at the same time neglecting details. The write-up lacks a clear statement of purpose but the goals seem to have been primarily phonetic. Wallin measured the duration of a large number of speech phenomena, such as empathetic and unempathetic syllables, and pauses.

The speech that was analyzed had been recorded by an unspecified number of people, and the reader is left with a notion of sample diversity:

The subjects were of varied characters, with different languages, from different countries, of different stages and walks of life (elementary and high school pupils, academic and graduate students, professors, poets, orators, musicians, etc.).

There are also suggestions of procedural heterogeneity:

The subjects were uninstructed in respect to the purposes of the experiment, *except where the nature of the experiment required otherwise,* in order to minimize the elements of unnaturalness and intentional change of the manner of speaking.[301] (Italics ours)

The speech was played back on a phonograph and the mechanical aspects of the experiment were conducted with as much exactness as possible. Wallin even devised a method of mechanically recording the length of the intervals, a refinement of the prior strategy of pressing a key and manually writing the duration.

Wallin seems to have experienced mixed feelings about continuing research on rhythm. He worked intermittently on problems allied with it, and ten years after the completion of the dissertation a series of three papers appeared.[302] They dealt with the amount of irregularity in rhythmical intervals before disrupting the sense of rhythm; the preferred tempo, that is, the length of intervals between auditory impressions judged to be the most pleasing; and the accuracy of estimations of a rate midway between two metronome-generated tempos. The stimuli for these investigations were tones and clicks, not meaningful speech.

Once again the instrumentation was stressed, while many other matters received less attention. For example, subjects were asked to compare "about a dozen" clicks. There was wide variation in the training of the observers. The participants included "Professor Warren" as well as enrollees in the first-year experimental course. Wallin used the term *introspection* with varying meaning. Often it referred merely to comparative judgments of experiences described with categorical adjectives such as pleasant or unpleasant. There are, however, references to the nuances of visual imagery, and at one point Wallin distinguishes between introspections about stimuli as opposed to those about sensations.

Wallin became interested in identifying the tempos that would induce the most vigorous motor responses, such as foot stamping, and studied the responses of theater audiences to "vaudeville, burlesque, minstrel, light opera and glee club performances."[303] The balcony was chosen because Wallin believed that people who occupied that section of a theater were less inhibited than those in other parts.

The enthusiasm displayed in collecting extra laboratory data did not lead to further research on rhythm. In his last publication on this topic Wallin is refreshingly straightforward about his lack of motivation to probe further:

I am obliged to lay out the data purely empirically. Moreover, other lines of work now so engross my attention that no other course is possible.[304]

The dissertation and these three supplementary papers provide 1,294 sets of figures in which calculations can be verified. Mistakes were discovered in 68, or 5 percent, of these computations and the mistakes ranged from 0.0002 through 2.00, with only two in excess of 1.00. This absolute range is in the case of Wallin's data misleadingly low, because with only a few exceptions the figures were decimals. Inaccuracy of digits loses significance as they move to the right of the decimal point. For example, a sum of 0.0293 that is correctly 0.0274 is actually in error by 19 digits, but interpretatively of no importance. The aura of inaccuracy once again outweighs the consequences.

Two additional investigations in the structuralist tradition were published,[305] as well as a book review and a reply to a criticism of it.[306] There is also an extensive work, *Optical Illusions of Reversible Perspective,* 330 pages, privately printed in 1905, but the authors have been unable to obtain a copy that could be used in this consideration of Wallin's work. The volume is described by Wallin as demanding the "lion's share" of the year he spent at Clark University. He was there during 1901–2 in order to study with Hall, and during the visit he gathered material on optical illusions and also coauthored, with Hall, a questionnaire study of children's reactions to clouds. This project also provoked a "decision not to devote much time to this method of investigation."[307]

Wallin was peripatetic. His autobiography, written in 1955, lists thirty-one institutions in which he had been in residence either as a full-time employee or on an extended visit. Wallin felt that in one year he had mastered all that Clark University had to offer. Seeking a post in which he could learn Titchener's approach, he accepted an appointment as assistant in experimental psychology at the University of Michigan, with the expectation of working with Walter B. Pillsbury. During the year at Ann Arbor, Wallin's attraction to "the functional direction" that had taken shape while he was in Worcester intensified and he accepted a position as demonstrator in experimental psychology at Princeton University as a means of coming to know J. Mark Baldwin.

Wallin spent three years at Princeton, and in 1906 he accepted the headship of the Department of Psychology and Education at East Stroudsburg State Teachers College in Pennsylvania. In this position he came in contact with "very backward" boys enrolled in the "model school." In 1910 his exposure to patients was intensified when he substituted for Goddard in teaching summer school at the New Jersey Training School for Feeble-Minded Girls and Boys. Most of the remainder of Wallin's career was devoted to educational and clinical pursuits. Wallin was as prolific as he was itinerant, and a self compiled bibliography of 1955—and this is neither complete nor totally accurate—lists 32 books or monographs and 220 articles and addresses, as well as 29 book reviews.

In October 1910 Wallin went to the New Jersey Village for Epileptics at Skillman as the first staff member in a laboratory of clinical psychology. This appointment was on the recommendation of Vineland personnel. In the game of competition for primacy it was "the first laboratory of clinical psychology in an institution for epileptics anywhere in the world. This was also the first such state supported laboratory in New Jersey."

During the eight months he was in residence at Skillman, Wallin spent most of the time collecting data. He, like Huey and Goddard, used both conventional laboratory equipment and Binet procedures. The former included a spirometer, a Smedley dynamometer, and an ataxiagraph.

The superintendent and Wallin became involved in a personality clash, and in June 1911 Wallin left the institution. Wallin's replacement reputedly resigned four times within sixteen months and finally left the laboratory in 1913. Publications from this facility were minimal and Wallin laments that much of the data he accumulated was never analyzed. He did, however, incorporate some results in four books and monographs published between 1912 and 1923.[308]

Wallin's account of the Binet methods is one of the five inaugural papers in *Psychological Clinic,* 1911–12. This was an administrative manual and was written because the author wanted to promote procedural consistency among the increasing number of examiners. Wallin comments that the need for uniformity was acute, because personnel who lacked scientific training were administering tests, and that the absence of "delicate instruments of precision" did not obviate the need for training in test administration.

Wallin's instructions fall short of the ideal in that there is a casualness about details that is reminiscent of laboratory methods. For example, the examiner is advised to "move lighted match slowly before the S.'s eye (*or* ring bell from behind S.)." (Italics ours.) For Test 46, Wallin advises presenting boxes weighing 6, 9, 12, 15, and 18 grams, but otherwise indistinguishable, and asking that the heaviest be identified. The equipment is specified, in this instance the exact grams, but the presentation is not. Merely, "Place the boxes fairly near together but out of correct order in a row before S."[309] There is no regulation of the distance between the stimuli, their distance from the edge of the desk, or the position of the correct choice. Thus, it would appear that Wallin was, at the end of the laboratory era of mental deficiency, offering more the idea than effective instruction in standardized procedures.

F. Kuhlmann

Fred Kuhlmann (1876–1941) received an A.B. in 1899 and an M.A. in 1901 from the University of Nebraska and then went directly to Clark University where he obtained a doctorate in 1903.

Kuhlmann's early postdoctoral years were spent in academia: 1903–5 and 1906–7 at Clark University, 1905–6 at the University of Wisconsin, and 1907–10 at the University of Illinois. In 1910 he was hired by A. C. Rogers to be director of research at the Minnesota School for Feeble-Minded. This apointment reactivated the laboratory in which Wylie worked, and Kuhlmann served there until 1921.[310] Rogers died in 1917, and his successor was characterized as hypercritical of research.[311] In 1921 Kuhlmann left the uncongenial atmosphere to become director of the Research Bureau of the State Board of Control in St. Paul where he remained until his death. His separation from academia was not as final as this log of major appointments suggests, inasmuch as he served as "Professional Lecturer" at the University of Minnesota over an extended period of time.[312]

The dissertation, "Experimental Studies in Mental Deficiency: Three Cases of Imbecility (Mongolian) and Six Cases of Feeble-Mindedness," was completed under Sanford and published in 1904 in the *American Journal of Psychology.* A shortened version, read by Wylie at the 1904 Annual Meeting of the American Association for the Study of the Feeble-Minded, was also printed in the *Journal of Psycho-Asthenics* during the same year.[313]

In the dissertation Kuhlmann warns:

The experimental enthusiast must learn first of all, that any pre-conceived plan of experimentation that has been the result of his training in a psycho-physics laboratory is doomed to fail.

Kuhlmann was acutely aware of the difficulties that Johnson and Wylie had encountered. In order to circumvent at least some of them, he restricted the number of subjects to nine residents of the Massachusetts School for Feeble-Minded Children. They ranged in age from eight through fourteen years and in duration of hospitalization from ten months to four years and six months, but this upper limit was the period of institutionalization of the youngest patient. He worked individually with the children for four months and selected methods that the patients were most likely to be able to manage. For example, memory was measured by the method of recognition, rather than recall, because so few patients had intelligible speech.

The sample size was restricted, but the number of topics that were investigated was not. They included visual memory span, practice curves for target throwing, tapping as an index of attention and effort, association and discrimination time, attention span, and visual discrimination. The apparatus included a tachistoscope, reaction keys, kymograph, metronome, and DePrez signals. Kuhlmann supplemented this widely available equipment with form and color discrimination stimuli that he had devised. He also used common items such as dominoes and Bradley's pictures of objects.

Like his colleagues, Kuhlmann indulged in breaches of experimental control. For example, in order to study the effects of competition he decided to pair the children, but since the number was nine, "C generally,—a few times A, and B—threw alone. . . ." At times the reasons for erraticism are omitted, as in the report of tapping: "On account of unavoidable omissions on the sixth day for some of them, the results for all cases are those of only the first five days."

Because Kuhlmann believed that being watched by a stranger improved effort, he asked a stranger to observe the patients, but during only the fifth and sixth weeks of a seven-week practice period. On the last day of the fifth week he also added "a maximum, systematic coaxing." Yet, the tabular data are grouped for "the first and second weeks, the third and fourth weeks, the first three days of the fifth week, the last day, average of the sixth week, average of the seventh week." Does the "last day" refer to the final day of the fifth week or to the concluding day? Why are the data grouped in intervals that are out of phase with changes in procedure?

Confusion is further compounded by measurements that are cumbersome and remote from the topic under investigation. For example, the scores for the practice curves are "the percentages of the number of times the correct number of taps were made in the different five-second intervals in the regulated tapping."[314]

With the exception of four accurate totals in one paper,[315] the dissertation is the only publication that allows reviewing arithmetic accuracy, and obviously incorrect digits occur throughout the document. For example, Kuhlmann reports the distances Wylie used in the measurements of muscular memory as 100, 200, and 300 mm., whereas Wylie notes them as 100, 300, and 500mm.[316] A score recorded as 2.25 in a table becomes 2.21 in the text. At least two calculation errors are obvious. One designates a mean of 39.97 for seven scores, the largest of which is 34.75. A second is an average printed as 36.61 but derived from a distribution in which the entries were a single score of 36, two of 38, and one each of 41.5, 43, and 49.

The dissertation offers 365 sets of figures, and mistakes were found in 42 instances or 12 percent. These vary from 0.01 through 9.93 and only eight are in excess of 1.0, ranging from 1.11 through 9.93. At least three of these mistakes would modify data interpretations and thus the pattern of pervasive but inconsequential carelessness is broken.

One calculation is in error by merely 2.5 points, but an appraisal of it arouses suspicion that an entire set of figures is wrong. The mean scores in the tapping test vary from 28.09 through 85.00, but the questioned digits, the mean for one subject, are reported as merely 10.2. A recount raises them merely to 12.7, still far below the averages of the other members of the sample. The text ignores this low order and reports that the individual who obtained it displayed the highest between-trial variations.

Kuhlmann was trying to assess the difference between the average "natural" tapping rate and that produced under instructions to tap very rapidly. The former is reported as 15.64, and the maximum rate as merely 12.28. A second reckoning, in Kuhlmann's pattern of averaging averages, increases the figure to 17.28, above the "natural" rate.[317] The correct values imply at least some favorable response to the pressure for speed and negate any "incapacity for voluntary effort in raising their maximum rate above their natural. . . ."[318]

Following the completion of the dissertation, Kuhlmann suspended work with patients in favor of theory oriented research. In 1905 he published a review of the literature on mental imagery and memory,[319] as well as a discussion of "Recent Studies of Normal Illusions of Memory." He reached several conclusions about the reliability of memory, including a statement that has a utilitarian flavor: "The average man is likely to be mistaken about one-fourth of the time when he reports a thing from memory, and conscientiously believes that he is speaking the truth."[320]

In 1906, Kuhlmann undertook an investigation of the memory for meaningless visual stimuli.[321] This was intended to comply with Titchener's plea made at the International Congress of Arts and Science in St. Louis in 1904 to deal directly with consciousness,[322] and Kuhlmann confined the investigation to the qualitative aspects of memory consciousness, specifically imagery and the nature of errors. Clusters of five to nine meaningless visual forms were presented only during the first trial, and introspections were obtained for this exposure, as well as for subsequent recollections. The participants were also asked during each recall session to draw the forms they had seen in the beginning—a tactic a bit beyond the boundaries of introspection. Kuhlmann made comprehensive analyses of the introspective reports, and his account of the nature of errors includes a description of various changes in the series of sketches, including a phenomenon that would later be labelled leveling.[323]

The pattern of procedural disorder and inexact writing was not violated by this article. For example, the intervals separating recall episodes are not clearly specified, but they apparently ranged from two through ninety days. Also, there is no concise account of the number of trials or of the number of subjects.

Kuhlmann's next paper dealt with the problems encountered in analyzing memory.[324] This was initially read at a joint meeting of the Western Philosophical

Association and the North Central Section of the American Psychological Association at Madison, Wisconsin, 1906.

Kuhlmann then supplemented the first paper on the memory of meaningless visual material with a study of meaningful content. Attraction to the practical is once again suggested, this time in the choice of stimuli—pictures of common objects. The experimental details are more explicit than in the prior paper, but there is still more a trend toward, then an attainment of, thoroughness and regularity. For example, the design initially specified the use of two groups and fifteen pictures each, but when these were found to require an undue amount of time for introspection, two observers were given only one group. For another two individuals, three pictures were removed from each series. The five observers were allowed from "six to twelve minutes" in which to memorize these series. The initial recall took place immediately after exposure; the second after "several days"; the third in "about ten days"; and the fourth "about four weeks" after the previous session. These intervals were arranged to accommodate to the schedule of the participants, "but nothing in the experiment required greater uniformity than was secured."[325]

Kuhlmann provides an in-depth presentation of many items. The following is a partial list: the order in which the pictures were memorized, the dominance of visual details, the use of names during learning and during recall, the spontaneity of imagery as a function of particular pictures, the reconstruction of details, and shifts from imagery of the picture to imagery of the object.

In 1908 Kuhlmann again reviewed the literature on memory. In this he made two laments, and these are not only contradictory but possibly reflect both sides of a conflict between the theoretical and the clinical. He complained that introspection was too rarely the method of choice and that laboratory tasks are too contrived to have much applicability outside of the laboratory.[326]

In the next year Kuhlmann published the results of an investigation of auditory memory, and again a taint of practicality is perceptible—the use of conditions "that approached as nearly as possible those of everyday experience."[327] The main data were introspective reports but again these were supplemented, in this instance with estimations of the duration of sound stimuli. This research was modeled after the studies of vision, but the author complains about the elusiveness of auditory images because they do not lend themselves either to drawings or to descriptions.

Kuhlmann's probes into structuralism were interrupted by two excursions into comparative psychology: "A Note on the Daily Life of the Honey Bee"[328] and "Some Preliminary Observations on the Development of Instincts and Habits in Young Birds."[329] The latter was concerned with "infancy," because it is the era in which associations, the basis of recall, are formed.

Kuhlmann's last publication in the formal laboratory tradition came more than a year after he first wrote about mental testing and was a description of a device for conducting research on visual memory.[330] He combined various pieces of available apparatus so as to allow, among other things, isolating the subject from extraneous stimuli and varying the size of retinal images independent of accommodation.

Kuhlmann's first publication on mental testing was a translation of a paper by Binet and Simon.[331] He acknowledged the existence of other translations and stated that he added one more because he believed that others were neglecting Binet's interpretations of individual items. Probably as an outgrowth of his sophistication about structuralism, Kuhlmann was concerned about the qualitative aspects of psychometrics. He believed that the use of the tests, particularly by untrained personnel, would contribute to the neglect of basic psychology. Accordingly, at the close of the laboratory era of mental deficiency, Kuhlmann was trying to direct at least some attention to the nature of psychological responses.

Initially, Kuhlmann tried dutifully to accomplish the impossible, that is, to apply brass instrument technology to mentally defective patients. He then turned toward the development of doctrine, but this posture was repeatedly tinged with applied matters, and finally he relinquished theory in favor of an explicit pursuit of clinical matters. Kuhlmann's career was a successful one and included the compiling of a well-standardized age scale. Kuhlmann edited the *Journal of PsychoAsthenics* for a brief period and in 1940 was president of the American Association on Mental Deficiency.

Comment

In brief, the research completed by those psychologists who formed a bridge between pioneer experimental psychology and mental testing does not in any distinct manner alter the record, including the blemishes, of their colleagues in psychiatric settings. Possibly in rare instances the procedures are less apt, such as Wylie's shift from a study of acuity to one of differences in saturation without acknowledging the change, and Kuhlmann's attempt to pair an odd number of subjects. The state of the science was immature and attempting to extend it to noncooperative patients served more to weaken than to strengthen the laboratory approach.

Each member of the group in the laboratory-testing span had either constructed new equipment or modified existent pieces. Witmer refined a chronoscope. Goddard built a microtome. Huey fashioned a method of recording eye movements. Wallin developed mechanical recording. Kuhlmann arranged equipment in a manner that would improve the study of visual memory. In spite of this productivity each participant was to become disenchanted and to turn away from brass instruments. Witmer and Huey even proclaimed gratification at the escape. Wallin condoned the abandonment. Goddard indicated that a failure to use apparatus was tolerable because more efficient tactics were at hand. Kuhlmann cautioned against believing the claims for apparatus.

This dissatisfaction with the symbols of scientific worthiness did not extend to all of the psychology of the period. Both Witmer and Kuhlmann joined Franz and Wells in endeavoring to promote an understanding of the qualitative nature of psychological responses. Witmer had a faith that the extreme conditions of the patients would help to bring experimental effects into focus. But these beliefs were strained and the residuals were ineffectual. Each of these men was forced to redefine the nature of psychology, and they handed to their intellectual descendants methods and techniques developed in their freshly structured enterprises. Both the psychometric methods and the behaviorist credo emerged when the ashes of structuralism were cooling and those of functionalism beginning to glow.

3. The Mental Testers

N. Norsworthy

The first to publish in the group of psychologists who were directly involved with mentally defective patients and lacked extensive experience in the pioneer research laboratories was Naomi Norsworthy (1877–1916). Norsworthy graduated from the New Jersey State Normal School at Trenton in 1896 and after three years of teaching in the public schools she enrolled in Teachers College, Columbia University, with the intention of majoring in chemistry. She attracted the attention of Thorndike and he encouraged her to become a psychologist. In 1900 she became a student assistant in educational psychology, received a B.S. in 1901, was chosen by Thorndike in 1902 to be his assistant, and in 1904 received the Ph.D. degree. She then joined the faculty at Teachers College, but biographers disagree about the date of promotion and whether or not the level was that of assistant or associate professor.[332] Whatever the rank, her influence was strong. Her classes were large and Thorndike is emphatic in attesting to her importance to the institution:

> At one time or another she taught a majority of the courses given in the department, both those for undergraduates and those for graduates—always with consummate success.[333]

Norsworthy's dissertation, "The Psychology of Mentally Deficient Children," is the first article in the inaugural issue of the *Archives of Psychology*.[334] A shortened version of it also appeared in the *Journal of Psycho-Asthenics* in 1907.[335] In this research Norsworthy compared normal and mentally defective children on a variety of tasks, posed the following three questions, and answered each in the negative: Are the mental and physical defects comparable in severity? Do idiots form a separate species? Is mental growth uniformly retarded? The writing discloses no pressure to enhance theory or to investigate the efficiency of laboratory procedures, but there is a declared wish to improve upon the procedures as reported in the literature, especially by Johnson and Wylie. Norsworthy criticizes her predecessors for not making certain that the subjects understood the instructions, for not reporting experimental details, and for a complex default: "In some cases the method used is indicated so roughly that one does not know how much the results mean."

Any improvements were more a matter of assertion and of sample restriction than of refinements in the methods of measurement. Six tests were administered in groups to residents of the School for the Feeble-Minded at Waverley, Massachusetts, "the Institution for the Feeble-Minded at Lakeville, Conn.,"[336] and members of classes for the mentally defective in the New York public schools.

Norsworthy, without indicating any criteria, picked 157 of the "brightest" of these children and gave each of them eight individually administered tests. This resulted in a very large number of measurements inasmuch as several of the items in this fourteen-unit battery were divided into two or more parts. The procedures were repeated one year following the initial administration and the scores were compared with literature reports as well as with the results of examinations of normal children that were conducted both by Thorndike and by Norsworthy.

Norsworthy's procedures show only a minor resemblance to conventional laboratory methods. There is simplification, as in the case of steadiness, which was measured by having the subjects draw a line inside the boundaries of a maze pathway. In one instance there appeared to be a modification, but not an improvement, of a customary laboratory procedure. In the determination of weight discrimination each participant was provided with an empty box and one weighing 100 grams as well as a supply of shot. The task was to add or to remove shot until the two boxes were equal in weight.

Only four anthropometric measurements were included: height, weight, pulse, and temperature. The battery is impressive, although not necessarily appropriate, because of the emphasis on the higher psychological processes. There are tests of analogies, of abstraction, and of perception, as well as of immediate memory for related and unrelated words and for statements. Also included is a "block test," a formboard originally developed by Bair.[337]

Norsworthy calculated the difference between the scores for each patient on each test and the median scores for the normal children of the same age and sex, and expressed the differences in PE units. These manipulations were antecedents of contemporary profiles or psychograms, and Norsworthy, probably correctly, assigned herself the status of pioneer in the development of strategies for quantifying intraindividual variations. She printed all raw scores, as well as transformations of them.

Determining the precision characteristic of psychometrics is not a task for this discussion, but a need for monitoring the accuracy of the reported results was provoked by the observation that the chronological ages of six patients varied among tables. These discrepancies suggested additional ones, but the overabundance of figures made it impractical to repeat all calculations and pointed toward the recomputing of merely a sample of them. A cancellation test was arbitrarily chosen for the first of these recomputations. The examination was scored by counting the number of A's canceled in two sets of thirteen lines of unseparated capital letters. The table of raw scores omits entries for 40 patients, presumably because they were uncooperative or, even with effort, made no correct cancellations. Yet, deviation scores are listed for 4 of these reputedly nonresponsive subjects. There were 117 participants for whom raw scores are listed, but for 29 of these deviation scores are lacking. That is, in the table of results of this one test there are 33, or 21 percent, obvious mistakes.

Consistency was also probed in the A-T test, an exercise that demanded the canceling of all words containing both the letters a and t in thirty-one lines of Spanish text. As might be anticipated, the attrition rate was higher than in the A test and, in fact, no scores were given for 82 patients. This left 75 raw scores, and for 24, or 15 percent, of the 157 patients transformed scores were either made up or omitted.

The summary tables for the block test (formboard) list the number and percentage of patients at each age level from eight through sixteen years and for adults who scored below the median of normal nine-year-olds. A checking of the summaries against the individual scores disclosed between table inconsistencies in 20, or 48 percent, of the 42 entries.[338] These differences are typically small in that the number of patients differed by only one or two, but the discrepancies for the percentages ranged from 1 percent through 10 percent with a mode of 3 percent.

Norsworthy's inaccuracies gain in importance in view of her responsibilities for teaching statistics. In 1902, two years prior to the doctorate, she took over a course that had been developed in 1899–1900 by Thorndike. This is described by Walker as the charter course in "Educational Statistics." Walker also notes that the text Thorndike wrote for this course contained no computational instructions or information as to where such assistance might be procured.[339] Speculation about the amount of assistance Norsworthy may have given in this matter is inevitable.

In the 1908 Festchrift for William James, Norsworthy reported a study of the distribution of the rankings by five individuals of several traits of one person and concluded that the consensus was sufficiently cohesive to permit the quantification of "character."[340] In 1912 she reported a relationship between acquisition rate and retention of German-English vocabulary.[341] Norsworthy's untimely death occurred in 1916.

Her most enduring work was directed toward educators. *The Psychology of Childhood*, written for a normal school audience, was published posthumously in 1918, with Mary Theodora Whitley as second author. This text was revised as late as 1933.[342]

The dissertation was Norsworthy's most extensive contribution to psychology, and her legacy to this discipline lies primarily in the adaptation of statistics to clinical purposes. Her censure of brass instrument technology is directed at the incompatibility between patients and instruments, as well as the lack of insight into what is actually being measured. Her corrections of these deficits are not materially successful, and the influence that she did exert on successors is more in the domain of mental testing than of mental deficiency.

I. Lawrence

This chronicle of the laboratory era of psychological research on mental deficiency closes with a series of five papers in the *Psychological Clinic*, 1911–12. One of these, "A Study of the Binet Definition Tests" by Isabel Lawrence (1853–?), is included in this monograph largely to complete the record. The paper reviews a project in psychometrics and one that is isolated from the theory of the period.[343]

Its author, an educator, was a member of the faculty of a normal school in St. Cloud, Minnesota, from 1879 to 1912, and this research appears to have been her only excursion into psychology.[344] The article reviews the written definitions of words on the Binet scale by children in grades two through eight. Lawrence found that some of the words, when translated from the French, were inappropriate and that a few terms yielded inversions in age progression curves. In spite of these shortcomings she concluded that a vocabulary test provided a satisfactory screening procedure.

L. P. Ayres

A second paper in the series was an appraisal of the Binet scale and was written by the statistician, Leonard Porter Ayres (1879–1946).[345] Ayres earned a Ph.B. in 1902, an A.M. in 1909, and a Ph.D. in 1910 from Boston University. He was at Teachers College, Columbia University, 1907–9, and later held various educational posts, including twelve years with the Russell Sage Foundation where he served as director of the departments of education and statistics.[346] In these positions he was confronted directly with the problems of mental deficiency and was a contributor to the *Psychological Clinic*.[347]

In 1920 Ayres became involved with banking and railroads and later served as consultant to the military and the government. In 1926 he was president of the American Statistical Association.

In the Binet treatise, Ayres criticizes specific items because they lack the face validity required for his concept of intelligence. Of more importance for this discussion than Ayres's demands for validity is the explanation of the phenomenal popularity of the scale. He attributes this to the fact that the scale is "universally intelligible" and "universally understood." These phrases are repeated and used to refer to the quality that distinguishes the Binet method: ". . . all previous tests of intelligence have been practically restricted in use to workers in psychological laboratories."[348] Ayres's condemnation does not single out either instruments or measurements. Possibly both are under fire. In any event, for him acceptance of the Binet method was due to its independence from the laboratory.

C. H. Town

The remaining three papers were all written by psychologists, and one was the previously described administrative guide that was authored by Wallin. A second was by Clara Harrison Town (1874–1967) who received a B.S. from Temple University in 1907 and two years later a Ph.D. from the University of Pennsylvania. She was resident psychologist at the Friends' Asylum for the Insane in Frankford, Pennsylvania, from 1905 to 1910, and an assistant in the University of Pennsylvania Psychological Clinic in 1910. In 1911 she replaced George Ordahl in the Department of Clinical Psychology at the Lincoln State School and Colony, formerly the Illinois Asylum for Feeble-Minded Children. This department had been initially directed by Huey, and in 1912 Town was appointed director. Her career included faculty appointments at the University of Pittsburgh, Rush Medical College, the Iowa Child Welfare Station, and the Colorado State Teachers College in Greeley, Colorado. In 1922 she became director of the Department of Psychology of the Children's Aid Society in Buffalo, New York, and in 1935 entered private practice in that city.[349]

Town's publication record parallels the employment history in that there is diversity within a clinical context. The dissertation, "The Train of Thought—An Experimental Study of the Insane," was complemented by a second paper on association.[350] Other articles that were published during the time span of this monograph included three on speech pathology,[351] one each on hallucinations and delusions,[352] and one on kinesthesia in endophasia (talking to oneself),[353] as well as an evaluation of an educational facility for mentally defective children.[354]

The Binet paper is essentially a reiteration that incorporates lengthy quotations of Binet, and Town generates an impression that the scale was more to be used than tampered with or improved. She joins Ayres in praising the freedom from the laboratory and Wallin in fearing that psychologists might be considered dispensable:

> Accustomed to the complicated apparatus of a psychological laboratory, the laity were pleased to find it unnecessary, and overlooked entirely the fact that the psychologist himself was not unnecessary.[355]

L. M. Terman

The last in the group of those whose exposure to an experimental laboratory was minimal is Lewis Madison Terman (1877–1956). Terman earned both a B.S. and a B.Pd. from Central Normal School at Danville, Indiana. He was employed first as a public school teacher and then as a principal, and in 1901 he enrolled in Indiana University in order to prepare for the teaching of psychology or pedagogy in a normal school. He was so successful as a student that he was awarded in 1902 an A.B. and an A.M. in 1903. He also developed a keen desire to pursue a doctoral degree. At that time the instruction in psychology at Indiana University was given by J. A. Bergström, W. L. Bryan, and E. H. Lindley—all Clark University students, whose common background dictated Terman's choice of institution. He earned the Ph.D. in 1905.[356]

Terman's initial publication was the master's thesis that had been directed by Lindley.[357] Part of this research was modeled after Binet's study of suggestibility and was the first expression of the pattern Terman would repeat in psychometrics, that is, following a design formulated by Binet but enhancing it by increasing the sample of both subjects and behavior.[358]

Terman's next article involved a method that he was not to adopt.[359] This research was prompted by Hall, and Terman lamented that at Hall's suggestion he had "inflicted upon the world a questionnaire on leadership among children. . . . I had had enough of the questionnaire method."[360]

The third paper was the dissertation, "Genius and Stupidity: A Study of Some of the Intellectual Processes of Seven 'Bright' and Seven 'Stupid' Boys."[361] The sponsorship of this study is a bit atypical. While at Clark, Terman began to read intensively about tests and decided, even in the face of mild disapproval from

Hall, to explore qualitative differences between samples divergent in intelligence. Terman commented that this topic was essentially outside of Sanford's field, and that he watched the progress of the research but contributed very little to it. His Clark peers, particularly Huey and Kuhlmann, were apparently influential. Terman reports that he had watched Kuhlmann's work with care, and the design he used resembled Kuhlmann's in that there was a small number of subjects but a relatively large number of measurements. There were, however, differences in that Kuhlmann utilized hardware and Terman did not. Also, Terman's subjects were in disjunctive subgroups, one intellectually superior and the second intellectually inferior, but not grossly deficient. Terman investigated such complicated processes as inventiveness, mathematics, interpretations of fables, and learning to play chess, as well as reading speed, accuracy, and fluency—the topics in which Huey was so well versed. There were also assessments of memory and motor ability.

Terman was a contributor to the 1911–2 sequence of articles dealing with Binet tests in the *Psychological Clinic*,[362] and this paper, invited by Witmer, was a preliminary and brief version[363] of an investigation that would be cited frequently.[364] Terman verbalized admiration for the scaling of groups of tests and stated a conviction that the Binet scale, when refined, would furnish a much needed tool for research on the relationship between intelligence and other variables. Missing from Terman's assessment is any reference to equipment, and the reasons for this were to be depicted later as intentional.

Terman, admits a mechanical ineptness as well as a concomitant aversion to apparatus. He comments about his experiences at Indiana University:

> The newness of the subject had its appeal, but neither that nor the gifted teachers I had could make me enjoy working with apparatus.

A move to Clark University did not alter this:

> . . . and a piece of 'machinery' always seemed to be an obstruction between me and the thing I was trying to get at. "Brass-instrument" psychology was all right for the other fellow, but was not intended for me. My dislike of apparatus doubtless had something to do later in turning me to tests and measurements of the kind that make no demands upon mechanical skill.[365]

Comment

This last group of psychologists lacked intimate experience with pioneer experimental psychology and hence had no legacy to transmit from this domain. Yet, the members were not content with a mere neglect of instrumentation but, rather, actively added to the criticisms that personnel who were experienced in the laboratory were beginning to voice. There was even a note of glory about the loss.

This was a renunciation of both a symbol and an achievement. The equipment was a sign of worthy membership in the fraternity of science, and the use of apparatus came the closest of all procedures to meeting the rules of the scientific method. The reasons for the repudiation in spite of these assets are complex, but undoubtedly include the affect that accrues to the perception of a discrepancy between the real and the ideal. Society at large may have found hardware reinforcing, but the scientist-clinician when confronted with patient capriciousness faced disillusion.

It is sad that this withdrawal from a once perceived triumph was somewhat welcome. In the academic laboratories a rush to the arms of behaviorism was a solution, but in the clinical area there was no conversion possible within a formal laboratory framework.

ACKNOWLEDGMENTS

The authors affirm their gratitude to Josef Brožek. He conceived this work and asked us to contribute to it.

This monograph has demanded compiling numerous bibliographical items, many of which are not in the literature. Many people have assisted in filling these lacunae and the authors wish to express appreciation to all those who have helped, and especially to Patricia L. Bodak, Gordon D. Collins, Clark A. Elliott, K. B. Hudgens, William A. Koelsch, and Andrea Mitchell.

The burden of collecting printed materials from a diversity of sources has been born willingly and efficiently by the staff of Bierce Library, the University of Akron. Margaret Guss and Valerie Johnson have been particularly helpful, and in a resourceful manner.

This project was assisted financially by the University of Akron Research Grant Program (Faculty Projects) on two occasions. These contributions are important because they helped to defray the cost of acquiring photocopies of obscure literature, essential to the gaining of an understanding of the pioneer psychology laboratories.

NOTES

1. Lynn White, Jr., "Cultural Climates and Technological Advance in the Middle Ages," *Viator* 2 (1971): 171–201.

2. Robert S. Harper, "The Laboratory of William James," *Harvard Alumni Bulletin* 5 Nov. (1949): 169–73; idem, "The First Psychological Laboratory," *Isis* 41 (1950): 158–61 (hereafter cited as "First Psychological Laboratory").

3. Edwin G. Boring, *A History of Experimental Psychology*, 2d ed. (New York: Appleton-Century-Crofts, 1957), p. 324 (hereafter cited as *History of Experimental*).

4. E. B. Titchener, *President's Address to the Cornell Chapter of the Society of the Sigma Xi, June 9, 1900* (Ithaca, N.Y., 1900), p. 5.

5. William O. Krohn, "Facilities in Experimental Psychology in the Colleges of the United States," *Report of the Commissioner of Education for Year 1890–91* (Washington, D.C.: Government Printing Office, 1894) (hereafter cited as "Experimental Psychology in United States"); E. B. Delabarre, "Les laboratoires de psychologie en Amérique," *L'Année psychologique* 1 (1894): 209–55; Edward Franklin Buchner, "A Quarter Century of Psychology in America: 1878–1903," *American Journal of Psychology* 14 (1903): 666–80; Burt G. Miner, "The Changing Attitude of American Universities toward Psychology," *Science*, n.s. 20 (1904): 299–307 (hereafter cited as "Changing Attitude"); Committee on the Academic Status of Psychology, *Report of the Committee on the Academic Status of Psychology* (American Psychological Association, 1914).

6. C. R. Garvey, "List of American Psychology Laboratories," *Psychological Bulletin* 26 (1929): 652–60 (hereafter cited as "American Laboratories").

7. Harper, "First Psychological Laboratory."

8. Edward W. Scripture, ed. "Elementary Course in Psychological Measurements," *Studies From the Yale Psychological Laboratory* 4 (1896): 89–139.

9. E. Bradford Titchener, "A Psychological Laboratory," *Mind,* n.s. 7 (1898): 311–31 (hereafter cited as "Psychological Laboratory").

10. Cora Friedline, "Experiences of a Graduate Student at Cornell," transcriptions of audio-tapes (4/11/60, 4/5/62, 5/3/66): Friedline Memoirs, Oral History Box 1, Archives of the History of American Psychology, University of Akron, Akron, Ohio.

11. Edwin G. Boring, "Experiences at Cornell University, Department of Psychology," non-transcribed audio-tape (ca. 1960); Catania Gift, Archives of the History of American Psychology, University of Akron, Akron, Ohio (hereafter cited as "Experiences at Cornell").

12. Edmund C. Sanford, "A Laboratory Course in Physiological Psychology," *American Journal of Psychology* 4 (1892): 141–55 (hereafter cited as "A Laboratory Course").

13. H. K. Wolfe, "The New Psychology in Undergraduate Work," *Psychological Review* 2 (1895): 382–87.

14. F. C. French, "The Place of Experimental Psychology in the Undergraduate Course," *Psychological Review* 5 (1898): 510–12.

15. James McKeen Cattell, "The Psychological Laboratory at Leipsic," *Mind* 13 (1888): 37–51.

16. George M. Stratton, "The New Psychological Laboratory at Leipzig," *Science,* n.s. 4 (1896): 867–68.

17. J. Mark Baldwin, "The Psychological Laboratory in the University of Toronto," *Science,* o.s. 19 (1892): 143–44.

18. Titchener, "Psychological Laboratory."

19. Lillien J. Martin, "The Electrical Supply in the New Psychological Laboratory at the Leland Stanford, Jr. University," *American Journal of Psychology* 17 (1906): 274–79.

20. Hugo Münsterberg, ed., *Emerson Hall,* Harvard Psychological Studies, vol. 2 (Cambridge, Mass.: Houghton Mifflin, Riverside Press, 1906), p. 2–39.

21. Edmund C. Sanford, "Some Practical Suggestions on the Equipment of a Psychological Laboratory," *American Journal of Psychology* 5 (1893): 429–38, quotation p. 436 (hereafter cited as "Some Practical Suggestions").

22. Hugo Münsterberg, *Psychological Laboratory at Harvard University* (Cambridge, Mass., 1893), pp. 14, 17 (hereafter cited as *Psychological Laboratory*).

23. E. B. Titchener, "The Equipment of a Psychological Laboratory," *American Journal of Psychology* 11 (1899–1900): 251–65, quotation p. 265.

24. Guy Montrose Whipple, *Manual of Mental and Physical Tests, Part I: Simpler Processes* (Baltimore: Warwick & York, 1914), pp. 351–52 (hereafter cited as *Manual Simpler Processes*).

25. Letter, R. S. Woodworth to Dear Sir, 20 September 1906, Dunlap Papers M570.1, Archives of the History of American Psychology, University of Akron, Akron, Ohio.

26. Münsterberg, *Psychological Laboratory.*

27. Miner, "Changing Attitude."

28. "Christian H. Stoelting," *American Journal of Psychology* 56 (1943): 450.

29. Philip J. Pauly, "Psychology at Hopkins: Its Rise and Fall and Rise and Fall and . . ." *Johns Hopkins Magazine* 30 (1979): No. 6, 36–41.

30. David P. Kuna, "A False Start for Experimental Psychology: Harlow S. Gale and the Laboratory at Minnesota" (Paper delivered at the Ninth Annual Meeting of Cheiron, Boulder, Colorado, 11 June 1977).

31. Sanford, "Some Practical Suggestions," p. 429.

32. Titchener, "Psychological Laboratory," p. 314.

33. Miner, "Changing Attitude," p. 303.

34. Christian A. Ruckmich, "The History and Status of Psychology in the United States," *American Journal of Psychology* 23 (1912): 517–31, quotation p. 531.

35. Boring, *History of Experimental,* p. 511.

36. S. S. Stevens, "Edwin Garrigues Boring: 1886–1968," *American Journal of Psychology* 81 (1968): 589–606, quotation p. 594.

37. W. B. Pillsbury, "The Psychology of Edward Bradford Titchener," *Philosophical Review* 37 (1928): 95–108, quotation p. 98 (hereafter cited as "Psychology of Titchener").

38. Boring, "Experiences at Cornell."

39. Martha L. Sanford, "Biographical Sketch," *Edmund Clark Sanford Nov. 10 1859–Nov. 22 1924,*

In Memoriam, ed. Louis N. Wilson (Worcester, Mass.: Clark University Press, 1925), Publications of the Clark University Library, vol. 8, no. 1, pp. 4–17 (hereafter cited as *Sanford Memoriam*).

40. Robert I. Watson, *The Great Psychologists,* 3d ed. (Philadelphia: J. B. Lippincott, 1978), p. 403.

41. Samuel W. Fernberger, "In Memory of G. Stanley Hall," *Granville Stanley Hall Feb. 1, 1844–April 24, 1924, In Memoriam,* ed. Louis N. Wilson (Worcester, Mass.: Clark University Press, 1925), Publications of the Clark University Library, vol. 7, no. 6, pp. 68–69 (hereafter cited as *Hall Memoriam*).

42. Edward Bradford Titchener, in *Hall Memoriam,* p. 92.

43. Miner, "Changing Attitude," pp. 304–5.

44. Gardner Murphy and Joseph K. Kovach, *Historical Introduction to Modern Psychology,* 3d ed. (New York: Harcourt Brace Jovanovich, 1972).

45. Daniel N. Robinson, *An Intellectual History of Psychology* (New York: Macmillan, 1976).

46. David Bakan, "A Reconsideration of the Problem of Introspection," *Psychological Bulletin* 51 (1954): 105–18, quotation p. 106.

47. Edwin G. Boring, "Introspection in Dementia Praecox," *American Journal of Psychology* 24 (1913): 145–70, quotation p. 145.

48. Pillsbury, "Psychology of Titchener," p. 100.

49. John B. Watson, "Psychology as the Behaviorist Views It," *Psychological Review* 20 (1913): 158–77, quotation p. 158.

50. George Malcolm Stratton, *Experimental Psychology and Its Bearing upon Culture* (New York: Macmillan, 1908), pp. 1–2, 4.

51. William James, *Psychology* (New York: Henry Holt, 1892).

52. Edmund C. Sanford, *A Course In Experimental Psychology* (Boston: D. C. Heath, 1898) (hereafter cited as *Course in Experimental*).

53. Sanford, "A Laboratory Course."

54. "Notes," ed. Edward W.Scripture, *Studies from the Yale Psychological Laboratory* 4 (1896): 140–41, quotation p. 141.

55. E. W. Scripture, *The New Psychology* (New York: Charles Scribner's Sons, 1897), p. 12 (hereafter cited as *New Psychology*).

56. James Rowland Angell, *Psychology,* 4th ed. rev. (New York: Henry Holt, 1908), p. 5.

57. Mary Whiton Calkins, *A First Book in Psychology* (New York: Macmillan, 1911), pp. 6, 7.

58. Edna Heidbreder, *Seven Psychologies* (New York: Appleton-Century, 1933), p. 119.

59. Cora Friedline Papers, M46, Archives of the History of American Psychology, University of Akron, Akron, Ohio, Interviews 10/17/17, 11/15/17, 11/22/17; Dissertation: "The Discrimination of Cutaneous Patterns below the Two-Point Limen," *American Journal of Psychology* 29 (1918): 400–419.

60. Edward Bradford Titchener, *Experimental Psychology, A Manual of Laboratory Practice Vol. I Qualitative Experiments Part II. Instructor's Manual* (New York: Macmillan, 1901), p. xix (hereafter cited as *Manual, Vol. I Part II.*).

61. E. B. Titchener, "The Problems of Experimental Psychology," *American Journal of Psychology* 16 (1905): 208–24, quotation p. 221 (hereafter cited as "Problems of Experimental Psychology").

62. Edward Bradford Titchener, *Lectures on the Elementary Psychology of Feeling and Attention* (New York: Macmillan, 1908), pp. 197–98. (hereafter cited as *Lectures on Feeling and Attention*).

63. E. B. Titchener, "The Schema of Introspection," *American Journal of Psychology* 23 (1912): 485–508, quotation p. 508.

64. James Mark Baldwin, *Handbook of Psychology. I. Senses and Intellect* (New York: Holt, 1889); idem, *Handbook of Psychology. II. Feeling and Will* (New York: Holt, 1891); idem, *Mental Development in the Child and the Race* (New York: Macmillan, 1895); idem, *The Story of the Mind* (New York: Appleton, 1898).

65. William James, *The Principles of Psychology,* 2 vols. (New York: Holt, 1890).

66. George Trumbull Ladd, *Elements of Physiological Psychology* (New York: Scribner, 1887); idem, *Psychology: Descriptive and Explanatory* (New York: Scribner, 1894).

67. E. W. Scripture, *Thinking, Feeling, Doing* (Meadville, Pa.: Chautauqua Century, Flood and Vincent, 1895); idem, *New Psychology.*

68. Edward Bradford Titchener, *An Outline of Psychology* (New York: Macmillan, 1896); idem, *A Primer of Psychology* (New York: Macmillan, 1898); idem, *Lectures on Feeling and Attention.*

69. Sanford, *Course in Experimental.*

70. Edward Bradford Titchener, *Experimental Psychology, A Manual of Laboratory Practice Vol. I Qualitative Experiments Part I. Student's Manual* (New York: Macmillan, 1901); idem, *Manual, Vol. I Part II;* idem, *Experimental Psychology, A Manual of Laboratory Practice Vol. II Quantitative Exper-*

iments Part I. Student's Manual (New York: Macmillan, 1905); idem, *Experimental Psychology, A Manual of Laboratory Practice Vol. II Quantitative Experiments Part II. Instructor's Manual* (New York: Macmillan, 1905).

71. Guy M. Whipple, *Manual of Mental and Physical Tests* (Baltimore: Warwick & York, 1910).

72. Lightner Witmer, *Analytical Psychology* (Boston: Ginn & Co., Athenaeum Press, 1902) (hereafter cited as *Analytical*).

73. Helen M. Walker, *Studies in the History of Statistical Method* (Baltimore: Williams & Wilkins, 1931) (hereafter cited as *History of Statistical Method*).

74. J. E. W. Wallin, "Uniformity of Page Numbering," *Psychological Bulletin* 3 (1906): 84; E. B. Titchener, "A Plea for Summaries and Indexes," *American Journal of Psychology* 14 (1903): 84–87, with footnote by E. C. Sanford, pp. 86–87; Louis N. Wilson, "Preparing Manuscript for the Press," *Pedagogical Seminary* 12 (1905): 55–68; Letter from E. B. Titchener to Weld, 29 June 1912, Morgan Papers M116, Archives of the History of American Psychology, University of Akron, Akron, Ohio.

75. Robert H. Haskell, "Mental Deficiency Over a Hundred Years," *American Journal of Psychiatry,* Centennial Anniversary Issue (1944): 107–18 (hereafter cited as "Mental Deficiency"); David Zubin and Joseph Zubin, "From Speculation to Empiricism in the Study of Mental Disorder: Research at the New York State Psychiatric Institute in the First Half of The Twentieth Century," in R. W. Rieber and Kurt Salzinger, eds. *The Roots of American Psychology: Historical Influences and Implications for the Future,* Annals of the New York Academy of Science, vol. 291 (1977), pp. 104–35 (hereafter cited as "Study of Mental Disorder").

76. Henryk Misiak and Virginia Staudt Sexton, *History of Psychology: An Overview* (New York: Grune & Stratton, 1966) (hereafter cited as *History of Psychology*); John M. Reisman, *The Development of Clinical Psychology* (New York: Appleton-Century-Crofts, 1966) (hereafter cited as *Development of Clinical*); J. E. W. Wallin, "Reminiscences from Pioneering Days in Psychology, with a Few Personality Portraits," *Journal of General Psychology* 67 (1962): 121–40; Robert I. Watson, "A Brief History of Clinical Psychology," *Psychological Bulletin* 50 (1953): 321–46 (hereafter cited as "Clinical Psychology").

77. David Shakow, "One Hundred Years of American Psychiatry, A Special Review,": *Psychological Bulletin* 42 (1945): 423–32.

78. August Hoch, "A Review of Some Psychological and Physiological Experiments Done in Connection with the Study of Mental Diseases," *Psychological Bulletin* 1 (1904): 241–57 (hereafter cited as "A Review of Experiments"); idem, "The Psychogenic Factors in the Development of Psychoses," ibid. 4 (1907): 161–69 (hereafter cited as "Psychogenic Factors").

79. E[dward] C[owles], "Book Reviews and Notices: The American Journal of Psychology, ed. G. Stanley Hall," *American Journal of Insanity* 44 (1887–88): 554–46; Dorothy Ross, *G. Stanley Hall: The Psychologist as Prophet* (Chicago: University of Chicago Press, 1972) (hereafter cited as *G. Stanley Hall*).

80. Wayne Dennis and Edwin G. Boring, "The Founding of the APA," *American Psychologist* 7 (1952): 95–97.

81. Gerald N. Grob, *The State and the Mentally Ill: A History of Worcester State Hospital in Massachusetts, 1830–1920* (Chapel Hill, N.C.: University of North Carolina Press, 1966); K. B. Hudgens, "Across the River: A Brief History of Kankakee Developmental Center," duplicated, Kankakee Developmental Center, Kankakee, Illinois [1976] (hereafter cited as "Across the River"); Alfred Lief, *The Commonsense Psychiatry of Adolf Meyer* (New York: McGraw Hill, 1948) (hereafter cited as *Adolf Meyer*); Zubin and Zubin, "Study of Mental Disorder."

82. George H. Kirby, "The New York Psychiatric Institute and Hospital: A Sketch of Its Development from 1895 to 1929," *Psychiatric Quarterly* 4 (1930): 151–67 (hereafter cited as "New York Psychiatric Institute"); Zubin and Zubin, "Study of Mental Disorder."

83. H. Addington Bruce, "Boris Sidis: An Appreciation," *Journal of Abnormal Psychology* 18 (1923–24): 274–76.

84. Boris Sidis, *The Psychology of Suggestion* (New York: Appleton, 1903 [1898]) (hereafter cited as *Suggestion*).

85. "Report of Special Committee for the Division of Philosophy: The Thesis of Boris Sidis," 26 May 1897, Harvard University Archives, Cambridge, Mass.; *Who's Who in America,* vol. 1, s.v. "Palmer, George Herbert."

86. Sidis, *Suggestion,* p. 2.

87. Zubin and Zubin, "Study of Mental Disorder."

88. William Alanson White, *The Autobiography of a Purpose* (Garden City, N.J.: Doubleday Doran, 1938).

89. Sidis, *Suggestion,* quotations on Plate II between p. 106 and 107.

90. Boris Sidis, "The Nature and Principles of Psychology," *American Journal of Insanity* 56 (1899): 41–52, quotations p. 42.

91. Kirby, "New York Psychiatric Institute."

92. Zubin and Zubin, "Study of Mental Disorder."

93. Boris Sidis, "An Inquiry into the Nature of Hallucinations. I," *Psychological Review* 11 (1904): 15–29; idem, "An Inquiry into the Nature of Hallucinations. II," ibid. 104–37.

94. Boris Sidis, "Are There Hypnotic Hallucinations?" *Psychological Review* 13 (1906): 239–57.

95. Boris Sidis, "The Hypnoidal State in Psychotherapeutics," *Monthly Cyclopaedia and Medical Bulletin* (23 1909): 1–3 (hereafter cited as "Hypnoidal State").

96. *Encyclopaedia of the Social Sciences*, vol. 14, s.v. "Sidis, Boris," by L. L. Bernard.

97. Boris Sidis, "The Doctrine of Primary and Secondary Sensory Elements. (I)," *Psychological Review* 15 (1908): 44–68; idem, "The Doctrine of Primary and Secondary Sensory Elements. (II)," ibid., pp. 106–21.

98. Boris Sidis, "An Experimental Study of Sleep, Part I," *Journal of Abnormal Psychology* 3 (1908): 1–32; idem, "An Experimental Study of Sleep, Chapter VIII," ibid., pp. 63–96; idem, "An Experimental Study of Sleep, Chapter XI," ibid., pp. 170–207.

99. Boris Sidis, "The Psychotherapeutic Value of the Hypnoidal State," *Journal of Abnormal Psychology* 4 (1909): 151–71; idem, "Hypnoidal State."

100. Boris Sidis and H. T. Kalmus, "A Study of Galvanometric Deflections due to Psycho-Physiological Processes. Part I," *Psychological Review* 15 (1908): 391–96; idem, "A Study of Galvanometric Deflections due to Psycho-Physiological Processes. Part II," ibid. 16 (1909): 1–35 (hereafter cited as "Galvanometric Deflections, Part II"); Boris Sidis and Louis Nelson, "The Nature and Causation of the Galvanic Phenomenon. Part I," ibid. 17 (1910): 98–146.

101. Sidis and Kalmus, "Galvanometric Deflections, Part II," pp. 1, 2, 3.

102. Knight Dunlap, "Galvanometric Deflections with Electrodes Applied to the Animal Body," *Psychological Bulletin* 7 (1910): 174–77.

103. Hudgens, "Across the River."

104. *Yale University Obituary Record, Graduate School*, s.v. "William Otterbein Krohn" (hereafter cited as *Yale Obituary*); *Who Was Who*, Vol. 14, s.v. "Krohn, William Otterbein" (hereafter cited as *Who Was Who*).

105. William O. Krohn, "Facilities in Experimental Psychology at the Various German Universities," *American Journal of Psychology* 4 (1892): 585–94; idem, "The Laboratory of the Psychological Institute at the University of Göttingen," *American Journal of Psychology* 5 (1893): 282–84; idem, "Experimental Psychology in United States."

106. *Yale Obituary*.

107. Krohn, "Experimental Psychology in United States."

108. William O. Krohn, "Pseudo-Chromesthesia, or the Association of Colors with Words, Letters and Sounds," *American Journal of Psychology* 5 (1893): 20–41, quotations pp. 20, 36.

109. William O. Krohn, "An Experimental Study of Simultaneous Stimulations of the Sense of Touch," *Journal of Nervous and Mental Disease* 18 (1893): 169–84, quotations p. 173.

110. William O. Krohn, "Sensation-Areas and Movement," *Psychological Review* 1 (1894): 280–81.

111. William O. Krohn, "Practical Child-Study: How to Begin," *Child Study Monthly* 1 (1895): 161–76, quotation p. 162 (hereafter cited as "Practical Child-Study").

112. Lief, *Adolf Meyer*.

113. *Yale Obituary*.

114. William O. Krohn, "Child-Study in Schools for Feeble-Minded Children," *Child Study Monthly* 1 (1895): 75–79; idem, "Nervous Diseases of School Children," ibid., pp. 354–68; idem, "Practical Child-Study."

115. William O. Krohn, "Child Study as Applied to Defective Children," *Charities Review* 6 (1897): 427–37.

116. Hudgens, "Across the River," p. 17.

117. William O. Krohn, "Laboratory Psychology as Applied to the Study of Insanity," *The Psychiater* 1 (1898?): 49–66, quotation p. 66.

118. *Yale Obituary; Who Was Who*.

119. *The Psychiater* 1, no. 1 (1898?) published by the Medical Staff of the Illinois Eastern Hospital for the Insane.

120. *National Union Catalog*, vol. 306, s.v. "Krohn, William Otterbein."

121. H. Douglas Singer and William O. Krohn, *Insanity and Law: A Treatise on Forensic Psychiatry* (Philadelphia: Blakiston's, 1924).

122. Maureen McKernan, *The Amazing Crime and Trial of Leopold and Loeb* (Chicago: Plymouth Court Press, 1924).

123. "In Borneo Jungles," *Saturday Review of Literature*, 2 July 1927.

124. Ross, *G. Stanley Hall*.

125. Shepherd Ivory Franz, "Shepherd Ivory Franz," *A History of Psychology in Autobiography*,

vol. 2, ed. Carl Murchison (Worcester, Mass.: Clark University Press, 1932) (hereafter cited as "Shepherd Ivory Franz").

126. G. Stanley Hall, "Laboratory of the McLean Hospital, Somerville, Mass." *American Journal of Insanity* 51 (1894): 358–64, quotation, p. 358 (hereafter cited as "McLean Laboratory").

127. Henry M. Hurd, "The New McLean Hospital," *American Journal of Insanity* 52 (1896): 477–502, quotation p. 502.

128. William Noyes, "A Counting Attachment for the Pendulum Chronoscope," *American Journal of Psychology* 3 (1891): 367–70; idem, "On Certain Peculiarities of the Knee-Jerk in Sleep in a Case of Terminal Dementia," ibid. 4 (1892): 343–61.

129. Hall, "McLean Laboratory."

130. Hoch, "A Review of Experiments."

131. Watson, "Clinical Psychology."

132. Hoch, "Psychogenic Factors."

133. Franz, "Shepherd Ivory Franz."

134. Harold Griffing and Shepherd Ivory Franz, "On the Conditions of Fatigue in Reading," *Psychological Review* 3 (1896): 513–30 (hereafter cited as "Fatigue in Reading"); Shepherd Ivory Franz, "On the Methods of Estimating the Force of Voluntary Muscular Contractions and on Fatigue," *American Journal of Physiology* 4 (1900): 348–72 (hereafter cited as "Force of Muscular Contractions").

135. Shepherd Ivory Franz, "The After-Image Threshold," *Psychological Review* 2 (1895): 130–36; idem, "After-Images," *Psychological Review, Monograph Supplements* 3, no. 2 (1899) (hereafter cited as "After-Images"); idem, "On After-Images—An Explanation," *Psychological Review* 7 (1900): 63–64.

136. Franz, "Shepherd Ivory Franz," p. 94.

137. Franz, "After-Images," pp. 16–17, 42.

138. Griffing and Franz, "Fatigue in Reading," p. 530.

139. Shepherd Ivory Franz and Henry E. Houston, "The Accuracy of Observation and of Recollection in School Children," *Psychological Review* 3 (1896): 531–35, quotation p. 534.

140. Franz, "Force of Muscular Contractions," p. 371.

141. Shepherd Ivory Franz, "On the Functions of the Cerebrum: I. The Frontal Lobes in Relation to the Production and Retention of Simple Sensory-Motor Habits," *American Journal of Physiology* 8 (1902): 1–22, quotation p. 8.

142. Shepherd Ivory Franz, "Observations on the Functions of the Association Areas (Cerebrum) in Monkeys," *Journal of the American Medical Association* 47 (1906): 1464–67.

143. Shepherd Ivory Franz, "On the Functions of the Cerebrum: The Frontal Lobes," *Archives of Psychology* 1, no. 2 (1906–8).

144. Shepherd Ivory Franz, "Anomalous Reaction-Times in a Case of Manic-Depressive Depression," *Psychological Bulletin* 2 (1905): 225–32, quotation p. 227.

145. Shepherd Ivory Franz and G. V. Hamilton, "The Effects of Exercise upon the Retardation in Conditions of Depression," *American Journal of Insanity* 62 (1905): 239–56, quotation p. 255 (hereafter cited as "Effects of Exercise").

146. Ibid., p. 243.

147. Shepherd Ivory Franz, "The Reeducation of an Aphasic, " *Journal of Philosophy, Psychology and Scientific Methods* 2 (1905): 589–97.

148. Shepherd Ivory Franz, "Psychological Opportunity in Psychiatry," *Journal of Philosophy, Psychology and Scientific Methods* 3 (1906): 561–67.

149. Shepherd Ivory Franz, "The Time of Some Mental Processes in the Retardation and Excitement of Insanity," *American Journal of Psychology* 17 (1906): 38–68, quotation p. 38 (hereafter cited as "Time of Some Mental Processes").

150. Ibid., p. 50.

151. Ibid., pp. 40, 46.

152. Ibid., p. 68.

153. [William Alanson White], *Report of the Government Hospital for the Insane to the Secretary of the Interior for the Fiscal Year Ended June 30, 1907* (Washington, D.C.: Government Printing Office, 1907) (hereafter cited as *Report of Government Hospital*).

154. Margaret Ives, "Psychology at Saint Elizabeths 1907–1970," *Professional Psychology* 1 (1970): 155–58.

155. *Who Was Who in America,* vol. 1, s.v. "MacDonald, Arthur."

156. [White], *Report of Government Hospital.*

157. Shepherd Ivory Franz, "The Physiological Study of a Case of Migraine," *American Journal of Physiology* 19 (1907): 14–38.

158. Shepherd Ivory Franz, "A Noiseless Room for Sound Experiments," *Science* 26, n.s. (1907): 878–81.

159. Shepherd Ivory Franz, "The Functional View of the Insanities," *Government Hospital for the Insane, Bull. No. 1* (1909): 30–42, quotation p. 33.

160. Shepherd Ivory Franz and William A. White, "The Use of Association Tests in Determining Mental Contents," *Government Hospital for the Insane, Bull. No. 1* (1909): 55–71.

161. Shepherd Ivory Franz, "Some Considerations of the Association Word Experiment," *Government Hospital for the Insane, Bull. No. 2* (1910): 73–80, quotation p. 73.

162. Franz, "Shepherd Ivory Franz," p. 109.

163. Samuel W. Fernberger, "Shepherd Ivory Franz 1874–1933," *Psychological Bulletin* 30 (1933): 741–42.

164. *Author Index to Psychological Index, 1894–1958 and Psychological Abstracts, 1927–1958*, vol. 2, s.v. "Franz, S. I."

165. Franz, "Shepherd Ivory Franz."

166. Laurance F. Shaffer, "Frederic Lyman Wells: 1884–1964," *American Journal of Psychology* 77 (1964): 679–82 (hereafter cited as "F. L. Wells").

167. Frederic Lyman Wells, "Linguistic Lapses with Especial Reference to the Perception of Linguistic Sounds," *Archives of Philosophy, Psychology and Scientific Methods*, no. 6, June 1906, ed. J. McKeen Cattell and Frederick J. E. Woodbridge, Columbia University Contributions to Philosophy and Psychology, vol. 14, no. 3, p. 17 (hereafter cited as "Linguistic Lapses").

168. Frederic Lyman Wells, "Linguistic Standards," *Journal of Philosophy, Psychology and Scientific Methods* 3 (1906): 431–35.

169. Frederic Lyman Wells, "Linguistic Ability and Intellectual Efficiency," *Journal of Philosophy, Psychology and Scientific Methods* 3 (1906): 680–87, quotations pp. 682, 683, 687 (hereafter cited as "Linguistic Ability").

170. Frederic Lyman Wells, "Standard Tests of Arithmetical Associations," *Journal of Philosophy, Psychology and Scientific Methods* 4 (1907): 510–12, quotation p. 510 (hereafter cited as "Standard Tests").

171. Frederic Lyman Wells, "A Statistical Study of Literary Merit," *Archives of Psychology* 1, no. 7 (1906–8) (hereafter cited as "Literary Merit").

172. Frederic Lyman Wells, "On the Variability of Individual Judgment," in *Essays Philosophical and Psychological in Honor of William James* (New York: Longmans Green, 1908), pp. 540–41, 548, 549 (hereafter cited as "Variability of Judgment").

173. Frederic Lyman Wells, "A Neglected Measure of Fatigue," *American Journal of Psychology* 19 (1908): 345–58; idem, "Normal Performance in the Tapping Test, before and during Practice, with Special Reference to Fatigue Phenomena," ibid., pp. 437–83, (hereafter cited as "Normal Performance in Tapping").

174. Frederic Lyman Wells, "Technical Aspects of Experimental Psychopathology," *American Journal of Insanity* 64 (1908): 477–512, quotations pp. 480, 487, 490, 495, 496.

175. Frederic Lyman Wells, "Studies in Retardation as Given in the Fatigue Phenomena of the Tapping Test," *American Journal of Psychology* 20 (1909): 38–59, quotation p. 44 (hereafter cited as "Studies in Retardation").

176. Frederic Lyman Wells, "Motor Retardation as a Manic-Depressive Symptom," *American Journal of Insanity* 66 (1909): 1–52.

177. Frederic Lyman Wells, "Sex Differences in the Tapping Test: An Interpretation," *American Journal of Psychology* 20 (1909): 353–63, quotations pp. 353, 362.

178. Wells, "Linguistic Lapses." Table, p. 28.

179. Wells, "Linguistic Ability," "Standard Tests," "Literary Merit," "Variability of Judgment," "Normal Performance in Tapping," "Studies in Retardation."

180. Shaffer, "F. L. Wells."

181. David Shakow. "The Contributions of the Worcester State Hospital and Post-Hall Clark to Psychoanalysis." In *Psychoanalysis, Psychotherapy, and the New England Medical Scene, 1894–1944*, ed. G. E. Gifford, Jr., pp. 29–62. New York: Neale Watson Publications, 1978, quotations pp. 44–45.

182. E. B. Titchener, "John Wallace Baird," *Science*, n.s. 49 (1919): 393–94; *Who Was Who in America*, vol. 1, s.v. "Baird, John Wallace." These biographies disagree on the birthdate. Titchener's date of 1869 is given preference in the text over the directory date of 1873.

183. J. W. Baird, "The Contraction of the Color Zones in Hysteria and in Neurasthenia," *Psychological Bulletin* 3 (1906): 249–54, quotation p. 249.

184. *Who's Who in America*, vol. 32, s.v. "Shepard, John Frederick."

185. Alfred C. Raphelson, "Psychology at the University of Michigan," mimeographed (1968): Raphelson File M 159, Archives of the History of American Psychology, University of Akron, Akron, Ohio.
186. Florence Berenice Barnes, "Some Aspects of Memory in the Insane," *American Journal of Psychology* 19 (1908): 43–57, quotation p. 43.
187. Robert H. Haskell, "Mental Deficiency" (1944); Leo Kanner, *A History of the Care and Study of the Mentally Retarded* (Springfield, Ill.: Charles C. Thomas, 1964) (hereafter cited as *History of Mentally Retarded*); *Sixth Annual Report of Harvard College Class of 1893*, s.v., "Arthur Rufus Trego Wylie."
188. Kanner, *History of Mentally Retarded*.
189. Haskell, "Mental Deficiency."
190. G. E. Johnson, "Contribution to the Psychology and Pedagogy of Feeble-Minded Children. I," *Journal of Psycho-Asthenics* 1 (1896–97): 90–107; idem, "Contribution to the Psychology and Pedagogy of Feeble-Minded Children. I. The Education of Idiots," ibid., pp. 141–51; idem, "Contribution to the Psychology and Pedagogy of Feeble-Minded Children. I. Results of Education," ibid. 2 (1897–98): 27–32; idem, "Contribution to the Psychology and Pedagogy of Feeble-Minded Children. I. Memory-Span of Feeble-Minded Children," ibid., pp. 63–81 (hereafter cited as "Memory Span of Feeble-Minded"); idem, "Contribution to the Psychology and Pedagogy of Feeble-Minded Children. II. Mental Association of the Feeble-Minded," ibid., pp. 107–20.
191. G. E. Johnson, "Contribution to the Psychology and Pedagogy of Feeble-Minded Children," *Pedagogical Seminary* 3 (1894): 246–301.
192. Misiak and Sexton, *History of Psychology;* Reisman, *Development of Clinical;* Watson, "Clinical Psychology;" M. Mike Nawas, "Landmarks in the History of Clinical Psychology from Its Early Beginnings through 1971," *Journal of Psychology* 82 (1972): 91–110.
193. Kathrine Regan McCaffrey, "Founders of The Training School at Vineland, New Jersey: S. Olin Garrison, Alexander Johnson, Edward R. Johnstone" (Ed.D. diss., Teachers College, Columbia University, 1965) (hereafter cited as "Founders of the Training School").
194. Samuel W. Fernberger, "The History of the Psychological Clinic," in *Clinical Psychology Studies in Honor of Lightner Witmer*, ed. Robert A. Brotemarkle (Philadelphia: University of Pennsylvania Press, 1931) (hereafter cited as "History of the Clinic").
195. Henry H. Goddard, "The Binet and Simon Tests of Intellectual Capacity," *Training School* 5 (1908): 3–9 (hereafter cited as "Binet and Simon Tests").
196. Henry H. Goddard, "Suggestions for a Prognostical Classification of Mental Defectives," *Journal of Psycho-Asthenics* 14 (1909–10): 48–54 (hereafter cited as "Suggestions for Prognosis").
197. Henry H. Goddard, "Four Hundred Feeble-Minded Children Classified by the Binet Method," *Journal of Psycho-Asthenics* 15 (1910–11): 17–30; also in *Pedagogical Seminary* 17 (1910): 387–97; (hereafter cited as "Four Hundred Children Classified"); F. Kuhlmann, "Binet and Simon's System for Measuring the Intelligence of Children," *Journal of Psycho-Asthenics* 15 (1910–11): 76–92 (hereafter cited as "Binet and Simon's System").
198. Leonard P. Ayres, "The Binet-Simon Measuring Scale for Intelligence: Some Criticisms and Suggestions," *Psychological Clinic* 5 (1911–12): 187–96 (hereafter cited as "The Binet-Simon Measuring Scale"); Lewis M. Terman, "The Binet-Simon Scale for Measuring Intelligence: Impressions Gained by its Applications," ibid., pp. 199–206 (hereafter cited as "The Binet-Simon Scale"); Isabel Lawrence, "A Study of the Binet Definition Tests," ibid., pp. 207–16 (hereafter cited as "Binet Definition Tests"); J. E. Wallace Wallin, "A Practical Guide for the Administration of the Binet-Simon Scale for Measuring Intelligence," ibid., pp. 217–38 (hereafter cited as "Practical Guide"); Clara Harrison Town, "The Binet-Simon Scale and the Psychologist," ibid., pp. 239–44 (hereafter cited as "Binet-Simon Scale and Psychologist").
199. *Who Was Who in America*, vol. 1, s.v. "Johnson, George Ellsworth" (hereafter cited as *Who Was Who*, "Johnson").
200. Johnson, "Memory-Span of Feeble-Minded," pp. 78, 80.
201. Ibid., p. 80.
202. Ibid., p. 68.
203. Ibid., p. 79.
204. *Who Was Who*, "Johnson."
205. George E. Johnson, "The Playground as a Factor in School Hygiene," *Psychological Clinic* 3 (1909–10): 14–20.
206. Letter from A. R. T. Wylie to President G. Stanley Hall, 4 March 1901, Clark University Archives, Worcester, Mass.
207. *Alumni Round Table*, 1894; *Revised Post-Graduate Courses*, 1897, College of Wooster, Wooster, Ohio.

208. Glenn Sonnedecker, *History of Pharmacy,* 4th ed. (Philadelphia: J. B. Lippincott, 1976).

209. *50th Anniversary Report Harvard Class of 1893,* s.v. "Arthur Rufus Trego Wylie" (hereafter cited as *50th Anniversary Report*). 210. A. R. T. Wylie, "Development of Institutional Care for the Feeble-Minded," *Bulletin of the Massachusetts Department of Mental Diseases, Fernald Memorial Issue* 14, Nos. 1 & 2 (1930): 57.

211. "Minutes of the Association, Twenty-Fourth Annual Meeting," *Journal of Psycho-Asthenics* 4 (1899–1900): 151–84, quotation p. 183.

212. A. R. T. Wylie, "Investigation Concerning the Weight and Height of Feeble-Minded Children," *Journal of Psycho-Asthenics* 4 (1899–1900): 47–57; idem, "Taste and Reaction Time of the Feeble-Minded," ibid., pp. 109–12 (hereafter cited as "Taste and Reaction Time"); idem, "A Study of the Senses of the Feeble-Minded," ibid., pp. 137–50 (hereafter cited as "Study of the Senses"); idem, "Memory of the Feeble-Minded," ibid., 5 (1900–1901): 17–27 (hereafter cited as "Memory of Feeble-Minded"); idem, "Motor Ability and Control of the Feeble-Minded," ibid., pp. 52–58 (hereafter cited as "Motor Ability"); idem, "Instincts and Emotions of the Feeble-Minded," ibid., pp. 98–107; idem, "Contribution to the Study of the Growth of the Feeble-Minded in Height and Weight," ibid. 8 (1903–4): 2–8 (hereafter cited as "Contribution to the Study of Growth").

213. Wylie, "Motor Ability," p. 57.

214. Wylie, "Taste and Reaction Time," p. 111.

215. Wylie, "Study of the Senses," pp. 139, 141, 145.

216. Wylie, "Memory of the Feeble-Minded."

217. Wylie, "Motor Ability."

218. Wylie, "Taste and Reaction Time," p. 110.

219. Wylie, "Memory of the Feeble-Minded," pp. 21, 23.

220. Wylie, "Study of the Senses," p. 147.

221. Wylie, "Motor Ability," Tables, pp. 53, 54.

222. Wylie, "Study of the Senses," Table, p. 140.

223. Wylie, "Contribution to the Study of Growth," Tables, pp. 3, 4.

224. A. R. T. Wylie, "Report of the Committee on Psychological Research: A Scheme for Psychological Investigation of the Feeble-Minded," *Journal of Psycho-Asthenics* 6 (1901–2): 21–26.

225. Letter from A. R. T. Wylie to Dr. Herbert Nichols, 18 January 1901, Clark University Archives, Worcester, Mass.

226. A. C. Rogers, "Reports from the States—Minnesota," *Journal of Psycho-Asthenics* 6 (1901–2): 96.

227. A. R. T. Wylie, "On the Psychology and Pedagogy of the Blind," *Pedagogical Seminary* 9 (1902): 127–60.

228. *50th Anniversary Report.*

229. Robert I. Watson, "Lightner Witmer: 1867–1956," *American Journal of Psychology* 49 (1956): 680–82; Joseph Collins, "Lightner Witmer: A Biographical Sketch," in *Clinical Psychology,* ed. Robert A. Brotemarkle (hereafter cited as "L. Witmer"); Michael Mark Sokal, "The Education and Psychological Career of James McKeen Cattell, 1860–1904" (Ph.D. diss., Case Western Reserve University, 1972) (hereafter cited as "James McKeen Cattell").

230. Mollie D. Boring and Edwin G. Boring, "Masters and Pupils Among the American Psychologists," *American Journal of Psychology* 61 (1948): 527–34.

231. Witmer, *Analytical,* p. v.

232. Collins, "L. Witmer"; Fernberger, "History of the Clinic"; and Joseph H. Penniman, "Preface," *Clinical Psychology,* ed. Robert A. Brotemarkle; *Directory of the American Psychological Association,* s.v. "Witmer, Lightner"; Misiak and Sexton, "History of Psychology"; Watson, "Clinical Psychology."

233. Miles A. Tinker, "Wundt's Doctorate Students and Their Theses 1875–1920," *American Journal of Psychology* 44 (1932): 630–37.

234. Samuel W. Fernberger, "Wundt's Doctorate Students," *Psychological Bulletin* 30 (1933): 80–83.

235. Sokal, "James McKeen Cattell."

236. Lightner Witmer, "Clinical Psychology," *Psychological Clinic* 1 (1907–8): 1–9 (hereafter cited as "Clinical Psychology").

237. Collins, "L. Witmer."

238. Garvey, "American Laboratories."

239. Robert A. Brotemarkle, "Clinical Psychology 1896–1946," *Journal of Consulting Psychology,* 11 (1947): 1–4.

240. Michael M. Sokal, "APA's First Publication: Proceedings of the American Psychological Association, 1892–1893," *American Psychologist* 28 (1973): 277–92.

241. Lightner Witmer, "Aesthetics of Form" (abstract of "Zur experimentellen Aesthetik einfacher räumlicher Formverhältnisse)," *Psychological Review* 1 (1894): 205–8.

242. Witmer, *Analytical*.

243. Lightner Witmer, "The Pendulum as a Control-Instrument for the Hipp Chronoscope," *Psychological Review* 1 (1894): 506–15.

244. Lightner Witmer, "Pleasure and Pain from the Psychologist's Standpoint," *American Medico-Surgical Bulletin* 7 (1894): 351–53; idem, "The Psychological Analysis and Physical Basis of Pleasure and Pain," *Journal of Nervous and Mental Disease* 19 (1894): 209–28; idem, "Pain," *Twentieth Century Practice of Medicine* 11 (1897): 905–45, quotation p. 940.

245. Lightner Witmer, "Practical Work in Psychology," *Pediatrics* 2 (1896): 462–71, quotation p. 463.

246. Lightner Witmer, "Courses in Psychology for Normal Schools, I," *Educational Review* 13 (1897): 45–57 (hereafter cited as "Courses in Psychology, I"); idem, "Courses in Psychology for Normal Schools, (II) Course II—Sensation and Perception," *Educational Review* 13 (1897): 146–62. (hereafter cited as "Courses in Sensation and Perception").

247. Fernberger, "History of the Clinic," p. 13.

248. Witmer, "Courses in Psychology, I."

249. Lightner Witmer, "University Courses in Psychology," *Psychological Clinic* I (1907–8): 25–35, quotation p. 28.

250. Lightner Witmer, "The Organization of Practical Work in Psychology," *Psychological Review* 4 (1897): 116–17.

251. Collins, "L. Witmer," p. 5.

252. Witmer, "Clinical Psychology," p. 4.

253. Fernberger, "History of the Clinic."

254. Arthur Holmes, *The Conservation of the Child* (Philadelphia: J. B. Lippincott, 1912), p. 35.

255. Gertha Williams, Oral History, 1965, Oral History Box 1, Archives of the History of American Psychology, University of Akron, Akron, Ohio.

256. Lightner Witmer, "Courses in Psychology at the Summer School of the University of Pennsylvania," *Psychological Clinic* 4 (1910–11): 245–73, quotation p. 271.

257. Fernberger, "History of the Clinic."

258. Witmer, "Courses in Sensation and Perception," p. 149.

259. Goddard Papers M33, M35.1, M38, Archives of the History of American Psychology, University of Akron, Akron, Ohio; H. E. Burtt and S. L. Pressey, "Henry Herbert Goddard: 1866–1957," *American Journal of Psychology* 70 (1957): 656–57.

260. Henry H. Goddard, "Are Drugs Unnecessary to the Cure of Disease?" *Hypnotic Magazine,* March 1897 pp. 155–58.

261. Henry H. Goddard, "The Effects of Mind on Body as Evidenced by Faith Cures," *American Journal of Psychology* 10 (1898–99): 431–502.

262. Henry H. Goddard, "A New Brain Microtome," *Journal of Comparative Neurology* 10 (1900): 209–15.

263. Henry H. Goddard, "Ideals of a Group of German Children," *Pedagogical Seminary* 13 (1906): 208–10.

264. McCaffrey, "Founders of the Training School."

265. "Professional Biography, Edward Ransom Johnstone," *Training School Bulletin* 44 (1947): 55.

266. Letter [Goddard] to Dear Friends (or "would be" Friends), 6 March 1952, Goddard Papers M35.2, Archives of the History of American Psychology, University of Akron, Akron, Ohio (hereafter cited as "Dear Friends").

267. Letter [Goddard] to My Dear Bob, 23 October 1950, Goddard Papers M33, Archives of the History of American Psychology, University of Akron, Akron, Ohio.

268. Henry H. Goddard, "In the Beginning," *Understanding the Child* 3 (1933): 22–26 (hereafter cited as "In the Beginning").

269. Letter E. C. Sanford to Goddard, 9 February 1906, Goddard Papers, M33, Archives of the History of American Psychology, University of Akron, Akron, Ohio.

270. Letter G. Stanley Hall to Goddard, 9 February 1906, Goddard Papers M33, Archives of the History of American Psychology, University of Akron, Akron, Ohio.

271. Letter Adolf Meyer to Goddard, 8 February 1906, Goddard Papers M33, Archives of the History of American Psychology, University of Akron, Akron, Ohio.

272. Diary, 17 September 1906 to 24 June 1907, Goddard Papers M43, Archives of the History of American Psychology, University of Akron, Akron, Ohio.

273. E. R. Johnstone, "The Institution as a Laboratory," *Twenty-Five Years, A Memorial Volume in Commemoration of the Twenty-Fifth Anniversary of the Vineland Laboratory, 1906–1931,* ed. Edgar

A. Doll (Vineland, N.J.: Publication of the Training School at Vineland, Series 1932–No. 2, February 1932), p. 11.

274. Henry Herbert Goddard, "Psychological Work Among the Feeble-Minded," *Journal of Psycho-Asthenics* 12 (1907–8): 18–30; "The Research Work," *Supplement to Training School* 4 (1907): 1–10 (hereafter cited as "Research Work"); "Teaching Numbers to Backward Children," *Training School* 5 (1908): 5–7; "Two Months among the European Institutions for the Mental Defectives," *Training School* 5 (1908): 11–16.

275. Henry H. Goddard, "A Side Light on the Development of the Number Concept," *Supplement to Training School* 4 (1907): 20–25; "A Group of Feeble-Minded Children with Special Regard to Their Number Concepts," *Supplement to Training School* 5 (1908): 1–6.

276. Goddard, "Research Work," pp. 6, 8.

277. Goddard, "Dear Friends," p. 4.

278. Goddard, "Four Hundred Children Classified."

279. Letter [Goddard] to Edwin D. Starbuck, 6 August 1912, Goddard Papers M615, Archives of the History of American Psychology, University of Akron, Akron, Ohio, p. 1.

280. Henry H. Goddard, "The Grading of Backward Children," *Training School* 5 (1908): 12; idem "Binet and Simon Tests"; idem, "Four Hundred Children Classified"; idem, "Suggestions for Prognosis."

281. Henry H. Goddard, "The Menace of the Feeble Minded," *Pediatrics* 23 (1911): 350–59; idem, "In The Beginning."

282. "Edmund Burke Huey," *American Journal of Psychology* 25, (1914): 319; "Lincoln State News, 10 October 1909" in *1909–10 Year Book, Illinois State Charitable Institutions;* John B. Carroll, "Foreword," in Edmund Burke Huey, *The Psychology and Pedagogy of Reading* (New York: Macmillan, 1908; reprinted Cambridge, Mass.: M.I.T. Press, 1968) (hereafter cited as *The Psychology of Reading*); *Hall Memoriam.*

283. Edmund B. Huey, "Preliminary Experiments in the Physiology and Psychology of Reading," *American Journal of Psychology* 9 (1897–98): 575–86; idem, "On the Psychology and Physiology of Reading. I," ibid. 11 (1899–1900): 283–302, quotation p. 283; idem, "On the Psychology and Physiology of Reading. II," ibid. 12 (1900–1901): 292–312, quotation p. 292.

284. Huey, *The Psychology of Reading.*

285. Ibid.

286. Garvey, "American Laboratories."

287. Letters Huey to H. H. Goddard, July 1910–November 1911, Goddard Papers M35.2, Archives of the History of American Psychology, University of Akron, Akron, Ohio (hereafter cited as "Huey to Goddard").

288. Edmund B. Huey, "The International Congress of Psychology," *American Journal of Psychology* 20 (1909): 571–75.

289. Edmund Burke Huey, *Backward and Feeble-Minded Children* (Baltimore: Warwick & York Educational Psychology Monographs, 1912) (hereafter cited as *Backward and Feeble-Minded*).

290. "Minutes of the Annual Meeting," *Journal of Psycho-Asthenics* 15 (1910–11): 131–36, quotation p. 133.

291. Edmund B. Huey, "Clinical Psychology," *Year Book Illinois Charitable Institutions,* 1909–10, pp. 31–35, quotations pp. 32, 34.

292. Edmund B. Huey, "The Binet Scale for Measuring Intelligence and Retardation," *Journal of Educational Psychology* 1 (1910): 435–44, quotation pp. 435–36.

293. Edmund B. Huey, "Retardation and the Mental Examination of Retarded Children," *Journal of Psycho-Asthenics* 15 (1910–11): 31–43, quotations pp. 34, 40.

294. Lewis M. Terman, "Trails to Psychology," in *A History of Psychology in Autobiography,* vol. 2, ed. Carl Murchison (Worcester, Mass.: Clark University Press, 1932) (hereafter cited as "Trails to Psychology").

295. Wilson, *Hall Memoriam;* Letter Goddard to Mrs. Z. Pauline Hoakley, 5 October 1920, Goddard Papers M35.2, Archives of the History of American Psychology, University of Akron, Akron, Ohio.

296. "Huey to Goddard."

297. Huey, *Backward and Feeble-Minded.*

298. Edmund B. Huey, "The Present Status of the Binet Scale of Tests for the Measurement of Intelligence," *Psychological Bulletin* 9 (1912): 160–68.

299. E. B. Huey, "The Education of Defectives and the Training of Teachers for Special Classes," *Journal of Educational Psychology* 4 (1913): 545–50.

300. *Directory American Psychological Association* 1968, s.v. "Wallin, Dr. J(ohn) E(dward) Wallace"; J. E. Wallace Wallin, *The Odyssey of a Psychologist* (Wilmington, Del.: Published by author,

1955) (hereafter cited as *Odyssey*); idem, "Researches on the Rhythm of Speech," *Studies from the Yale Psychological Laboratory* 9 (1901): 1–142 (hereafter cited as "Rhythm of Speech").

301. Wallin, "Rhythm of Speech," p. 8.

302. J. E. Wallace Wallin, "Experimental Studies of Rhythm and Time. I. Qualitative Limens or Grades of Rhythm, and the Difference Limen in the Perception of Time," *Psychological Review* 18 (1911): 100–131; idem, "Experimental Studies of Rhythm and Time. II. The Preferred Length of Interval (Tempo)," ibid., pp. 202–22 (hereafter cited as "Preferred Length of Interval"); idem, "Experimental Studies of Rhythm and Time. III. The Estimation of the Mid-rate Between Two Tempos," ibid. 19 (1912): 271–98 (hereafter cited as "Estimation of Mid-rate").

303. Wallin, "Preferred Length of Interval," p. 217.

304. Wallin, "Estimation of Mid-Rate," p. 273.

305. J. E. Wallace Wallin, "The Size Illusion of the Depressed Letter P," *Scientific American* 93 (1905): 315; idem, "The Duration of Attention, Reversible Perspectives, and the Refractory Phase of the Reflex Arc," *Journal of Philosophy, Psychology and Scientific Methods* 7 (1910): 33–38.

306. J. E. Wallace Wallin, "Accommodation and Convergence—A Reply," *Psychological Bulletin* 1 (1904): 208–10.

307. J. E. Wallace Wallin, *Optical Illusions of Reversible Perspective* (Stanton, Iowa: Stanton Call Press., 1905). G. Stanley Hall and J. E. W. Wallin, "How Children and Youth Think and Feel About Clouds," *Pedagogical Seminary* 9 (1902): 460–506; Wallin, *Odyssey*, p. 19.

308. Wallin, *Odyssey*, pp. 23, 31, 40.

309. Wallin, "Practical Guide," pp. 219, 228, 235.

310. Francis N. Maxfield, "Fred Kuhlmann 1876–1941," *American Journal of Mental Deficiency* 46 (1941): 17–18; K(arl) M. D(allenbach), "Frederick Kuhlmann: 1876–1941," *American Journal of Psychology* 54 (1941): 446–47; Neil A. Dayton, "Introduction of the Speaker of the Evening, President Frederick Kuhlmann," *American Journal of Mental Deficiency* 45 (1940): 3–7. Note the inconsistency in designating the first name. Kuhlmann's most common signature as author is F. Kuhlmann, but *Directory of the American Psychological Association* and the roster of Ph.D.'s at Clark University in Wilson, *Sanford Memoriam,* identify him as Fred, not Frederick.

311. Correspondence Caroline M. Crosby with H. H. Goddard, July 1921, Goddard Papers M35.2, Archives of the History of American Psychology, University of Akron, Akron, Ohio (hereafter cited as "Crosby-Goddard").

312. F. Kuhlmann, *The Kuhlmann-Binet Tests for Children of Pre-School Age* (Minneapolis, Minn.: University of Minnesota Press, 1928); "Crosby-Goddard."

313. F. Kuhlmann, "Experimental Studies in Mental Deficiency: Three Cases of Imbecility (Mongolian) and Six Cases of Feeble-Mindedness," *Journal of Psycho-Asthenics* 9 (1904): 1–7.

314. F. Kuhlmann, "Experimental Studies in Mental Deficiency: Three Cases of Imbecility (Mongolian) and Six Cases of Feeble-Mindedness," *American Journal of Psychology* 15 (1904): 391–445, quotations pp. 393, 414, 415, 421–22 (hereafter cited as "Experimental Studies in Mental Deficiency").

315. F. Kuhlmann, "On the Analysis of the Memory Consciousness for Pictures of Familiar Objects," *American Journal of Psychology* 18 (1907): 389–420 (hereafter cited as "Memory for Pictures of Familiar Objects").

316. Wylie, "Memory of Feeble-Minded," p. 24.

317. Kuhlmann, "Experimental Studies in Mental Deficiency," pp. 404, 415, 422, 425.

318. Ibid, p. 425.

319. Fred Kuhlmann, "The Place of Mental Imagery and Memory among Mental Functions," *American Journal of Psychology* 16 (1905): 337–56.

320. F. Kuhlmann, "Recent Studies of Normal Illusions of Memory," *American Journal of Psychology* 16 (1905): 389–98, quotation p. 392.

321. F. Kuhlmann, "On the Analysis of the Memory Consciousness: A Study in the Mental Imagery and Memory of Meaningless Visual Forms," *Psychological Review* 13 (1906): 316–48.

322. Titchener, "Problems of Experimental Psychology."

323. Friedrich Wulf, "Tendencies in Figural Variation," in *A Source Book of Gestalt Psychology,* ed. Willis D. Ellis (London: Routledge & Kegan Paul, 1938).

324. F. Kuhlmann, "Problems in the Analysis of the Memory Consciousness," *Journal of Philosophy, Psychology and Scientific Methods* 4 (1907): 5–14.

325. Kuhlmann, "Memory for Pictures of Familiar Objects," pp. 392, 393.

326. F. Kuhlmann, "The Present Status of Memory Investigation," *Psychological Bulletin* 5 (1908): 285–93.

327. F. Kuhlmann, "On the Analysis of Auditory Memory Consciousness," *American Journal of Psychology* 20 (1909): 194–218, quotation p. 195.

328. F. Kuhlmann, "A Note on the Daily Life of the Honey Bee," *American Bee-Keeper* 17 (1907): 127–32.

329. F. Kuhlmann, "Some Preliminary Observations on the Development of Instincts and Habits in Young Birds," *Psychological Monographs* 11, no. 44 (1909): 49–84.

330. F. Kuhlmann, "A New Memory Apparatus," *Psychological Review* 19 (1912): 73–80.

331. Kuhlmann, "Binet and Simon's System."

332. Frances Caldwell Higgins, *The Life of Naomi Norsworthy* (Boston: Houghton Mifflin, 1918) (hereafter cited as *N. Norsworthy*); Geraldine Joncich, *The Sane Positivist: A Biography of Edward L. Thorndike* (Middletown, Conn.: Wesleyan University Press, 1968).

333. Higgins, *N. Norsworthy*, p. 229.

334. Naomi Norsworthy, "The Psychology of Mentally Deficient Children," *Archives of Psychology* 1, no. 1 (1906–8) (hereafter cited as "Psychology of Mentally Deficient").

335. Naomi Norsworthy, "Suggestions Concerning the Psychology of Mentally Deficient Children," *Journal of Psycho-Asthenics* 12 (1907–8): 3–17.

336. Norsworthy, "Psychology of Mentally Deficient," pp. 16, 26.

337. Joseph Hershey Bair, "The Practice Curve," *Psychological Review, Monograph Supplement* 5 (1902), no. 2.

338. Norsworthy, "Psychology of Mentally Deficient," Table, p. 53.

339. Walker, *History of Statistical Method*, p. 154.

340. Naomi Norsworthy, "The Validity of Judgments of Character," in *Essays Philosophical and Psychological in Honor of William James* (New York: Longmans Green, 1908), p. 553.

341. Naomi Norsworthy, "Acquisition as Related to Retention," *Journal of Educational Psychology* 3 (1912): 214–18.

342. Naomi Norsworthy and Mary Theodora Whitley, *The Psychology of Childhood* (New York: Macmillan, 1918).

343. Lawrence, "Binet Definition Tests."

344. *Woman's Who Was Who of America*, 1914–15, s.v. "Lawrence, Isabel."

345. Ayres, "The Binet-Simon Measuring Scale."

346. *Who's Who in America*, vol. 25, s.v. "Ayres, Leonard Porter."

347. Leonard P. Ayres, "Irregular Attendance—A Cause of Retardation," *Psychological Clinic* 3 (1909–10): 1–8; idem, "The Money Cost of the Repeater," ibid., pp. 49–57; idem, "The Effect of Physical Defects on School Progress," ibid., pp. 71–77; idem, "A Simple System for Discovering some Factor Influencing Non-Promotion," ibid. 4 (1910–11): 189–92.

348. Ayres, "The Binet-Simon Measuring Scale," pp. 187, 194.

349. *Buffalo Evening News*, 27 November 1967; *University of Pennsylvania Graduate School Roster*, s.v. "Town, Clara Harrison."

350. Clara Harrison Town, "Association Tests in Practical Work for the Insane," *Psychological Clinic* 2 (1908–9): 276–81.

351. Clara Harrison Town, "An Infantile Stammer (Baby Talk) in a Boy of Twelve Years," *Psychological Clinic* 1 (1907–8): 10–20; "The Training of a Case of Infantile Stammer," ibid. 4 (1910–11): 136–40; "Congenital Aphasia," ibid. 5 (1911–12): 167–79.

352. Clara Harrison Town, "The Negative Aspect of Hallucinations," *American Journal of Psychology* 17 (1906): 134–36; "A Psychological Analysis of Three Delusional States: The Belief in the Control of Thought from Without, in the Unreality of the External World, and in the Unreality of the Self," *Psychological Clinic* 1 (1907–8): 198–209.

353. Clara Harrison Town, "The Kinaesthetic Element in Endophasia and Auditory Hallucination," *American Journal of Psychology* 17 (1906): 127–33.

354. Clara Harrison Town, "Public Day Schools for Backward Children," *Psychological Clinic* 1 (1907–8): 81–88.

355. Town, "Binet-Simon Scale and Psychologist," p. 239.

356. Terman, "Trails to Psychology"; May V. Seagoe, *Terman and the Gifted* (Los Altos, Calif.: William Kaufmann, 1975); Ernest R. Hilgard, "Lewis Madison Terman: 1877–1956," *American Journal of Psychology* 70 (1957): 472–79.

357. Lewis M. Terman, "A Preliminary Study in the Psychology and Pedagogy of Leadership," *Pedagogical Seminary* 11 (1904): 413–51.

358. Lewis M. Terman and H. G. Childs, "A Tentative Revision and Extension of the Binet-Simon Measuring Scale of Intelligence. Part I. Introduction," *Journal of Educational Psychology* 3 (1912): 61–74; idem, "A Tentative Revision and Extension of the Binet-Simon Measuring Scale of Intelligence. Part II. Supplementary Tests," ibid., pp. 133–43; idem, "A Tentative Revision and Extension of the Binet-Simon Measuring Scale of Intelligence. Part II. Supplementary Tests—Continued," ibid., pp.

198–208; idem, "A Tentative Revision and Extension of the Binet-Simon Measuring Scale of Intelligence. Part III. Summary and Criticisms," ibid., pp. 277–89 (hereafter cited as "Tentative Revision and Extension"); Lewis M. Terman, *The Measurement of Intelligence* (Boston: Houghton Mifflin, 1916); Lewis M. Terman and Maud A. Merrill, *Measuring Intelligence* (Boston: Houghton Mifflin, 1937).

359. Lewis M. Terman, "A Study in Precocity and Prematuration," *American Journal of Psychology* 16 (1905): 145–83.

360. Terman, "Trails to Psychology," p. 318.

361. Lewis M. Terman, "Genius and Stupidity. A Study of Some of the Intellectual Processes of Seven 'Bright' and Seven 'Stupid' Boys," *Pedagogical Seminary* 13 (1906): 307–73.

362. Lewis M. Terman, "Medical Inspection of Schools in California," *Psychological Clinic* 5 (1911–12): 57–62; idem, "School Clinics for Free Medical and Dental Treatment," ibid., pp. 271–78.

363. Terman, "The Binet-Simon Scale."

364. Terman and Childs, "Tentative Revision and Extension."

365. Terman, "Trails to Psychology," p. 311.

James McKeen Cattell
and
American Psychology in the 1920s

MICHAEL M. SOKAL

Worcester Polytechnic Institute

Introduction

As James McKeen Cattell concluded his 1925 presidential address before the American Association for the Advancement of Science, "Some Psychological Experiments,"[1] he casually mentioned that "the experiments used in this address as illustrations of work in psychology may seem like an autobiographical obituary notice."[2] And like an obituary, much of the talk focused on the past. In it, Cattell raised various issues that vitally concerned his generation of psychologists at the turn of the century—arguing, for example, that psychology could be as experimentally quantitative as any physical science.[3] Also, most of the experiments discussed dated from before 1900, as Cattell reviewed his own work first published in the 1890s[4] and that of some of his students from the same period.[5] The reasons for Cattell's concern with the past are clear.

Cattell was the first psychologist elected president of AAAS, but he was not elected as a student of what are now called the behavioral sciences. From at least 1900 he was best known in the American scientific community as the editor of *Science,* the official weekly of the association and probably the country's most important scientific journal. He had purchased it late in 1894, and from 4 January 1895, when he issued the first number of its "new series" with the cooperation of the editorial committee, composed of outstanding members of this community, the affairs of *Science,* and of the various other journals that he edited, took more and more time away from his psychological activities.[6] At the same time, the weaknesses of his early program for mental testing, to which he had devoted a good deal of himself for over a decade, gradually became clear.[7] As early as 1905, Cattell's day-to-day interests were not those of the typical American research psychologist, who continued to experiment regularly. Also, in 1917, three years before he turned sixty, he was dismissed from Columbia University in what soon became a celebrated academic freedom case,[8] and so lost his institutional base in academia. He continued to participate in the activities of the American psychological community throughout his life, despite all the setbacks relating to his ideas and affiliation, but clearly by 1925, and probably much earlier, he did not keep up with the latest experimental work in psychology. Of course, the phenomenon of the elder statesman of a science losing touch with the work of his younger colleagues is not unknown, but in Cattell's case, as noted, there were many reasons for this beyond the usual course of events. No wonder, then, that the experiments discussed in his presidential address were at least twenty-five years old.

All of this is not to say, however, that Cattell lost touch with the science of psychology in the United States, or with the community of psychologists. He participated actively in this community throughout the 1920s. For example, he personally arranged for the American Psychological Association to be incorporated in the District of Columbia in 1924,[9] and was elected by the American psychologists as president of the Ninth International Congress of Psychology, at Yale in 1929, the first ever held in this country.[10] Many of the issues he discussed in his AAAS Presidential address, though he referred to older experiments, were of as much concern in the 1920s as they were when Cattell first was appointed professor of psychology in 1889 and, interestingly enough, greatly concern psychologists today. Furthermore, a survey of how the psychologists of the 1920s approached many of these issues reveals an interesting pattern within the structure of the psychological profession, the ideas held by the psychologists, and the actual confidence that they had in these ideas. Cattell's presidential address, therefore, provides both direct and indirect access, though not the most obvious one, to the interests and concerns of American psychology in the 1920s, which is the general topic of this essay.[11]

The intellectual boundaries of the decade of interest here are not, of course, those of the chronological decade, 1920–1930. American psychology received a tremendous developmental impetus as a result of World War I, and the years that followed 1918 saw the growth and decay of at least three psychological movements—testing, industrial psychology, and the certification of consulting psychologists. The Ninth International Congress of 1929 marks a natural end to the period, and the years immediately before it saw the growth of large-scale support for child psychology and the beginnings of the migration of Gestalt psychology to the United States. In all, the period from 1918 through 1929 was an exciting one for American psychology, and historians can learn much by examining just what went on within the community of psychologists.

A number of conclusions emerge readily from such a study, and some may appropriately be suggested here, to clarify the direction that the rest of this essay will take. First, the psychologists of the 1920s shared many of the attitudes that characterized the vast majority of middle-class, native-born, white Anglo-Saxon Protestants. This group—and most psychologists were members of it[12]—shared a great deal of self-confidence, derived in part from America's economic success during the period and the country's major role in helping to "make the world safe for democracy."[13] In the same way, the psychologists typically shared the xenophobic smugness of the period, well illustrated by Sinclair Lewis in *Babbitt*.[14] The fact that the psychologists of the 1920s, like most people, reflected the world in which they lived should surprise nobody. But apparently it has shocked several psychologists of the 1970s. One has complained that *Even the Rat Was White*,[15] while others seem to believe that the earlier psychologists, with their scientific "pretensions," should have transcended their milieu.[16] Whatever the merits of these charges in the 1970s, to read them back into the 1920s is ahistorical and distorts the past.

A second conclusion that emerges from a study of the 1920s is that psychologists of the period shared a confidence possibly not seen at any other time in their science's history. Even graduate students could feel that they worked in "exciting times," with the "journals bristling with controversy."[17] One reason for this confidence was, at least in the early years of the decade, the belief that psychology had done much to win the Great War. This belief was reinforced by the attention paid in the popular press and in such journals as *Harper's* and the *New Republic* to the psychology of the period, in all of its aspects. Scientific methods of child care, philosophical implications of behaviorism, and practical applications of mental testing were all regularly discussed in articles written for the literate layman.[18] Humorists wrote about "the outbreak of psychology" and of ways to avoid it.[19] With such attention, it is no wonder that psychologists thought well of what they were doing. Another reason for their confidence was the high academic status that many of their colleagues were reaching. For example, between 1919 and 1921, Northwestern, Yale, Cornell, and the University of North Carolina all appointed psychologists to their presidencies.[20] For many, this confidence also reflected a belief in the validity of the "school" with which large numbers of psychologists identified themselves. The behaviorists, whose ideas have been well discussed by others,[21] knew that they had the answer to all, or at least most, of the world's problems, and some of them believed so strongly in their approach that they regularly read a chapter from John B. Watson's latest book before going to bed each night.[22] The Gestalt psychologists, who became an important force in American psychology long before Hitler drove many German intellectuals off the continent, felt to some degree that they were missionaries called to save the scientific souls of the poor benighted Americans.[23]

But another important conclusion of this paper is that the importance of warring "schools" in the history of American psychology has been greatly exaggerated,[24] and that, in many ways, American psychologists of the 1920s formed a small, fairly tightknit community whose members were usually quite friendly with each other, whatever systematic disagreements they might have had. For example, one psychologist who later stressed the differences between *Contemporary Schools of Psychology*,[25] concluded in an overview of the systematic approaches of the last half of the decade that:

There is a curious contrast in present-day psychology between the mutual hostility of the several schools, on the one hand, and the solidarity of the group of psychologists, on the other. From the insistence of each school on the futile and reprehensible tendencies of the others, you would scarcely expect to find them meeting in associations and congresses on a footing of mutual respect and interest, nor see them laboring together on abstract journals and the like; yet this cooperation is just what you find.[26]

This "mutual respect" and "cooperation" rested on, in large measure, what has been described as an "inborn eclecticism" shared by most American psychologists of the period.[27] This eclecticism played a major role in the early reception of Gestalt psychology in the United States. In all, American psychologists were clearly psychologists first, and only after that behaviorists, structuralists, or whatever.

The final major conclusion that comes out of this study of the 1920s is perhaps the most significant, but at the same time cannot be illustrated readily without reference to specific examples. Conversely, this conclusion is tied to a pattern that will emerge at several points in this essay, so that to connect it to one or another example would prevent its general importance from becoming clear. One way around this dilemma is to sketch this pattern here, and then, in the detailed discussions that follow, to indicate just how this pattern appears in the specific episode under consideration.

Specifically, this pattern saw the American psychologists of the 1920s approach one or another problem with extreme confidence, buoyed by the factors that had led to their faith in psychology in the first place. This confidence led, in some cases, to important scientific, theoretical advances, and to results of genuine practical applicability. But more importantly, this confidence went further, and thus the psychologists often vastly overstated their claims for the validity of their results and the usefulness of their work. These overstatements in turn led to exaggerated and unrealizable expectations of what psychology could do, on the part of the public, educators and other professionals, and often other scientists. Even before these expectations were created, many more critical psychologists, less involved in overstating the value of their work, attacked those who did claim that they could do more than they actually could. And the unfulfilled expectations often led to attacks from outside the community of psychologists as well. These attacks—both from within and without the discipline—led usually to disclaimers and sometimes public apologies by some psychologists, and portions of the field actually underwent what might be called scientific retrenchment. In any event, this pattern will become clear in the detailed analyses of this paper.

Mental Testing

To many historians and psychologists, the 1920s are best known as the first period of large-scale, nonmilitary psychological testing, and this aspect of the psychology of the period has been well treated by several observers.[28] Cattell, of course, is best known in the history of psychology as one of the pioneers of psychological testing. At the 1923 meetings of the American Association for the Advancement of Science he claimed to have originated the terms "mental tests" and "individual differences."[29] The failure of these early tests has been referred to above, and in his AAAS presidential address Cattell spoke of the results he obtained as "disappointing."[30] But around 1910, American psychologists became familiar with other tests, derived not from Cattell's work but from that of Alfred Binet, that gave more useful, if not more precisely defined results.[31] These tests were used primarily in schools and colleges, and many students were examined individually, mainly to segregate from the mass of students those who could not benefit from regular instruction, and those for whom exposure to advanced material would be useful.[32] By 1916, so many psychologists were devoting so much of their time to the use and development of tests that a number of them attempted to standardize them for all users,[33] and some progress was made toward organizing a journal devoted solely to such mental tests.[34]

However, psychology and its tests were not really well known in the United States until World War I, and it was the role that they played during the war that first brought them national attention. When America entered the War in 1917, the governing body of the American Psychological Association met to decide how the nation's psychologists could best come to the aid of their country.[35] The outcome of this meeting was multifaceted,[36] but perhaps the best known and probably most important results of these deliberations were to be the development of two standardized group tests of "intelligence," given to most recruits taken into the army. These were the Alpha test for men literate in English, and the Beta test for those literate only in another language, or totally illiterate. The results of these tests were quite useful to the army in the limited areas of selecting men for officer training and eliminating men unfit for various types of service, and Cattell quoted an estimate of the value of the tests at one billion dollars. He also said that the tests cost about fifty cents per man to administer, thus claiming that psychology gave to the war effort much more than it received.[37]

As a recent historian of intelligence testing in the United States put it, "psychology was on the brink of a boom that was to prove financially profitable. . . . The work on the army tests . . . was a powerful stimulant to intelligence testing and to psychology" in general. Right after the war, many more jobs for psychologists opened up than there were men and women to fill them. As one of the leading members of the psychological community wrote to another, who was looking for a young psychologist to fill a position, "I am afraid it will be difficult to find the right person. . . . Men with any substantial training in psychology are scarce and very much in demand."[30]

Psychological testing also boomed. The first heavy users of the group tests developed for the army were the schools and colleges, which found them more efficient than the individual tests. Even before the armistice, various colleges and even high schools approached psychologists connected with the army testing program about getting copies of the examinations, but due to their confidential nature, all such requests were discouraged during the war. The first official announcement of the tests made after the war, however, in *Science* in March 1919, stressed "the applicability of mental measurement" to education.[39] Only three weeks later, John B. Watson, then at Johns Hopkins, wrote to Robert M. Yerkes, who headed the team of psychologists who developed the Army tests, about the possibility of obtaining test forms for use in a school in Baltimore.[40] That fall similar tests were used as part of the entrance procedure at such colleges as

Columbia and the University of Rochester, and by April 1921 at least ten institutions of higher education were using the Army Alpha Test (and many others were using other sets of tests) for similar purposes.[41] Such tests were also used at the high school level. Various school officials—for example, B. M. Stigall of the Kansas City, Missouri, school system—apparently contacted prominent psychologists and Army officials involved with the earlier tests to inquire just how they could use the testing material then becoming available.[42] A distinguished psychologist, Carl E. Seashore of the University of Iowa, used his term as resident chairman of the Division of Anthropology and Psychology of the National Research Council in 1920–21 to travel around the country and urge educators to use such tests to section their student bodies by ability, and thereby give each student the education most suited to his or her capabilities.[43] Helen Thompson Woolley worked with the Cincinnati Public Schools during this period to establish a Vocational Guidance Bureau, using tests to direct students to special vocational and remedial classes, and in general to augment the guidance role that many public schools were then beginning to play.[44]

The aim of most of the educators in using these tests was at least twofold. They wanted both to tailor the education received by each student, insofar as possible, to his or her capacities, and to increase the efficiency of the educational process.[45] Both of these goals reflected the ideas of the progressive education movement, which remained an important force in American education long after John Dewey wrote *The School and Society* in 1899. The first aim derived from the movement's basic assumptions, and the second, at first seemingly antithetical to its goals, came from an application of the principles of scientific management to education. Standardized group tests quickly became an objective way to measure school and teacher efficiency and were soon installed in many public schools.[46]

On an individual basis, the use of these tests by educators probably proved beneficial to many of those students tested, by directing some to remedial classes, or by discovering in others abilities that had previously lay hidden and thus opening various educational possibilities. For example, in 1910, only 20 percent of all freshmen entering Princeton were graduates of public high schools, as opposed to Eastern preparatory academies. By 1935, this fraction had grown tremendously, primarily due to the use of examinations given by the College Entrance Examination Board, and the Scholastic Aptitude Test, first given in 1926, was purposely introduced for scholarship examinations so as not to bias the selection in favor of prep school graduates.[47] Cattell himself spoke of such tests as being "of untold value to our schools and to the children who are the ultimate origin and end of all our efforts," and Seashore spoke of "the measurement of talent" as one of the "central factors in this scientific movement," leading to "giving scientific advice in regard to the treatment of precocious children."[48] The use of such tests by psychologists and educators playing the role of counselor reflected the assumption that "psychology knows best," or, more generally, "science knows best," explicitly seen in Seashore's comments. In this respect, the educational testing movement of the 1920s reflected the open concern of many psychologists with "social control," an important aspect of the popular program of behaviorism, discussed elsewhere.[49] And when psychologists generalized the results of these tests from individuals to groups, and extrapolated on the basis of various assumptions, this concern with "social control" became explicitly important.

The results of the tests that had the greatest immediate social implications indicated, quite simply, that whites scored higher than blacks, that native-born whites scored higher than immigrant whites, and that immigrants from northern and western European countries scored higher than those from southern and eastern Europe.[50] These facts were not disputed by anyone. What led to a great deal of controversy were the interpretations attached to these data. For example, it has been shown that educators used these results to justify ethnic segregation and mediocre education for Chicanos in southern California during this period,[51] thus providing a counterexample to the argument that testing often led to increased educational opportunity. But as the largest collection of data resulted from the army testing program, it was their interpretation that was most controversial.

In preparing their final report, Robert M. Yerkes and his fellow psychologists made at least three major assumptions: that their tests measured actual innate "intelligence"; that this intelligence was hereditary and was passed in some way from parent to child; and that those individuals from various social groups—e.g., Northern blacks; Southern blacks; Northern native-born whites; English-born immigrants; Italian-born immigrants—who were recruited into the army and tested, represented an actual sample of these groups in American society at large.[53] These assumptions led them to interpret their data in various ways, arguing, for example, that those individuals with more years of schooling scored higher than those with fewer years of schooling because their native intelligence led them to stay in school longer, or that Southern blacks scored lower than Northern blacks because the brighter the black individual the more apt he or she would be to migrate north.[53] And of course the generally lower scores of the entire black group tested were used to argue that blacks were an inferior race.[54]

Although the official report of the army testing program did not discuss the data from foreign-born recruits, they were soon picked up by many avowed racists to argue for the superiority of the "Nordic" race over the "Alpine" and "Mediterranean" races, and for restrictions on the immigration to the United States of members of these "less-favored races." The best known of these racists, Madison Grant, never referred to test results, even in the last editions of his well-known book, *The Passing of the Great Race*.[55] But many others of his persuasion, such as Lothrop Stoddard and Seth K. Humphrey,[56] cited the test results continually. Their interpretations received support from by such psychologists as William McDougall (who answered his rhetorical question *Is American Safe for Democracy?*[57] in the negative, basing his opinion on the results of the tests), Carl C. Brigham (whose book *A Study of American Intelligence* neatly summarized the army test data on immigrants in accordance with views of Charles W. Gould),[58] and Yerkes himself, who summarized his interpretation of the tests as follows:

> Whoever desires high taxes, full almshouses, a constantly increasing number of schools for defectives, of correctional institutions, penitentiaries, hospitals, and special classes in our public schools, should by all means work for unrestricted and non-selective immigration.[59]

Yerkes also wrote to the chairmen of both the House and Senate Immigration Committees, citing the data of the army tests. Such activities have led several historians to claim that the psychologists played a major role in the passage of immigration-restriction legislation in the 1920s, and at least one psychologist in the 1970s has been quick to shout "mea culpa."[60]

More probably, like the social-Darwinian arguments of fifty years earlier, the results of the tests were taken merely as scientific proof of opinions long held. Even without these data, the social climate created by the Red scare and race riots of the early 1920s, the activities of the Ku Klux Klan, the pressure of labor unions to protect the jobs of their members, and the propaganda of various eugenicists, would probably have resulted in the passage of the immigration restriction laws of 1921 and 1924.[61]

The confidence of the testers, and in general of most psychologists was, however, never greater than in the middle of the 1920s. Terman, for example, required letters of recommendation for graduate students to include their scores on "standard intelligence tests," and he even published an article entitled "Adventures in Stupidity: A Partial Analysis of the Intellectual Inferiority of a College Student." He also posed the rhetorical question "Were We Born That Way?" in a popular journal, and answered it with an unequivocal yes.[62] This arrogance spread beyond the psychologists who identified themselves as testers. Even Carl E. Seashore, a man beloved by generations of students and colleagues at the University of Iowa, made many enemies in the university's School of Religion in the mid-1920s by habitually suggesting to its best students that they change their majors to psychology and study the psychological aspects of religion, arguing that "there is no other method" of value than that of experimental psychology.[63]

One disconcerting attitude—an almost casual anti-Semitism—was shared by psychologists with much of American culture of the period. During a period when Jewish quotas were introduced at Columbia, Princeton, and New York Universities and talented Jewish physicists and philosophers had trouble finding employment,[64] some psychologists were openly anti-Semitic. One, for example, wrote to a close friend that he "did not want to return to the 'ghetto' [i.e., New York] just yet," and a distinguished biologist with close personal ties with many psychologists complained about articles in the liberal magazine he called "The Jew Repub lic."[65] Other psychologists typically did not object to Jews, as such, and were probably more open than the general milieu in which they worked. But at the same time they typically objected to those individuals who exhibited what they referred to as Jewishness. Thus, through the 1920s, graduate students were recommended for jobs as "noticeably Jewish, but not obnoxiously so," or as "vastly more agreeable as a fellow-worker than one might suspect from his [Jewish] name," or as "brilliant, and his race is not objectionable."[66] In the 1930s, many of these psychologists were particularly concerned that their Jewish students found it especially difficult to find employment. And most ironically, in the 1920s, Terman felt he had to tell a graduate student from a Christian family—Harry Israel—to adopt his mother's maiden name and change his name to Harry Harlow. But even with his old name, before the change became official, he won his first position at the University of Wisconsin.[67]

Before the end of the decade, pressure began to build that eventually forced the testers to reevaluate their assumptions, and the psychological community in general to limit its claims. Such pressure came not only from nonpsychologists, but also often from psychologists themselves, and even sometimes from those who supported testing. For example, though he urged extensive use of psychological tests, Cattell stressed that he believed the tests measured "alertness" as a specific cluster of abilities, rather than a generalized "intelligence," and felt that "when it is found that Italian children in our schools do not do so well in certain tests as native American children, this may be due simply to lack of familiarity with the language or to ease in understanding the instructions." But he still argued that such tests predicted what and how well "the individual will do in a given situation," an operational definition of the results of the test.[68]

A more explicitly operational definition of "intelligence" was offered by Edwin G. Boring, who argued that "intelligence [is] . . . the capacity to do well on an intelligence test," and that this *intelligence* is analogous to the physicist's term *power;* i.e., the ability to do a given amount of work in a given time.[69] Boring also attacked Brigham's book, though he was a good friend of both Yerkes and Brigham, and Yerkes had gone out of his way to help arrange for Boring to review it in the *New Republic*. Specifically, Boring attacked Brigham's assumptions that the tests measured innate intelligence, and that the foreign-born recruits tested were an accurate sample of the various European races. He did not conclude that Brigham was wrong—"he may be right"—but rather felt that there were "so many other possibilities that I think we can say little more than we do not know; or, if . . . we have to make a judgment, we may say that the chances are that he is wrong."[70]

In general, the reaction to Brigham's book among professional psychologists was negative,[71] and his contemporaries attacked all of his assumptions. Also attacked were the internal inconsistencies among parts of the Alpha and Beta tests, which, some psychologists thought, made it questionable that the tests measured any such thing as general intelligence.[72] But these reviews did not prevent the *Literary Digest* from using Brigham's results to argue for immigration restriction, or other professional groups from accepting his arguments as fact.[73]

Pressures from outside the narrowly defined psychological community also forced a reevaluation of the tests and their results. William C. Bagley, an educator at Teachers College, Columbia University, whose training in experimental psychology had involved him in the interpretation of Cattell's tests about thirty years earlier,[74] argued against the tests. He claimed that all they really measured was the extent of the individual's education, and that to accept their results without question would lead to a deterministic self-fulfilling prophecy, an argument that Terman of course rejected.[75]

On a more popular level, Walter Lippmann's long series of articles in the *New Republic* attacked all of the testers' basic assumptions before a wide audience.[76] And even a long reply by Lewis M. Terman, whose Stanford-Binet was the most widely used individual (as opposed to group) test,[77] an editorial in the *New York Times* supporting Terman's position over Lippmann's,[78] and a fairly extensive correspondence between Lippmann and Yerkes[79] could not counteract the effects of Lippmann's attacks. To be sure, American psychologists did not stop their testing,[80] but by about 1925, in most cases, their claims for the tests had toned down. Tests were still used by guidance counselors and in college admissions procedures, and in 1926, the College Entrance Examination Board first gave the Scholastic Aptitude Test, developed by Brigham and others. But such was the change of climate of opinion that within a few years the CEEB dismissed any claims that the SAT measured intelligence, but rather said that it measured verbal ability.[81] As early as 1921, at least two of Terman's assistants began even to question his reliance on the individual Stanford-Binet tests alone to measure intelligence, and by 1927, one of his colleagues, Truman L. Kelley, published a statistical analysis of the internal consistency of intelligence tests that raised much doubt as to their validity.[82]

Meanwhile, many anthropologists and psychologists trained or influenced by Franz Boas at Columbia challenged the concept of European races supported by Brigham.[83] Boas himself wrote of "The Nordic Nonsense,"[84] and had his students attack problems related to Brigham's ideas. With a grant from the Columbia University Council for Research in the Social Sciences, which had itself been funded by the Laura Spelman Rockefeller Memorial, he and his students carried out a long-term project on "Hereditary and Environmental Influences upon the Development of Man."[85] For example, Margaret Mead measured "the effect on intelligence test scores of the language spoken in the home."[86] But probably the most influential of Boas's students in this area was Otto Klineberg, who had come to Columbia with an M.D. from McGill University convinced of the validity of McDougall's arguments in *Is America Safe for Democracy?* Boas had Klineberg give various tests to American Indian groups, and this experience convinced the student that cultural factors were important in any testing situation.[87] Klineberg later developed different versions of these tests that were among the most sensitive of the period,[88] and with the help of fellowships from the National Research Council and the Laura Spelman Rockefeller Memorial, he gave these tests to children in France, Germany, and Italy. He showed that there was no correlation between the results on the tests and the characteristics that Grant and others had used to distinguish the Nordic, Alpine, and Mediterranean races.[89] Later, he used similar tests to argue that any difference between the scores of Northern blacks and Southern blacks on earlier tests was due to the better education that the former had received.[90] Even Brigham began to change his mind. By 1927, work on the internal inconsistencies of the army tests had led him privately to reconsider his earlier statements, and in 1929 he told Klineberg, that he "didn't stand by a word" of his book on American intelligence. By 1930, he openly concluded that "one of the most pretentious of these comparative racial studies—the writer's own—was without foundation."[91]

Of course, this work did not settle the question of any relationship between race and intelligence. By 1941, Raymond B. Cattell (who is *not* related to James McKeen Cattell) published what he felt to be "A Culture-Free Intelligence Test,"[92] and the past fifteen years have seen the writings of Arthur Jensen, Richard Herrnstein, William Shockley, H. J. Eysenck, and others.[93] Clearly, the question is still not settled, despite the fact that such psychologists as Anne

Anastasi have developed approaches that allow the study of *how* heredity and environment *interact* in one individual, and that these approaches are part of a broader intellectual "climate of opinion" that has recently been described as "the triumph of evolution."[94]

Clearly the tests of the 1920s failed to answer important questions, and this episode is the first that illustrates the general pattern of confidence, overstatement, and failure. In some ways, this pattern can also be seen in the failure of James McKeen Cattell's testing program of the 1890s.[95] In both, the psychologists approached the problem of testing with confidence, buoyed by the recognition their work had earned them in the years immediately preceding. This was especially true in the 1920s, when the psychologists could point to the success of their work in the important, if restricted, area of selecting men suitable for officer training.[96] This confidence led in both instances to vastly overstated claims for the tests, despite the fact that, again in both cases, the testers knew that there were important aspects of what they were measuring about which they knew little.[97] And of course the problems to which the testers tried to apply their work were more complicated than the selection of men for officer training. The failure of the tests to deliver what the testers claimed they could readily led to attacks on their use, first by psychologists who were not involved with the testing movements, and then by related specialists, such as educators and anthropologists.[98] However, only in the later period did such public figures as Lippmann attack the tests, perhaps because the psychological testing of the 1890s was not well known to the public. And while by the late 1920s the general scientific climate of opinion in the United States had clearly shifted away from the testers' point of view,[99] the main reason for the decline of the testing movement of the 1920s was the psychologists' overstatement of what their tests could do.

Industrial Psychology

Before the testing movement as such declined, it contributed extensively to the rise of a broadly defined "applied psychology," which used tests and similar procedures to attack problems in clinical, educational, and industrial areas.[100] In this work, those who called themselves "consulting psychologists" often did not simply apply the results of their more academically oriented colleagues. Instead, they developed their own applied science and behavioral technology.[101] Cattell was deeply involved in this movement, as will be seen. But probably the most significant point to make about the development of applied psychology in the United States during the 1920s—at least industrial psychology—was that it followed the same pattern that testing had followed: limited success, overconfidence and overstatement, and retrenchment.

Industrial psychology did not begin with the application of the earliest tests.[102] As early as 1895, in his psychology classes at the University of Minnesota, Harlow Gale used advertisements to illustrate the various phenomena of involuntary attention.[103] But the first person who identified himself as a psychologist to approach the problems of advertising directly and who attempted to improve the effectiveness of advertising copy was Walter Dill Scott.[104] Scott had been educated in Germany, where he worked with Wilhelm Wundt in Leipzig, and, in 1901, while teaching at Northwestern University, he was approached by a Chicago copywriter to speak to a local advertising club on the psychology of advertising.[105] This talk led to others, and to the serial publication of his book *The Theory of Advertising*—carefully avoiding the word psychology in its title, to prevent offending other psychologists—in an advertising agency's house organ.[106] Meanwhile, other psychologists began working on psychological problems of advertising,[107] and Scott's second book on this topic explicitly referred to psychology in its title.[108] Problems of advertising led directly to problems of salesmanship, and Scott soon involved himself in the development of methods to select and train salesman,[109] an effort which soon expanded to attempts to use psychological techniques in the selection of individuals for other jobs and professions.[110] This work paralleled similar studies by other distinguished psychologists such as Hugo Münsterberg, who had lectured on this topic as early as 1912, and Edward Lee Thorndike.[111] Other studies of worker selection by 1915, received support on a large scale at Carnegie Institute of Technology, where the H. J. Heinz Company, the Equitable Life Assurance Society, and the Burroughs Adding Machine Corporation, among others, contributed to the Division of Applied Psychology, under Walter Van Dyke Bingham. By 1916, the two leading industrial psychologists in the United States joined forces, for in that year Scott came to Carnegie Tech as professor of applied psychology—apparently the first such chair ever created—and as the director of the Bureau of Salesmanship Research within Bingham's division.[112] By 1917, the *Journal of Applied Psychology* appeared, and the fact that it survived America's participation in World War I, when, for example, the *Journal of Experimental Psychology* suspended publication for two years, shows how alive the new field was.

When the United States entered the First World War, Scott and Bingham offered their services to the War Department, based on their experience in selecting salesmen, and presented a "rating scale for selecting captains," a modification of Scott's earlier scales for rating business personnel. By August 1917, a Committee on the Classification of Personnel in the Army had been established, with Scott as director, and Bingham as executive secretary.[113] Like the Army Alpha and Army Beta tests, the work of this Committee attracted a great deal of attention to what psychology could do, and its work was quite successful. By Armistice Day, it had classified and rated the job qualifications of more than three million men, and was lauded in such journals as the *New Republic* as an instrument to prevent politics from entering into the appointment and promotion of officers.[114]

After the war, psychology in all of its aspects boomed, and such was the public interest in the field that psychologists found themselves discussing "Psychology as a Life Work"[115] before audiences of young men interested in the science and its practice as a career. Many firms, involved in businesses as diverse as retail sales and heavy manufacturing, grew interested in psychology and began to hire psychologists to study their personnel practices.[116] R. H. Macy and Company, for example, hired a Columbia psychologist to study its recruitment, training, and management procedures for sales and clerical positions,[117] and the U.S. Civil

Service Commission, interested in Scott's work during the war, hired Beardsley Ruml, another member of the committee's staff, as a consulting examiner to study its testing procedures. One result of this study was the establishment of a Research Division for the commission in 1922.[118] Meanwhile, in 1919, hoping to apply much of what he learned during the war, Scott himself organized many of the men who had worked with him in the Army Committee on Classification into a private personnel management consulting firm, the Scott Company. Working closely with more than forty industrial and commercial firms by 1923, the company developed special tests for particular jobs in such fields as meat packing, machine assembly, and the like, and even worked directly with both companies and unions to stimulate efficient practices. Its "active members" included most of the men who had worked with Scott during the war, as well as many of his students from Carnegie Tech. In addition, its list of "associates" included such prominent psychologists as James R. Angell, Bingham, Thorndike, John B. Watson, and Yerkes.[119]

Such was the situation with respect to industrial psychology in 1919, when James McKeen Cattell first began to make plans for what was to be founded in 1921 as the Psychological Corporation, his attempt at applying psychology on a large scale.[120] Today the company is probably the best known commercial firm involved in applied psychology, but in the early 1920s it started slowly. Its growth was retarded by a rather strange organizational scheme that Cattell imposed on it.[121] He often referred appropriately to the corporation as a "holding company for psychologists." Under Cattell's plan, the Psychological Corporation was to act as a sort of publicity agent, referral service, and supply company for applied psychology, in its largest sense. For example, besides personnel studies, Cattell envisioned that the corporation would administer, at a nominal fee, tests for those persons who wished to know how intelligent they were, or how well they scored on such standardized tests as the Army Alpha. The corporation was to make the availability of its services known through judicious publicity—e.g., the issuance of press releases and the circularization of reprinted newspaper stories about its activities—and was to make available to its stockholders supplies of test forms and other such items. Those individuals and business firms who felt the need of the services of a psychologist and who approached the corporation were to be referred to one of its psychologist-stockholders, or more likely, to one of its branches, which were planned for most American cities. Each individual stockholder, or branch member, would perform the required service, and charge the client a fee. This fee was to be split evenly between the individual performing the service and the corporation, subject to two understandings. One was that the stockholder agreed to devote at least half of his or her fee to the psychological research in which he or she was currently involved. The other was that the dividends to be paid by the corporation were strictly limited by law, and that any excess of profits over expenses and dividends was to be devoted, in some unspecified way, though probably through grants, to the advancement of scientific research. In this way, Cattell hoped not only to drive psychological charlatans out of business, but also to promote psychological research, add to the financial standing of psychologists, expand the public's familiarity with psychology, and improve the social standing of psychologists throughout the United States. His program was a confident one, and it claimed a great deal.

All of the goals of applied psychology meshed well with the typical concerns of the period for efficiency and with the "progressive" concerns for "scientific" reform that continued into the 1920s from the "Progressive Era."[122] This similarity of approaches suggests that there were ties between the growing profession of industrial psychology and the previously existing Scientific Management movement.[123] To be sure, members of the two groups knew each other, and Bingham was fairly well acquainted with Frank B. Gilbreth. He even solicited a gift of a set of Gilbreth's apparatus for Carnegie Tech, and arranged for a similar set to be exhibited at the American Psychological Association in 1917.[124] Similarly, as part of his investigation of extremely intelligent individuals, Terman measured the IQ's of the entire Gilbreth family, and found that while Frank's was higher than all but 1.33 percent of the white recruits tested in World War I, his wife, Lillian, had a higher IQ than all but 0.12 per cent of such recruits.[125] Lillian Gilbreth *did* have a Ph.D. in psychology, but always referred to herself as an industrial engineer, and kept her membership in the American Psychological Association primarily for the business contacts it gave her.[126] In the same way, Elsie Bregman, the psychologist who had been employed by Macy's, was once invited to take part in a study of "The Application of Scientific Management to the Home" at Teachers College, Columbia University.[127] But as these contacts suggest, there was no real intellectual or substantive interaction between the professions. That is, at least during this period, neither group really learned much from the other, nor did they work together to apply "science" to industrial problems. Scientific management, whether practiced by a strict disciple of F. W. Taylor or by a more eclectic follower of the Gilbreths, concerned itself with the work and the task, via time or time-and-motion studies. Industrial psychology, on the other hand, was interested in the worker and his or her selection, motivation, and training. It is true that the two movements shared the same goal—increased production and efficiency—but they approached this goal in different ways. Still, as another historian has indicated, "scientific management had accustomed industrialists to the idea that a study of the production process would pay. . . . For this, the industrial psychologists would be eternally in debt to Taylor's movement."[128]

Much more important to the development of industrial psychology were links the emerging profession had with both the business community and, to a lesser extent, the labor movement. The ties with the business community were particularly clear. Bingham wrote of Edward A. Woods of the Equitable Life Assurance Company as "the leading spirit" behind the organization of the Personnel Research Bureau at Carnegie Tech. Likewise, many of Scott's associates, including Robert C. Clothier, who wrote with him a book on personnel management, were by experience and training businessmen and industrialists. Parallel to this situation, John B. Watson, an academic for twenty years, became a vice-president of the J. Walter Thompson Advertising Agency after the scandal following his divorce forced him to leave Johns Hopkins.[129] The industrial psychologist and the businessman shared the same goals and worked well together.

These ties between business and psychology in the early 1920s have led a number of historians to suggest that one reason for the growth of industrial psychology in the early 1920s was its use by business in an attempt "to kill unionism with kindness."[130] That is, industrial psychology provided an alternative to scientific management, which treated the worker as part of the machinery of production. There may be something to this view, especially as the psychologists were not political radicals. Cattell, however, had once issued "A Program of Radical Democracy," proposing, for example, a confiscatory tax on all inheritances.[131] This interest led him to enter into a long correspondence with Samuel Gompers, of the American Federation of Labor, as to the nature of intelligence tests and industrial psychology, and how psychology could contribute to the goals of unionism.[132] The Scott Company worked well with unions to insure industrial peace, mainly as a factor in improving the efficiency of production. Scott himself refused to work with any company determined to fight the unions, and his company lost several important contracts when it told its prospective employers that it would not work to destroy organizations of employees.[133] Scott and his colleagues preferred to work through trade associations—groups combining representation of both the unions and the different firms involved in each industry—hoping to get the benefit of as many different viewpoints as possible, while having access to all labor and personnel policies practiced by both management and the unions.[134] The Scott Company's greatest success in following this procedure was in Chicago in the early 1920s when it worked closely with both sides to settle a longstanding major dispute in the men's clothing industry. Others have suggested that Scott's work led to the relatively long peace in the industry and, undoubtedly, it did play a role. But probably a much more important factor was the "moderation and realism" of Sidney Hillman, the head of the Amalgamated Clothing Workers of America.[135] In any event, industrial psychologists had subtle, and not necessarily antagonistic, relations with the unions.

But like the various programs of mental testing of the 1920s, by the middle of the decade industrial psychology showed signs that it had overextended itself. The field had developed strongly during World War I, and in the years immediately afterward. But even during the War, James R. Angell, dean at the University of Chicago and a former president of the American Psychological Association, expressed his doubts to Bingham as to the viability of the program of the Army Committee on the Classification of Personnel. And General John J. Pershing, Commander-in-Chief of the American Expeditionary Force, thought that the committee overstated the value of its work.[136] In 1921, a young industrial psychologist, trained outside of the Bingham-Scott tradition at Carnegie Tech, argued that the tests then used by most applied psychologists were limited in that they did not consider such factors as attention span, reaction speed, and "planfulness," and urged the development of tests for such specific abilities.[137]

By 1923, the Scott Company dissolved itself, having been relatively successful for at least a part of its four years of existence. But by that year the team Scott had organized during the war had disbanded, as its "active members" took advantage of opportunities elsewhere. Scott himself had become president of Northwestern University by 1921, and the company's secretary, Beardsley Ruml, had left to become director of the Laura Spelman Rockefeller Memorial. Financial factors undoubtedly played a part in the company's closing, as the relative recession of 1922 cut deeply into its activities. Several of its officers claimed that its dissolution also reflected the development of personnel departments in many industrial firms, thus reducing the need for outside consultants.[138] But an important factor in the Company's demise was probably its policy of not fighting unions and, perhaps even more significantly, the subtle approach it took to personnel problems. Scott and his colleagues never claimed to be able to answer all of management's problems immediately, and its sophisticated tools, including the analysis of "the worker in his work" as a unit, were not the simple, straightforward, and easy-to-administer tests that many industrialists apparently expected. The Scott Company offered no easy answers, and its honesty apparently cost it much business.[139]

Only one year later, in 1924, the Division of Applied Psychology at Carnegie Tech also closed. During its existence, it had sponsored a Bureau of Salesmanship Research, a Research Bureau for Retail Training, and a Bureau of Personnel Research, all well supported by the business community of Pittsburgh. The reasons for the discontinuance of this division are many, and none are entirely clear. Certainly personal animosities were involved, as well as an effort to make the most efficient use of the scholarly resources of Pittsburgh. But except for the Research Bureau of Retail Training—i.e., a practical business school—which was transferred to the University of Pittsburgh, it appears that the industrial community of the city did not believe it was getting its money's worth from the support it gave the division.

As early as 1917, in response to a visit to Carnegie Tech at the invitation of Bingham, James R. Angell expressed his doubts as to the division's ability to do all that it had planned to do, just as he questioned the program of the Army Committee on Classification at about the same time. In 1920, Edward A. Woods, one of the businessmen who helped found the division, noted that "it is by no means certain that the present Intelligence Tests given to applicants for positions as salesmen are valuable," and sketched a research program for Bingham and Scott. He suggested studies to determine which qualities of good salesmen were ascertainable by physical examination, experience, and educational record, and which were measurable only by psychological tests. These studies were to be followed by the design of tests to determine these traits, without wasting time devising mental tests for "qualities that are comparatively unimportant." But nothing came of Woods's proposal, and four years later the division was disbanded.[140]

The Psychological Corporation, in the 1920s at least, failed even more spectacularly. Cattell's organizational scheme concentrated more on how the expected profits were to be used than on how the corporation was actually to apply psychology, and therefore there was literally no coordination between the various branches.[141] More than that, Cattell's own approach to industrial psychology was as unsophisticated as his approach to psychological testing had been in the 1890s. For example, he believed that simple tests could be developed that could easily pick out various traits in individuals that would qualify, or disqualify, them for specific positions. From his point of view, the role of industrial psychology was to select the proper person for the proper job, or, analogously, to select the best position in a magazine or newspaper for an advertisement.[142] An example he often used in describing this approach was to classify individuals into those interested primarily in: (1) persons; (2) material objects; and (3) "abstractions such as words and figures." He claimed that a transportation company could use the services of a psychologist to select the first type of individual as conductors and pursers, the second as motormen and engineers, and the third as clerks and bookkeepers.[143] While carrying out his early testing program, he explicitly ignored what were known as the "higher mental processes," at least partially because he could not easily quantify them. In the 1920s, he again concentrated on simple aspects of the problem that he could measure, or thought he could measure. That an individual's performance on a given job could depend on much more than his or her aptitude for it is a question that finds no concern in his writings. His approach was the "square peg in a square hole" industrial psychology that the "worker in his work" concept of the Scott Company was designed to combat.

The Psychological Corporation, unlike the Scott Company, never did show a profit at any time during the 1920s. For ten months of 1924 and 1925, the total *gross* income of the New York office of the corporation—one of the busiest, apparently—was $215.00, and the net income, after royalties and salaries, was $51.75.[144] Meanwhile, the corporation was keeping offices in one of the prime commercial buildings in New York—Grand Central Terminal—and was paying a secretary $2,500.00 per year.[145] By 1925, Cattell had to lend the corporation a total of $5,000.00 so that it could meet its expenses,[146] and it is doubtful if this debt was ever paid off.

By the end of 1926, the situation had gotten so bad that a drastic reorganization of the corporation took place. Cattell resigned, either under pressure or by choice, as president, and was "kicked upstairs" as chairman of the board. The new president was Walter Van Dyke Bingham, a man who had had over a decade of experience with industrial psychology and its problems. Dean R. Brimhall, who had been appointed secretary of the corporation as Cattell's protégé, left, and was replaced by Paul S. Achilles, an industrial psychologist who had had close ties to Bingham since the beginning of the Army Committee on Classification.[147] The board of directors drew up detailed plans for what they hoped the corporation would accomplish over the next five years, including such subtle problems as "mental aspects of the prevention of industrial accidents" as part of its program. But this program cost much—an estimated $540,000.00 for the five years[148]—and in 1929, just before the Great Depression, the corporation's gross income totaled $1,642.33.[149] The Depression hit the corporation hard, of course, as most businesses cut all but their most necessary expenditures.[150] Throughout the 1930s, even though a full-time staff had been hired, it "had to fight for its existence," and at least one methodologically sophisticated observer despaired at what he considered the "simple-minded approach" the corporation took to most of its problems.[151]

In general, then, by the middle of the 1920s, the interest of businessmen and industrialists in applied psychology had decreased greatly. The reasons for this again are not totally clear, but they are at least partially related to the stabilization of the business and employment atmosphere during this period, after the period of high labor turnover immediately after the war. Other reasons included the presence of various fraudulent and pseudoscientific consultants, and, more importantly, the fact that the reputable psychologists who conscientiously practiced their profession could offer no immediate solutions to any of the problems that business faced. The Psychological Corporation was, to be sure, an extreme example, but, in general, the psychologists again confidently overstated what they could do, and were, therefore, subject to disappointment.

Certification of Consulting Psychologists

The same pattern of confidence, based upon success with handling a limited problem, leading to overstatement, and, in turn, to disenchantment, appeared in the movement for the certification of psychologists engaged in nonacademic, professional practice of one sort or another that emerged in the years immediately following World War I. This movement saw the establishment of an American Association of Clinical Psychologists,[152] the absorption of this group into the American Psychological Association,[153] and an abortive attempt to have the APA itself certify what it broadly called consulting psychologists.[154] This story is much too complex to be told in full here, but as early as 1917, a committee of the American Psychological Association was established to investigate "the qualifications for psychological examiners and psychological experts," including clinical, educational, and industrial psychologists.[155] However, many psychologists believed that such an investigation was unnecessary—i.e., that enough was known about what clinical psychology, at least, should be—and at the same meeting of the APA at which this committee was formed a group of nine men and women organized an American Association of Clinical Psychologists, which discussed such standards for qualification at its organizational meeting.[156] Many members of the APA feared that this new group would split from the American Psychological Association, and debate between the two groups continued through December 1918, when the newer group met with the older. The Association of Clinical Psychologists had planned both a business session and scientific symposium for the meeting, but interest in the relations between the two groups forced the postponement of the formal papers.[157] The business meeting led to the formation of a joint committee of both associations to study problems of certification, and a year later the clinical psychologists were merged into the American Psychological Association. At that time, an APA Committee on the Certification of Consulting Psychologists was formed, with a mandate broader than clinical psychology.[158]

Throughout this episode both groups of psychologists were trying to protect, or establish, the reputation of psychology as a service profession, able to administer individual intelligence tests, offer vocational guidance, and help industries solve their personnel problems. A related important goal was the defense of psychology—especially industrial psychology—from the claims of such pseudoscientific or even fraudulent services as "psychanalysis" [sic], phrenological psychography, the Blackford School of Character Analysis, and the like.[159] The *Literary Digest* even organized a "Society of Applied Psychology," whose president, Warren Hilton, was acquainted with the science of psychology only through one under-graduate course in the area taken at Harvard.[160] But both groups were also ex-plicitly concerned with establishing the psychologist as an expert in a legal sense, analogous to the physician's position before the courts.[161] In the 1920s, this desire of the applied psychologists was opposed by academic psychologists, who were afraid of having their science "dirtied" by contact with practical problems, and who probably also realized many of the problems of applying a fledgling sci-ence.[162] In the same way, psychiatrists opposed the professionalization of psy-chology, in part because they saw their monopoly in the diagnosis and treatment of certain disorders threatened, and in part because of some real doubts that they had about the usefulness of psychology.[163] In any event, the issue of the certification of psychologists is still not settled, at least in part as a result of the opposition of "scientific" psychologists and psychiatrists. Still, the Committee on the Certification of Consulting Psychologists started with high hopes despite its charge to limit its expenses to the funds it raised by requiring fees for certification.[164] By 1922, however, it found itself with little or no role to play as less than two dozen (of more than four hundred) members of the association applied for certification.[165] After the agitation of the previous five years, the committee at first could not understand why more psychologists did not apply for certification, and then finally decided that this low number was a result of the relatively high fee ($35.00) it charged for certification, and of some confusion about the meaning of certification. It therefore decided to recommend that the certification fee be reduced, and to develop a list of "distinguished" psychologists who would be invited to apply for certification.[166]

The issuance of a large number of invitations to certification clashed with the whole philosophy of certification itself, and many members of the APA were "perturbed" by the committee's action. Most of those circularized did not apply for certification—"puzzlement" was the typical reaction[167]—and the association's president, Knight Dunlap, refused to sign any diplomas of certification until the matter had been thrashed out at the annual meeting.[168] At that meeting, the committee sought to clarify its role, but its report, recommending fundamental changes in the concept of certification—suggesting, for example, that certification be granted in either clinical, educational, or industrial psychology—was not ac-cepted.[169] From that point on, the committee was moribund, and after an attempt in 1926 to establish a definite policy with regard to unprofessional conduct on the part of APA members—stimulated by a report that an unnamed clinical psycholo-gist engaged in sexual intercourse with his patients[170]—the committee was finally dissolved in 1927.[171] In its six-year history it had certified as consulting psycholo-gists only twenty-five members of the APA.[172]

It is striking how many of the issues raised by the history of this committee still face psychology today.[173] But the pattern of overstatement followed by disen-chantment is perhaps more interesting, and certainly more significant. But if the attempts by psychologists to apply their science were disappointing, the confidence that the psychological community shared throughout this decade was hardly dampened. The reasons for this continued confidence and good feeling were many.

Financial Support of Child Psychology

Perhaps the main reason for the continued good feeling and confidence among psychologists through the 1920s was the large amount of money invested in their science throughout the decade. Large sums were granted for work in many areas of psychology, especially child study, by several large philanthropic foundations. The Commonwealth Fund was especially active, supporting Truman L. Kelley's "Study of the Structure of the Intellect" at Stanford, and, from 1921 through the Depression, the Harvard Growth Study. This last project, funded heavily, saw Walter F. Dearborn and his colleagues "assess the nature of physical and mental growth by making annual measurements on the same individuals over a period of twelve years."[174] Even more spectacular were Terman's "Genetic Studies of Genius," which saw Stanford match the major grant from the Fund. Begun in 1921, this study identified one thousand young "geniuses" in California public schools, and, since that date, has traced its subjects' lives and careers through the present. Employing a large number of student and postdoctoral assistants, Terman's work in this area is perhaps the earliest example, in psychology, of what has come to be called "Big Science."[175]

Perhaps the largest amount of money given to psychologists for their work came from the Rockefeller Foundation and its associated agencies.[176] For example, in 1926, the Laura Spelman Rockefeller Memorial gave $76,500 to the American Psychological Association to subsidize, for ten years, the publication of *Psychological Abstracts*. It also regularly provided funds for European psychologists to work in the United States.[177] And in 1929, the foundation pledged a total of $4,500,000 to Yale over ten years to establish an Institute of Human Relations, dominated by psychologists, while including work in psychiatry, law, and the social sciences. Including funds for child study and for an "anthropoid breeding station," these grants established a center for psychological study that in later years produced some of the most exciting research to appear in America before World War II.[178]

But like most philanthropic agencies that supported psychology during the 1920s, the Laura Spelman Rockefeller Memorial was interested primarily in "Child Study and Parent Education."[179] Headed by Beardsley Ruml, a psychologist who had earlier been associated with James R. Angell at the University of Chicago and the Carnegie Corporation, with Bingham at Carnegie Tech, and with Scott at the Scott Company, the Memorial funded work in this area via grants to home economists, nursery school educators, nutritionists, and education teachers, as well as to child psychologists. Besides funding National Research Council fellowships and scholarships for child study,[180] and providing direct and indirect grants in support of *Parents' Magazine*,[181] the Memorial also gave much support for various child study research centers, following the model established in Iowa in 1917. In that state, a well-known clubwoman, Cora B. Hillis, had argued since 1913 that the state legislature should spend as much for the study of children as it did for research on hogs and cattle. With the support of Carl E. Seashore and other psychologists at the state university, Hillis lobbied at the legislature regularly through 1917. In that year, the failure of many young men from Iowa to meet the minimum standard set for draftees convinced the state legislators to establish a Child Welfare Research Station at the university.[182] At first a fief of the university's Department of Psychology, the station had a strong director, Bird T. Baldwin, a psychologist.

He soon established important research programs in child health and institutional and social patterns of rural and urban families, as well as important extension programs for parent education and the training of kindergarten teachers.[183] To aid its work, Hillis arranged for the Women's Christian Temperance Union to grant the station $50,000 over five years, and at her death left it $10,000.[184]

In 1920, Baldwin began corresponding with officers of the memorial about the possibilities of obtaining funding for the station's work, and early in 1921 he wrote optimistically to Hillis that he expected such funding "sooner or later." In 1922, $22,500 was granted to the station by the Memorial over a three-year period, representing its first large-scale investment in child-study research. Other grants were made in 1925 (ca. $100,000 over five years), 1926 (an additional $15,000 for a "study of the rural child"), and 1928 (ca. $850,000 over ten years).[185] In addition, smaller grants were made to the Iowa State College of Agriculture at Ames (in 1925, $22,500 over three years; in 1928, $30,000 over five years), where child-study work and extension education programs were centered in the School of Home Economics under a strong dean, Anna Richardson, and to the Iowa State Teachers College at Cedar Falls (in 1925, $22,500 over three years; in 1929, $32,000 over six years) for nursery-school education.[186] By the end of the decade, then, Rockefeller money supported a unified program of child-study and parent education in many different areas, under several auspices, throughout the state of Iowa.[187]

Once the Iowa model was established, the Memorial followed it, and supported other centers of child research at such institutions as Teachers College of Columbia Univerity, the University of California, and the University of Minnesota.[188] At Yale, Arnold Gesell received some support for his photographic studies of children's behavior quite early, but the Memorial soon—by 1924—supported this work only as part of the Yale Psycho-Clinic, and later as part of the Institute of Psychology, established by 1925, which set the pattern later to be followed by the Institute of Human Relations.[189] Other smaller institutions of various kinds also received grants for psychological work with children of one kind or another. Mills College in California, for example, received $36,600 over three years for a program in nursery school education, and the University of Cincinnati was granted $15,000 for similar work. And at the Agricultural College of the State of Georgia, a program in preschool education was established with a grant of $12,000 over three years through the intervention of Rosa M. Walker, a woman much like Cora B. Hillis, an officer of the state Parent-Teacher Association and the wife of the governor.[190] In many ways, psychologists had arrived, and the acceptance of their work did much to support the good feeling and confidence that permeated the profession.

The Psychological Community and E. B. Titchener

Another reason for the confidence and good feeling of the 1920s was the fact that the community of psychologists was still quite small, and most of its members knew many of their colleagues well and could speak of them as friends and coworkers, even if they sometimes disagreed with one another. Robert S. Woodworth's comment on this point has already been quoted, but nothing illustrates the unity of the profession during the 1920s better than a sketch of the role played in the community of psychologists by Edward Bradford Titchener.

By 1919, Titchener's "structural" psychology stood in almost total isolation from the views of the rest of the profession and, as during the first years of the century, many American psychologists defined their theoretical positions by how far they stood from Titchener.[191] Yet Titchener was loved and respected even by the most ardent behaviorists. Many leading psychologists came long distances to attend the meetings of the Society of Experimental Psychologists, which he organized and over which he presided with a kindly paternalism.[192] He never really took part in the formal activities of the American Psychological Association and even let his membership in it lapse every few years, yet in 1921 various of his students and their contemporaries urged their colleagues to elect him president of the APA. Many agreed with Margaret Floy Washburn's opinion—"T. is the ablest living American psychologist"—but even she had to note that "that fact is irrelevant to the presidency," and in fact he was not elected. In the same year he again let his membership in the association lapse, and its members reacted with a unanimous resolution asking him to reconsider his decision. He did so, only to let his membership lapse five years later.[193] This personal affection was reciprocated, and Titchener went out of his way, for example, to take a stand against the A. N. Marquis Company, when it dropped Watson from *Who's Who* after his divorce in 1920 and the scandal that followed.[194]

When Titchener died in 1927, the reaction of his colleagues showed how much he was loved. His beard had grown extremely white a year or two earlier, and his normally perfect lectures, just before his death, were interrupted by sudden pauses while he struggled to regain his train of thought. The death was totally unexpected, although members of his family had suspected the existence of the cerebral tumor, which "fortunately" hemorrhaged before it incapacitated him completely.[195] Upon receiving the news, Edwin G. Boring of Harvard, who long before had adopted Titchener as a surrogate father, immediately telegraphed the leaders of the profession, reporting the death, and followed this action with almost identical letters supplying the details of the actual disease, the autopsy, and the cremation.[196] To "forestall" all other candidates, he also immediately sat down to write a long, analytic, and cathartic obituary of his mentor, published only a few short months later.[197] None of this reaction seemed overdone at the time, and even those without a strong personal tie to him felt his loss. Cattell wrote that "Titchener's death leaves the world more empty," while Yerkes indicated that "his death . . . came as a terrible shock. I feel as though half my professional world were gone. Never before have I experienced such a sense of combined professional and personal loss."[198] A former student of Titchener's, Karl M. Dallenbach, who had quarreled furiously with him just before his death over the policies of the *American Journal of Psychology,* felt the death of his mentor keenly. "In spite of the estrangement between us, his death hit me pretty hard."[199] And even a nineteen-year-old student at Barnard College, a psychology major who had never met Titchener, reacted strongly to the news. When told by her mother, who was reading the daily newspaper, that a famous psychologist named Titchener had died, Anne Anastasi could do nothing for a few minutes but repeat aloud, "I can't believe he's dead."[200] One of the giants of American psychology had fallen, and his loss was felt by all.

The Ninth International Congress of Psychology

The end of the decade saw a reaffirmation of the self-confidence of American psychology with the Ninth International Congress of Psychology, held at Yale in September 1929.[201] The Institute of Human Relations had just opened officially, and the stock market crash was still a month away. Chronologically, the setting could not have been better. The congress meant much to many of the older psychologists, who had been greatly embarrassed when plans for an international congress in America in 1913 fell through completely, and the invitation had to be withdrawn, because of intramural squabbling within the profession.[202] In 1923, Cattell and others tried to have the 1926 congress invited to the United States, and the APA even formed a Committee on an International Congress of Psychology in America. But these plans fell through as the Americans soon realized that the financial situation in Europe in 1923 was such that many Europeans probably could not afford a trip to America even three years later.[203] The 1929 congress, therefore, was a realization of the hopes of many Americans and Europeans, and Edouard Claparède, permanent secretary of the International Congress, expressed this feeling well by opening his address at the congress with the exclamation, "Enfin, enfin en Amérique!"[204]

The congress itself was an immense success, and the more than one thousand registrants interacted socially and took part in stimulating scientific discussions that were reflected in their work for many years. Even the *New Republic* editorialized as to its importance.[205] Cattell, of course, was the congress's president—chosen by the members of the American Psychological Association—and his address reviewed the development of American psychology in a way that impressed some of his auditors favorably and struck others as self-aggrandizement. He highlighted the talk by distributing copies of it at the meeting, printed in a large format, and illustrated with photographs of Wundt, William James, G. Stanley Hall, and other important early psychologists. In many ways, it was a bravado performance.[206]

The social history of the congress is also interesting, but here only Cattell's own actions can be discussed. They struck the participants so forcefully that forty-five years later those who attended the congress, and were still living, remembered them. While the various memories differ with respect to many details, all remember a public insult of some sort hurled by Cattell at William McDougall, the English psychologist who had taught at Harvard from 1920 to 1927 before moving to Duke.[207] McDougall had recently been studying learning in successive generations of rats, hoping to show that the learned ability to swim a water-maze was heritable, and hence a Lamarckian trait.[208] His early experiments appeared to show that this acquired ability was indeed inherited. Later McDougall realized that the data upon which he based these conclusions were falsified by a student hoping to please his professor. It was either at a general session, at which McDougall commented while Cattell was in the chair, or at a symposium on physiological psychology, in which McDougall presented the findings bearing on the Lamarckian theory, that the confrontation took place. Cattell stood up when McDougall finished and said, in just about so many words, that he personally would not believe any results coming from McDougall's laboratory. Paul Farnsworth remembered that he reacted by turning to the person sitting next to him and saying, "My God, the old boy was certainly crude on that, wasn't he?" Unfortunately, he found himself speaking to Cattell's daughter, Psyche, herself a prominent psychologist, and immediately apologized, but he remembered that she responded, "That's perfectly all right. He was crude, terribly crude. That was an awful thing to do." Anne Anastasi remembered a "horrified gasp" from the audience, followed immediately by a hushed silence, and eventually by comments about Cattell's lack of tact. Roswell P. Angier, a professor of psychology at Yale, the host of the Congress, felt especially bad about it.

Cattell was certainly outrageous. His treatment of McDougall was insufferable. . . . I looked round for McDougall in order to let him know what we all thought of Cattell's behavior, but did not find him. [Raymond] Dodge [another Yale psychologist] did speak to McDougall about it. He seemed very grateful.[209]

Of course, it was the scientific program on which most of the success of the congress rested, and here the hopes of its organizers were well fulfilled. Many Americans took part in formal sessions and relatively informal symposia on such topics as "Learning Theory" and "General Intelligence" and "Psychology of Industry and Personnel."[210] But the most exciting feature of the congress was the participation of many Europeans at all levels of the program, including informal presentations, formal papers, and invited addresses. Perhaps the most famous foreign speaker was Ivan Pavlov, who spoke, through an interpreter, on "The Highest Nervous Activity."[211] Despite his reliance on a translator, "he spoke with such enthusiasm and dramatic fervor that . . . his gestures and voice alone would have held the interest of the audience."[212] Twelve other papers were presented by Russians, and other Europeans filled the program, with twenty-six German and seventeen British papers being presented.[213]

Gestalt Psychology in America

The theoretical perspective that attracted the most attention at the congress was that of Gestalt psychology. Even Karl Lashley, in his presidential address before the American Psychological Association (which met at the congress), reflected in many ways the Gestalt point of view in his discussion of the "Basic Neural Mechanisms in Behavior."[214] Of course, most of the American papers at the congress reflected the "normal science" of a middle-of-the-road applied, behavioristically oriented functionalism. But many of those papers which explicitly took—or challenged—a systematic point of view concerned themselves with Gestalt psychology. Many of these, of course, were by Europeans, and the American committee had explicitly tried to attract as many Germans—and hence mostly Gestalt psychologists—to the congress as possible, often by arranging summer-school positions in this country for them to cover the costs of their visits.[215] At the congress, these psychologists held important positions on the program. For example, the only other psychologist to speak at the same formal session as Pavlov was Wolfgang Köhler, who spoke "Über einige Gestalt probleme,"[216] and the accounts of the congress published in various psychological journals stressed their attendance.[217] Many Americans also spoke on Gestalt psychology. Some, like Harry Helson, used its approach to psychological problems, and others, like Margaret F. Washburn, attacked its point of view.[218] Besides Köhler, other European psychologists with a Gestalt point of view who attended the congress included Kurt Lewin, David Katz, and Edgar Rubin. The prominence of Gestalt psychology at the congress was such that one of Lewin's leading students has said that it did more to bring this movement to the United States than Hitler ever did.[219] If nothing else, then, the 1929 International Congress left a major legacy to American psychology through the Gestalt school.

Despite a kernel of truth in that statement, the situation was not that simple. To be sure, at least one prominent German psychologist with close ties to the Gestalt movement—Kurt Lewin—won his first American position, at Stanford University, as a result of the impression he made at the congress.[220] But the transfer of Gestalt psychology to the United States was a complicated episode in the social history of ideas, which began in the 1920s and even earlier, and is too vast a topic to be considered in depth here.[221] Recent literature on this topic has stressed the problems that Gestalt psychologists had in being accepted in the United States[222] and, although this emphasis is somewhat misleading, as will be shown below, many of them undoubtedly did face problems. Thus Lewin never held a long-time position in a psychology department, serving instead in such settings as a Department of Education, a School of Home Economics, a Child Welfare Research Station, and a Research Center for Group Dynamics.[223] Köhler and Kurt Koffka never held the chairs at the major universities that many of their followers felt they deserved. There *was* some opposition to Gestalt psychology in the United States in the late 1920s and early 1930s, but this opposition was in general not based on any deep antipathy to their ideas. But more importantly, a focus on this opposition obscures a good many more significant points.

In fact, probably the most interesting aspect of the transmission of Gestalt psychology from Europe to the United States was the readiness with which most of the German ideas, and psychologists, were listened to, studied, and to at least some degree accepted. The "ingrained eclecticism" of many Americans, such as that that led to their respect for Titchener, played a major role in this phenomenon. More important, probably, several Americans had studied in Europe during the early years of this century, knew the Gestalt psychologists personally, and considered them their friends. For example, Herbert S. Langfeld of Princeton had studied in Berlin from 1904 to 1909, where he met and befriended Kurt Koffka, who later became a leading member of the Gestalt school. In 1912, Langfeld (then at Harvard) sent one of his students, Edward C. Tolman, to Giessen, where Koffka was then teaching, and eleven years later, when the opportunity next presented itself, Tolman returned to Giessen and Koffka for a few months.[224] In the same way, Robert M. Ogden of Cornell studied at Würzberg from 1901 to 1903 with Oswald Külpe. Ogden also knew Koffka well, included some Gestalt ideas in some of his own work, and, as early as 1922, solicited Koffka's first American paper, "Perception: An Introduction to the *Gestalt-Theorie*," for the *Psychological Bulletin*.[225] Similarly, in the early 1920s, Gordon Allport spent a year in Germany on a Sheldon Traveling Fellowship from Harvard, and took advantage of this opportunity to acquaint himself with the various psychological movements that sprang up after the War. Though especially impressed with William Stern's personalistic psychology, then being developed at Hamburg, he also appreciated "the brilliance of the Lewinian approach" and thought much of "the high quality of experimental studies by the Gestalt school" in general.[226] In 1923, he reported on latest currents in German psychological thought in the *American Journal of Psychology* and the following year presented "The Standpoint of *Gestalt* Psychology" in a leading English journal at the invitation of its editor.[227] None of these four men—Langfeld, Tolman, Ogden, and Allport—ever specifically identified himself as a Gestalt psychologist, but they all played a major role in its transmission to the United States. In 1922, Ogden delivered a paper at the meeting of the American Psychological Association relating to Gestalt theory, and three years earlier, Tolman, carrying out standard behaviorist experiments, "was already becoming influenced by Gestalt psychology and conceived that a rat in running a maze must be learning a lay-out pattern."[228]

By 1924, other psychologists were studying the work of the Gestalt psychologists, and getting excited about it. Few Americans during this early period identified themselves with Gestalt psychology but many found things in the work of Köhler and Koffka to stimulate them. Even Watson in the mid-1920s "struggl[ed] with Köhler's presentation of Gestalt-psychologie [but] failed to get a kick out of" it. Boring was more impressed with their experimental work, and wrote in 1924 of "its power to stimulate the great deal of research which I call good research and which I find very interesting."[229] His commitment to Titchener's structuralist approach began to weaken long before his mentor's death and, unimpressed by the various attempts to apply psychology to practical problems, he was in the early 1920s open to different views of psychology, demanding only that they be "scientific" and rigorous.[230]

As early as 1923, his graduate student Harry Helson began a dissertation on Gestalt psychology—despite his initial opposition—and by 1925 Boring was flirting seriously with Gestalt ideas.[231] That year, after a summer at Harvard, a Vassar student reported to her professor, Margaret Floy Washburn, that Boring had become a "configurationalist."[232] Boring denied the charge—"so I am a contortionist, or whatever the word is"[233]—but two months later, in reporting to Koffka that "rumor is beginning to drift in that I am a Gestalt psychologist," he seemed quite impressed with the German's ideas; "Very well, so be it. At least what I get from Köhler, added to the little I get from you, seems to be eminently good scientific sense."[234] But strong as this statement was, it was not as strong as one he had made more than six months earlier in a letter to Köhler: "I have decided that I am not a *Gestalt* psychologist but merely a scientist. *Gestalt* psychology seems to me to be nothing more than the introduction of science into psychology!"[235]

In the mid-1920s, also, the Gestalt psychologists began visiting the United States themselves and the Americans could hear first hand the ideas that excited them so. Max Wertheimer, the leader of the Gestalt school, did not cross the Atlantic during this period, and the fact that he published much less than his colleagues, especially Koffka and Köhler, kept him in the background as far as the Americans were concerned.[236] For example, in 1924, Ogden arranged a visiting appointment for Koffka at Cornell, followed by visiting professorships at Chicago and Wisconsin.[237] In 1925, "on the invitation of the program committee," he spoke before the American Psychological Association, and took part in a well-attended "Round Table Conference on the 'Gestalt-Psychologie.' "[238] During the next three years, he gave at least thirty lectures on Gestalt psychology before various groups around the United States, including the Philosophical Society at Harvard[239] and Boring tried to arrange for him to take his—Boring's—place at Harvard while he took a sabbatical leave.[240] By late 1926 it became clear that Koffka would probably settle in America, especially as he was then getting a divorce from his wife, who was planning to return to Germany, and rumors began to circulate about the salary offers he was receiving from various universities.[241] By February 1927, Wisconsin had offered him a professorship with a salary of $7,500, at a time when Boring's salary, at Harvard, was $5,500.[242] Within three months, Koffka accepted a professorship at Smith College, in Northampton, Massachusetts, with a salary rumored to be around $10,000.[243] Several commentators have complained that Smith did not give Koffka the institutional base in American psychology that a man of his stature deserved. But he seemed happier at a smaller institution than he had been at such large schools as Cornell and Wisconsin, and if the rumors about his salaries were correct, he had financial reasons to go to Northampton.[244] Meanwhile, he continued his extensive lecturing, and he and his friends continued to publish in the area of Gestalt psychology. At Smith, he even developed a small graduate program and played a major role in training such distinguished psychologists as Molly Harrower and Eleanor J. Gibson.[245] As Boring noted much later, at Smith Koffka "had great influence."[246]

Karl Bühler was not a member of the Gestalt school, but as a German in America he was often sympathetic to its cause. He was at least as talented as

Koffka, and in the eyes of many Americans, such as Terman, he was a better scientist than either Koffka or Köhler. He had been professor at the University of Vienna since 1922, and while visiting Stanford in the late 1920s he greatly impressed both the faculty and his students. But even Terman had to admit Bühler "lacked . . . culture and aristocratic bearing," factors that played, and still play, important roles in academic appointments. Worse than this, Bühler's command of the English language was "wretched," and wherever he taught he had to read his lectures "almost entirely from manuscript."[247] Previous accounts of Bühler's interactions with American psychologists have stressed his tenure in the 1940s at such colleges as St. Scholastica College in Duluth and the College of St. Thomas in St. Paul, and concluded that "he was certainly one man whom America did not welcome with open arms."[248] He returned to Europe in the early 1930s, where such Americans as Boring and Terman followed his career closely. In 1938, they and Edward C. Tolman helped him return to this country, and arranged positions for him and his wife, Charlotte Bühler, a distinguished child psychologist. For many years thereafter, Terman, at least, helped look after the Bühlers' interests.[249] Karl Bühler was *not* accepted as part of the leadership of the American psychological community, but that is no reason to conclude, as others have implied, that this lack of recognition was scandalous.

Kurt Lewin's case is in many ways more interesting, and more gratifying, than Koffka's or Karl Bühler's. As noted, Lewin's presentations at the 1929 International Congress were great successes, particularly the two films he showed of children, including his son, behaving in various situations. Like Karl Bühler's, his English was not good, but he was not afraid to use any slang or gesture in an attempt to communicate, and his audiences, both formal and informal, always seemed able to understand him.[250] Almost immediately, various American universities attempted or planned to arrange visiting appointments for him, but not until 1931 was a term at Stanford arranged for the following year. Meanwhile, psychologists described him as "the man of the hour," and "the young dynamo" of Berlin, and during the summer of 1931, when a group of six New England psychologists met for dinner, they found that the principal topic of conversation was Lewin's work.[251]

Despite this great reputation, and the fact that he thought quite highly of Lewin and his work, Terman still had to make various inquiries about Lewin before even a visiting appointment could be made at Stanford. For example, he wrote to Boring and asked

> whether Lewin is a Jew. It would not necessarily be fatal to his appointment here if he were, but it would be best for me to know the facts if I were recommending him. The few Jews we have on our Stanford faculty have no trace whatever of the objectionable traits usually attributed to Jews, and against this kind I haven't the slightest prejudice in the world.[252]

Boring had to ask around to answer Terman's question, and finally a former student of his, Carroll Pratt, who had just returned from Berlin, informed him that Lewin *was* a Jew.[253] Apparently, this did not matter, and his appointment as a visiting professor at Stanford was a success from all points of view. Terman and his students and colleagues were greatly impressed with Lewin's psychological ideas and teaching, but, more than this, grew to like him in a warm and personal way. Of all of the Gestalt psychologists, Lewin was, in Boring's words, "anything but self-important after the German manner," and, in general, was the least formal of this group. Even in Germany, while his "careful systematic building . . . [was] being carefully watched with the greatest respect by everyone," and he was having "a great many students working under him," he "seemed to be on the most friendly terms with everyone . . . a most agreeable person."[254] In 1933, when Hitler came to power, Lewin was visiting Japan, and cabled both Boring and Terman in hopes of getting a position in the United States. Both were concerned about the situation, and Terman's words about what Lewin meant to him stand in contrast to his earlier inquiries about his ethnic background:

> I have always been intending to write to you particularly to tell you how highly we appreciated Lewin. . . . His work commanded the respect of our students, both graduate and undergraduate, and of our department faculty. . . . Faculty and students became so fond of him that it was hard to let him go. I have known few people who were so alive to everything about them, or so genial and friendly."[255]

Neither Boring nor Terman was able to get Lewin a position in the United States, despite Terman's personal appeal to Alvin Johnson of the New School's University in Exile and some frantic if ineffective efforts on the part of Boring and Koffka.[256] Ogden finally arranged for him a position in Cornell's School of Home Economics—an institutional base that previous writers sympathetic to the Gestaltists have complained about—which allowed him to continue his studies of child development at the Nursery School. This was to be only the beginning of his permanent and outstanding career in the United States, which Terman and Boring followed and assisted as friends and admiring colleagues.[257]

But to many people in the United States, Gestalt psychology in the 1920s meant the work of Wolfgang Köhler, and the history of his interaction with American psychology through the mid-1930s reveals much about the way in which Gestalt ideas and Gestalt psychologists were received in America. This fact, as well as the fact that many rumors have recently been circulating concerning Köhler's relations with several American psychologists, justifies a fairly extensive treatment of this topic.[258] Köhler first had contacts with American psychology as early as 1914, before World War I began, when he was working with chimpanzees at the Anthropoid Research Station on Tenerife, in the Canary Islands. Early that year, Yerkes, then a young assistant professor at Harvard, wrote to Köhler, expressing interest in his work, asking for further information about it, and hoping to be able to join the German off the coast of Africa at the station. The outbreak of the European War, and Köhler's internment on Tenerife, soon brought an end to Yerkes's travel plans, but the two psychologists soon began to exchange reprints, and the American even arranged for John B. Watson to send Köhler a set of his articles. Yerkes also arranged to have Köhler's motion picture films of his chimpanzee experiments processed in the United States when this became impossible on the Islands. This friendly and mutually profitable exchange was marred in 1916, when Yerkes published *The Mental Life of Monkeys and Apes* and did not cite Köhler's work. And with the American entry into the War in 1917 the relationship came to a temporary close.[259]

Soon after the War, Yerkes utilized his temporary position with the National Research Council to reestablish contacts with Köhler. By 1921 the two psychologists were again exchanging books, reprints, and congratulations on each other's appointments: Köhler's at Berlin and Yerkes's at Yale. Yerkes even offered to send money to Köhler to cover the cost of the books and reprints, in view of the deterioration of the economic situation in Germany and "the unfairness of the exchange situation" but Köhler would not accept.[260] By 1923, the two men were again learning much from a correspondence they both apparently enjoyed.

Then, in 1924, Carl Murchison at Clark University arranged for Köhler to serve as visiting professor at the Worcester institution during 1925, and the reaction of most American psychologists was joyful. Terman, a Clark alumnus who had been bemoaning the condition of psychology at his alma mater, was especially pleased. As he wrote to a Clark official, "It was a splendid stroke to get Dr. Koehler to come over."[261] Both Boring and Yerkes wrote to congratulate Köhler on his appointment and were among the first to write him letters of welcome to America. Boring's welcome was particularly enthusiastic: "the psychological stock of America took a jump upward as soon as I heard you were safely on shore."[262] Once Köhler arrived in Worcester, Boring and Yerkes saw him regularly, and the visitor spoke at least once at both Harvard and Yale.[263] Boring even attended a weekly seminar led by Köhler at Clark, which he described as "great fun."[264] Meanwhile, Köhler met with other members of the American psychological community, and impressed most of them. For example, Köhler, with Koffka, attended a meeting of the Society of Experimental Psychologists as its guests, two of the very few ever to do so. During a visit to Stanford, Köhler impressed Terman as "an intellectually active man" with "youth and vigor."[265] Yerkes also recommended Köhler and Koffka to the home secretary of the National Academy of Sciences as "two of the foremost German psychologists," in an effort to get for them a place on the Academy's programs, and an official of the Rockefeller Foundation referred to Köhler's movies on apes as "interesting scientifically . . . [and] . . . highly entertaining."[266] By 1926 Ogden began arrangements for the translation and publication in English of several of Köhler's German books. He never completed these arrangements, but the fact that he began them indicates the importance to American psychology of Köhler's ideas at that time.[267]

Soon after Köhler started lecturing at Clark in January 1925, Boring and James H. Woods, the chairman of the Department of Philosophy and Psychology at Harvard, began making plans to invite Köhler to Cambridge the following fall as a Visiting Professor. Köhler himself was intrigued with the idea for a while, and wrote of being particularly interested in working with Harvard graduate students. Boring himself presented to Köhler many details about the situation at Harvard, including lists of facilities available, and concluded that "I am very anxious for you to come."[268] These plans fell through that spring, however, as Köhler concluded that his responsibilities to his colleagues in Germany were pressing and, as Boring wrote to Yerkes, he "did not feel he could extend his leave from Berlin."[269]

Köhler indicated, however, that he would welcome a visiting position at Harvard some time in the future, and Boring and Woods reacted positively to this idea, projecting such an appointment for the fall of 1926. The two Americans even began planning a curriculum into which lectures and seminars that Köhler might teach would fit, and by March 1926 were pressuring the German to accept their offer. Köhler cabled, "Sorry can not decide before May," but wrote soon afterward to explain that financial considerations made it impossible for him to teach at Harvard, as had been proposed.[270] Throughout this episode, all correspondence was polite and even cordial, and both Boring's hopes and Köhler's regrets were apparently honest. But it was a trying experience for all three men.

Another possibility for Köhler to come to Harvard opened up in December 1926, when McDougall resigned his position, and left Cambridge for Duke. Both Boring and Woods immediately thought of Köhler as McDougall's successor, and such members of their department as the distinguished philosopher Ralph Barton Perry urged that Köhler be offered the position immediately. But Boring was beginning to doubt Köhler's suitability for Harvard. The university's major need, Boring thought, was for an experimentalist working in the mainstream of American experimental psychology, unlike McDougall or Köhler. Sometime in 1925 Köhler had visited Harvard from Clark, and spoke at a departmental colloquium. Boring was greatly disappointed in the talk, and later described it as being full of "general theoretical analogies [and] unformulated psychological events [with] not [one] bit of experimentation."[271] But Harvard's philosophers, especially Woods and Perry, admired Köhler greatly and Boring, for the moment, agreed to ask the Gestalt psychologist to join the Harvard faculty.[272]

It was not easy, however, to invite Köhler to Harvard, as he did not respond to two of Boring's letters on the subject. A third letter from Boring, and one from Woods, did bring a reply, but it did not clarify the situation extensively. To be sure, some of the correspondence between these three men has apparently been lost, so the details of the episode are unclear, but even those who saw all the letters could not agree what Köhler, at least, intended. As Boring wrote to Terman, "my own interpretation of the correspondence is that he will not accept . . . [but] some at Harvard interpret the same letters as meaning that he is coming." And in the one letter of Köhler's that has survived, he was clearly ambivalent about the invitation: "When I think of you and my other friends at Harvard the choice looks simple. But when I look at the economic situation and the number of lectures to which an American Professor tends to be obligated, then my face drops."[273] In August 1927, the situation was unresolved and not until that fall did Köhler definitely notify Harvard that he would keep his Berlin professorship. He apparently wrote to Boring to apologize for keeping Harvard in suspense for as long as he had. Boring tried to be conciliatory, but he could not totally hide his annoyance at what had happened. As he wrote to Köhler, "after all what is Harvard against Berlin? . . . That you have left us in the lurch and we are still limping along is certainly not your fault, but is entirely our responsibility." It is no wonder then that he later described this period as "the summer that Köhler blew up on us."[274]

Harvard still had to appoint a successor to McDougall and the philosophers continued to urge that a European be chosen for the position. Boring still wanted an American and an experimentalist and wrote critically of European psychologists who performed "the scissors and cardboard kind of experiments [that] do not reflect favorably upon Harvard's psychology in America." In fact, he was greatly concerned about the reputation of psychology at Harvard and about "criticism from the men whose opinion I respect, and in whose judgment I concur."[275] When Köhler's name was again mentioned for the position, he blew up. "American psychologists who felt that Harvard had made a mistake with both Münsterberg and McDougall would feel that it again erred."[276] But Boring's outburst got him nowhere, as his colleagues in philosophy still wanted Köhler for Harvard. As he expressed the situation in the fall of 1928.

> The issue is out in the open. It is between A and B.
> A. Breadth of interest, vision and imagination
> B. Technical skill and knowledge within a given field.
> We want both. We can not have them. Actually they are negatively correlated.
> . . .
> Hocking, Perry and Woods are for A and thus for a renewal of the offer to Köhler.
> I am for B and thus can not conscientiously agree to Köhler.[277]

Boring was also annoyed that the philosophers were trying to tell the psychologists how to manage their affairs. His protests over the way in which the entire situation had been handled were later a major reason why philosophy and psychology at Harvard were administratively reorganized in the early 1930s.[278]

Meanwhile, Boring had been devoting all of the time that he could spare from Harvard matters to the study of the history of psychology, in preparation for the writing of his well-known book, published in 1929. This research, and his quarrels with his Harvard colleagues about Köhler, led him to reconsider his early enthusiasm for Gestalt psychology, which, after all, he had never expressed in print. Several of his friends had always been critical of the school—e.g., Margaret Floy Washburn[279]—and Boring had always been sensitive to the opinions of other psychologists. Some of them thought highly of the work of one or another Gestalt psychologist, but criticized that of others. Terman, for example, found the work of Lewin exciting, but by 1927 began to have qualms about Koffka's and Köhler's. He described a talk by Koffka at Stanford as "piffle," and, though somewhat impressed by Köhler's writings, thought little of Köhler's future as a psychologist: "I doubt . . . he will ever do much more experimenting."[280] Terman was also put off by what he felt was the propagandizing of the Gestalt psychologists, which he thought detracted from the merit of their school's ideas, and Boring began to be bothered by this aspect of his relationships with Koffka and Köhler.[281]

Of course, the Gestalt psychologists were not the only ones of the 1920s to argue that their school possessed the only valid approach to psychology, but something about their attitude especially bothered the Americans. To many, it appeared that the Gestalt psychologists had come to the United States almost as intellectual missionaries, spreading the new gospel. Wertheimer's biographer and son writes of his father as a "Gestalt Prophet" and of his views of Gestalt psychology as "indeed an all encompassing religion." In 1967, Köhler just about admitted sharing a similar perspective by quoting a remark by Lashley about Gestalt psychology: "Excellent work—but don't you have religion up your sleeve?" And as late as 1943, Köhler still implied that Gestalt psychology helped civilize American psychology.[282] The term *Mandarin* has been well used to characterize the attitudes and behavior of many of the German university professors of the period,[283] and while in some ways the entire Gestalt movement represented a revolt against traditional German university culture, in other, deeper ways the Gestalt psychologists shared many of the traits of their colleagues who made up the faculty of most German universities.[284] None of the Americans of the period ever described a Gestalt psychologist as a "Mandarin," but they probably would have easily recognized the characterization.

In 1929, *A History of Experimental Psychology* was published, and throughout the ten-page discussion of Gestalt psychology, Boring's tone was critical. Apparently he believed that he tried to be fair to the school—he later noted that "it is a question as to whether I have been favorable or unfavorable"—but such friends of Gestalt psychology as R. M. Ogden had little doubt as to Boring's actual feelings.[285] His analysis of the school continually stressed its origins as a "psychology of protest" against the older, atomistic theories of psychology. And while he admitted that "if this negative element were all that there is to *Gestalt* psychology, it would never have become an important movement," most of his discussion revolved around its criticisms of older ideas. Furthermore, he regularly stressed the continuity of Gestalt ideas with older theories, and criticized the Gestalt psychologists because they "made little effort to show the antiquity of the[ir] objection."[286] One can readily see why Ogden felt attacked.

The following year, Boring published a note on "The *Gestalt* Psychology and the *Gestalt* Movement," in which he wrote well of the former, but criticized the latter.[287] He tried to explain the note to Köhler before it appeared, sending galley proofs of it to Berlin, and expanding a bit on his own ambivalence. As he noted:

Sometimes I seem to be so enthusiastic about it and sometimes so negative. My enthusiasm is for the research that has come out under this label. . . . On the other side I get very angry about the label of *Gestalt* psychology and its solidarity as a new movement.[288]

If Köhler responded to Boring's letter or to the article, his answer has been lost, but Koffka's reaction was calm, reasoned, and cordial. He argued "that the Gestalt *movement* has been created not by the Gestalt psychologists but by their opponents," stressing that he had been "overwhelmed with the intrinsic beauty and fruitfulness of Wertheimer's new approach and . . . wanted to share the gift I received with all other psychologists." He further claimed that "many misunderstandings may have been caused by the fact that Köhler and I were invited to give so many public lectures," from which "concrete details" had to be omitted.[289] There was some validity in Koffka's points, especially in view of the long list of critical papers on Gestalt psychology that Boring presented in his history, and Koffka's attitude towards his public lectures might certainly explain why Terman thought the one he heard was "piffle."[290] Boring conceded at least some validity to

Koffka's rebuttal. But at the same time he harked back to the seminar that Köhler had given in 1925 at Harvard that had impressed him so unfavorably. Boring made sure to stress that these specific criticisms did not apply to Koffka, but though he was cordial, Boring clearly was not happy with Gestalt psychology, or at least the Gestalt school.[291]

In the years that followed, the number of articles in American psychology journals critical of Gestalt psychology, and especially of Köhler's work, increased, perhaps as more and more psychologists became familiar with the school.[292] Meanwhile, Koffka continued teaching at Smith, Boring remained at Harvard, and Köhler returned to Berlin, while still carrying a heavy load of popular lecturing. These three men all continued to correspond regularly, and cordially, with each other and all continued their scientific work. Boring for example, drifted toward behaviorism and published *The Physical Dimensions of Consciousness,* an attack on dualism that he later spoke of as "immature" and which a friendly colleague later called a "silly little thing."[293] In Germany, the rise of Hitler did not immediately affect Köhler, as he was an "Aryan," but he clearly felt uncomfortable under the Nazis and was one of the few non-Jewish scientists in Germany to oppose the regime.[294] In December 1933, the Harvard Division of Philosophy and Psychology asked Köhler to come to Cambridge as the third William James Lecturer, after John Dewey and Arthur O. Lovejoy, to deliver a course of ten or twelve public lectures, and conduct a seminar for graduate students. Boring himself wrote to Köhler that *both* the philosophers and psychologists in the division wanted the Gestalt psychologist to accept the appointment, and that he himself was especially hopeful of hearing Köhler again. Köhler responded as he did to so many previous invitations from Harvard, writing that he would love to accept "this invitation, which I regard as an unusual honour," and stressing that "it should have been impossible for me to accept without knowing about your point of view." He did not accept immediately, citing the difficult problems he faced at the University of Berlin with regard to the Nazi-controlled administration.[295]

Köhler soon afterward accepted the invitation, and arrived in Cambridge in September 1934 to begin his lectures and seminar. Boring attended the series of formal talks and apparently hoped to see a good deal of Köhler, arranging at least one social event for the visitor and his wife. But on the whole he was greatly disappointed in that Köhler spent most of his time with Harvard's distinguished philosophers, especially Perry, and the two psychologists rarely interacted. By November, the situation became so bad that Boring felt that he had to write to Köhler, because "things are so disposed that we are not thrown together for conversation," in order to discuss some points that had been raised in the lectures.[296] But, worst of all from Boring's perspective, he felt strongly that Köhler's lectures were very, very poor. Other psychologists agreed with Boring, and when the lectures were published four years later as *The Place of Value in a World of Facts,*[297] despite some very favorable reviews in philosophy journals and in the popular press,[298] the reaction from professional psychologists was typically quite negative.[299] In 1934, at least one psychologist wrote to Boring that the single lecture of Köhler that he heard did not impress him, and Boring's reply reveals much:

> You commented on being disappointed in a lecture which you heard recently. I can say only that I heard the whole series and am terribly disappointed, and a little humiliated at the knowledge that I took the time to go to them. The content was not well informed nor related to current knowledge. The ideas were not important or clear. Most of the argument was childishly elementary, although I caught suggestions of something sinister behind the scenes once in a while—but I was never sure. The vocal presentation was dull and tiresome, although the literary exposition was, if you could grasp it, exceptionally able. This then is what we applaud so heartily![300]

To be sure, Boring himself was at a critical point in his life, and was soon to undergo psychoanalysis in an attempt to free himself from the despondency that plagued him throughout the mid-1930s.[301] But his criticisms of Köhler were as much intellectual as personal. Apparently, soon after Köhler completed his William James lectures, the philosophers at Harvard again urged that he be appointed professor at the university and, apparently, with the situation in Germany worsening, Köhler was more open to such an appointment than he ever had been before. But Boring, as director of the Psychological Laboratory, and as head of the Department of Psychology within the Division of Philosophy and Psychology, again adamantly opposed the appointment.[302] This opposition was final and lost him several of his Harvard friends, which in turn contributed to his despondency, and led also to the rumors about the relations between Köhler and Boring that are still heard in the late 1970s.[303] In any event, by the end of 1935 Köhler had settled at Swarthmore College where he established an institutional base for his work comparable to Koffka's at Smith. There he played a major role in training such distinguished psychologists as Mary Henle, Solomon Asch, and Robert B. MacLeod. Within a year or two Boring and Köhler were again corresponding cordially, and by the mid-1940s Boring readily admitted Köhler's great influence on American psychology. In fact, as soon as he became a U.S. citizen, Köhler was immediately elected to the National Academy of Sciences.[304]

Closing Comments

It is difficult, of course, to end an essay gracefully when its conclusions have already been presented and discussed in its Introduction. However, for one appearing in a volume of similar papers, a few historiographic remarks may be appropriate. If this essay does nothing else, it at least illustrates that the social history of psychology can be written. That is, psychologists do not work in a social vacuum, and a history of the people who identified themselves as psychologists, and of the community and profession in which they worked, can, perhaps, be as interesting as any discussion of the history of psychological ideas. Moreover, such a social history of psychology can reveal the ways in which psychological ideas originated, developed and changed through time, and influenced the world in which they emerged, in a way that a traditional history of psychological ideas may miss. The point here is *not* that the history of ideas is unimportant, or that it should be abandoned, or that its practitioners write mediocre history. The other articles in this volume well illustrate the very real strengths of such an "internal" approach to the history of psychology. But there are other ways to write this history and, when this essay was first written—in 1974—few of those who wrote the history of psychology realized the possibility of other approaches. Since that date, other historians and psychologists have begun writing excellent social history of psychology, and this essay may therefore be viewed as one of a several examples of the emergence of the new historiographic approach. Therefore, if it serves as a marker in the growth of the historiography of psychology, this paper will have well served its exploratory purpose.

ACKNOWLEDGMENTS AND NOTE ON SOURCES

The first version of this essay was prepared while the author was Visiting Post-Doctoral Research Fellow in History of Science and Technology, Division of Medical Sciences, National Museum of History and Technology, Smithsonian Institution. It was first presented as part of a symposium on "The Development of American Science in the Nineteenth and Twentieth Century," at the 140th meeting of the American Association for the Advancement of Science, 1 March 1974, San Francisco, California. It could not have been written without the help of many individuals. A large number of psychologists granted the author interviews, and these men and women are cited in the notes to this essay where appropriate. Others took the time to read and comment on all or part of earlier drafts, and this final version, different in many respects from the text that was first presented in San Francisco, incorporates the author's serious consideration of their very helpful and insightful criticisms. Among those who have contributed to this monograph in this and other ways are such distinguished scholars as Michele Aldrich, Mitchell G. Ash, Josef Brožek, John C. Burnham, James H. Capshew, William Coleman, Hamilton Cravens, Robert C. Davis, Helen F. Eckerson, Leonard W. Ferguson, Laurel Furumoto, Robert H. Kargon, Kathleen Kelly, Cedric Larson, Elizabeth Lomax, Nicholas Pastore, John A. Popplestone, Franz Samelson, and especially the author's colleagues at Worcester Polytechnic Institute. Finally, the foundation of this essay is the documentary richness of a large number of manuscript collections, listed below. Grateful acknowledgment is made of the very kind and extensive help of the custodians of these collections, and to the literary heirs of the authors of the documents, who gave the author the permission that he needed to quote from unpublished material.

American Psychological Association (APA) Papers, Manuscript Division, Library of Congress, Washington, D.C.

James R. Angell Papers, Yale University Archives, New Haven, Conn.

Bird T. Baldwin files, Faculty Information Records, University of Iowa Archives, Iowa City, Iowa

Walter Van Dyke Bingham Papers, Carnegie-Mellon University Archives, Pittsburgh, Penn.

Edwin G. Boring Papers, Harvard University Archives, Cambridge, Mass.

Elsie O. Bregman Papers, Archives of the History of American Psychology, University of Akron, Akron, Ohio

Leonard Carmichael Papers, American Philosophical Society Library, Philadelphia, Penn.

James McKeen Cattell Papers, Manuscript Division, Library of Congress, Washington, D.C.

Harry L. Hollingworth Papers, Archives of the History of American Psychology, University of Akron, Akron, Ohio

Institute of Child Welfare Papers, University of Iowa Archives, Iowa City, Iowa

Truman L. Kelley Papers, Harvard University Archives, Cambridge, Mass.

Kurt Koffka Papers, Archives of the History of American Psychology, University of Akron, Akron, Ohio

Wolfgang Köhler Papers, American Philosophical Society Library, Philadelphia, Penn.

Laura Spelman Rockefeller Memorial (LSRM) Archives, Rockefeller Archive Center, North Tarrytown, New York

Kurt Lewin files, Faculty Information Records, University of Iowa Archives, Iowa City, Iowa

George and Jean Mandler Papers, Archives of the History of American Psychology, University of Akron, Akron, Ohio

Hugo Münsterberg Papers, Boston Public Library, Boston, Mass.

Department (and Division) of Philosophy Papers, Harvard University Archives, Cambridge, Mass.

Rockefeller Foundation (RF) Archives, Rockefeller Archive Center, North Tarrytown, New York

Walter Dill Scott Presidential Papers, Northwestern University Archives, Evanston, Illinois

Carl Emil Seashore files, Faculty Information Records, University of Iowa, Iowa City, Iowa

B. M. Stigall Papers, University of Missouri Archives, Columbia, Missouri

Lewis M. Terman Papers, Stanford University Archives, Stanford, California

Edward B. Titchener Papers, Cornell University Archives, Ithaca, New York

Robert M. Yerkes Papers, Yale University Archives, New Haven, Conn.

NOTES

Details concerning manuscript collections cited will be found at the end of this essay under the heading "Acknowledgments and Note on Sources."

1. Cattell, "Some Psychological Experiments," *Science* 63 (1 January 1926): 1–8; (8 January 1926): 29–35. This paper, with many others by Cattell, is reprinted in *James McKeen Cattell, Man of Science*, 2 vols., ed. A. T. Poffenberger (Lancaster, Pa.: The Science Press, 1947), 2: 381–406. In general, the

versions of Cattell's papers cited in this essay will be those found in these volumes. (Hereafter cited as *Man of Science.*)

2. Ibid., 2: 404.

3. E.g., ibid., 2: 381. Cattell's concern with quantification runs throughout his career, and relates directly to an early exposure to the ideas of Comtean Positivism. See Michael M. Sokal, ed., *An Education in Psychology: James McKeen Cattell's Journal and Letters from Germany and England, 1880–1888* (Cambridge, Mass.: MIT Press, 1981), p. 16; idem, "The Education and Psychological Career of James McKeen Cattell, 1860–1904" (Ph.D. dissertation, Program in History of Science and Technology, Case Western Reserve University, 1972; University Microfilms order no. 73-6341).

4. E.g., Cattell, "Some Psychological Experiments," pp. 384, 389. See also Cattell, "Über die Zeit der Erkennung und Benennung von Schriftzeichen, Bildern und Farben," *Philosophische Studien* 2 (1885): 636–50; idem, "On the Time Required for Recognizing and Naming Letters and Words, Pictures and Colors," in *Man of Science* 1: 13–25; idem, "The Time Taken Up By Cerebral Operations," *Mind* 11 (1886): 220–42, 377–92, 524–38; *Man of Science,* 1: 41–94.

5. E.g., Cattell, "Some Psychological Experiments," p. 395; Edward Lee Thorndike, "Animal Intelligence," *Psychological Review Monographs* 2, no. 8 (1898).

6. Besides *Science,* Cattell edited the *Psychological Review* (1894–1904), *Popular Science Monthly* (1900–1915), the *American Naturalist* (1907–44), *Scientific Monthly* (1915–43), *School and Society* (1915–39), and the first six editions (1906, 1910, 1921, 1927, 1933, 1938) of *American Men of Science.*

7. On the failure of Cattell's testing program, see Michael M. Sokal, "James McKeen Cattell and the Failure of Anthropometric Mental Testing, 1890–1901," in *The Problematic Science: Psychology in Nineteenth-Century Thought,* ed. William R. Woodward and Mitchell G. Ash (New York: Praeger, 1982), pp. 322–45.

8. See Carol Singer Gruber, "Academic Freedom at Columbia University, 1917–1918: The Case of James McKeen Cattell," *AAUP Bulletin* 58 (1972): 297–305.

9. See "Proceedings of the Thirty-Second Annual Meeting of the American Psychological Association," *Psychological Bulletin* 21 (1924): 69–120; Cattell to Henry Cabot Lodge, 24 May 1923, 1 June 1923, 16 June 1923, Cattell Papers.

10. Edwin G. Boring to Cattell, 9 December 1927, Boring Papers; *Ninth International Congress of Psychology: Proceedings and Papers* (Princeton, N.J.: Psychological Review Co., 1930).

11. Of course, the overview of this topic presented in this essay reflects the author's own interests and perspective, and a totally different paper could be, and, in fact, has been, written on the same general topic. See the brilliant paper by John C. Burnham, "The New Psychology: From Narcissism to Social Control," in *Change and Continuity in Twentieth-Century America: The 1920's,* ed. John Braeman, Robert H. Bremner, and David Brody (Columbus, Ohio: Ohio State University Press, 1968).

12. It can be argued—with much justification—that American psychology was more open than most other academic areas during the 1920s and even in the years before the decade. After all, a Roman Catholic priest—Edward A. Pace—was a charter member of the American Psychological Association, and two women—Mary W. Calkins and Margaret F. Washburn—had served as its president. But of the other leaders of psychology who did not fit into the general pattern, most conformed in more ways than they differed. For example, among the readily identifiable Jews, one—Joseph Jastrow—was the son of a leading "Liberal" rabbi, and another—Hugo Münsterberg—had himself baptized when he came of age. See *DAB,* 13: 337–39; 3d supp., 383–84; Matthew Hale, Jr., *Human Science and Social Order: Hugo Münsterberg and the Origins of Applied Psychology* (Philadelphia: Temple University Press, 1980), pp. 19–20. In the same way, of the very few individuals who were not native born, at least two— George S. Fullerton and Charles H. Judd—were born in India of missionary parents and another two— Edward B. Titchener and Münsterberg—came to the United States as professors. See *DAB,* 7: 66–67; 18: 564–65; 4th supp., 443–46.

13. A popular history that well illustrates this aspect of the 1920s is Frederick Lewis Allen, *Only Yesterday: An Informal History of the Nineteen-Twenties* (New York: Harper and Brothers, 1931).

14. Lewis, *Babbitt* (New York: Harcourt, Brace and Company, 1922).

15. Robert V. Guthrie, *Even the Rat Was White: A Historical View of Psychology* (New York: Harper and Row, 1976).

16. Leon Kamin, *The Science and Politics of I.Q.* (Kensington, Md.: Lawrence Erlbaum Associates, 1974); Stephen Jay Gould, *The Mismeasure of Man* (New York: W. W. Norton, 1981).

17. Anne Anastasi, "Reminiscences of a Differential Psychologist," in *The Psychologists,* ed. T. S. Krawiec, vol. 1 (New York: Oxford University Press, 1972), pp. 3–37.

18. See the articles cited in Burnham, "The New Psychology"; in Lucille C. Birnbaum, "Behaviorism in the 1920's," *American Quarterly* 7 (1955): 15–30; and below.

19. Stephen Leacock, "A Manual of the New Mentality," *Harper's* 148 (1924): 471–80.

20. Cattell, "University Presidents Who Have Been Psychologists," *Scientific Monthly* 45 (1937): 473–77.

21. See Burnham, "The New Psychology," and Birnbaum, "Behaviorism in the 1920's."

22. Interview with Anne Anastasi, 20 November 1973.

23. Jean Matter Mandler and George Mandler, "The Diaspora of Experimental Psychology: The Gestaltists and Others," in *The Intellectual Migration: Europe and America, 1930–1960,* ed. Donald Fleming and Bernard Bailyn (Cambridge, Mass.: Belknap Press of Harvard University Press, 1969), pp. 371–419. See also Wolfgang Köhler, "The Scientists from Europe and Their New Environment," in *The Cultural Migration: The European Scholar in America,* ed. W. Rex Crawford (Philadelphia: University of Pennsylvania Press, 1953), pp. 112–37.

24. For a similar conclusion, see also *some* of the papers in *Schools of Psychology: A Symposium,* ed. David L. Krantz (New York: Appleton-Century-Crofts, 1969).

25. Robert S. Woodworth, *Contemporary Schools of Psychology* (New York: Ronald Press Co., 1931).

26. Woodworth, "Dynamic Psychology," in *Psychologies of 1930,* ed. Carl Murchison (Worcester, Mass.: Clark University Press, 1930), pp. 327–36.

27. Burnham, "Psychology, Anthropology and Sociology: Change in American Thought in the 1920's" (M.A. thesis, Department of History, University of Wisconsin, 1952).

28. The wide range of books, dissertations, and articles on this topic, both older and recent, makes an elaborate history of psychological testing during the 1920s unnecessary here. What follows, therefore, is a largely interpretive overview. Among the more important general discussions of testing during this period are: Hamilton Cravens, *The Triumph of Evolution: American Scientists and the Heredity-Environment Controversy, 1900–1941* (Philadelphia: University of Pennsylvania Press, 1978), chap. 7, "Mental Testing," pp. 224–65; Joseph Peterson, *Early Conceptions and Tests of Intelligence* (Yonkers, N.Y.: World Book Co., 1925); Thomas Pogue Weinland, "A History of the I.Q. in America, 1890–1941" (Ph.D. dissertation, Joint Committee on Graduate Instruction, Columbia University, 1970; University Microfilms, order no. 73-8991); Russell Marks, "Testers, Trackers and Trustees: The Ideology of the Intelligence Testing Movement in America, 1900–1954" (Ph.D. dissertation, School of Education, University of Illinois, 1972; University Microfilms, order no. 73-17,311); Andrew T. Wylie, "A Brief History of Mental Tests," *Teachers College Record* 23 (1922): 19–33. Other important specific discussions are cited below where appropriate.

29. Cattell, "The Interpretation of Intelligence Tests," *Scientific Monthly* 18 (1924), 508–16; *Man of Science,* 2: 376.

30. Cattell, "Some Psychological Experiments," p. 396.

31. E.g., Lewis M. Terman, *The Measurement of Intelligence: An Explanation of and a Complete Guide for the Use of the Stanford Revision of the Binet-Simon Intelligence Scale* (Boston: Houghton Mifflin, 1916); Robert M. Yerkes et al., *A Point Scale for Measuring Mental Ability* (Baltimore, Md.: Warwick and York, 1915).

32. Weinland, "The I.Q. in America," pp. 120–25.

33. Yerkes to Bingham, 13 January 1916, Yerkes Papers; Melvin E. Haggerty to Bingham, 22 March 1916, 1 April 1916; Bingham to Haggerty, 30 March 1916; A. H. Sutherland to Bingham, 4 November 1916; Bingham Papers.

34. See Yerkes to Bingham, 15 January 1917, Yerkes Papers; J. W. Baird to Bingham, 19 January 1917; Bingham to J. Carleton Bell, 23 January 1917; Bell to Bingham, 25 January 1917; Bingham Papers.

35. Yerkes to Bingham and Scott, 6 April 1917, 25 April 1917; Scott to Yerkes, 14 April 1917; Bingham to Yerkes, 23 April 1917, 10 May 1917; Bingham Papers.

36. See Thomas Marley Camfield, "Psychologists at War: The History of American Psychology and the First World War" (Ph.D. dissertation, Department of History, University of Texas, 1969; University Microfilms, order no. 70-10,766); Daniel J. Kevles, "Testing the Army's Intelligence: Psychologists and the Military in World War I," *Journal of American History* 55 (1968): 565–81.

37. Cattell, "Practical Psychology," *Science* 53 (14 January 1921): 30–35; *Man of Science,* 2: 359. Some psychologists, however, have argued recently that the tests in general were not very useful to the army. For example, see Franz Samelson, "World War I Intelligence Testing and the Development of Psychology," *Journal of the History of the Behavioral Sciences* 13 (1977): 274–82.

38. Weinland, "The I.Q. in America," p. 132; Bingham to Frederic L. Wells, 2 July 1919, Bingham Papers.

39. Margaret F. Washburn to Bingham, 5 October 1917; Ernest H. Koch, Jr., to Bingham, 23 October 1917; Bingham to Koch, 31 October 1917; Bingham to E. P. Frost, 6 November 1917; Bingham Papers. "The Measurement and Utilization of Brain Power in the Army," *Science* 49 (7 March 1919): 221–26; (14 March 1919), pp. 252–59. Even before the war had ended, however, a little-known pamphlet, entitled *Army Mental Tests,* was published in Washington under the editorship of Terman and Mabel R. Fernald. See Nicholas Pastore, "The Army Intelligence Tests and Walter Lippmann," *Journal of the History of the Behavioral Sciences* 14 (1978): 316–27.

40. Watson to Yerkes, 29 March 1919, Yerkes Papers.

41. *New York Times*, 17 July 1919, p. 8; 23 September 1919, p. 17; Lewis M. Terman, "Intelligence Tests in Colleges and Universities," *School and Society* 13 (1921): 481–94; Weinland, "The I.Q. in America," p. 147. See Bingham to Frederic Palmer, 20 April 1921; Pennsylvania State Educational Association to A. A. Hamerschlag, 8 July 1919; Memorandum, "Society for the Promotion of Engineering Education; Committee No. 22 on Intelligence Tests," 1 November 1919; Bingham Papers.

42. H. C. Morrison to Stigall, 29 September 1920; P. C. Harris to Stigall, 1 February 1921; J. Carlton Bell to Stigall, 23 February 1921; Stigall Papers.

43. Seashore, "Sectioning Classes on the Basis of Ability," *School and Society* 15 (1922): 353–58.

44. Weinland, "The I.Q. in America," pp. 154–57; William M. Proctor, "The Use of Psychological Tests in Educational and Vocational Guidance of High School Pupils," *Journal of Educational Research Monographs*, June 1921, no. 1. See also Roger F. Aubrey, "Historical Development of Guidance and Counseling and Implications for the Future," *Personnel and Guidance Journal* 55 (1977): 228–95.

45. Weinland, "The I.Q. in America," pp. 150–52.

46. Dewey, *School and Society* (Chicago: University of Chicago Press, 1899); Lawrence A. Cremin, *The Transformation of the School: Progressivism in American Education, 1876–1957* (New York: Random House, 1961); Raymond E. Callahan, *Education and the Cult of Efficiency: A Study of the Social Forces that Have Shaped the Administration of the Public Schools* (Chicago: University of Chicago Press, 1962); Helen L. Horowitz, "The Progressive Education Movement After World War I," *History of Education Quarterly* 11 (1971): 79–84.

47. Lee J. Cronbach, "Mental Tests and the Creation of Opportunity," *Proceedings of the American Philosophical Society* 114 (1970): 480–87; Weinland, "The I.Q. in America," pp. 154–57; Matthew T. Downey, *Carl Campbell Brigham: Scientist and Educator* (Princeton, N.J.: Educational Testing Service, 1961), p. 23. It was not until after World War II, however, when college applications rose tremendously, that the older CEEB essay examinations were generally replaced by the SAT. See Diane Ravitch, "The College Boards," *New York Times Magazine*, 4 May 1975, pp. 12ff.

48. Cattell, "Some Psychological Experiments," p. 394; Seashore to Cora B. Hillis, 14 February 1920, Institute of Child Welfare Papers.

49. Burnham, "The New Psychology," pp. 357, 373, 377; Birnbaum, "Behaviorism in the 1920's."

50. Yerkes, editor, *Psychological Examining in the Army*, National Academy of Sciences, *Memoirs* 15 (1921): 698–707.

51. Gilbert G. Gonzalez, "Racism, Education, and the Mexican Community in Los Angeles, 1920–30," *Societas—A Review of Social History* 4 (1974): 287–301.

52. Weinland, "The I.Q. in America," pp. 157–65.

53. Yerkes, *Psychological Examining*, pp. 707, 735.

54. Ibid.; Weinland, "The I.Q. in America," pp. 162–63.

55. Grant, *The Passing of the Great Race; or, The Racial Basis of European History* (New York: Charles Scribner's Sons, 1916, 1918, 1920, 1926).

56. Stoddard, *The Revolt Against Civilization* (New York: Charles Scribner's Sons, 1923); Humphrey, "Men and Half-Men," *Scribner's Magazine* 73 (1923): 284–87. It is interesting to note that Scribner's published much of the avowedly racist literature of this period. See also Mark Aldrich, "Progressive Economists and Scientific Racism," *Phylon* 40 (1979): 1–14.

57. McDougall, *Is America Safe for Democracy?* (New York: Charles Scribner's Sons, 1921).

58. Brigham, *A Study of American Intelligence* (Princeton, N.J.: Princeton University Press, 1923); Gould, *America: A Family Matter* (New York: Charles Scribner's Sons, 1920). The close friendship shared by Brigham, Gould, and Yerkes, which helped shape the views of each, can be traced in detail in the Yerkes Papers.

59. Yerkes, "Testing the Human Mind," *Atlantic Monthly* 121 (1923): 358–70.

60. Yerkes to Albert Johnson, 11 February 1921, Yerkes Papers; Thomas F. Gossett, *Race: The History of an Idea in America* (Dallas, Tex.: Southern Methodist University Press, 1963), p. 373; Leon J. Kamin, "The Science and Politics of I.Q.," *Social Research* 41 (1974): 387–425; idem, *The Science and Politics of I.Q.* For a more balanced analysis, see Franz Samelson, "On the Science and Politics of the I.Q.," *Social Research* 42 (1975): 467–88.

61. John Higham, *Strangers in the Land: Patterns of American Nativism, 1860–1925* (New Brunswick, N.J.: Rutgers University Press, 1955), pp. 306–24; Helen F. Eckerson, "Immigration and National Origins," *Annals* 367 (1966): 4–14.

62. Terman to Bingham, 27 May 1921, Bingham Papers; Terman, "Adventures in Stupidity," *Scientific Monthly* 14 (1922): 24–40; "Were We Born That Way?" *World's Work* 40 (1922): 656–60.

63. Eddie Baker to E. D. Starbuck, 1 November 1926, Seashore files.

64. Gossett, *Race*, pp. 372–73; Heywood Broun and George Britt, *Christians Only: A Study in*

Prejudice (New York: Vanguard Press, 1931); Daniel J. Kevles, *The Physicists: The History of a Scientific Community in Modern America* (New York: Alfred A. Knopf, 1978), pp. 211–13, 278–79; Bruce Kuklick, *The Rise of American Philosophy: Cambridge, Massachusetts, 1860–1930* (New Haven, Conn.: Yale University Press, 1977), pp. 455–58.

65. Brigham to Yerkes, 7 November 1927, Yerkes Papers; Edwin G. Conklin to Terman, 6 February 1923, Terman Papers.

66. J. W. Baird to Bingham, 17 June 1916, Bingham Papers; Boring to Leonard Carmichael, 8 January 1931, Boring Papers.

67. Boring to Carmichael, 2 June 1925, 26 September 1935; Carmichael to Boring, 28 June 1934, Carmichael Papers; Carol Travis, interview with Harry Harlow, *Psychology Today* 6, no. 11 (April 1973): 72–73.

68. Cattell, "The Interpretation of Intelligence Tests," pp. 377–80.

69. Boring, "Intelligence as the Tests Test It," *New Republic*, 6 June 1923, pp. 35–37.

70. Boring, "Facts and Fancies of Immigration," ibid., 25 April 1923, pp. 245–46. See also Yerkes to Boring, 2 September 1922, Boring Papers; Yerkes to Brigham, 3 January 1923; Boring to Yerkes, 23 March 1923, 2 April 1923, Yerkes Papers; Boring to Brigham, 23 March 1923, Boring Papers.

71. Frank N. Freeman, "An Evaluation of American Intelligence," *School Review* 31 (1923): 627–28; A. J. Snow, *American Journal of Psychology* 34 (1923): 304–7; Kimball Young, *Science* (8 June 1923): 666–70.

72. Truman L. Kelly, *Interpretation of Educational Measurement* (Yorkers, N.Y.: World Book Co., 1927). This book summarizes many of the inconsistencies of these tests, and had a great effect on Brigham's later work. See Weinland, "The I.Q. in America," pp. 241–42. An earlier analysis of these tests, stimulated by Brigham's book, made many similar points, but was written by a social worker and a psychiatrist. See Maurice B. Hexter and Abraham Myerson, "13.77 versus 12.05: A Study in Probable Error," *Mental Hygiene* 8 (1924): 69–82.

73. *Literary Digest*, 9 June 1923, pp. 56–57; Charles Leonard Stone, *American Economic Review* 13 (1923): 523.

74. Bagley, "On the Correlation of Mental and Motor Abilities in School Children," *American Journal of Psychology* 12 (1901): 193–205.

75. Bagley, "Educational Determinism; or Democracy and I.Q.," *School and Society* 15 (1922): 373–84; Terman, "The Psychological Determinist; or Democracy and the I.Q.," *Journal of Educational Research* 6 (1922): 57–62; Bagley, "Professor Terman's Determinism: A Rejoinder," ibid., pp. 372–85. See also Weinland, "The I.Q. in America," pp. 197–205.

76. Lippmann, "The Mental Age of Americans," *New Republic*, 25 October 1922, pp. 213–15; idem, "The Mystery of the 'A' Men," ibid., 1 November 1922, 246–48; idem, "The Reliability of Intelligence Tests," ibid., 8 November 1922, pp. 275–77; idem, "The Abuse of the Tests," ibid., 15 November 1922, pp. 297–98; idem, "Tests of Hereditary Intelligence," ibid., 22 November 1922, pp. 328–30; idem, "A Future for the Tests," ibid., 29 November 1922, pp. 9–11. Lippmann's attacks, and the controversy that followed them, have been well analyzed by Nicholas Pastore, in "The Army Intelligence Tests and Walter Lippmann," and "In Defense of Walter Lippmann," *American Psychologist* 30 (1975): 940–42. See also Weinland, "The I.Q. in America," pp. 184–97.

77. Terman, "The Great Conspiracy, or The Impulse Imperious of Intelligence Testers, Psychoanalyzed and Exposed by Mr. Lippmann," *New Republic*, 27 December 1922, pp. 116–20; Lippmann, "The Great Confusion: A Reply to Mr. Terman," ibid., 3 January 1923, pp. 145–46. (It should be noted that Terman's reference to psychoanalysis was sarcastic, since he shared with most American psychologists of this decade an extreme distaste for what they felt to be the totally unscientific work of Freud and his disciples. Of course, this general topic could well form a section of this paper, but that is now impossible. For Cattell's own view, see "Some Psychological Experiments," *Man of Science*, 2: 389.) Lippmann and Terman continued their debate for a while, and other correspondents also made their views known. See "Correspondence," *New Republic*, 17 January 1923, pp. 201–2; 7 February 1923, pp. 289–90.

78. "Another War Beginning," *New York Times*, 28 December 1922, p. 16. See Terman to Yerkes, 8 January 1923, Yerkes Papers.

79. Yerkes to Lippmann, 28 November 1922, 4 January 1923, 23 January 1923; Lippmann to Yerkes, 6 December 1922, 9 January 1923; Yerkes Papers. Another account of the Lippmann-Terman controversy is Lee J. Cronbach, "Five Decades of Public Controversy Over Mental Testing," *American Psychologist* 30 (1975): 1–14.

80. See Yerkes to Terman, 2 January 1923; Terman to Yerkes, 8 January 1923; Yerkes Papers. Boring, meanwhile, had written to Terman, telling him that he agreed with most of Lippmann's arguments. In response Terman sent an undated postcard claiming to have received "30 or 40 letters" supporting his position. See Boring Papers.

81. Weinland, "The I.Q. in America," pp. 248–51. See Brigham et al., "Second Annual Report of the Commission on Scholastic Aptitude Tests," *Twenty-Seventh Annual Report of the Secretary of the College Entrance Examination Board* (New York: CEEB, 1927).

82. Helen Marshall to Terman, 22 October 1921; Florence Fuller to Terman, 11 March 1922, 3 April 1922; Terman Papers. See also Kelley, *The Interpretation of Educational Measurement.*

83. See Cravens, *The Triumph of Evolution,* pp. 230–35; Weinland, "The I.Q. in America," pp. 210–24.

84. Boas, "This Nordic Nonsense," *Forum* 74 (1925): 502–11. See also Boas, "Fallacies of Racial Inferiority," *Current History* 25 (1927): 676–82.

85. Arthur Woods to Nicholas Murray Butler, 28 May 1925; Boas, "An Investigation of Hereditary and Environmental Influences upon the Development of Man," LSRM Archives.

86. Mead, "Group Intelligence Tests and Linguistic Disability among Italian Children," *School and Society* 25 (1927): 465–68; idem, "Autobiography," in *A History of Psychology in Autobiography,* vol. 6, ed. Gardner Lindzey (Englewood Cliffs, N.J.: Prentice-Hall, 1974), pp. 295–326.

87. Klineberg, "Autobiography," in *A History of Psychology in Autobiography,* vol. 6, pp. 161–82; idem, "Racial Differences in Speed and Accuracy," *Journal of Abnormal and Social Psychology* 22 (1927): 273–77.

88. See Quinn McNemar, "Sampling in Psychological Research," *Psychological Bulletin* 37 (1940): 331–65.

89. Klineberg, "A Study of Psychological Differences Between 'Racial' and National Groups in Europe," *Archives of Psychology,* 1931, no. 132.

90. Klineberg, *Negro Intelligence and Selective Migration* (New York: Columbia University Press, 1934).

91. Brigham to Terman, 27 December 1927, Terman Papers; Klineberg, "Autobiography," p. 167; Downey, *C. C. Brigham,* pp. 26–27; Brigham, "Intelligence Tests of Immigrant Groups," *Psychological Review* 37 (1930): 158–65.

92. R. B. Cattell, "A Culture-Free Intelligence Test," *Journal of Educational Psychology* 31 (1940): 161–79; 32 (1941): 81–100.

93. E.g., Jensen, "How Much Can We Boost I.Q. and Scholastic Achievement?" *Harvard Educational Review* 39 (1969): 1–123.

94. Anastasi, "Heredity, Environment, and the Question 'How?'" *Psychological Review* 65 (1958): 197–208; Cravens, *The Triumph of Evolution,* pp. 269–74.

95. Sokal, "James McKeen Cattell and the Failure of Anthropometric Mental Testing." Much of this discussion follows this article.

96. In the 1890s, psychology was the new science, and universities were regularly establishing new laboratories—twenty-six were created between 1890 and 1899; see C. R. Garvey, "List of American Psychology Laboratories," *Psychological Bulletin* 26 (1929): 652–60—and offering high salaries to psychologists. Cattell, for example, doubled his salary in moving to Columbia University from the University of Pennsylvania in 1891.

97. In the 1890s the testers knew that by concentrating on physical measurements they were ignoring what was known as the "higher mental processes." See James Mark Baldwin, et al., "Physical and Mental Tests," *Psychological Review* 5 (1898): 172–79. Throughout the 1920s, many psychologists admitted that they did *not* have a precise definition for intelligence. See Cattell, "The Interpretation of Intelligence Tests"; Boring, "Intelligence as the Tests Test It."

98. In the 1890s, one of the first attacks on the testing movement came from a student of Edward Bradford Titchener (Stella Sharp, "Individual Psychology: A Study in Psychological Method," *American Journal of Psychology* 10 (1898): 329–91), and the statistical analyses of Cattell's data that showed them to be useless were performed by Clark Wissler ("The Correlation of Mental and Physical Tests," *Psychological Review Monographs,* 1901, no. 6), who had been trained by Boas. In the 1920s, the attacks by Boring were sooned followed by those of Bagley, an educator, and Boas, an anthropologist.

99. This point, of course, is the major thrust of Cravens, *The Triumph of Evolution.*

100. See Donald S. Napoli, *Architects of Adjustment: The History of the Psychological Profession in the United States* (Port Washington, N.Y.: Kennikat Press, 1981).

101. For a brilliant analysis of the parallel situation regarding the physical sciences, technology, and the engineering sciences, see Edwin. T. Layton, Jr., "Mirror-Image Twins: The Communities of Science and Technology in Nineteenth Century America," *Technology and Culture* 12 (1971)): 562–80.

102. In addition to Napoli, *Architects of Adjustment,* two general histories of industrial psychology in the United States are Leonard W. Ferguson, *The Heritage of Industrial Psychology* (Hartford, Conn.: Finlay Press, 1963–68), and Loren Baritz's interesting if one-sided analysis, *The Servants of Power: A History of the Use of Social Science in American Industry* (Middletown, Conn.: Wesleyan University Press, 1960).

103. Frank G. Coolsen, "Pioneers in the Development of Advertising," *Journal of Marketing* 12 (1947): 80–86; Gale, "On the Psychology of Advertising," *Psychological Studies* (Minneapolis: by the author, 1900).

104. See Jacob Z. Jacobson, *Scott of Northwestern* (Chicago: Louis Mariano, 1951); Edmund C. Lynch, "Walter Dill Scott: Pioneer Industrial Psychologist," *Business History Review* 42 (1966): 149–70; David P. Kuna, "The Concept of Suggestion in the Early History of Advertising Psychology," *Journal of the History of the Behavioral Sciences* 12 (1976): 347–53; Kuna, "The Psychology of Advertising, 1896–1916" (Ph.D dissertation, Department of Psychology, University of New Hampshire, 1976; University Microfilms, order no. 76-26,875).

105. Jacobson, *Scott*, pp. 70–74; Coolsen, "Pioneers," pp. 83–84.

106. Scott, *Theory of Advertising* (Boston: Small, Maynard, 1903), first appeared serially in John Lee Mahin's *Mahin's Magazine*. See Coolsen, "Pioneers," pp. 83–84.

107. See Harry L. Hollingworth, "Prospectus for the Ad League Study Courses in Advertising, 1911–1912," Hollingworth Papers; Hollingworth, *Advertising and Selling* (New York: D. Appleton, 1913). See also Ludy T. Benjamin, Jr., "Harry Levi Hollingworth: Reluctant Pioneer in Applied Psychology" (unpublished paper, American Psychological Association, Chicago, Ill., August 1975).

108. Scott, *The Psychology of Advertising* (Boston: Small, Maynard, 1908); A. Michal McMahon, "An American Courtship: Psychologists and Advertising Theory in the Progressive Era," *American Studies* 13, no. 2 (1972): 5–18.

109. Lynch, "Scott," p. 155; Scott, "Selection of Employees by Means of Quantitative Determinations," *Annals* 65 (1916): 182–93; idem, "The Scientific Selection of Salesmen," *Advertising and Selling* 25, no. 5 (October 1915): 5–6, 94–96; 25, no. 6 (November 1915); 25, no. 7 (December 1915): 11, 69–70.

110. E.g., Elsie Oschrin Bregman, "Vocational Tests for Retail Saleswomen," *Journal of Applied Psychology* 2 (1918): 148–55.

111. Münsterberg, *Psychology and Industrial Efficiency* (Boston: Houghton Mifflin, 1913); Thorndike, "Fundamental Theorems in Judging Men," *Journal of Applied Psychology* 2 (1918): 67–76. See also Baritz, *The Servants of Power*, pp. 35–40.

112. Ferguson, "Industrial Psychology and Labor," in *Walter Van Dyke Bingham Memorial Program*, ed. B. von Haller Gilmer (Pittsburgh, Pa.: Carnegie Institute of Technology, 1962), pp. 7–22; Bingham, "Autobiography," in *A History of Psychology in Autobiography*, vol. 4, ed. Edwin G. Boring et al. (Worcester, Mass.: Clark University Press, 1952), pp. 1–26; Jacobson, *Scott*, pp. 88–97; Bingham to Guy M. Whipple, 5 October 1915, Bingham Papers.

113. Lynch, "Scott," pp. 160–65; Bingham, "Autobiography," pp. 14–15. See also Memorandum, "Committee on Classification of Personnel in the Army," 5 May 1917; Thorndike to Bingham, 1 August 1917, Bingham Papers.

114. *The Personnel System of the United States Army*, vol. 1, *History of the Personnel System Developed by the Committee on Classification of Personnel in the Army (Subsequently the Classification Division, Adjutant General's Department)* (Washington, D.C., 1919); Scott to Newton D. Baker, 4 August 1917; undated memorandum on "The Work of the Committee," "Memorandum on Duties and Personnel of the Committee on Classification of Personnel," 28 September 1918; Scott Papers. See also William Hard, "Captain Smith–77," *New Republic*, 6 July 1918, pp. 283–85.

115. Raymond Dodge, Edward L. Thorndike, Shepherd I. Franz, and Walter V. Bingham, "Psychology as a Life Work," *Science* 57 (13 April 1923): 429–31.

116. Camfield, "Psychologists at War," p. 283, writes of the application of psychology becoming "something of a fad in the nation's business and industrial world in the period following the war." But see also Baritz, *The Servants of Power*, pp. 44–76.

117. Bregman, "The Development and Application of Tests for the Indication of Special Abilities," unpublished report, R. H. Macy and Company, March 1920, Bregman Papers; idem, "Studies in Industrial Psychology," *Archives of Psychology*, no. 54 (September 1922).

118. Samuel Kavruck, "Thirty-Three Years of Test Research: A Short History of Test Development in the U.S. Civil Service Commission," *American Psychologist* 11 (1956): 329–33; Ruml to Bingham, 12 April 1921, Bingham Papers.

119. Leonard W. Ferguson, "The Scott Company: Chapter 15 of *The Heritage of Industrial Psychology*," *JSAS Catalog of Selected Documents in Psychology*, vol. 6, no. 4, (1976), p. 128, MS number 1397.

120. See Sokal, "The Origins of The Psychological Corporation," *Journal of the History of the Behavioral Sciences*, 17 (1981): 54–67.

121. One major problem with Cattell's program for the Psychological Corporation was that it was apparently never spelled out clearly, perhaps because its details were continually in flux, and perhaps

because Cattell never really understood many of the problems involved in the application of psychology, as will be shown below. The closest Cattell ever came to a clear statement of this program was in a special issue of the *Annals of the American Academy of Political and Social Science* on "Psychology in Business." See Cattell, "The Psychological Corporation," *Annals* 110 (1923): 165–71. The discussion of the program presented here is derived from this article and from various unpublished and undated memoranda—e.g., "A Corporation for the Advancement of Psychology," "Memorandum for the Directors of the Psychological Corporation," and "Confidential for Psychologists—The Psychological Corporation"—in the Cattell Papers.

122. Burnham, "Psychiatry, Psychology, and the Progressive Movement," *American Quarterly* 12 (1960): 457–65.

123. Samuel Haber, *Efficiency and Uplift: Scientific Management in the Progressive Era, 1890–1920* (Chicago: University of Chicago Press, 1964).

124. Bingham to Gilbreth, 17 October 1916, 20 November 1916; Gilbreth to Bingham, 25 October 1916, 19 January 1917; J. B. Miner to Gilbreth, 10 November 1917, 17 November 1917, 15 December 1917, 3 January 1918; Miner to Bingham, 15 November 1917; Herbert S. Langfeld to Miner, 17 November 1917; Bingham Papers.

125. "Collection of Data on Child Prodigies—Gilbreth," Terman Papers.

126. Edna Yost, *Frank and Lillian Gilbreth: Partners for Life* (New Brunswick, N.J.: Rutgers University Press, 1949).

127. Emma H. Guntler to Bregman, 14 February 1927, Bregman Papers.

128. Baritz, *The Servants of Power,* pp. 30–31.

129. Bingham to J. J. Apatow, 20 May 1916; Ruml to Bingham, 7 April 1917; Watson to Bingham, 16 April 1921; Bingham papers.

130. See Burnham, "The New Psychology," p. 390; Baritz, *The Servants of Power,* pp. 11, 59–60.

131. Cattell, "A Program of Radical Democracy," *Popular Science Monthly* 80 (1922): 606–15. See also Sokal, "The Unpublished Autobiography of James McKeen Cattell," *American Psychologist* 26 (1971): 626–35.

132. Cattell and Gompers exchanged at least ten letters between 20 December 1922 and 9 January 1923. See Cattell Papers.

133. Ferguson, "The Scott Company," pp. 361–62.

134. Ibid., p. 363.

135. Ferguson, "Industrial Psychology and Labor," pp. 7–22. See also *DAB,* 4th supp., pp. 364–77.

136. Angell to Bingham, 8 June 1917; Bingham to Angell, 13 June 1917; Memorandum, Commander-in-Chief to Adjutant General, 2 January 1918; Committee on the Classification of Personnel to "All Personnel Supervisors," 5 April 1918; Bingham Papers.

137. Morris S. Viteles, "Tests in Industry," *Journal of Applied Psychology* 5 (1921): 57–63; idem, "Industrial Psychology: Reminiscences of an Academic Moonlighter," in *The Psychologists,* ed. T. S. Krawiec, vol. 2 (New York: Oxford University Press, 1974), pp. 440–500.

138. Clothier to Yerkes, 5 June 1923, Yerkes Papers; "Development of the Scott Company," undated memorandum, Scott Papers. See also Ferguson, "The Scott Company," pp. 373–75.

139. Ferguson, "The Scott Company," pp. 339–43.

140. Bingham, "Autobiography," pp. 17–18; Ferguson, "Industrial Psychology and Labor," pp. 7–9. See also Angell to Bingham, 25 March 1917, 30 July 1917, 2 August 1917; Woods, "Suggestion in Relation to Salesmanship Tests," 5 October 1920; Bingham Papers.

141. Sokal, "Origins of the Psychological Corporation," pp. 59–60.

142. Untitled and undated interview about the Psychological Corporation, Cattell Papers.

143. Cattell, "The Psychological Corporation," p. 169.

144. A. M. Johnson, "Report of Examinations Given in this Office," 31 August 1925, Cattell Papers.

145. Cattell to Dean R. Brimhall, 11 December 1920, Cattell Papers.

146. Untitled Memorandum, 15 January 1926, Cattell Papers.

147. Yerkes to Bingham, 3 December 1926; Bingham to Yerkes, 8 December 1926; Yerkes Papers; Cattell to Bregman, 4 December 1926, Bregman Papers; Achilles to Bingham, 9 July 1917, Bingham Papers; Achilles, "A Statement of the Present Status and Possible Future Development of the Psychological Corporation and the Personnel Research Foundation," 9 December 1926; Bingham to "the Members of the Board of the Psychological Corporation," 20 December 1926; Minutes, Meeting of the Board of Directors, 29 December 1926; Cattell Papers. See also "Notes and News," *Journal of Applied Psychology* 11 (1927): 81.

148. "Report of the Committee on Programs, Ways and Means," Psychological Corporation, 29 December 1926, Cattell Papers.

149. Treasurer's Report, Psychological Corporation, 2 November 1929, Cattell Papers.

150. Achilles, "Commemorative Address on the Twentieth Anniversary of the Psychological Corporation and to Honor Its Founder, James McKeen Cattell," *Journal of Applied Psychology* 25 (1941): 609–18; "The Role of the Psychological Corporation in Applied Psychology," *American Journal of Psychology* 50 (1937): 229–47.

151. Paul F. Lazarsfeld, "An Episode in the History of Social Research: A Memoir," in *The Intellectual Migration: Europe and America, 1920–1960,* pp. 270–337.

152. It must be stressed that in the American psychological community of the 1920s, clinical psychology referred *not* to psychotherapy, but to various testing and diagnostic procedures. See Virginia Staudt Sexton, "Clinical Psychology: An Historical Survey," *Genetic Psychology Monographs* 72 (1965): 401–34, and Robert I. Watson, "A Brief History of Clinical Psychology," *Psychological Bulletin* 50 (1953): 321–46.

153. The history of this group has been sketched in various articles by one of its leaders, J. E. Wallace Wallin. For example, see "A Note on the Origin of the APA Clinical Section," *American Psychologist* 16 (1961): 256–58; "A Red-Letter Day in APA History," *Journal of General Psychology* 75 (1966): 107–14; and *The Odyssey of a Psychologist* (Wilmington, Del.: by the author, 1955), pp. 119–22.

154. The history of the APA's efforts in this direction may be traced in summary in Samuel W. Fernberger, "The American Psychological Association: A Historical Summary, 1892–1930," *Psychological Bulletin* 29 (1932): 1–89; in some detail in "Proceedings" of the Annual Meetings of the Association, published in the *Psychological Bulletin;* and in great detail in the file headed "Committee on the Certification of Consulting Psychologists," APA Papers; and in the Terman Papers. Another recent secondary account, totally independent of the one presented here, is Napoli, *Architects of Adjustment,* pp. 57–61.

155. "Proceedings . . . 1917," *Psychological Bulletin* 15 (1918): 25–56.

156. Wallin, *Odyssey,* pp. 191–221. See especially Leta S. Hollingworth to Terman, 6 January 1918, Terman Papers.

157. Wallin, *Odyssey,* pp. 121–22; "The Field of Clinical Psychology as an Applied Psychology: A Symposium," *Journal of Applied Psychology* 3 (1919): 81–95.

158. "Proceedings . . . 1919," *Psychological Bulletin* 17 (1920): 37–38.

159. These services were used extensively throughout the 1920s and afterwards, despite the attempts by psychologists to discredit them. See A. W. Kornhauser and A. W. Jackson, "A Note on the Extent to which Systems of Character Analysis are Used in the Business World," *Journal of Applied Psychology* 6 (1922): 302; Guenter B. Risse, "Vocational Guidance during the Depression: Phrenology versus Applied Psychology," *Journal of the History of the Behavioral Sciences* 12 (1976): 130–40. See also Napoli, *Architects of Adjustment,* pp. 31, 58, 67, 82.

160. B. O. Taylor to Bingham, 29 October 1917; "The Literary Guild" and "The Society of Applied Psychology" to Bingham, 26 January 1920; Bingham to I. B. Davies, 25 February 1920; Bingham Papers.

161. "Report of the Committee on the Qualifications of Psychological Experts," December 1919; Minutes, Meeting of the Committee on Qualifications and Certification of Consulting Psychologists, August 1920; Leta S. Hollingworth to Frederic L. Wells, 15 April 1920; Committee file, APA Papers.

162. See Napoli, *Architects of Adjustment,* pp. 46–47.

163. See ibid., pp. 54–55.

164. "Proceedings . . . 1920," *Psychological Bulletin* 18 (1921): 119–22.

165. In 1920, at least sixty-two psychologists indicated that they were in favor of certification. "Memorandum on Letters from Psychologists Concerning Accrediting of Consulting Psychologists," 13 September 1920, Committee file, APA Papers.

166. Frederic L. Wells, circular letter to the other members of the committee, 9 March 1922; "Memorandum on Meeting of the Committee in New York," 9 May 1922; Committee file, APA Papers.

167. On 5 October 1922, as executive officer of the committee, F. L. Wells wrote to at least twenty-two distinguished psychologists asking them to apply for certification. Many of these—for example, Raymond Dodge, Knight Dunlap, G. Stanley Hall, William McDougall, and Margaret Floy Washburn (whose reply is quoted)—could not under any circumstances be considered consulting psychologists. See Washburn to Wells, 15 October 1922, Committee file, APA Papers.

168. Dunlap to Wells, 10 October 1922, 17 October 1922, 25 October 1922, Committee file, APA Papers.

169. "Proceedings . . . 1922," *Psychological Bulletin* 20 (1923): 61–108. See Wells to Dunlap, 24 October 1922, Committee file, APA Papers; Boring to Terman, 25 January 1923, Boring Papers.

170. "Confidential Memorandum to the Council," 11 December 1926, Committee file, APA Papers; "Proceedings . . . 1926," *Psychological Bulletin* 24 (1827): 137–201.

171. "Proceedings . . . 1927," ibid. 25 (1928): 125–98.

172. Fernberger, "The American Psychological Association, 1892–1942," *Psychological Review* 50 (1943): 33–60.

173. See Cheryl M. Fields, "What Kind of Training Should be Required for a Psychologist?," *Chronicle of Higher Education,* 23 October 1978, pp. 9–10.

174. Financial Statement, Commonwealth Fund Grant, Expenditures to December 31, 1924, Kelley Papers; Leonard Carmichael, *Walter Fenno Dearborn and the Scientific Study of Reading* (Cambridge, Mass.: Harvard Graduate School of Education, 1957), p. 7.

175. Terman to S. P. Capen, 23 February 1921; Terman to Max Farrand, 18 May 1921; E. P. Cubberly to Terman, 22 May 1921; Terman Papers. See Terman et al., *Genetic Studies of Genius,* vol. 1, *Mental and Physical Traits of a Thousand Gifted Children* (Palo Alto, Calif.: Stanford University Press, 1925); vol. 5, *The Gifted Group at Mid-Life: Thirty-Five Years' Follow-up of the Superior Child* (Stanford, Calif.: Stanford University Press, 1959).

176. Of course, a history of the Rockefeller Foundation is outside the scope of this essay, but clarity requires the following notes. In the early 1920s, three agencies deriving their funds from the Rockefeller family made grants to psychologists for their work: the Rockefeller Foundation, the Laura Spelman Rockefeller Memorial, and the General Education Board. These groups and several others underwent a number of permutations in the years that followed, to emerge in the 1940s as the unified Rockefeller Foundation. See Robert Shaplen, *Toward the Well-Being of Mankind: Fifty Years of the Rockefeller Foundation* (London: Hutchinson, 1964); Raymond B. Fosdick, with Henry F. Pringle and Katharine Douglas Pringle, *Adventure in Giving: The Story of the General Education Board, A Foundation Established by John D. Rockefeller* (New York: Harper and Row, 1962).

177. George M. Stratton and Walter S. Hunter to Laura Spelman Rockefeller Memorial, 29 March 1926; Lawrence K. Frank, memorandum of interview with Stratton and Hunter, 29 March 1926; Beardsley Ruml to Stratton, 10 May 1926; "Foreign Fellowship 'Yellow Sheets'"; LSRM Archives. See also The Rockefeller Foundation, *Directory of Fellowships and Scholarships, 1917–1970* (New York: Rockefeller Foundation, 1972).

178. Minutes of the Rockefeller Foundation, 3 January 1929, 22 January 1929, 22 May 1929, RF Archives; John A. Dollard, "Yale's Institute of Human Relations: What Was It?," *Ventures* (The Magazine of the Yale Graduate School), 1964, pp. 32–40. Among the products of the Institute's first ten years were: Dollard, Neal E. Miller, Leonard W. Doob, O. H. Mowrer, and Robert R. Sears, *Frustration and Aggression* (New Haven, Conn.: Yale University Press, 1939); Arnold L. Gesell, *An Atlas of Infant Behavior: A Systematic Delineation of the Forms and Early Growth of Human Behavior Patterns . . . Illustrated with 3200 Action Photographs,* 2 vols. (New Haven, Conn.: Yale University Press, 1934); and Yerkes, *The Great Apes: A Study of Anthropoid Life* (New Haven, Conn.: Yale University Press, 1929).

179. An excellent overview of the Memorial's activities in this area is Elizabeth Lomax, "The Laura Spelman Rockefeller Memorial: Some of Its Contributions to Early Research in Child Development," *Journal of the History of the Behavioral Sciences* 13 (1977): 283–93.

180. Lawrence K. Frank to Stratton, 9 November 1925; Stratton to Frank, 20 January 1926; Ruml to Stratton, 3 March 1926; Minutes of the Meeting of the Committee on Child Development . . . National Research Council, 21 March 1926; LSRM Archives.

181. Grants were made directly to George J. Hecht, the founder of the Parents Publishing Association, in 1925, and to Teachers College of Columbia University, Yale University, and the University of Iowa, among others, so that the institutions could purchase stock in the association. Frank, memorandum of interview with Hecht, 6 November 1924; Hecht to Ruml, 7 November 1925; Angell to Frank, 8 October 1929; Hecht to Ruml, 18 October 1927; Hecht to Walter A. Jessup, 7 June 1929; LSRM Archives. See Marilyn Bender, "A Dr. Spock of Magazines," *New York Times,* 21 September 1975.

182. Hillis to Seashore, 2 December 1913; Seashore to Hillis, 21 November 1914; Minutes of the Child Welfare Committee, 22 December 1914; Hillis to Seashore, 27 May 1916; Hillis, Child Welfare Circular, 6 April 1917; Institute of Child Welfare Papers. See also *Pioneering in Child Welfare: A History of the Iowa Child Welfare Research Station, 1917–1933* (Iowa City, Iowa: State University of Iowa, 1933) and *The Institute of Child Behavior and Development: Fifty Years of Research, 1917–1967* (Iowa City, Iowa: University of Iowa, 1967), both of which will soon be superseded by the definitive and critical history of the station now being prepared by Hamilton Cravens.

183. Walter A. Jessup to Baldwin, 17 July 1917; Baldwin to Jessup, 6 August 1917; Seashore to Baldwin, 13 August 1917; Seashore to Hillis, 13 August 1917; Institute of Child Welfare Papers; Lawrence K. Frank, memorandum of interview with Baldwin, 25 October 1927; Amy L. Daniels to Jessup, 24 December 1928, LSRM Archives.

184. Baldwin to Ruml, 13 December 1922, LSRM Archives; Margaret C. Munns to Baldwin, 7 October 1924, Institute of Child Welfare Papers.

185. Baldwin to Hillis, 18 January 1921, Institute of Child Welfare Papers; Baldwin to W. S. Richardson, 8 December 1920; Ruml to Jessup, 22 November 1922; Baldwin and Jessup to LSRM, 2 April 1925; Arthur Woods to Jessup, 14 April 1925; Ruml to Baldwin, 7 January 1926; Frank, memorandum of interview with Baldwin, 25 October 1927; Baldwin to Frank, 1 November 1927; Ruml to Jessup, 2 March 1928, 27 April 1928; LSRM Archives. For the work of the station during these years, see *Pioneering in Child Welfare,* and *The Institute of Child Behavior and Development.*

186. Frank, memorandum of interview with Richardson, 2 March 1925; Arthur Woods to R. A. Pearson, 14 April 1925; Ruml to R. M. Hughes, 2 March 1928; Ruml to Homer H. Seerley, 4 February 1926; Revell MacCallum to G. R. Latham, 30 April 1929; LSRM Archives.

187. This unified program was not achieved without a power struggle, as the psychologists at the State University argued forcefully that all child study work in the State should be under their control. It was only the powerful position of Richardson, and the Memorial's explicit desire to use all available resources in the state, that enabled the program to emerge as it did. See Baldwin, "Memorandum to the Laura Spelman Rockefeller Memorial," 11 December 1924, Institute of Child Welfare papers. Frank to Ruml [May 1924]; Frank, memorandum of interview with Richardson, 2 March 1925; Baldwin to Frank, 28 May 1927; Frank, memorandum of interview with Baldwin, 25 October 1927; LSRM Archives.

188. Frank, "Child Study Program," memorandum, 22 March 1924; Edward L. Thorndike to Ruml, 14 June 1927; Frank, memorandum of interview with "Faculty and Officers, University of California," 6–12 March 1925; Frank to Warner Brown, 27 May 1925; Ruml to W. W. Campbell, 31 May 1927; Frank, "University of Minnesota," memorandum, 6 October 1924; L. D. Coffman to Frank, 29 January 1925; Arthur Woods to Coffman, 14 April 1925; LSRM Archives.

189. Angell to Ruml, 13 June 1923, 23 June 1923, 29 June 1923; Gesell to Ruml, 9 February 1924; Frank to Gesell, 18 February 1924; Frank, memorandum of interview with Gesell, 20 January 1925; Arthur Woods to Angell, 19 May 1925; Ruml to Angell, 28 May 1925; Gesell, "Memorandum for Mr. Frank," 2 April 1927; LSRM Archives.

190. Ruml to Aurelia H. Reinhardt, 2 December 1927; Ruml to Herman Schneider, 3 March 1928; Walker to Laura Spelman Rockefeller Memorial, 26 March 1924; Syndor Walker, memorandum of interview with Mary Cresswell, Department of Home Economics, Georgia Agricultural College, 27 February 1925; Ruml to Andrew Soule, 28 March 1925; LSRM Archives.

191. E.g., Angell, "The Relations of Structural and Functional Psychology to Philosophy," *Philosophical Review* 12 (1903): 243–71; "The Province of Functional Psychology," *Psychological Review* 14 (1907): 61–91.

192. Boring, "The Society of Experimental Psychologists, 1904–1938," *American Journal of Psychology* 51 (1938): 410–21.

193. Bingham to Yerkes, 12 December 1913, Yerkes Papers; Yerkes to Terman, 21 July 1921, Terman Papers; Boring to Yerkes, 18 January 1921; Washburn to Boring, 17 September 1921; Boring to Bingham, 24 November 1922; Bingham to Boring, 27 November 1922; Boring Papers. "Proceedings . . . 1921," *Psychological Bulletin* 19 (1922): 65–115; "Proceedings . . . 1926," ibid. 24 (1927): 137–201.

194. See Cedric A. Larson and John J. Sullivan, "Watson's Relation to Titchener," *Journal of the History of the Behavioral Sciences* 1 (1965): 338–54.

195. Boring, "The Society of Experimental Psychologists," p. 416; Karl M. Dallenbach to Boring, 3 August 1927, Boring Papers.

196. Boring, Telegrams to Cattell, Yerkes, Raymond Dodge, et al., 3 August 1927; Boring to Cattell, Yerkes, Dodge, 11 August 1927; Boring Papers. The two letters to Yerkes and Dodge were actually produced by use of carbon paper.

197. Boring to Yerkes, 11 August 1927; Yerkes Papers; Boring, "Edward Bradford Titchener, 1867–1927," *American Journal of Psychology* 38 (1927): 489–506. In his autobiography, Boring explicitly compared the effect of Titchener's death on him to the release that John Stuart Mill felt on the death of his father. See Boring, *Psychologist at Large: An Autobiography and Selected Essays* (New York: Basic Books, 1961), p. 49.

198. Cattell to Boring, 6 August 1927; Yerkes to Boring, 10 August 1927; Boring Papers.

199. Dallenbach to Boring, 3 August 1927, Boring Papers. See also Boring to Terman, 9 August 1927, Terman Papers.

200. Interview with Anne Anastasi, 20 November 1973.

201. See also Sokal, "Enfin in Amerique: First U.S. International Congress," *APA Monitor,* July/ August 1979, p. 3; Carl P. Duncan, "A Note on the 1929 International Congress of Psychology," *Journal of the History of the Behavioral Sciences* 16 (1980): 1–5.

202. See Rand B. Evans and Frederick J. Down Scott, "The 1913 International Congress of Psychology: The American Congress that Wasn't," *American Psychologist* 33 (1978): 711–23.

320   EXPLORATIONS IN THE HISTORY OF PSYCHOLOGY

203. John E. Anderson to Council of the American Psychological Association, 27 April 1923, 12 May 1923, 22 June 1923, Terman Papers. "Proceedings of the . . . American Psychological Association . . . 1923," *Psychological Bulletin* 21 (1924): 69–120.

204. Claparède, "Address by the Secretary of the International Congress," *Ninth International Congress of Psychology*, pp. 33–47.

205. *New Republic*, 18 September 1929, pp. 112–13.

206. Cattell, "Psychology in America," *Science* 70 (11 October 1929): 335–47; *Scientific Monthly* 30 (1930): 114–26. That Cattell printed this address in *two* of his journals, besides publishing it separately, shows how much he thought of it. See also *Man of Science*, 2: 441–84, and Paul Farnsworth and Ernest Hilgard, unpublished informal memoirs, July–August 1967, Archives of the History of American Psychology.

207. This discussion is based primarily on the following interviews and oral histories: A. T. Poffenberger, interview, 4 November 1972; Hudson Hoagland, interview, 7 November 1972; David Shakow, interview, 29 October 1973; Anne Anastasi, interview, 20 November 1973; Farnsworth and Hilgard, informal memoir. See also Duncan, "A Note on the 1929 International Congress."

208. McDougall, "An Experiment for Testing the Hypothesis of Lamarck," *British Journal of Psychology* 17 (1927): 267–304; "Second Report on a Lamarckian Experiment," *Ninth International Congress*, pp. 302–3; *British Journal of Psychology* 20 (1930): 201–18. See also Harry Helson, "E. G. B.: The Early Years and Change of Course," *American Psychologist* 25 (1970): 625–29.

209. Angier to James R. Angell, 18 September 1929, Angell papers.

210. *Ninth International Congress*, pp. xvi–xxi, xxxiii–xxxiv.

211. Ibid., 331–33.

212. Herbert S. Langfeld, "The Ninth International Congress of Psychology," *Science,* 70 (18 October 1929): 364–68.

213. Katharine Adams Williams, "Psychology in 1929 at the International Congress," *Psychological Bulletin* 27 (1930): 658–63.

214. *Ninth International Congress,* p. xxviii; *Psychological Review* 37 (1930): 1–24.

215. E. g., Langfeld to Kurt Koffka, 16 December 1927, 20 January 1928, 27 January 1928, 15 February 1928, 4 June 1928, 7 November 1928, 15 December 1928, 8 March 1929, Koffka Papers. Boring to Seashore, 25 June 1928, 21 August 1928, Boring Papers. See also "Subjects of Morning Lectures and Afternoon Discussions by Six Foreign Psychologists, First Summer Session, 1929, State University of Iowa," Institute of Child Welfare Papers.

216. *Ninth International Congress*, pp. 270–72.

217. E.g., Langfeld, "The Ninth International Congress," pp. 364–68.

218. Helson, "The Effects Obtained from Rotation of Irregularly Formed Regions," *Ninth International Congress,* pp. 219–20; Tolman, "Maze-Performance as a Function of Motivation and of Reward as well as of a Knowledge of the Maze-Paths," ibid., pp. 439–40; Washburn, "Köhler's Discussion of Association," ibid., p. 470.

219. Interview with Tamara Dembo, 14 November 1973.

220. Ibid. See also below.

221. This topic is treated in greater detail, in a slightly different perspective, in Sokal, "The Gestalt Psychologists in Behaviorist America," *American Historical Review*, forthcoming.

222. Mandler and Mandler, "The Diaspora of Experimental Psychology." The material collected by these authors in the preparation of their paper is available at the Archives of the History of American Psychology, and has provided some of the information, and much of the background, for this discussion.

223. Ibid., pp. 409–11.

224. Tolman, "Autobiography," *A History of Psychology in Autobiography*, vol. 4, p. 327.

225. Koffka, "Perception: An Introduction to the *Gestalt-Theorie*," *Psychological Bulletin* 19 (1922): 531–85; Boring to the Mandlers, 7 June 1967, 14 February 1968, Mandler Papers. See also Frank S. Freeman, "The Beginnings of Gestalt Psychology in the United States," *Journal of the History of the Behavioral Sciences* 13 (1977): 352–53.

226. Allport, "Autobiography," *A History of Psychology in Autobiography*, vol. 5, pp. 7–11.

227. Allport, "Leipzig Congress for Psychology," *American Journal of Psychology* 34 (1923): 612–15; "The Standpoint of *Gestalt* Psychology," *Psyche* 4 (1924): 354–61.

228. Ogden, "The Phenomena of Meaning," in "Proceedings of the American Psychological Association . . . 1922," *Psychological Bulletin* 20 (1923): 61–108; Tolman, "Autobiography," p. 329.

229. Watson to Boring, 15 September 1924; Boring to Watson, 20 September 1924; Boring Papers.

230. Helson, "E. G. B.: The Early Years and Change of Course." According to the excellent paper by John O'Donnell, "The Crisis of Experimentalism in the 1920s: E. G. Boring and His Uses of History," *American Psychologist* 34 (1979): 289–95, Boring's concern led him to write his *History of*

Experimental Psychology (New York: Century, 1929), which ignored most branches of applied psychology.

231. Helson, "E. G. B.," pp. 627–28; idem, "Some Highlights of an Intellectual Journey," *The Psychologists*, pp. 94–95; idem, "The Psychology of the *Gestalt*," *American Journal of Psychology* 36 (1925): 342–70, 494–526; 37 (1926): 25–62, 189–223.

232. Washburn to Boring, 16 September 1925, Boring Papers.

233. Boring to Washburn, 19 September 1925, Boring Papers.

234. Boring to Koffka, 17 November 1925, Boring Papers.

235. Boring to Köhler, 30 April 1925, Boring Papers.

236. See Michael Wertheimer, "Max Wertheimer: Gestalt Prophet," *Gestalt Theory* 2 (1980): 3–17.

237. Boring to the Mandlers, 7 June 1967, 14 February 1968, Mandler Papers.

238. "Proceedings . . . 1924," *Psychological Bulletin* 22 (1925): 69–138.

239. Register, Koffka Papers; Boring to James H. Woods, 12 November 1924, 24 November 1924, Boring Papers.

240. Boring to Woods, 8 November 1926, 11 November 1926, 16 November 1926, 7 February 1927, 28 February 1927; Boring to Koffka, 2 March 1927, 9 March 1927; Koffka to Boring, 13 November 1926; Boring Papers.

241. Boring to Woods, 8 November 1926; Boring to Koffka, 22 November 1926; Boring Papers.

242. Koffka to Boring, 23 February 1927; Boring to Woods, 28 February 1927, Boring Papers.

243. Koffka to Boring, 1 April 1927, Boring Papers.

244. Seth Wakeman to Koffka, 5 October 1926, 12 October 1926, 16 November 1926, 1 January 1927, 11 January 1927, 28 February 1927, 2 March 1927, 19 March 1927, 1 June 1927, Koffka Papers.

245. Ogden, "The Gestalt-Hypothesis," *Psychological Review* 35 (1928): 136–41; Ogden to Koffka, 17 June 1927, 2 January 1928, 30 March 1928, 4 April 1928, 15 October 1928, 11 November 1928, 22 November 1928, Koffka Papers.

246. Boring to the Mandlers, 7 June 1967, Mandler Papers.

247. Terman to Boring, 3 August 1927; E. C. Tolman to Terman, 5 April 1938; Boring to Terman, 14 December 1927, 22 December 1941; Terman Papers.

248. Mandler and Mandler, "The Diaspora of Experimental Psychology," pp. 409–11; A. Hunter Dupree, "The Coming of the Refugees," *Science* 166 (19 December 1969): 1495–97.

249. Bühler to Terman, 24 June 1941, 8 December 1941; Terman to Bühler, 11 December 1941, 8 May 1951; Terman Papers. See also Charlotte Bühler to the Mandlers, 9 September 1967, Mandler Papers.

250. Interview with Tamara Dembo; Boring to Terman, 31 July 1931, 6 October 1931, Terman Papers. See also Grace Heider, "News and Notes," *Newsletter of the Division of the History of Psychology* (American Psychological Association) 7 (1974): 10.

251. Mandler and Mandler, "The Diaspora of Experimental Psychology," pp. 400–405; Boring to Terman, 31 July 1931, Boring Papers.

252. Terman to Boring, 13 August 1931, Boring Papers.

253. Boring to Terman, 18 August 1931, 6 October 1931, Terman Papers.

254. Terman to Boring, 19 November 1934; Boring to Terman, 31 July 1931, 6 October 1931; Terman papers.

255. Boring to Terman, 7 April 1933; Terman to Boring, 11 April 1933; Terman Papers.

256. Terman to Johnson, Terman Papers; Boring to Koffka, 5 April 1933, 7 April 1933, 2 May 1933, 15 May 1933, 18 May 1933; Koffka to Boring, 6 April 1933, 1 May 1933, 16 May 1933; Boring Papers.

257. Terman to Lewin, 4 February 1942; Lewin to Terman, 28 March 1942, 8 February 1944; Terman to E. C. Tolman, 14 February 1944; Terman Papers. See also Mandler and Mandler, "The Diaspora of Experimental Psychology," p. 401; Boring to George D. Stoddard, 7 October 1941, Lewin files.

258. A more detailed and extensive discussion of this same topic is found in Sokal, "The Gestalt Psychologists in Behaviorist America."

259. Yerkes to Köhler, 27 March 1914, 20 May 1914, 17 July 1916, 10 October 1916, 21 December 1916, 10 January 1917; Köhler to Yerkes, 17 April 1914, 15 February 1916, 19 May 1916, 10 September 1916, 13 December 1916, 2 March 1917; Yerkes Papers.

260. Yerkes to U.S. Department of State, 14 February 1921; Yerkes to Köhler, 13 April 1921, 8 October 1921, 6 March 1922, 6 November 1923; Köhler to Yerkes, 19 May 1921, 23 October 1921, 29 January 1922; Yerkes Papers.

261. Terman to C. H. Thurber, 26 May 1924, Terman Papers.

262. Yerkes to Köhler, 22 October 1924, 26 January 1925, 7 May 1925; Köhler to Yerkes, 8 February 1924, 15 February 1925; Yerkes Papers; Boring to Köhler, 9 June 1924, 6 February 1925, Boring Papers.

263. Yerkes to Köhler, 7 May 1925, Yerkes Papers; Boring to Köhler, 31 March 1925; Köhler to Boring, 2 April 1925, 20 April 1925; Boring Papers.

264. Boring to Yerkes, 28 October 1925, Yerkes Papers.

265. Boring, "The Society of Experimental Psychologists," p. 415; Terman to Boring, 26 January 1927, Terman Papers.

266. Yerkes to David White, 5 March 1925, Yerkes Papers. Lawrence K. Frank to Terman, 7 April 1925, LSRM Archives.

267. Kegan Paul Trench Trubner and Company to Köhler, 16 November 1926, 19 January 1927, 15 February 1927, 14 June 1927, 22 July 1927, 11 October 1927, Köhler Papers.

268. Boring to Woods, 15 April 1925, 16 April 1925; Boring to Köhler, 25 March 1925, 31 March 1925; Köhler to Boring, 2 April 1925; Boring Papers; Boring to Köhler, 4 June 1925, Köhler Papers.

269. Köhler to Boring, 12 July 1925, Boring Papers; Köhler to Woods, undated draft (ca. 10 July 1925), Köhler Papers; Boring to Yerkes, 28 October 1925, Yerkes Papers.

270. Boring to Woods, 22 July 1925, 6 January 1926, 21 January 1926, 18 March 1926; Woods to Boring, 18 July 1925, 15 March 1925; Boring to Köhler, 17 March 1925; Boring Papers; Köhler to Woods, 15 March 1926, undated draft (Spring 1926), Köhler Papers.

271. Boring to Koffka, 23 April 1930, Boring Papers.

272. Woods to Boring, 17 December 1926; Boring to Woods, 27 December 1926; Boring Papers; Boring to Terman, 17 January 1927, Terman Papers.

273. Boring to Woods, 13 January 1927; Köhler to Boring, 13 May 1927 (translated from the German); Boring Papers; Boring to Terman, 11 July 1927, Terman Papers.

274. Boring to Terman, 9 August 1927, 14 December 1927, Terman Papers; Boring to Köhler, 6 January 1928, Boring Papers. See also Boring to Clarence I. Lewis, 2 August 1927, 14 August 1927, Department of Philosophy Papers.

275. Boring to Lewis, 4 December 1927, 4 April 1928, 30 October 1928, Department of Philosophy Papers.

276. Boring to Lewis, 7 December 1927, Department of Philosophy Papers. See also Kuklick, *The Rise of American Philosophy*, p. 460.

277. Boring to Lewis, 30 October 1928, Department of Philosophy Papers.

278. Boring to Perry, 15 November 1928, Department of Philosophy Papers.

279. Washburn, "Gestalt Psychology and Motor Psychology," *American Journal of Psychology* 37 (1926): 516–20; Washburn to Boring, 16 September 1925, Boring Papers.

280. Terman to Boring, 3 August 1927, 27 January 1927, Terman Papers.

281. Boring to Seashore, 25 June 1928, 21 August 1928, Boring Papers.

282. Michael Wertheimer, "Max Wertheimer, Gestalt Prophet"; Köhler, "Gestalt Psychology," *Psychologische Forschung* 31 (1967): xviii–xxx; "A Perspective on American Psychology," *Psychological Review* 50 (1943): 77–79.

283. Fritz K. Ringer, *The Decline of the German Mandarins: The German Academic Community, 1890–1933* (Cambridge, Mass.: Harvard University Press, 1969).

284. Ash, *Gestalt Psychology in Two Cultures*, makes this point well.

285. Boring, *A History of Experimental Psychology*, pp. 570–80, 591–93; Boring to Köhler, 27 February 1930, Boring Papers.

286. Boring, *A History of Experimental Psychology*, pp. 570–71, 576–78, 593.

287. Boring, "The *Gestalt* Psychology and the *Gestalt* Movement," *American Journal of Psychology* 42 (1930): 308–15.

288. Boring to Köhler, 27 February 1930, Boring Papers.

289. Koffka to Boring, 22 April 1930, Boring Papers.

290. Boring, *A History of Experimental Psychology*, p. 593.

291. Boring to Koffka, 23 April 1930, Boring Papers.

292. E.g., F. H. Lund, "The Phantom of the Gestalt," *Journal of General Psychology* 2 (1929): 307–23; William McDougall, "Dynamics of Gestalt Psychology," *Character and Personality* 4 (1930): 232–44, 319–34; S. C. Fisher, "A Critique of Insight in Köhler's Gestalt Psychology," *American Journal of Psychology*, 43 (1931): 131–36; F. M. Greg, "Materializing the Ghost of Köhler's Gestalt Psychology," *Psychological Review* 39 (1932): 257–70.

293. Boring, *The Physical Dimensions of Consciousness* (New York: Century, 1933); Julian Jaynes, "Edwin Garrigues Boring: 1886–1968," *Journal of the History of the Behavioral Sciences* 5 (1969): 99–112.

294. Mary Henle, "One Man Against the Nazis—Wolfgang Köhler," *American Psychologist* 33 (1978): 939–44.

295. Boring to Köhler, 7 December 1933; Boring to Koffka, 13 December 1933; Köhler to Boring, 22 January 1934; Boring Papers.

296. Boring to Köhler, 19 March 1934, 2 October 1934, 7 November 1934, Boring Papers; Boring to the Mandlers, 14 February 1968, Mandler Papers.

297. New York: Liveright Publishing Co., 1938.

298. *Journal of Philosophy* 36 (1939): 107–8: "Keen, wide-ranging, and original," *New York Times,* 5 February 1939, p. 6.

299. Harry L. Hollingworth, *American Journal of Psychology* 53 (1940): 146–52; J. R. Kantor, *Psychological Bulletin* 36 (1939): 292–96.

300. Carmichael to Boring, 15 December 1934, 22 December 1934; Boring to Carmichael, undated card (ca. 20 December 1934); Carmichael papers.

301. Boring, *Psychologist at Large,* pp. 53–54; Jaynes, "Boring," p. 107. See also Boring and Hanns Sachs, "Was This Analysis a Success?" *Journal of Abnormal and Social Psychology* 35 (1940): 4–16.

302. Helson to the Mandlers, 27 February 1968, Mandler Papers.

303. Jaynes, "Boring," p. 107.

304. Boring to Terman, 7 March 1947, Terman Papers; Boring to the Mandlers, 14 February 1968, Mandler Papers.

Notes on Contributors

JAMES G. BLIGHT contributed to this collection a monograph entitled "Jonathan Edwards's Theory of the Mind: Its Applications and Implications." Mr. Blight received his A.B. from the University of Michigan (1970) and his Ph.D. from the University of New Hampshire (1974). Since then he has published on some of the major figures of American psychology prior to William James, including articles on Solomon Stoddard (seventeenth century), Jonathan Edwards (eighteenth century), and Asa Burton (nineteenth century). Formerly a Mellon Faculty Fellow, and a National Endowment for the Humanities Fellow in the department of the history of science at Harvard University, he is currently an editor for The Guilford Press.

JOSEF BROŽEK, the initiator and editor of the *Explorations in the History of Psychology in the United States,* is the author of the contribution on "David Jayne Hill: Between the Old and the New Psychology." Brožek became deeply interested in the history of psychology during his student years at Charles University, Prague, around 1935. However, only in the last two decades did the history of psychology become one of his dominant concerns, with "Current Historiography of Psychology around the World" as a major, long-range project. He is coeditor and coauthor, with Maarten S. Sibinga, of *Origins of Psychometry* (1970); with Dan I. Slobin, of *Psychology in the USSR: An Historical Perspective* (1972); with Rand B. Evans, of *R. I. Watson's Selected Papers on the History of Psychology* (1977); with L. J. Pongratz, of *Historiography of Modern Psychology* (1980); and coauthor, with Solomon Diamond, of *Le Origini della Psicologia Obiettiva* (1982). A past president of the American Psychological Association's Division 26, History of Psychology (1973–1974), Brožek is a member of the Editorial or Advisory Boards of the *Journal of the History of the Behavioral Sciences,* the German *Archiv für Psychologie,* the Italian *Storia e Critica della Psicologia,* and the Spanish *Revista de Historia de la Psicologia.*

RAND B. EVANS contributed to the present volume a monograph on "The Origins of American Academic Psychology." Currently he is head of the department of psychology at Texas A&M University. Prior to that he was codirector of the History of Psychology Program at the University of New Hampshire. His research interests began with the early systematic psychology of the twentieth century, particularly E. B. Titchener and structuralism. These interests have extended to the pre-experimental psychology of the nineteenth-century America. He has recently published an historical introduction to the new Harvard edition of William James's *Principles of Psychology* (1981). Evans's book on E. B. Titchener (1867–1927)—Cornell University's experimental psychologist par excellence—is nearing completion.

JOHN A. POPPLESTONE and MARION WHITE MCPHERSON are, respectively, Director and Associate Director of the Archives of the History of American Psychology (founded in 1965) at the Bierce Library of the University of Akron. While they are both clinicians, they are also deeply involved with the history of psychology, particularly historical methodology. Beginning with the publication in 1971 of the *Prolegomena to the Study of Apparatus in Early Psychological Laboratories Circa 1875–1915* they have been concerned with the facts of pioneer experimental psychology laboratories. Their treatise is entitled "Pioneer Psychology Laboratories in Clinical Setting."

MICHAEL M. SOKAL, a historian of science and technology (Ph.D., Case Western Reserve University, 1972), has written extensively on the history of psychology in the United States and contributed to this volume a monograph entitled "James McKeen Cattell and American Psychology in the 1920s." Currently professor of history in the department of humanities, Worcester Polytechnic Institute, Worcester, Massachusetts, he has been visiting scholar in the department of the history of science, Harvard University; visiting postdoctoral research fellow at the National Museum of History and Technology, Smithsonian Institution; national lecturer for Sigma Xi, the Scientific Research Society; and American Psychological Association centennial lecturer. Sokal is the editor of *An Education in Psychology: James McKeen Cattell's Journals and Letters from Germany and England: 1880–1888* (1981) and compiler, with Patrice A. Rafail, of *A Guide to Manuscript Collections in the History of Psychology and Related Areas* (1982). He is completing a full biography of Cattell, and his long-term research interests include the history of psychological testing in the United States.

WILLIAM R. WOODWARD, associate professor of psychology at the University of New Hampshire, wrote for this collection "William James's Psychology of Will: Its Revolutionary Impact on American Psychology." With degrees in history and science (Harvard, 1967), experimental psychology (Princeton, 1969) and history of science and medicine (Yale, 1975), at New Hampshire he codirects and teaches undergraduate and graduate students in the History and Theory of Psychology Program. Professor Woodward's research traces present-day social behaviorism back to functional psychology, and from there to a revolutionary shift in scientific thought through the confluence of the Darwinian and Kantian intellectual traditions. In 1981–82 he was a Humboldt Research Fellow in Heidelberg, Germany, preparing an intellectual biography of Hermann Lotze.

Index

Acquired connections, law of: E. L. Thorn-dike, 170

Advertising: psychological approach. *See* Psychology, American, in the 1920s

Allen, A. V. G.: on J. Edwards, 100

Allport, F.: and W. James, 179; *Social Psychology* (1924), 179

Allport, G.: and W. James, 176–77; functional autonomy, 176–77; and Gestalt psychology, 298; theory of personality, 176

Angell, J. R.: and W. James, 166; and James-Lange theory of emotions, 173; sensori-motor reactions, 166; transition from random to controlled movements, 167

Anti-Semitism: and psychologists, 280

Apparatus: choice of instruments, 224; at the Minnesota School for Idiots and Imbeciles at Fairbault, 249; at the Psychological Clinic, University of Pennsylvania, 237–38; at the research laboratory in the New Jersey Training School for Feeble-Minded Girls and Boys at Vineland, 241–42

Association of ideas: C. L. Morgan, 167

"Athenian creed": J. Witherspoon's parody of deism, 31

Attention and volition: and W. James, 165–67; and J. Dewey, 165–66; and J. M. Baldwin, 165–66; and J. R. Angell, 166–67; and A. W. Moore, 166

Ayres, L. P.: critique of the face validity of specific items of the Binet-Simon scale, 256

Baird, J. W.: color sensitivity in hysterics and neurasthenics, 226

Baldwin, B. T.: director of the Child Welfare Research Station, State University of Iowa, 293

Baldwin, J. M.: and W. James, 160–65; and A. Binet, 165; sensory and motor types of reaction, 166

Bard, P.: neuro-humoral theory of emotions, 174

Barnes, F. B.: memory in psychotics, 227

Binet (-Simon) scale, 229, 238, 242, 245, 252; J. E. W. Wallin's administrative manual, 248; word definitions, 256; critique of face validity, 256; and psychologists, 257

Bingham, W. Van Dyke: and applied psychology, 284

Blight, J.: "Jonathan Edwards's Theory of the Mind: Its Applications and Implications," 61–119

Blind, psychology of the: A. R. T. Wylie, 234

Body-soul relations: D. J. Hill, 131

Boring, E. G.: operational definition of "intelligence," 281; and Gestalt psychology, 298–99, 303–7

Bowen, F.: for Sir William Hamilton and against (1878) W. James's elective course on "Psychology," 50

"Brass instrument" psychology: transition to mental testing, 235–53

Brigham, C. C.: and critique of his *A Study of American Intelligence* (1923), 281

Brožek, J.: "David Jayne Hill: Between the 'Old' and the 'New' Psychology," 121–47; Preface, 13–14. *See also* Hill, D. J.

Bühler, K.: academic appointments, 299–300

Calkins, M. W.: theory of personality, 175

Candland, Douglas K., 11

Cannon, W. B.: and theories of emotion, 173–74

Carnegie Institution of Technology, Pittsburgh: its Applied Psychology Division, 288

Cattell, J. McKeen: on the history of American psychology prior to the 1880s, 17–18; confrontation with W. McDougall, 297; mental testing, 276–77; and Psychological

327

Corporation, 285; president of the Ninth International Congress of Psychology (1929), 295

Certification: of consulting psychologists, 290–92

Cherry, C.: on J. Edwards, 105

Child Welfare Station: at State University of Iowa, 293

Clapp, T.: supporting mathematics and "experimental philosophy" in the curriculum of Yale College, 23

Cognitive development: and J. M. Baldwin, 160–65; and A. Binet, 165; and W. James, 160–65

Commonwealth Fund: and financial support of child psychology, 292

Congress of Psychology, the Ninth International (1929), 295–96; and J. McKeen Cattell, 295–96; and W. McDougall, 296; and I. P. Pavlov, 296; and Gestalt psychology, 297

Conversion: the focal concern of J. Edwards's psychology, 63–84; essence of, 81; validity of, 79–84; spurious and "true" (holy) affections, 79–81; "marks" and "signs" of valid conversion, 81–84

"Correlations of sciences": I. Van Giessen, 209

Cousin, V.: as source of German idealist views, 46–47

Cross-cultural studies: H. H. Goddard's "Ideals of a Group of German Children" (1906), 239

Curriculum: continuing differentiation in the early nineteenth century (U.S.), 42; changes in, at Yale College, 23; changes in, at King's College, 27–28; changes in, at College of Philadelphia, 28–29; scholastic, 19–22; scholastic, and psychological topics at Harvard College (establ. 1636), 21

Deism: "Athenian creed" (a parody), 31

Dewey, J.: and W. James, 165; reflex arc concept in psychology, 165

Dualism v. monism: D. J. Hill, 128–29

Edwards, J.; and Locke, 23, 98, 110, 111; and Hume, 88–91; and James, 91; biographical sketch, 61–62; the theory of the mind, 62–96; review of the literature on Edwards's psychology, 97–119

Edwards's psychology under scrutiny, 97–119: A. V. G. Allen, 110–11; J. Haroutunian, 113–14; P. Miller, 99–102; A. A. Roback, 104; C. Cherry, 105

Edwards's theory of conversion, 61–69, 97; motives to seek conversion ("first awakenings"), 63–67; growing need to *receive* the saving grace, 67–69; infusion of the divine love, 73–78

Edwards's theory of the mind, 69–73; the unity of "understanding" and of "will-affections," 69, 71, 79, 81; illusion of "choices," 70, 79; "notional understanding" v. "a sense of the heart," 72–73; alteration in the cognitive-attitudinal structure of the mind in conversion, 76, 80; emotional involvement, 79; debate over Edwards's view of human nature, 105–11

Eighteenth century: J. Edwards's theory of the mind, 61–97; the "New Learning," 22–29; the rise of Scottish thought in America, 29–33

Elective system: its introduction into American colleges, 48; implementation at Harvard, 49

Elemental powers of the soul: D. J. Hill, 130; Sir William Hamilton, 132

Emotions, theories of: C. S. Sherrington, 172; W. B. Cannon, 173; P. Bard, 174

Enlightenment, American: the seeds of, 22; its scientific foundations in the Yale curriculum, 23; King's College (Columbia University) curriculum under S. Johnson, 27–28

Equipment. *See* Apparatus

Evans, R. B.: "The Origins of American Academic Psychology," 17–60

Fay, J. W. (*American Psychology before William James,* 1939): comment on D. J. Hill's *The Elements of Psychology* (1888), 143

Financial support: of child psychology, 292–94

Foundations, 292–93: The Commonwealth Fund, 292; Laura Spelman Rockefeller Memorial Fund, 292

Franz, S. I.: and afterimages, 217; visual fatigue, 218; training-extirpation studies, 218–19; experimental research on psychotics, 219–21; research on associations, 221–22

Functional autonomy of motives: G. Allport's concept, 176–77

Gestalt psychology: in America in the 1920s, 297–307; and K. S. Lashley, 297; at the Ninth International Congress of Psychology (1929), 297; K. Lewin, 297, 300–1; and

American psychologists studying in Europe, 298; and H. Helson, 299; and E. G. Boring, 298–99, 303–7; and K. Koffka, 299; and Max Wertheimer, 299, 304; and K. Bühler, 299–300; and W. Köhler, 301–7

Goddard, H. H.: "Ideals of a Group of German Children" (1906), 239; as director of the research laboratory at the New Jersey Training School for Feeble-Minded Girls and Boys at Vineland, 239–43; mental tests, 242–43

Hall, G. S.: first Harvard Ph.D. in psychology (1878), 54; professor of psychology (and pedagogics, 1884), at Johns Hopkins University (1884), 54; founder of the *American Journal of Psychology* (1887), 54

Haroutunian, J.: on J. Edwards, 113–14

Harvard College: scholastic curriculum, 19–22

Hedonism: of E. L. Thorndike, 169

Hickock, L. P.: expositor of German idealism, 47; *Rational Psychology* (1848) and *Empirical Psychology* (1854), 47

Hill, D. J., 121–43: chronology, 123; college years, 123–25; teaching, 125–28; professor of psychology (and ethics, 1881, University of Lewisburg), 126; publications, 129; *Elements of Psychology* (1888), 129–36; *Genetic Philosophy* (1893), 136–39; from dualism to monism, 139–42; applying psychology, 142–43

Historiography of psychology: social (v. "internal"), 307–8

Hoch, A.: as psychologist at McLean hospital, Laboratory of Pathological Physiology, 216

Honor studies in psychology: D. J. Hill, 128

Huey, E. B.: *The Psychology and Pedagogy of Reading* (1908), 243; as director of the Department of Clinical Psychology at the Illinois Asylum for Feeble Minded Children at Lincoln, Illinois, 244; translation (1910) of the 1908 Binet-Simon scale, 244

Idealism, German (and its introduction to America by): J. Marsh, 44–45; V. Cousin, 46–47; L. P. Hickock, 47

Immigration, restrictive: and R. M. Yerkes, 279–80

Institutionalization of psychology as an independent, experimental discipline, 18

Intelligence: operational definition, 281. *See* Binet (-Simon) scale

Introspection: in the view of early American psychologists (1892–1913), 203–5; E. B. Titchener, 205

James, W.: early courses on psychology at Harvard University, 51

James-Lange theory of emotions: defended by J. R. Angell (1916), 173; critically examined by W. B. Cannon (1927), 173–74; replaced by the Cannon-Bard model, 174

James's theory of will, account of: habit and ideomotor action, 149–50; fiat as inhibition and consent, 151; subjective interest and attention, 151–53; refutation of feelings of innervation, 153–55; critique of the association of ideas, 155–58

James's theory of will, impact of: on physiological psychology, 158–60; on cognitive development, 160–65; on attention and volition, 165–67; on learning, 167–71; on motivation, 171–72; on social psychology, 177–81; on abnormal psychology, 181–84; overview, 184–86

Johnson, G. E.: early (1894) experimental research with feebleminded children, 230–31

Johnson, S.: and the "New Learning" (1714–15), 23; *Elementa Philosophica* (1752), 23–26; president of the College of New York (later renamed Columbia University), 27–28

Journal of Applied Psychology, 284

Journals in the field of mental deficiency: *Journal of Psycho-Asthenics* (1896), 228; *Training School* (1904), 228; *Psychological Clinic* (1907), 228

Kant, I. (introduction of his views to America by): J. Marsh, 44–45; V. Cousin, 46–47; L. P. Hickock, 47

King's College (Columbia University): curriculum under S. Johnson, 27

Koffka, K.: academic appointments, 299

Köhler, W.: academic appointments, 302–4, 307

Krohn, W. O.: experimental psychologist working in a psychiatric setting, 212–16; and G. S. Hall, 214; Illinois Eastern Hospital for the Insane, 214; *Practical Lessons in Psychology* (1894), 215; article on "Laboratory Psychology as Applied to Insanity" (1898), 214

Kuhlmann, F.: at the Minnesota School for Idiots and Imbeciles at Fairbault, 248–50; and mental testing, 252

Laboratories of psychology, in academic settings: growth of laboratories, 197–99; equipment, 199–200; support, 201; experimentalists turned administrators, 201–2; experimentation and conceptualization, 202–3; to introspect or not to introspect, 203–5; literature on, 205
Laboratories of psychology, in the context of mental deficiency, 228–53; Minnesota School for Idiots and Imbeciles at Fairbault (1896, 1898), 228, 232–34; Psychological Clinic, University of Pennsylvania (1896), 235; The New Jersey Training School for Feeble-Minded Girls and Boys at Vineland (1906), 239, 240; Department of Clinical Psychology at the Illinois Asylum for Feeble Minded Children at Lincoln (1909), 244; Laboratory of Clinical Psychology, New Jersey Village for Epileptics at Skillman, 247
Laboratories of psychology, in psychiatric settings: New York Pathological Institute in New York City (1895), 207; Illinois Eastern Hospital for the Insane (1897), 214; McLean Hospital, Laboratory of Pathological Physiology (1904), 215, 216, 222; Government Hospital for the Insane, Washington, D.C. (1907), 221
Ladd, G. T.: Elements of Physiological Psychology (1887), 158; and W. James, 158–60; and H. Lotze, 159
Lamarckian theory: and W. McDougall, 296
Lashley, K. S.: and the Gestalt point of view, 297
Law of acquired connections: E. L. Thorndike, 170
Lawrence, I.: definition of words in the Binet scale, 256
Learning: and W. James, 167–71; E. L. Thorndike, 167–71; C. L. Morgan, 167; G. J. Romanes, 169
Lecture system: replacing the recitation system, 43
Lewes, G. H.: critique of, by D. J. Hill, 140; Problems of Life and Mind (1880), 139–40
Lewin, K.: academic appointments, 297, 300–1
Lewisburg, The University at (renamed Bucknell University): and D. J. Hill, 125–27
Locke, J.: early impact on American

philosophical thought, 23; division of sciences, 23–24; and J. Edwards, 23, 98, 110, 111

McPherson, M. W. See Popplestone, J. A. and M. W. McPherson
McCosh, J.: president of Princeton University (1868), 52–53; Psychology of Cognitive Powers (1886), 53
McDougall, W.: and the Lamarckian theory, 296; confrontation with J. McKeen Cattell, 206
Macy, R. H. & Co.: and personnel psychology, 284
Marsh, J.: introducing Kantian views to America, 44–45
Memorial Fund, Laura Spelman Rockefeller: support of child psychology, 292
Mental deficiency, experimental psychologists working in the area of: G. E. Johnson, 230–31; A. R. T. Wylie, 231–35; L. Witmer, 235–38; H. H. Goddard, 238–43; E. B. Huey, 243–45; J. E. W. Wallin, 245–48; F. Kuhlmann, 248–52
Mental deficiency, mental testers in the area of: N. Norsworthy, 253–55; I. Lawrence, 255–56; L. P. Ayres, 256; H. C. Town, 256–57; L. M. Terman, 257–58
Mental philosophy: T. C. Upham's Elements of Mental Philosophy (1832), 40; listing of topics, 40–42; differentiation from moral philosophy, 43
Mental science: as a synonym of psychology, 43
Mental testers in the area of mental deficiency. See Mental deficiency, mental testers in the area of
Mental testing, 276–83: major assumptions, 279; L. M. Terman, 280; E. G. Boring, 281; critique, 281
Mental tests: pre-Binet, 254–55; Binet (-Simon) scale, 229, 238, 242, 244, 245
Meyer, A.: and early psychological study and care of psychotics, 208
Miller, P.: on J. Edwards, 99–102, 107–8, 112–13
Mind: J. Edwards's theory of, 61–91
Monism: C. L. Morgan, 141; D. J. Hill, 141; N. S. Schaler, 142
Moral philosophy: T. Reid's division of the human mind into intellective and active powers, 38
"Moral therapy" of W. James: and J. J. Putnam, 184
Morgan, C. L.: kinetic (physical) and meta-

kinetic (psychological) phenomena, 141; and E. L. Thorndike, 167

Motivation: and W. James, 171–72; and R. S. Woodworth, 171–72

Murphy, G.: on W. James's psychology of voluntary action, 148

Münsterberg, H.: and W. James, 184; physiological theory of subconscious, 184

Neural mechanisms of behavior: K. S. Lashley, 297

"New Learning": British sources of, 22

"New Psychology": Harvard's W. James, 51; Yale's G. T. Ladd and E. Scripture, 52; Princeton's J. M. Baldwin, 53–54; Johns Hopkins's G. S. Hall, 54; mind-as-content v. mind-in-use, 55

Nineteenth century: Scottish philosophy and academic orthodoxy, 34–42; consolidation and development of academic psychology, 42–48; academic reform and the coming of the "New Psychology," 48–59; D. J. Hill (ca. 1879–96), between the "Old" and the "New" psychology, 121–47; W. James's psychology of the will, 149–57

Norsworthy, N.: at Columbia University's Teachers College, 253; "The Psychology of Mentally Deficient Children" (1906), 253–55; E. L. Thorndike's course on Educational Statistics, 255; *The Psychology of Childhood* (with M. T. Whiteley, 1918), 255

Noyes, W.: instrumentation and research in experimental psychology, 216

O'Brien, Dennis, 11

Pavlov, I. P.: at the Ninth International Congress of Psychology, 296

Peirce, C. S.: critique of D. J. Hill's *Genetic Philosophy* (1893), 138–39

Personality: and W. James, 175–77; M. W. Calkins, 175; G. Allport, 176

Philadelphia, College of (University of Pennsylvania): curriculum under W. Smith, 28–29

Piaget, J.: and J. M. Baldwin, 165–66

Popplestone, J. A., and M. W. McPherson, "Pioneer Psychology Laboratories in Clinical Settings," 196–271

Porter, N.: *The Human Intellect* (1868), 43, 51; *The Elements of Moral Science: Theoretical and Practical* (1885), 43

Prince, M.: and W. James, 182–83; theory of association neuroses, 182–83

Professorships of psychology: D. J. Hill (1881, The University at Lewisburg, renamed Bucknell University), 126; G. S. Hall (1884, Johns Hopkins University), 54; J. McKeen Cattell (1889, University of Pennsylvania), 274

Psychiatric settings, psychologists working in, 207–28: B. Sidis, 209–12; W. O. Krohn, 212–16; S. I. Franz, 216–22; F. L. Wells, 222–26. *See also* Laboratories of psychology, in psychiatric settings

Psychiatry: and early psychological study and care of psychotics, 207; A. Meyer, 208

Psychogenesis: D. J. Hill, 139

Psychological Corporation: in the 1920s, 285, 288–89

Psychologists: and anti-Semitism, 280

Psychologists: as university presidents, 275

Psychology, abnormal: T. C. Upham's *Outlines of Disordered Mental Action* (1840), 40; and W. James, 181–84; as a root of W. James's theory of will, 181; M. Prince, 182–83: H. Münsterberg, 184; J. J. Putnam, 184

Psychology, academic: its consolidation and early development, 42–48; and curriculum differentiation, 42; textbooks, 43; replacing recitation system by a lecture system, 43; impact of Continental philosophies, 44–48

Psychology, advertising and. *See* Psychology, American, in the 1920s

Psychology, American, prior to the 1880s: according to J. McKeen Cattell, 17; according to E. B. Titchener, 18

Psychology, American, in the 1920s, 273–323: advertising, 283–84; mental testing, 276–83; industrial, 283–90; consulting, 290–92; child, 292–94; and E. B. Titchener, 294–95; and the Ninth International Congress of Psychology, 295–96; and Gestalt psychology, 297–307

Psychology, application of: by D. J. Hill, 142–43

Psychology, child: in the 1920s, 292–94

Psychology, consulting: certification, 290–92; American Psychological Association, Committee on the Certification of Consulting Psychologists, 290–91

Psychology, elementary: D. J. Hill, 127

Psychology, experimental: early textbooks, 205; manuals, 206; limitations of, 207

Psychology, genetic: D. J. Hill, 136–38

Psychology, Gestalt: in America in the 1920s, 297–307

Psychology, industrial: in the 1920s, 283–90
Psychology, "Old" and "New": and D. J. Hill, 132–34
Psychology, physiological: D. J. Hill, 127; W. James, 158–60; G. T. Ladd, 158–60
Psychology, social: and W. James, 177–81; G. H. Mead, 177–79; F. Allport, 179
Putnam, J. J.: and W. James's "moral therapy," 184

Rating scales: for selection of business and army personnel, 284
Rauch, F. A.: as source of German philosophical ideas in America, 45; *Psychology or a View of the Human Soul* (1840), 46
Recitation system: replacement by the lecture system, 43
Reform, academic: secularization of education in America, 49; introduction of elective system at Harvard (1984), 49; "optionals" at Yale, 51
Regenting system: its abandonment in the eighteenth-century American colleges, 27–28
Reid, T.: *Essays* (on the intellectual and active powers of the human mind), 38; influence on the arrangement of psychological topics in college textbooks, 39
Roback, A. A.: on J. Edwards, 103
Rochester, University of: and D. J. Hill, 127–29
Roger, A. C.: editor, *Journal of Psycho-Asthenics*, 228

Schaler, N. S., *The Interpretation of Nature* (1893): concept of the "soul-bearing capacity of matter," 142
Scientific management: and psychology, 286
Scott Company: a personnel management consulting firm, 285; its dissolution, 287–88
Scott, W. D.: Psychology of advertising, 283–84
Scottish thought in America: its rise, 29–34; the norm in the American colleges in the nineteenth century, 34; "safe books," 27; T. Reid's *Essays* and moral philosophy, 38–39; T. C. Upham's series of textbooks, 39–42; T. Brown, 44; Sir William Hamilton, 44; N. Porter, 51–52; J. McCosh, 52–53

Scripture, E.: *Studies from the Yale Psychological Laboratory*, 52

Sergi, G.: *L'Origine dei fenomeni psichici* (1885): and D. J. Hill's genetic psychology, 139
Seventeenth century: psychological topics in the scholastic curriculum, 19–22
Sherrington, C. S.: and theories of emotions, 172
Siciliani, P., *Psychogénie moderne* (1880): and D. J. Hill's genetic psychology, 139
Sidis, B.: and W. James, 182–84; *The Psychology of Suggestion* (1897), 182; experimental psychological research in a psychiatric setting, 209–12
Smith, S. S.: Americanization of Scottish psychology, 32–33
Smith, W.: *A General Idea of the College of Mirania* (1753), 28; division of the departments of knowledge, 29
Sokal, M. M.: "James McKeen Cattell and American Psychology in the 1920s," 273–323. *See also* Psychology, American, in the 1920s

Terman, L. M.: a study of "bright" and "stupid" boys, 257; revision and extension of the Binet-Simon scale of intelligence, 258; requirements of scores on standardized intelligence tests for applicants for admission to graduate study, 280; *Genetic Studies of Genius* (1925), 292; and Gestalt psychology, 304
Terminology: of D. J. Hill, 130, 131, 132, 139
Textbooks of psychology: American "firsts," 39; T. C. Upham's series, 39–42; differentiation between intellectual and moral philosophy, 43; proliferation of textbooks on mental philosophy between 1827 and 1860, 43; N. Porter's *The Human Intellect* (1868), 43; textbooks of psychology published between 1886 and 1890, 134
Theory of association neuroses: M. Prince, 182–83
Theory of social stimulation and response: G. H. Mead, 178
Thorndike, E. L.: and W. James, 169–71; and C. L. Morgan, 167; trial-and-error learning, 167; critique of associationist tradition, 167–69; hedonism, 169
Titchener, E. B.: on American psychology prior to the 1880s, 18; on introspection, 205; and American psychological community, 294–95: obituary by E. G. Boring, 294
Town, C. H.: Binet-Simon scale and the psychologists, 257

Twentieth century: pioneer psychological laboratories in clinical settings, 196–272; the impact of W. James's theory of the will on American psychology, 158–88; J. McKeen Cattell and American psychology in the 1920s, 273–323

University of Iowa, State: Child Welfare Station, 293
University of Pennsylvania: the Psychological Clinic, 235, 237, 238. *See also* Philadelphia, College of
University presidents: drawn from the ranks of psychologists, 275
Upham, T. C.: *Elements of Intellectual Philosophy* (1827), 39–40; *Elements of Mental Philosophy* (1832), 40; *Philosophical and Practical Treatise of the Will* (1834), 40; *Outlines of Disordered Mental Action* (1840), 40
U.S. Army tests: in the First World War, 277; R. M. Yerkes, 277
U.S. Civil Service Commission: establishment of a Research Division (1922), 285

Van Giessen, I.: as director of the New York Pathological Institute, 209; "correlation of sciences," 209

Wallin, J. E. W.: rhythm of speech, 245–46;

Optical Illusions of Reversible Perspectives (1905), 247; administrative manual for the Binet-Simon scale (1911–12), 248
Wells, F. L.: technique of ranking, 223; fatigue, 223, 225; experimental research in psychopathology, 224
Wertheimer, Max: academic appointments, 299
Witherspoon, J.: adversary of Berkeley's philosophy, 31; faculties of the mind, 32; introducing the Scottish philosophy of common sense to the College of New Jersey (Princeton University), 31–32
Witmer, L.: Psychological Clinic, University of Pennsylvania (1896), 235, 237, 238; sustained surveillance of behavior, 238
Woodward, W. R.: "William James's Psychology of Will: Its Revolutionary Impact on American Psychology," 148–95
Woodworth, R. S.: and W. James, 171–72
Wylie, A. R. T.: research at the Minnesota School for Idiots and Imbeciles at Faribault, 232–33; "A Scheme for Psychological Investigation of the Feeble-Minded" (1901), 234; psychology of the blind, 234

Yale College: changes in the curriculum, 23; T. Clapp's support of mathematics and "experimental philosophy," 23
Yerkes, R. M.: and U.S. Army tests, 277; and restrictive immigration, 279–80

NOV 0 3 1987

WITHDRAWN

Sale of this material benefits the Library

JAN. 1 1 1987

BOSTON PUBLIC LIBRARY

3 9999 00325 840 5

WITHDRAWN
No longer the property of the
Boston Public Library.
Sale of this material benefits the Library.

Boston Public Library

**COPLEY SQU
GENERAL LIB**

BF108
.U5E96
1983

88800733-01

The Date Due Card in the pocket indicates the date on or before which this
book should be returned to the Library.

Please do not remove cards from this
pocket.